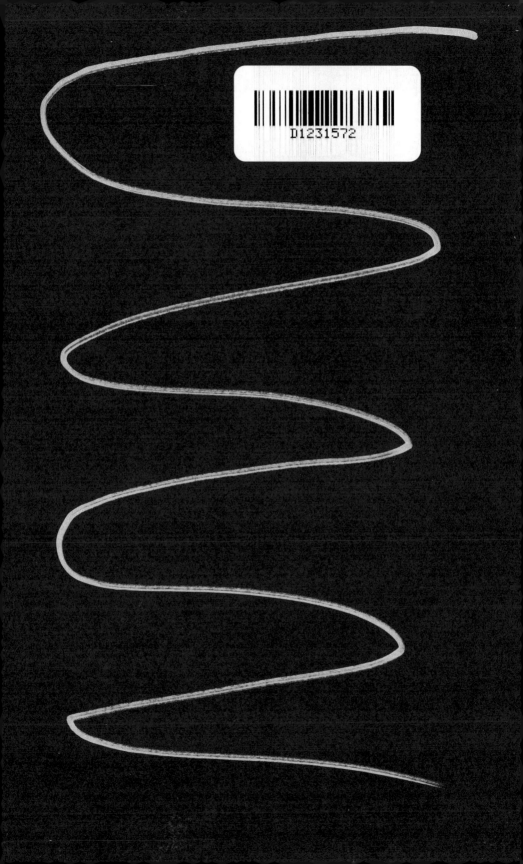

D1231572

# FILM CRITICISM
## A COUNTER THEORY

# FILM CRITICISM
## A COUNTER THEORY

## William Cadbury
## Leland Poague

The Iowa State University Press
AMES

## ACKNOWLEDGMENTS

*Anavysos Kouros, Diskobolos* by Myron, and *Bronze Seated Hermes from Herculaneum.* Photographs reproduced by permission of Hirmer Verlag, Munich.

*La Musique,* oil on canvas, 1939, 45³⁄₈″ x 45³⁄₄″, by Henri Matisse. Albright-Knox Art Gallery, Buffalo, New York, Room of Contemporary Art Fund. Reproduced by permission.

Frame enlargements from *La Notte.* Reproduced courtesy Corinth Films.

Frame enlargements from *Young Mr. Lincoln.* © 1939 Twentieth-Century Fox Film Corporation. Reproduced by permission.

Publication of this work has been made possible in part by a grant from the **Andrew W. Mellon Foundation.**

Printed by The Iowa State University Press, Ames, Iowa 50010

First edition, 1982

---

**Library of Congress Cataloging in Publication Data**

Cadbury, William.
   Film criticism.

   Bibliography: p.
   Includes index.
   1. Moving-pictures—Philosophy. 2. Moving-pictures—Aesthetics. I. Poague, Leland A., 1948–
II. Title.
PN1995.C27    1982     791.43′01′5     82–9896
**ISBN 0–8138–0352–7**     AACR2

---

For Maxine Scates and for William and Charlotte Cadbury

—W.C.

And for Rudy and Sylvia Rucker

—L.P.

# CONTENTS

# P R E F A C E

---

What can we say about films: about the whole class or about
particular films? What should we say? Are all statements about
films of equal value or relevance? By what criteria do we judge
particular acts or concepts of film criticism? By what criteria
should we judge them?

In Film Criticism: A Counter Theory we attempt to provide
defensible answers to such questions. Though we ourselves differ
in the degree of our objectivism with respect to the defining
of aesthetic objects, we share an instrumentalist theory of
aesthetic value, namely the theory that art objects are good (if
they are) because it does people good to have aesthetic experience
of them, and we share the belief that it is in their capacity
to provide aesthetic experience to people who know how to have
it that aesthetic objects are defined. We employ a "mentalistic"
model of cognition, of that aspect of human nature that allows
us to know things and have experiences, including aesthetic ones,
and so we share a deep distrust of the more literal
interpretations, such as we often find expressed in recent film
criticism and theory, of the notion that social being determines
consciousness. Put another way, we believe in aesthetic
experience as a primary and constitutive category of knowledge
about films--particularly, of the knowledge we think one should
want to have about films--and hence as a principal term in film
criticism. The essays here collected, some reprinted and some
newly fashioned for the purpose, may be understood as an
exploration of the implications of such an approach for the
criticism and interpretation of film.

The book is organized into two sections. The first, "Film,
Language, and Criticism," focuses on various categories of
criticism--on the problem, that is, of the "language" of film
as criticism abstracts its elements and features; and it considers
the validity of various models for the description of film

language:  aesthetic (Beardsley), ontological (Bazin), generic (Tudor), and semiotic (Barthes, Lacan, etc.).  The second section, "Authorship, Meaning, and Interpretation," is more practical in its orientation, as evidenced by extended discussions of Hitchcock and Antonioni, but it also pursues further the consequences for criticism of an acceptance of a Cartesian subject:  as "author," as "theme," and most crucially as "viewer" or "reader"--as someone who has the capacity to "think about" films, to "make sense" of films in ways which are responsive to their properties while at the same time maintaining a necessary measure of independence from the objects under consideration (we are not the films we see).

Therein lies both the indebtedness and the novelty of our approach.  The contention that we are capable of thinking productively and objectively about films we ground quite explicitly, as best we can, in the aesthetics of Monroe Beardsley and the linguistics of Noam Chomsky--neither one a newcomer to philosophy.  Such an approach is novel, however, because the current trend in advanced film theory denies any such picture of the mind/screen relationship by declaring "the subject" to be so thoroughly a product of ideology and the texts reproducing it that "language speaks, not man."  We reject that contention and believe the time has come to offer a counter theory of film criticism grounded in a counter theory of human cognition.

Readers will note that individual chapters are initialed rather than signed to encourage the view that this is a single book with two authors rather than simply a collection of topically related essays.  However, many debts of kindness and insight require acknowledgement, making it necessary to specify who wrote what.

The Introduction and Chapters 3, 5, 7, and 8 are the work of Lee Poague.  His research was carried on with the support of the State University of New York Research Foundation, the University of Rochester (especially Richard Gollin and the Film Study Program), the National Endowment for the Humanities, and Iowa State University (special thanks to Frank Haggard, chairman of the Department of English).  Many friends and colleagues read and critiqued his sections of the manuscript:  Richard Gollin, Gary Hooper, Alan Lutkus, Rick Ramsey, and Rudy Rucker (in New York); NEH Seminar Director David Bordwell and fellow seminarians Jim Jubak, Bill Bywater, and Robert Self; and ISU colleagues Charles L. P. Silet, Douglas Catron, Scott Consigny, and Susan Galenbeck--to all of whom are owed sincere thanks, though not always for agreeing with or endorsing what they read.  He is grateful to Ron Gottesman for his advice on the Introduction and to Joe Kupfer for his advice on Chapter 8.  Chapter 3, "The Problem of Film Genre," originally appeared in Literature/Film Quarterly; thanks to James Welsh for permission to reprint. More personal thanks are due, in abundant measure, to Amy, Melissa, and Susan for their gifts of love and patience.

William Cadbury wrote Chapters 1, 2, 4, 6, 9, and 10.  He

wishes especially to thank, for readings and critiques and for
much-appreciated interest, support, and encouragement, Joseph
A. Hynes (whose unflagging patience and concern have helped
enormously, often with detailed readings); Don Levi; Wayne A.
O'Neil; and Don Fredericksen, who as Book Review Editor for the
Journal of the University Film Association solicited and
published as "Human Experience and the Work Itself: A Review
of Beardsley's Aesthetics for Film Critics" what is now, much
revised, Chapter 1; thanks also to Tim Lyons, editor, for
permission to reprint it from Journal of the University Film
Association, 29, no. 1 (Winter 1977): 25-32. Thanks also to
Don Fredericksen for soliciting, for a panel he chaired at the
Society for Cinema Studies meetings in 1977, the paper that is
now, though in substantially different form, Chapter 4. Chapter
2, "The Cleavage Plane of Andre Bazin," is reprinted with some
changes and additions by kind permission of Maurice Beebe, editor,
from Journal of Modern Literature, 3 (1973); 253-68, the issue
"Film as Literature and Language," Guest Editor: Norman
Silverstein. Thanks are due to Ernest Callenbach for suggestions
about that chapter and about Chapter 6. Special thanks go to
Linda Blackaby for inventing, in 1969, and implementing thereafter
Cadbury's teaching and study of film at the University of Oregon,
and to the students who have been contributors to and sounding
boards for what is developed here, especially (to name only former
students, more colleagues than students) Bill and Linda Batty,
Alice Blanchard, Dave Coursen, Michele Piso, Bob Bibler, and Tom
Hyde.
        It is especially appropriate that we conclude this Preface
by acknowledging our mutual indebtedness and gratitude to two
patient editors. First, to Doug Holm, editor of Cinemonkey.
Three of our chapters--"Semiology, Human Nature, and John Ford,"
"Auteurism: Theory as against Policy," and "Intentionality,
Authorship, and Film Criticism"--originally appeared in the pages
of his journal, and are reprinted here with his kind permission.
Over and above that, however, we are grateful for the support
that he has consistently expressed not only by publishing our
work but also in his conversations and correspondence. Lee
Poague's chapter on Alfred Hitchcock, for instance, owes much
to Doug's concerned advice. His enthusiasm helped considerably
to bring this project to completion; our thanks to Doug are well
deserved and sincerely tendered. Finally, our thanks go to Judith
Gildner of the Iowa State University Press, for tact, patience,
and creative suggestions during the preparation of this book.
Its faults are entirely our own, but they would have been more
glaring without her help, and we feel a special debt of gratitude
to her.
        Financial assistance from the University of Oregon
Foundation, Douglas M. Wilson, Director, for the preparation of
the illustrations is gratefully acknowledged, as are the many
courtesies and assistances of Ronald E. Sherriffs, Head, and the
staff of the Department of Speech, University of Oregon.

# INTRODUCTION

This book is a "counter theory" of film criticism in a sense similar to that in which Christian Metz's <u>Film Language</u> is a "semiotics of cinema." Neither book is a fully worked out, move by move, proposition by proposition exposition of its subject area. Rather, both books are collections of essays, some very speculative and risk-taking, others less so, all of them complete within the bounds of specific occasions and particular arguments, yet all of them relying to a greater or lesser degree on a general body of knowledge, European structural linguistics in the case of Metz, Anglo-American aesthetics and linguistic theory in our own case. Nevertheless, even if we make no claim to the sort of elegance occasionally found in works on aesthetics, and despite the fact that the essays were originally written independently and evidence certain differences of emphasis and approach, we believe that the pieces here collected and revised do point toward and effectively embody a theory of film criticism which can stand, in its present form, as a philosophically viable alternative to the general brand of cultural semiotics which currently dominates in the realms of film theory and film aesthetics.

Our basic thesis, stated in positive terms throughout the essays here included, is that aesthetic objects exist in some "phenomenally objective" sense and that human minds are capable of understanding such works, including films, in a very active, productive, yet nonsubjective manner. It is very much the trend in advanced film studies, however, to deny the truth of this position, to say, for example, that there simply is no such thing as aesthetic experience and therefore no point in discussing as aesthetic objects those artifacts whose most important aspect is their capacity to provide that experience; or to say that all perception is precoded and predetermined, so that everything we might say about a work of art will be hopelessly contaminated by our own subjectivity; or to say that aesthetic objects exist, but in terms that effectively deny the productivity of the perceiving mind. The essays in this book, however, undertake to demonstrate that many such denials of the objectivity of aesthetic objects and the creativity of human minds are problematic, especially, as William Cadbury points out, to the degree that they are founded on a mistaken view of language and language use derived from Ferdinand de Saussure and carried forward into the views of Claude Levi-Strauss, Jacques Lacan, and Roland Barthes, with damaging results.

Several Saussurian theses--as extended and generalized by his disciples and successors--are crucial to the semiological point of view with which we take issue. Perhaps the most crucial of them all is that which suggests that synchronic or structural linguistics, of the sort developed in Saussure's Cours de linguistique générale, could serve as the master pattern of a larger "science of signs." There are two separate but related questions here: 1) Is such a science possible? That is, are various kinds of signs similar enough in their functioning to justify equating the kinds of communication which are made possible by semiological systems, like natural languages or dreams, which do not give rise to aesthetic experience in knowledgeable audiences, with the kinds of communication of information--of meaning--characteristic of systems which do make such experience possible? 2) Are the linguistic theories of Saussure and his followers powerful enough to provide the foundation for such a science? We believe the answer to both questions is no.

Thus in his review of Beardsley, William Cadbury suggests that aesthetic objects are characterized by specific and describable qualities which enable them to give rise to aesthetic experience. Other kinds of semiotic artifacts can also give rise to experience of a similar sort, but aesthetic objects as a class are good for little else, while other kinds of semiotic behavior or artifacts (football games and restaurant menus) are good for other ends and accordingly become less rewarding to aesthetic contemplation. In other words, we have serious doubts about dissolving aesthetics into semiotics, however much aesthetic objects may share certain characteristics with nonaesthetic artifacts. At best, we believe that the category of "aesthetic experience" must be maintained as a special instance of sign behavior; but the general trend in advanced film studies these days is in the opposite direction.

Furthermore, as Cadbury also points out, there are serious questions to be raised about the adequacy of Saussurian linguistics to the task of describing the faculty of language--in which instance the extension of Saussurian concepts into other realms of analysis will be called into serious doubt. The basic Saussurian thesis at issue here involves the very concept of "language." For Saussure, language is defined largely in terms of phonetics and morphemics, i.e., in terms of sounds and words, with little explicit or sustained regard for the principles of generation which enable human beings to put sounds and words

together into comprehensible strings.  Furthermore, at the level
of these minimal linguistic "units" or "signs," Saussure defines
la langue as an impersonal cultural system, imposed upon
individuals without their knowledge or consent, where "meaning"
is essentially "arbitrary" (there being no necessary relation
between the signifying sound and the signified concept) and is
derived almost entirely from a series of otherwise insignificant
relational shifts:  we recognize fit by virtue of the fact that
it is not hit or bit.

Even in Saussurian terms, then, the linguistic reality of
a word is not solely or primarily a function of its status as
a material object (a sequence of sound waves) but rather involves
its status in a cultural system.  But the Althusser/Lacan
extension of Saussure comes near to eliminating any concept of
the objective reality of aesthetic objects by decreeing that the
structure of consciousness is identical to the structure of
language as Saussure described it.  All perception is therefore
coded according to culturally imposed and arbitrarily constructed
categories which lend to relational shifts an illusion of positive
meaning.  In which case it becomes essentially impossible to speak
objectively of aesthetic objects:  we cannot perceive them apart
from our "always already" precoded view of the world; and even
if we could, nothing we might subsequently say would carry any
logical authority.  In the "prison house" of language we can do
no better than shift from one arbitrary meaning to another.  It
is an endless and therefore pointless process.

There is no denying, we think, the systematic nature of human
perception or of human language.  But we believe that the present
state of knowledge in the fields of aesthetics and linguistics
is such as to cast serious doubts on the picture of those systems
which has been derived from Saussure.  To begin with, as Cadbury
points out in "Semiology, Human Nature, and John Ford," the
structuralist view of language is inadequate in its genesis for
it largely ignores matters of grammar and of language
acquisition.  Serious study of language use has shown that the
mental processes involved are far more active and complicated
than that process of relational shifts posited by Saussure.
Understanding even a simple sentence, as Chomsky demonstrates,
is not simply a matter of noting relational shifts and tallying
them up by some simple linguistic calculus.  Such a view of
language could hardly account for our ability to distinguish the
profound difference in meaning between "John is easy to please"
and "John is eager to please."

It is rather the case that in even the simplest act of
linguistic comprehension a whole variety of mental operations
are involved that enable us to relate surface structures
(syntactical organizations that underlie realizations of their
relations in speech acts) to two things:  1) deep structures
(syntactical organizations that underlie realizations of their
relations in apprehensible meanings) and 2) the processes of
"transformation" that may make the surface look different from

what it means in the same way that the images of, say, a dream
may look different from what they stand for.  And the same is
true, we hold, in the comprehension of aesthetic objects
generally.  To comprehend an aesthetic object is not simply to
relate the units of its surface to any storehouse or set of
storehouses of "components of aesthetic objects" that we might
have learned to recognize and to interpret on the basis of
differences, but rather to relate surface features to a complex
set of processings of representations of many sorts, some
involving learned skills and recognition of culturally established
"codings," some not.  The process of interpretation, in other
words, is a matter of relating parts to wholes on many levels,
on most (if not all) of which the Saussurian system of differences
is a demonstrably inadequate explanatory tool.  In fact,
Saussurian linguistics is at its weakest in providing explanation
of "the sense of the whole," as for instance in explaining
relations among the meanings of whole sentences.  But it is with
our ability to arrive at a sense of the whole aesthetic object
that most of the essays here are concerned.

Furthermore, we believe it inaccurate to assert that the
system of language is a sort of absurdist prison house imposed
upon us by culture such that our only ethical recourse is to
embrace absurdity and take pleasure in shifting from one set of
terms to another.  Rather, we believe, with Chomsky, that
linguistic competence is a resource of which the most powerful
aspects are biologically not culturally acquired.  Thus, even
if our perception of the world, our ability to relate the surface
structures of appearance to a set of senses of the nature of
things, is in some degree precoded, it is not arbitrarily so in
the Saussurian sense, and should not be expected to differ from
one culture to the next anywhere near so much as radical
semiologists, echoing the old Whorf/Sapir hypothesis, would have
us believe.  In other words, within the realm of the human we
can find a sense in which it is proper to speak of the
objectivity of aesthetic objects and to hope to come to an
agreement (which will be more than merely verbal stipulation)
as to their qualities and values.  We are not so much the
playthings of language or culture that rational discourse is
impossible--which is not of course to seek to conceal that we
may well be so much the prisoners of our biological inheritance
as to make the limits of that discourse hard to make out.  There
may well be, as Chomsky has often pointed out, aspects of reality
which the structure of the human mind simply disqualifies us from
comprehending.  But of these we must perforce be silent.

One final issue relating to our ability to be actively and
productively involved in the comprehension of aesthetic objects
remains to be introduced, though it is not unrelated to the
linguistic/aesthetic issues discussed above.  A distinction is
frequently made in film studies, and in literary studies, between
works that allow for "passive" enjoyment and those that require
"active" collaboration on the part of the viewer or reader.  Much

of the discussion implies, wrongly we believe, that the matter
of viewer activity depends upon the text rather than the reader.
In film studies this distinction is generally associated with
André Bazin and with the distinction he draws in "The Evolution
of the Language of Cinema" between classical editing and deep
focus mise-en-scène, between the cinema of the image and that
of reality. Bazin is quite explicit on the point that the cinema
of the image, of montage and graphic expressionism, functions
to "impose its interpretation[s] of events on the spectator."
To this he contrasts the cinema of reality where framing or
composition does not "impose" a meaning on reality but "forces
it to reveal its structural depth." Accordingly, the cinema of
the image "only calls for [the spectator] to follow his guide,
to let his attention follow along smoothly with that of the
director who will choose what he should see"; while the cinema
of reality implies "both a more active mental attitude on the
part of the spectator and a more positive contribution on his
part to the action in progress."[1]

To Bazin, of course, all film scholars owe an incalculable
debt, for allowing us even to speak of mise-en-scène, and for
his contributions to genre and auteur studies. It must be said,
however, as we do here in our essays on Bazin and Hitchcock, that
Bazin's view of the "use" of film language by film viewers, like
Saussure's view of the use of verbal language, is in error, and
for essentially the same reason:  both assign too much weight
to organizations of apprehensible elements, structurable in terms
that need not refer to underlying representations and from which
it is assumed far too easily that a correlation with
representations of meaning can be "read off" directly; and at
the same time far too little weight is given to the complexity
of the processes by which rules must operate over representations
to yield any correlation whatever of apprehension with meaning.
The creativity of the mind, which resides precisely in its ability
to use complex systems of recursive rules to generate
representations of relations among the apprehensible and the
meaningful, is therefore undervalued if not denied altogether.
There is, in reality, very little sense to any distinction between
activity and passivity of perceptions or other cognitive
processes, very little meaning to the notion of "let[ting] the
attention follow along smoothly" on any track at all.

It is demonstrable, then, as I endeavor to point out in "The
Problem of Film Genre," that even in fairly simple instances of
language or cinema the mind must be very actively
engaged--otherwise neither language nor cinema would exist. To
be sure, some films reward greater activity than do others. But
the real distinction to be made, a distinction upon which the
validity of film criticism and study may be said to rest, is not
between passive and active films but between passive and active
viewers--viewers who differ not in the operation of their
perceptual and other cognitive processes per se, but in their
willingness to put those processes to vigorous use, to engage

films with them, and to set representations of films against and with representations of the world in the full richness of interplay which is connoted by the notion of interpretation. Such vigorous processing will not change the films, since it is exactly the point of such processing to find out what the world (including films) is like and what can be said of it, to build representations which will embody the quality of the objects they represent. But we can change habits of viewing, our own and those of our students. Only if that capacity for action is in some sense independent of the films we see is there any possibility for education. Were it absolutely true that certain film styles automatically or tyrannically invoke identical responses in every individual, then there would be no need for education and criticism. We believe, however, that human minds are capable of independent and creative action--and it is in that belief that these essays were written.

L.P.

NOTES
1. André Bazin, <u>What Is Cinema?</u>, vol. 1 (Berkeley: Univ. of California Press, 1967), pp. 25, 27, 35-36.

P A R T

I

---

# FILM, LANGUAGE, AND CRITICISM

# 1

# Beardsley's *Aesthetics* and Film Criticism

Aesthetics, and Monroe C. Beardsley's Aesthetics, concern what we can and should say about aesthetic objects--single works, sets like films or works of music, or the whole class. We learn from Beardsley not to take some tempting approaches. It is, for instance, critical error to describe a work, interpret its meaning, or estimate its value, in terms of its author's intention. We can seldom determine intention (even where we can determine an author!), but if we could, we would not have found out about the work but about the intention with regard to it, and that would leave what we cared about unexplained.[1] On the other hand, we learn that other approaches are safer than they might seem. We learn, for example, that we can ignore animadversions on "the myth of objective criticism," in Andrew Tudor's phrase, and confidently speak of the forms and qualities of parts and wholes of aesthetic objects.[2]

In addition to learning about approaches, we learn from aesthetics about critical procedures. From the philosopher's organization of arguments about art, the critic can infer a sound critical method for properly assessing the objects of his or her interest. Our interest is film, and Beardsley speaks of it only in passing. But his treatments of music, visual design, and literature, and of the relations among them, provide criteria for sensible statements about film. And, in detailing the moves that proper treatments of the different arts have in common, Beardsley allows us to construct a well-grounded film criticism.

But objective criticism is often rejected because people think that there is no such thing as an aesthetic object to be objective about. One reason for this belief is that it is hard to find common qualities among disparate arts and thus to claim that different sorts of work may all be called aesthetic objects on grounds of their common nature. There is nothing in works of visual art like the structure characteristic of music in which melodies are established and then developed through variation, inversion, and other elaborations (p. 202). There is nothing in music like the implicit movement, balance, and equilibrium

3

among simultaneously perceived areas that are characteristic of visual design. And there is nothing in music to compare with the capacity of words, the elements of literature, to have both sound and sense and hence to develop a web of meanings, distant from the surface of the work as the qualities of melodies are not, as well as webs of sensible and narrative qualities (p. 115). Yet representational visual design does have something very like this capacity. Thus literature must be representational because words must have sense as well as sound, but visual design may be representational or not, and music is representational only in theme songs, leitmotifs, and the like.

Yet there are some terms with which we can deal with all the arts in ways appropriate to each, and much of Aesthetics is devoted to showing their consistently related applications. All art objects may be seen in terms of parts and wholes, and indeed should so be seen--those are the most important terms of any analysis. All arts have minimal parts or elements. In literature they are words. In visual design they are areas, which have shape, size, position, and tone; also among the elements of visual design are line and figure. In music the elements are tones and melodies, from which derive rhythm, scale, and harmony. Further, elements have emergent qualities: dominance and density in visual design, contour and cadence for the melodies of music. Elements, moreover, fuse into complexes or regions, which likewise have emergent qualities: depth, mass, implicit movement and tension in visual areas, and rhythm, harmony, and tonality in music.

To say that areas are the elements of visual design does not commit us to the theory recently advanced by Bill Nichols that the visual field itself may be seen in "bracketed perception," as "sensory impressions." E. H. Gombrich says in Art and Illusion that "the innocent eye is a myth," and that "nobody has ever seen a visual sensation." James J. Gibson also claims that "no one ever saw the world as a flat patchwork of colors." But since, in Gibson's view, "a picture is both a surface in its own right and a display of information about something else," and since "we can distinguish between a surface as an aesthetic object and a surface as a display of information," we can safely say that areas are the elements of the treated surface as such, without impugning our ability to say with Gibson that what we see in pictures, as in reality, are "not visual sensations but only the surfaces of the world that are viewed now from here." In the world we see objects, in pictures "virtual objects." Yet these virtual objects, Beardsley could say without essential disagreement from Gibson, emerge from the areas of the treated surface. In Gibson's formulation, "the picture is both a scene and a surface, and the scene is paradoxically behind the surface" where its layouts of invariants may be ordered just like the areas of the surface, to aesthetic effect.[3]

ELEMENTS OF FILM
    We will rely on these fundamental concepts, concepts of
emergence in which parts with their qualities fuse in each others'
lights to become new parts with new qualities and do it of their
own nature, not because of any projection by the perceiver. The
foremost exponent of the projection theory of depictions is E. H.
Gombrich, who in Art and Illusion argues for "the beholder's
share" in perception both of pictures and of the world. But we
think James J. Gibson successfully refutes his argument when he
says that Gombrich "assumes that sensations are depthless and
that the third dimension of space has to be added to sensations,
whereas I deny this and assert that the way the surfaces of the
world are laid out is seen directly."[4]
    But a problem surfaces at once regarding film. What are
the elements? Most film aestheticians seem to think they have
to start by identifying unique elements of film, thus defining
cinematic specificity in terms of attributes and capacities of
the medium or of what is urged as the viewer's properly cinematic
experience. Thus we have Rudolf Arnheim's "distortions" or
"restrictions" "of the images we receive of the physical world,"
which properly exploit the "peculiar possibilities of
cinematographic technique"; Eisenstein's "shot and montage,
[which] are the basic elements of cinema"; F. E. Sparshott's
"technologically determined" "alienated vision" of dreamlike film
space and time; Bazin's "filtered" imprintings, which are
"fragments of imaged reality"; V. F. Perkins's "opportunities
of the medium," which amount to the discipline implied by cinema's
recording/realistic and creating/illusionistic aspects in
narrative mainstream film; Siegfried Kracauer's "basic" and
"technical" properties of the medium; and such precise
specification of the cinematic elements as Christian Metz's
"audio-visual, moving, multiple, mechanical, iconic images."[5]
    We agree on the importance of all of these aspects of film.
Analyzing them, we can say much about what makes films filmic.
But it seems to us that they are not minimal, but emerge from
elements. What elements? Areas for the visual aspects of film
design, sounds for the auditory, words for the verbal. We don't
think we need define special elements of film, though it is quite
natural to use terms like those above in a very different context
from determination of the elements of film. To use them is to
discuss film history, to consider and report on what has been,
is, or could be most characteristic of films. The terms are for
what Christian Metz calls the "language" that has developed from
film's "fine stories," a language of connotations deposited with
the knowledgeable film viewer like Bazin's "fine carpet of silt
and gold dust," as a set of special expectations of film
experience.[6]
    But the most obvious thing about modern sound film is that
the elements are mixed. We can't say that the word "good" isn't
an element of Rio Bravo; nor that the melodies of Thus Spake

Zarathustra aren't elements of 2001; nor that the area
representing a rock formation is not an element of the shot of
Sandy and Travis discovering the show folks in Wagon Master
(Fig. 1.1). So the problem is easy enough, as it is for theater
and other mixed forms. The visual and auditory elements, and
the elements of the language, are the elements of the film. They
may fuse with other elements of their own kind or of different
kinds to yield complexes with emergent regional qualities. The
shot in Wagon Master is such a complex, with strong qualities
deriving both from the visual similarity of wagon and butte and
from the human action that takes place in that scene.

The wagon has the look of a simultaneous front and back view
of a pioneer woman in her sunbonnet, incongruously hovering over
her golden bed. Yet the elegant and richly connotational
silliness of this image is endorsed, not derogated as we think
at first, by the ungainly delicacy of the rocks. They have the
same top-heavy but tracery outline, as if they were a distant
echo of the wagon, yet they are placed in the frame as if they
hovered over the wagon as the wagon hovers over the bed. And
this quality of mockery that gives way to appreciation--nature
echoing and ratifying the absurdities of human beings--is enhanced
by the sequence it introduces. The show folk, drunk, ask for
a drink, but Travis and Sandy are chagrined to find their
inference wrong: the show folk want water, not liquor. They
have lost their water supply and drunk the "Lightning Elixir"
that was all they had. So we are not observing Sandy and Travis
observing opposites here: socially corrupted wagon and naturally
innocent butte. Rather we are observing human nature and external
nature share a certain fragile independence, a certain comical
beauty. What we find later casts back on and enriches the shot
in which we have our first view, though it will turn out that
its beauty needs to be supplemented by the Mormons' purpose not
to linger in this elegant desert but to gather at the river.

There is no reason to appeal to specifically cinematic
elements in describing a scene like that, though every reason
to appeal to the specific qualities of Wagon Master in
describing what film complexes can be. In film, as in the other
arts, the complexes matter most to critic and theorist: the
discourse emergent from a set of sentences; the tensions among
complexes in their isolation within some visual frame and their
interaction with it; the emergence, from the design of elements,
of representations of persons, places, and things. What matters
most in most films, in fact, is that these representational design
complexes interplay among each other as representations, so that
together they make up large-scale complexes, the qualities of
which derive from what they depict and how they depict.

But this is not for a moment to say that the complexes large
or small, or their elements, lose their status as elements of
design when depiction emerges from them. As parts of the design,
they may be sources of glow or gloom in a film scene, of
preternatural stillness or vigorous movement, of dominant

horizontality or verticality of a shot, a scene, or a whole film
as it develops as a sequence. Of course, the pivotal claim of
Gombrich's Art and Illusion is that we cannot see the plane
surface of a picture and its depiction at the same time; therefore
"in illusionist painting . . . the ambiguity of the canvas
destroys the artist's control over his elements." But James J.
Gibson argues that on the contrary "a picture always requires
two kinds of apprehension . . . at the same time, . . . a direct
perceiving of the picture surface along with an indirect awareness
of virtual surface--a perceiving, knowing, or imagining, as the
case may be." And we may add, why should we not understand in
each other's lights the qualities of design and subject, or even
of two percepts for which a design carries incompatible kinds
of pictorial information--e.g., the familiar goblet/faces
illusion--even if we couldn't perceive them at the same
time?[7]
     The problem of change over time, which seems to differentiate
film from other visual arts, is in fact only apparent. There
is often actual movement or change across time in a visual
design: the play of light that alters with the advancing times
of day or seasons in architecture or sculpture; the mobility of
a mobile; the dynamics of mise-en-scène in theater or film; the
progression of the images in film itself. In cases like these
we simply notice that the elements of the design combine with
each other in sequences as well as all at once, and that the
qualities of the visually perceptible object can no more be
experienced all at the same time than can the theme and the
variations of a piece of music. (But then, attention being the
concentrated thing it is, not even a small painting can be
perceived all at once.)[8] But the elements that combine into
sequences haven't become different elements, they have just become
combined into a whole in which their sequence matters. We have
no new elements here, we simply have complexes that should be
apprehended in sequence. And these complexes, these emergent
larger parts of the design, may be, like the larger parts of a
whole painting, attended to and experienced, as we think about
a work, either as having been presented in sequence or as simply
being the larger parts they are.[9]
     The example of sculpture is instructive, though Beardsley
does not discuss it. A work of sculpture is obviously a three-
dimensional visual design and we have to move around it to see
it all. That only enriches our notion of what visual designs
can be--layouts in space, in which complex variations of
frontality and linearity, quadrifaciality and stereomorphic
fidelity, and so on, can be observed. Design is design; none
of these variations is privileged, more specifically sculptural
than another, except by the qualities it achieves on its own.
The elegant tensions and balances of the Diskobolos by Myron
appear only in the silhouette views; viewed from the side it is
shapeless, incoherent (Fig. 1.2). On the other hand, the spirally
posed Bronze Seated Hermes from Herculaneum gives what Rhys

Carpenter calls "omnifacial stereomorphic presentations," with
every viewpoint yielding "simultaneous silhouetted and
foreshortened aspects" (Fig. 1.3).[10] We might think we'd have
to say the Hermes is the more sculptural of the two.

But the one sculpture is not more sculptural than the other,
because there are no special sculptural elements to the
implications of which a monument should be true. What you lose
on the swings you gain on the roundabouts: the Diskobolos gains
formality and loses stereomorphic fidelity just as Archaic
kouroi gain power and lose verisimilitude from their air of
offering us exactly four silhouetted views (Fig. 1.4). The
Hermes gains that verisimilitude along with the vigor that
attends the implicit movement of its torsion, but loses the
dignity that tends to accrete to any stylization, the implication
of freedom from and (in a sense) superiority to mere
representationalism. And as we notice these facts we are a long
way from elements, as we should be. To notice them is to consider
these sculptures as wholes, complex designs of layouts to which,
because of what Beardsley calls the "perceptual conditions"
presented to us by their "physical bases" (but which could come
from many other physical bases—from holograms, for example),
we can attend in the round though not all at once, and for just
the qualities each has to offer.

A sculpture is present before us all at once, but we usually
see it and explore its design and qualities in time. Film is
presented to us in time, as is music. We can't move around a
film at leisure to consider the visual qualities of the layouts
it presents, except metaphorically, as a matter of reflection.
The fact remains that there is no more reason than there is in
the case of sculpture to think that because the film is not a
painting, its visual elements are different from those of any
visual design. What we see in film is still the layout of visual
elements of its surface and of its depicted world. And if the
familiar issue of film's usual dependence on photography appears
here, it dissolves under inspection in this light.

That photography is the usual source of the film image is
unimportant when discussing films as aesthetic objects. Beardsley
makes plain that the physical basis is never germane to
description of aesthetic objects, though like the development
of the plastic in sculpture, the development of alterations in
the photographic image may be interesting historically, as a
matter of the interlocking of changes in style with changes in
technology. But for questions of aesthetic analysis, it's what
something looks like that counts, not how it happened to get its
looks. "What matters is the visible result" (p. 34). As
Beardsley generalizes the principle, "I propose to count as
characteristics of an aesthethic object no characteristics of
its presentations that depend upon knowledge of their causal
conditions, whether physical or psychological" (p. 52). If an
exact replica of a Gothic cathedral were constructed with a steel
frame, we would have no reason to discuss the relation of that
fact to the design if the frame were not perceptible.

The visible result of photography is usually that photographic images have characteristic textures that we correlate with the physical bases of their production. We recognize their styles as photographic (p. 172) and so quite rightly count among their connotations those of photographic images. Gibson points out that a "photographic picture" is "a record of perception, of what the picture maker was seeing at the time she made the picture at the point of observation she then occupied." But when we look to photographs for information about the world they present to us, we are not attending as one does to aesthetic objects, any more than when one consults Gibbon for details of the late Roman Empire. When we attend to photographs or Gibbon for aesthetic experience, it does not matter whether they are veridical. Still, photographic and cinematic images connote a certain verisimilitude, or rather that interplay among types of verisimilitude and formalization which is so often remarked, and this fact is entirely relevant to questions of the qualities of photographic and cinematic design.[11]

Oil paintings, too, have textures that we correlate with the physical bases of their production. It would be a curiosity to find that someone was so clever as to have done in watercolor what we thought was done in oil; it would be a curiosity to find that someone was so expert in animation as to have painted on film what we thought was an ordinarily photographed film scene. We would feel odd about it, as we do when we read poems we are told are computer-generated. But curiosities are all these cases are. Description of the curious film, for instance, would still be of the design of its surface and of its world, and of the qualities that emerge from both designs and their interaction.[12]

So our critical practice would not change if we found that we had been fooled about the sources of a film's images. It is not affected, after all, when we realize that studio settings, costume, makeup, graphic alteration of the photographic image, the articulating montage itself, play variations upon that "bias of exposition" that F. E. Sparshott claims we assume toward photographic representations, that bias with which we "take what we see as the record of something that took place as we see it taking place."[13] Design and the visual world it depicts always have all the connotations that go with their appearing the way they do. But the visible elements of film are nonetheless those of any visual design, and what counts for us viewing it is how those elements fuse with others so that complexes with more comprehensive and more intricate designs and qualities emerge.


DESIGN AND FORM
If film's elements are those of visual, verbal, and auditory design, cinematic specificity is historical fact and possibility rather than the nature or the opportunities of the medium itself, and all is smooth sailing. We can and should discuss the larger units of film and other arts in exactly the same ways, while of course considering the consequences of such differences as those

among temporal, spatial, and logical designs in the various arts.
With regard to relations among elements and complexes, we should
use the term "design" when we want to emphasize qualities and
content, and to enumerate or compare the parts and describe the
shape of the composition. And we should use the term "form" when
we want to discuss structure and texture. Texture is repetition
of any set of small-scale relations, and style is "recurrent
features of texture" (p. 173). Structure, which concerns large-
scale relations, is of a particular kind for each sort of design.
    Structural analysis of visual design deals with dominant
pattern. The relations among the parts of a design that yield
a sense of composition in this formal sense are the "dual
relations" (p. 174) of balance, color-tonality, and equilibrium,
and the "serial relations" (p. 176) of repetition and directional
change: complexes of all sorts and magnitudes pair with or
antagonize each other; more complexes than two form series, the
changes or repetitions within which are often the most important
components of an entire work's form.
    But as well as the structure that is a formal ordering of
major parts there is a sort of structure that is an ordering of
parts that could be more or less structured, more or less in
good order (p. 190). Balance and equilibrium figure in this
well-ordering too, but also important to it are focus and harmony.
And these four kinds of relation among the major design parts--
balance, equilibrium, focus, harmony--establish the completeness
and coherence of a design, the principal aspects of its unity.
But if the unity of a design is one of its most important global
attributes, it is not the only one. There is also a design's
complexity, which we find by counting up the parts: first, the
major parts, determined by stopping places and points of greatest
change; then the smaller parts, found by counting up the elements
that recur in the texture. But any aspect of design (for example,
line or figure) may be an aspect of structure. It is only
necessary that the aspect contribute to large-scale relations.
The long takes with a moving camera and the frenzied montage
sequences in The Miracle of Morgan's Creek are textural
elements, but they are in such balance across the film that they
emerge as major structural elements of its visual design. They
are strongly connotative, bearing heavily on the qualities of
the whole film.
    Structural analysis of music deals with structure-types and
with relations, analogous to the major relations of visual design,
like similarity, nearness, and contrast. But there are also
relations possible only in designs that are apprehended in
sequence: repetition, inversion, development, and kinetic pattern
with its four qualities of movement. The interplay of these
qualities --Introduction Quality, Exhibition Quality, Transition
Quality, and Conclusion Quality--throughout a piece makes up its
dominant kinetic pattern, which is analogous to the kinetic
pattern of visual design, and analogous also to dramatic structure
in literature.
    As Eisenstein always emphasized, film is commonly organized

by alterations in the pattern of changes in its progressive
images--for implicit movement can emerge from relations among
actual movements as readily as from the dynamics of static
images. Rudolf Arnheim, in fact, suggests that "if we want to
do justice to visual dynamics, we had better speak of 'movement'
as little as possible" and, with Wassily Kandinsky, "replace the
almost universally accepted concept 'movement' with 'tension.'"
Thus "directed tension . . . is what.we are talking about when
we discuss visual dynamics."[14]  Often there are massing,
balancing, and contrasting, across the space of the composition,
of visual blocks that should be apprehended as phases of a film's
sequence and as parts of its kinetic pattern. These orderings
reveal that while without separate elements from either visual
or auditory design, film's visual complexes, its major parts,
are composed in ways having attributes of both.

Literature, too, has aspects of composition in sequence and
in conceptual space. Its narrative structure is like visual
composition since it emerges from similarities in the patterns
of major parts. Its dramatic structure is like music since it
emerges from similarities and developments in the properties of
the dynamics of sequences, contoured and cadential like melodies
themselves. In this, film is no different from literature. But
literature also has unique properties of logical structure, since
language makes assertions but visual and musical designs do not,
facts we will consider further in Chapter 9.

Considering what Beardsley calls the "world projected by
a literary work" rather than the design or "discourse" made up
by its words, structural analysis assesses two set of relations.
One set is implied by the notion that "something is being said
by somebody about something" (pp. 237-38). Thus, structural parts
of the projected world are the speaker and his or her pragmatic
context; the situation, which is also in a slightly broader usage
the "subject"; the attitude of the implied speaker; and the
analogous attitude of the implied receiver, or tone. From these
properties of discourse that project a world emerge literature's
structures involving perspective, which are point of view and
tense.

But the other set of relations assessed by structural
analysis of literature is more important for film. The literary
situation or subject, what the speaker talks about, has structure
too. The perspectival controls of language, in literature, permit
the presentation of a world by means of assertions about it.
Images make no assertions, but what Christian Metz describes as
the "current of induction" that flows among a series of pictures
yields a design of representations as well as of structures of
visual surface, just as the literary discourse yields both a web
of meanings and a depicted world.[15]

The complexes of this depicted world--its characters, events,
settings--fuse into a design that has dramatic and narrative
structures. Within the latter we can distinguish plot, the
natural order of the represented events, and story, their ordering
in the work. And like the structures of surface design, the

structures of the projected worlds of literature and film may be discussed as well or ill ordered in terms of unity with its aspects completeness and coherence, of complexity, and of intensity of qualities in and among the parts.

Formal analysis of design, form, and content yields descriptions appropriate to the perceptual conditions of each art. Interpretation, possible for literature and representational visual design but not for music or nonrepresentational visual design, assesses the relation between a design of representations and the real world, a relation of meaning. In literature, theme, thesis, and symbol are the objects of interpretation. In representational visual design the objects are depiction and portrayal and also symbol, though symbols are different in literature and visual design. Nonrepresentational visual design has by definition no depiction, and hence no interpretable relation to the world, but it may have "suggestion," when "a design . . . has some notable and quite distinctive characteristic . . . in common with [an] object, but does not have enough in common with that object to represent it" (p. 283). As we shall see later, we can say much the same about music as well.

AESTHETIC EXPERIENCE AND AESTHETIC OBJECTS

But discriminating the parts of aesthetic objects, and the terms for their description and interpretation, does not prove that aesthetic objects exist. And such a proof is what film critics need most, so that descriptions, interpretations, and evaluations of films using the terms of aesthetic analysis will not seem unwarranted effusions. As well as providing terms for proper analysis of aesthetic objects of different kinds, Beardsley shows that there is a common property of aesthetic objects that does distinguish them from other perceptual objects and hence warrants our claiming their existence. That property derives from an object's relation to a particular kind of human experience.

Beardsley argues that when we speak of the aesthetic object we refer to some phenomenally objective thing in the "field" that we are "aware of, or conscious of, at a given time." It is something "persisting 'out there,' self-contained, independent of your will, capable of owning its own qualities" (p. 37), and therefore coughs and whispers in the audience or dust in the film gate aren't part of it even though they are parts of the field. It is also something different from what we feel or think about it, though that too may be in our field, as a phenomenally subjective part of the "presentation" (p. 44) of the object in that field. In short, an aesthetic object, like other perceptible objects, is something we experience, yet it is different from our experiencing it; its qualities are its own and not ours. The argument for the existence of aesthetic objects thus asserts the <u>objectivity</u> of perceptible presentations whose elements <u>fuse</u> into complexes with <u>qualities</u> among which can be those capable of providing <u>aesthetic experience</u>.

Beardsley demonstrates that the qualities belong to the object by pointing out that it makes perfect sense to say "the Matisse painting is cheerful," rather than "it makes me feel cheerful" (Fig. 1.5). For "even when, under some circumstances, the sight of a cheerful painting only increases my own melancholy by reminding me of what I lack, I can perceive its cheerfulness nevertheless, and in fact it is precisely this perception that makes me sad" (p. 38). There is a corollary--that I may be made to feel cheerful by a picture that is sad if, for instance, it reminds me of someone about whom I like to think. Thus there is a difference between saying that the work has qualities and that I respond to it in a particular way. And thus the work is different from my experience of it. As Beardsley puts it, "When we say, therefore, that Debussy's melody is sad, with an unutterably lost and hopeless sadness, we are talking about something phenomenally objective, not about ourselves" (p. 39). And that may well be the most important single claim of his book.

The aesthetic object is a perceptual object. Therefore it may have presentations, occasions when it is perceived by individual people. Presentations have in common "that they are caused by some exposure to the stimuli afforded by the physical basis of that aesthetic object" (p. 47). These facts establish the objectivity of the object, while at the same time relating it to people's experience. But they do not establish the relation, if any, between the object and its presentations. That is, they do not establish the existence of the object as distinct from its presentations.

Beardsley does something odd at this point, or at least odd at first glance. He sidesteps the question, or rather translates it. It will not do to say that the object is the class of its presentations, since one can conceive of but not perceive a class, and aesthetic objects are perceptual. And it is obvious that the object is no definable set of presentations--mine, yours, "competent critics'." Beardsley's temporary solution is simply to recast most object-talk into presentation-talk. "The ending of the Bartók composition is vigorous, but last evening's performance was slack" becomes "There have been, or will be, vigorous presentations of the end of the Bartók composition, but last evening's presentations were slack." Likewise the statement, "Bartók composed the Music for String Instruments, Percussion, and Celesta," is recast as "The first presentation of that composition occurred in Bartók's phenomenal field" (pp. 54-55).

This procedure postpones the question whether aesthetic objects are distinct from their presentations. Having established that aesthetic objects are phenomenally objective, though not what they are, Beardsley calls them aesthetic objects throughout his book. Yet the connection between presentations and the objects they present is nonetheless central, and it is with this that Beardsley concludes. To reach that conclusion we must emphasize that there are three kinds of statement we make about works: descriptive, interpretive, and evaluative. Beardsley exempts evaluative statements from translation into presentation-

language since "'This is good music' cannot be directly put into
the form 'Some presentations of this music are good'" (p. 55).
But evaluation is nonetheless dependent upon experience of the
presentation.  In fact, the quality of the experience available
for the attentive observer in the presentation of the object is
a measure of the object's worth, if the presentation may be taken
as of the object.  And "if it be granted that aesthetic experience
has value, then 'aesthetic value' may be defined as 'the capacity
to produce an aesthetic experience of some magnitude'" (p. 533).

This is an "instrumentalist definition" in that the value
comes from the work's capacity to do something.  It is not a
psychological definition, since it does not claim that whatever
people like is good.  Claims like that always leave as an "open
question" the possibility that perhaps people ought to like what
for some reason they don't, that maybe they're missing
likableness they oughtn't miss (pp. 518-20).

Of course, with its if-clause, the definition just given
of "aesthetic value" itself leaves as an open question the
possibility that perhaps aesthetic experience does not have
value.  If it did not, then aesthetic value could not be said
to exist on its grounds, and in turn there would be no reason
to claim existence for the objects defined through being said
to have that value.  But leaving that question open rather
simplifies than confuses things.  Put that way, the problem is
not hard to solve--find what aesthetic experience is, and see
if it's worth anything in terms of its effects, if it has value.
Does it improve our lives, in any respects other than the
improvement which consists simply in the pleasure of having it,
if we do have it?  Beardsley's last chapter argues that art does
help, and we will consider that claim shortly.  More important
here, however, his definition of aesthetic value as the capacity
to produce experience of a particular kind settles the question
of the existence and qualities of aesthetic objects.  But to
understand that, we should be clear about what kind of experience
aesthetic objects, if they exist, can produce.

Aesthetic experience is available only to people who know
how to apprehend the appropriate elements of perceptual objects
as fusing into complexes with qualities.  That is, we don't get
the full aesthetic experience that the calligraphy of Ryokwan
can provide if we don't know Japanese, although we may get some
from the formal and vital qualities of its nonrepresentational
visual design.  Again, we don't get full aesthetic experience
from classical Indian music if we haven't learned to follow the
count of an alap or hear the tonalities of ragas.  And we don't
get full aesthetic experience from nonrepresentational painting
if we haven't learned to see that areas of a visual design that
depict nothing can have human regional qualities, such as
cheerfulness, hesitancy, and forcefulness, just as depictions
can.

But to argue that a perceiver must know something in order
to have aesthetic experience does not make aesthetic objects

subjective.  Beardsley settles this in the context of music, when
he suggests that melody has to

> be defined in a relative way:  a series of notes is a melody
> at a certain stage in the history of music, or in a certain
> culture, if it can be heard as fusing together by people
> at that place or time who have had whatever training is
> available.  This is not an individual matter, for the word
> "can" makes the definition impersonal.  When Brahms'
> contemporaries complained that some of his series of
> notes were not melodies, they were mistaken, for others,
> and perhaps later they themselves, could hear them that
> way. . . . The distinction between what is a melody and what
> is not is objective and discoverable within the context of
> a given musical period or the music of a given culture. (p.
> 103)

This accounts for the importance of connotations among the
qualities of musical elements and complexes, and by analogy for
the importance of connotations among the qualities of the other
arts.  Yet it might seem as well to permit claims, such as Umberto
Eco's and Bill Nichols's, for a theory of "ideological
determination" of perception, recognition, and iconicity itself.
But it does not, for perceptual objects have many other qualities
besides their connotations, and these guarantee that what an
object is to be for us is not solely what its place in our culture
makes it.[16]
     There are reasons, different from the capacity of social
practice to accrete connotations, for the emergence of qualities
from perceptual complexes.  And these are thus reasons, different
from the existence of connoting conventions, for saying that
aesthetic experience is not solely determined by the state of
the experiencer.  Intervals in music cannot help but have a
relation to what Leonard Bernstein calls the "built-in preordained
universal known as the harmonic series," and this relation is
profoundly important for the qualities of music.  Music in a minor
key, for instance, has "a 'disturbed' quality" just from the
importance in it of a tone, the minor third, so far along in the
series, and so much "at variance with the major third which is
implicitly present in the fundamental," as to make those
resolutions that feature it "'troubled,' 'sad,' 'unstable,'
'dark,' 'passionate,' or whatever."  This "so-called 'affective'
phenomenon," Bernstein points out, is "not an extrinsic
metaphorical operation at all; it is intrinsic to music, and its
meaning is a purely musical one."[17]
     Concerning visual design, James J. Gibson has shown that
"a picture is a surface so treated that a delimited optic array
to a point of observation is made available that contains the
same kind of information that is found in the ambient optic arrays
of an ordinary environment."  Thus the areas of a picture cannot
help but have a relation to the "formless and timeless invariants

that specify the distinctive features of the object."[18]  When
we consider the information in the pictured optic array, its
deviations from and agreements with what we might pick up in the
world must emerge as the characterizing qualities of that pictured
surface quite apart from any contribution of cultural
connotations.  Even E. H. Gombrich, who urges against Gibson the
"beholder's share" in visual perception, notes that "if all seeing
is interpreting, all modes of interpretation could be argued to
be equally valid," and he rejects that conclusion as "nonsense."
For him, visual representation cannot help but be related to that
"eye-witness principle" that eliminates "all that the eye-witness
could not see" from images possessing "visual credibility."  Their
qualities are not exclusively, in Gombrich's view, contributed
by the beholder's share, but are in part those of the visible
world.[19]
     Patterns in verbal discourse, moreover, cannot help but have
a relation to the grammar of the language in which they are cast,
and grammar is not in any simple sense learned from social
practice but is constrained by biological determinants.[20]  So
in literature too there are both connotative qualities and
qualities of adhesion to and deviation from norms that are not
directly associated with culture or patterns of learning.  In
the sense suggested by all these considerations about music,
visual design, and literature, aesthetic experience should be
understood not as entirely subjectively determined, nor learned
as a matter of social symbolism, but as experience of objective
qualities in the perceptual objects that can give rise to it.
     The aesthetic experience that works of art have the capacity
to produce, Beardsley shows, is usually and rightly described
in ways that are readily collapsible into three familiar terms.
Aesthetic experience is highly unified, complex, and intense.
It is possible to obtain unified, complex, and intense experience
from sources other than works of art, for instance, from athletic
events, and there is no reason to restrict the definition of
aesthetic experience to experience of works of art.  George Dickie
points out that Beardsley, concerning himself with criticism of
art, does not and need not "include an account of natural objects
as aesthetic objects."  But Dickie suggests that one "might be
developed along these lines:  a natural object is an aesthetic
object when it functions in someone's experience in a manner
similar to the way a work of art functions when it is taken as
an object of appreciation and/or criticism."[21]
     But it is the rare athletic event that can give rise to
experience sufficiently unified, complex, and intense in its human
qualities to warrant calling it an aesthetic object, and it is
from works of art, many of which can provide a high degree of
it, that aesthetic experience usually comes.  We can attempt to
see a car, for instance, as an aesthetic object, if we constrict
our minds and ignore the car's fitness for something other than
inducing aesthetic experience.  But such a constrained
presentation of a car is less than unified in its qualities, since
the car itself has so many qualities that are at cross purposes

with the set to which we are primarily attending.  Moreover, we
cannot respond to the car fully, since to do so requires an
unconstrained mind.  Having an obvious and ordinary use in the
world, the car lacks an essential quality of aesthetic objects:
disinterestedness, the quality of cutting themselves off from
the rest of the world and gaining thereby a "multiple relatedness"
that is an aspect of their unity (p. 128).  Aesthetic objects,
Beardsley says, are "objects manqués.  There is something
lacking in them that keeps them from being quite real, from
achieving the full status of things . . . and upon this depends
their capacity to call forth from us the kind of admiring
contemplation, without any necessary commitment to practical
action, that is characteristic of aesthetic experience" (p. 529).
     If we persist in seeing the car as an aesthetic object, we
ignore about it what we shouldn't, and that is that a full
experience of it soon draws us from contemplation toward action.
To ignore that fact about it is as quirky as to ignore the fact
that aesthetic objects possess focussed and articulated structures
that maximize their emergent contemplatable qualities at the same
time that they minimize their use for something other than
contemplation.  Of course, we can go to the movies to experience
what Jurij Lotman handsomely describes as the "unquestionably
base emotions which are typical of the passive observer of genuine
catastrophes," just as we can fail to contemplate Hamlet or
The Naked Dawn from headache or preoccupation.  But as in all
cases where objects have qualities that can induce aesthetic
experience we should, if aesthetic experience has value, attend
to them for it.  It's truer to the qualities of Rio Bravo, for
example, to find a unity in its relations of parts to parts and
to exhaust our interest in the act of contemplating that unity,
than to gratify the "base emotions" of enjoyment at seeing people
in the work's world blown up by dynamite.  Unity is a set of
qualities of coherence and completeness, and aesthetic experience
is, in large part, contemplation of that set as such.[22]
     The understanding of aesthetic objects is grounded in
aesthetic experience, but it is the objects, and not the
experience, with which we are concerned.  A curious fact about
aesthetic experience is that, while it defines aesthetic objects,
what counts for us who have it is not the experiencing itself
so much as the objects that cause it.  Aesthetic experience is
a certain kind of attentiveness, but a kind in which the state
of attending is less important to us than the natures of the
objects to which we attend.  What we are concerned with is
whether, to what extent, and in what ways in the different arts,
objects in our phenomenal fields can provide aesthetic
experience by rewarding our attention.
     The measure is then, Beardsley says, like the one we use
when we say that and how a particular foodstuff is "nutritious"
(p. 531).  To creatures that know how to use it (e.g., for cows,
grass) it can provide nutriment.  But it doesn't have to do so
to be nutritious, and we'd never think of saying that grass was
nutritious only if, in fact, cows were nourished by it.  And no

one has to have an aesthetic experience from Rio Bravo for the
film to have the capacity of providing one. We may even suspect
that fewer early viewers did have the aesthetic experience it
can provide than did those of later runs, something we have seen
that we could also say about the melodies of Brahms.

What attributes, then, enable objects to provide aesthetic
experience? Why just the ones, naturally enough, that could be
expected to supply the different aspects of that experience.
The aesthetic experience, critics have always agreed, is markedly
self-contained. It is more disinterested contemplation than goal-
directed thought or purposive action, and the experience is of
more rather than fewer linkages among its aspects. Just so, the
objects that provide the experience are complete and coherent,
and these are the aspects of their unity, just as completeness
and coherence are principal aspects of aesthetic experience.
Likewise, just as aesthetic experience is marked by the sense
that we are balancing many aspects of a complex attitude as we
respond to the work, so one of the attributes of objects that
enables them to provide aesthetic experience is their complexity.

And as aesthetic experience is always attentiveness to human
relevance, just so aesthetic objects have a certain intensity
of human qualities, the flow and change and interaction of which
are the very substance of what we go to art for. Consider the
human richness of these passages:  the compassionate but savage
finality of the concluding montage in Eclipse; the ironic and
cool detachment of the bird's-eye view of Bodega Bay's burning
gas station in The Birds; the witty delirium of the locket
cascading through the silvered trees in The Scarlet Empress; the
divided flow at the end in The Searchers, as the staggering
grief of the excluded Ethan Edwards is closed from our view by
the door that includes us in the primitive darkness where the
new couple, and the redeemed Debbie, will recreate a hearthside
civilization equivocally to replace the cold but gorgeous desert.
Describing the richness of such human qualities as these is almost
impossible, but this is exactly why we treasure them so much.

So the existence in aesthetic objects of unity, complexity,
and intensity of human qualities resolves the question of the
relation of presentations to works of art, exactly because it
links the experience the objects can provide with properties of
the objects themselves. Beardsley's thematically climactic
passage is this:  "in short, appeal to the three General Canons
[of Unity, Complexity, and Intensity] that seem to underlie so
much of critical argument can itself be justified in terms of
an Instrumentalist definition of 'aesthetic value.' For these
Canons refer to characteristics of aesthetic objects that enable
them to evoke aesthetic experiences" (p. 534). Thus aesthetic
objects are defined as well as evaluated in terms linked to our
experience of them. But these terms are not of our experience
itself, but rather of their capacity to provide it because of
their properties. Aesthetic objects are simply phenomenally
objective things in the world that have the three canonical
characteristics in some magnitude. The objects are real. It

is to them we refer, not to ourselves, when we point out their structures and emergent qualities. But we know that they are aesthetic objects through our comprehension of them as capable of producing aesthetic experience on account of their characteristics.

Aesthetic value, then, may be defined in terms of aesthetic experience. The experience of attending to how a good film works is a matter of understanding the composition and the inexhaustible flow of "aboutnesses," relevancies to the world that emerge from the interaction of qualities of meaningfulness that attend such a web of forms and connotations, such a design. This experience is concentrating, refreshing, enlivening, illuminating, as good for the mind and spirit as physical exercise is for the body and spirit. As experience, aesthetic experience may be distinguished from other sorts of experience, such as sexual, religious, or intellectual. For in experiencing the aesthetic object there is in the quality of one's attention a quite particular kind of wholeness and pointedness. It includes, as a result of focus and kinetic pattern, a certain orientation to consummation, but not at the cost of the multiple relatedness among all the aspects of the experience. It thus remains pointed in on itself as an experience we are having, for we treasure our own experience when attending like this, and feel its ties with the rest of our lives, of which it is indeed simply and unmysteriously a part. But it is always an experience of the object, for we feel it and value it with our attention to it, even more than we value our attending--first things first, after all, and we came for the movie. There is pointedness in such focus and direction, yet wholeness in that it is not pointedness towards conclusion or action, but towards preserving the phenomenal object as something that can be contemplated as a whole within the experiencing of it. The end is for us in the preservation of all the relations among the means. Experience of that sort is not like other kinds.

But it is not out of the ordinary. It happens all the time, in various degrees and durations. Its reality is, Beardsley shows, well attested. But to someone who doubts its existence we can only say, "Come now, hasn't this sort of alert and sympathetic observation, this awareness and understanding of objects as simply possessing the qualities of their designs, ever happened to you?" Of course someone could say, "Yes, I've been deluded like that, prisoner of ideology as I am." But to that more "theoretical" issue we will have to return.

As we claim the existence of aesthetic experience on empirical grounds, so its value. We can ask with Beardsley the crucial question: "But does aesthetic experience do people any good?" (p. 573). And it does seem that there is some "worth of art to the consumer, so to speak," and that we can "use the term 'inherent value' for the capacity of aesthetic objects to produce good inherent effects--that is, to produce desirable effects by means of the aesthetic experience they evoke" (p. 573).[23]

There is reason to think that aesthetic experience "relieves

tensions and quiets destructive impulses," on the Aristotelian
model.  By checking our mental state before and after it, we can
discover that aesthetic experience provides "a remarkable kind
of clarification, as though the jumble in our minds were being
sorted out," a jumble having little evident connection with the
content of the object evoking the experience.  It is less easily
shown, but we hope it true, "that aesthetic experience refines
perception and discrimination" in that it calls for an "unusual
degree of attention to subtle differences in regional quality,
not only in the emotions and attitudes of characters in
literature, but in the human qualities of paintings and musical
compositions"--surely practice makes better, if not perfect.
Probably aesthetic experience "develops the imagination, and along
with it the ability to put oneself in the place of others" (p.
574), even if only because people otherwise so different can share
it--Ester (seated, listening):  "Bach"; The Waiter (standing,
listening too):  "Sebastian Bach."
     Most important, "in aesthetic experience we have experience
in which means and ends are so closely interrelated that we feel
no separation between them.  One thing leads to the next and finds
its place in it; the end is immanent in the beginning, the
beginning is carried up into the end.  Such experience allows
the least emptiness, monotony, frustration, lack of fulfillment,
and despair--the qualities that cripple much of human life" (p.
575).  After such experience, then, how can we help but think
that "if some of the satisfyingness of the end could be brought
into the means, and the means at every stage felt as carrying
the significance of the end, we should have in life something
more of the quality of aesthetic experience itself" (p. 576)?
If to be reminded of that is an inherent effect of aesthetic
experience, then aesthetic experience has value, and so do the
objects that evoke it.  Of course, if we are wrong, and if there
is no such thing as aesthetic experience, or if it does not have
the effects we think it has, or if it is not connected as we say
to the qualities of aesthetic objects, then perhaps not dust and
ashes all that is, but at least precious little excuse for
studying films for the sake of alerting ourselves and others to
the aesthetic experience that they can provide.  But we are not
wrong.


THE PROCEDURE OF CRITICISM AND YOUNG MR. LINCOLN
     Critical practice as Beardsley suggests it, then, is a
process of accounting for the interaction between the perceptual
conditions of the work and the qualities that emerge from their
forms and contents.  Here is how the work is shaped, and how its
shaping gives it qualities like these--that is the critical claim
in a nutshell.  Thus a Beardsleyan critical procedure is this:
we observe the formal and representational aspects of the design
and the qualities that emerge from them and we note the
interaction of the qualities in the different parts of the work,

thus building a sense of structure. From structure emerge
qualities that in turn we observe: formal qualities like
looseness, dynamic development, or textural variation; human
qualities like lassitude, passion, or serenity. Thus we achieve
a sense of the whole, which we can describe in terms of the formal
relations of the work and their emergent qualities, interpret
in terms of the implications of the qualified structure concerning
the real world as the work represents or suggests it, and evaluate
in terms of the degree to which the structure has the capacity
to provide aesthetic experience.

The best thing about this procedure is its insistence that
the work itself be defined by just the most finely tuned and
closely perceived qualities that the responder finds in himself
or herself in his or her presentation of the work. Beardsley's
approach lets us appeal at every instant to what we actually see
happening in a film, rather than imposing upon it any deductive
grid or interpretation in the light of a preestablished and
distorting system of thought. A significant example of such a
distorting imposition is the famous reading of John Ford's Young
Mr. Lincoln by the editors of Cahiers du Cinéma.[24]

Ford's film, in the Cahiers view, is about violence and
erotic repression. Their reading, though they would not wish
to be paraphrased like this, implies that the film is at root
about Americans' ostensible respect for law as an excuse for
violence, which is made necessary by the emasculation of the
American male. The reading is achieved by an elaborate
translation of the film's implications into congruence with a
psychoanalytic model of psychological process. But the
interpretive grid, far from revealing the meaning of the film,
conceals it in two ways. Only the facts come through that the
grid allows. And even those that come through are taken not for
their qualities but for their significance to the model that
supplies the grid, as if the film's meaning were not in it, but
were a secret to be teased out by a method of seeing through its
cover stories. The actual qualities of the film, passage by
passage and also as they should be seen in each other's lights,
are programmatically suppressed, or seen at best as signals of
a truer meaning for which they act as masks.

For example, Cahiers reads the moment when Lincoln takes
the Almanac out of his hat to confront Palmer Cass with facts
about the moon's phase as seeming like a magician springing a
rabbit out of his hat. Its point for Cahiers is that it is
a gag. Like any gag, by its "occultation" as a joke it is
automatically in the realm of the erotic, since, with their
economy of expenditure of psychic energy, gags evade a repression
and release some energy from the erotic repressed. Taking the
Almanac from the hat is, in Cahiers's view, a "phallic
signifier": "it is not Lincoln who uses the signifier to manifest
the truth," for he would have to admit to doing it and face up
to the repression, "but the signifier which uses Lincoln as
mediator to accede to the status of the sign of truth." From

its perspective we can understand Cahiers's point. The
resolution by hat trick is just either a distortion of the
"ideological project," which was to show Lincoln praiseworthy
because of the way he could act to bring truth, or a strange
replacement of the praise of work with an eroticization of work,
an absorbing of its effectors into the social power of the
signifier.[25] The signifier would thus be the phallus in the
place of the subject in the film's Imaginary. The replacement
would be strange, yet common, since "man thinks with his object,"
Lacan says, and the Almanac here is to Lincoln as the cotton-reel
to the child in the "Fort! Da!" game.[26]

     Cahiers's point is thus the falsity of the image, the
way it cheats on its film. The image replaces real praise of
Lincoln, Cahiers implies, with a trivialized absorption of
achievement into mere destiny. It translates a man into a monster
of legend, the Other's pawn: "the improbable levity with which
Ford brings the trial to its close really can only be read as
a masking effect which conceals to the end the 'human' context,
. . . a final consequence of Lincoln's re-enactment of the
Mother's role." That role is both to present to the world and
to be represented by the phallus, her phallus, her son. But what
a paradox. As son, he is the phallus for his mother the Law
and resembles the cavalry or Ethan Edwards--ecstatic, scalping/
castratable, "expendable." But in the role of the mother, he
has the phallus--the Almanac that signifies truth. The film's
lesson, then, its "properly scriptural projection," is that the
insistence on masking Lincoln's violence subverts the text, writes
in the violence but disowns it. We learn from the film "the
effects of the repression of violence," and these effects are
the qualities Cahiers finds in it. The effects are of
incoherence, a "fantastic contrast which contributes considerably
to the subversion of the deceptively calm surface of the text."
It is an incoherence itself troubled and violent, hence (we extend
Cahiers) a kind of mirror of the society for which it is objet
petit a, like the Almanac, like any Imaginary signifier.[27]

     The case is coherent, but it depends on taking the Almanac
as something different from and using Lincoln, taking over from
him the key role in causing events. Cahiers implies that its
revelation of Lincoln as complex and disturbing undercuts his
place in the film's manifest structure, his contribution to its
perceptible meaning. But the Almanac does not come out of the
blue when it appears in what Cahiers takes to be a meaningless
and incomprehensible co-presence with Lincoln in the "three scenes
where it is present without Lincoln knowing what to do with it
in terms of the truth." Rather, it comes out of Lincoln's hat!

     Lincoln doesn't always tell us what he's up to, he keeps
it under his hat. But his plans are still his. What he keeps
under his hat doesn't use him, we can see; he uses it (Fig. 1.6).
The Cahiers reading explicitly claims to be superior to other
readings because it is open to the film just as it is. But while
Cahiers mentions, though quite without comment, a few other
appearances of hats in the film--Lincoln doffing his to the

Revolutionary veterans and to the final crowd, for instance--it misses Lincoln's hat carried before him at the dance, the pioneer coonskin knocked off by the bailiff at the trial, and many others. And Cahiers, as if willfully, refuses to attend to a striking quality emergent from the many emphases on hats. It is a quality that comes to have everything to do with the effect of that scene that Cahiers sees with its tin eye only as an "improbable levity" because of its air of being like a magician's trick.[28]

The trial is not the first time "the Law" is in Lincoln's hat. After he intimidates the "brothers" Woolridge and Hawthorne, Lincoln folds the paper concerning their case and puts it carefully into his hat, as he stares at them for offering false coin. From his hat we can see peeking scraps of paper as he tells the loiterers who watch that his law office is "in my hat" and rides off toward the Clay farm. Nor is taking the law out of one's hat new in this film. In The Iron Horse the traveling judge keeps his law book in his top hat and takes it out with a flourish at the trial. There is hat-play of an evocative kind as early as Three Bad Men and as late as Seven Women. The Cahiers reading, far from freeing itself to understand the film by relating its episodes to scenarios justified by psychoanalysis, binds itself to the perceptions of only those aspects that fit its purpose. Of course many good but partial readings do just that--but Cahiers claims from the start to get it all, not to present "(yet another) commentary" or "interpretation" that is a "translation of what is supposed to be already in the film into a critical system (metalanguage) where the interpreter has . . . absolute knowledge."[29]

Lincoln's assurance is grounded in both the sorts of law he has received as a virtual inheritance from the Clay family, and from the pioneer tradition for which they stand and by which he is linked to them. These are the law of society and the law of nature. Lincoln gets from the Clays books concerning both sorts, Blackstone's Commentaries and the Almanac. Law books connote the social medium in which alone justice can be effected; the Almanac connotes the rootedness of that justice in nature. There is no doubt which one takes precedence. Beyond the bar at the side of the courtroom, bareheaded and with hat nowhere in sight, Lincoln fingers law books from the shelves behind him and mockingly baits the prosecutor Felder, who is crippled as if he were deficient in one of the legs of the law and who is shown as stooge for Springfield's power structure. But in the middle of the courtroom, the bar of justice divides the total space before the judge's bench as the fence divides the space before the tree and river in Lincoln's scene with Ann Rutledge (Fig. 1.7). When Lincoln is across the bar his hat is always prominent in the frame, reservedly crown up on the trial's first day, expectantly brim up on the second.

Beyond the bar, then, in the space associated with the river and with Ann's urging Lincoln to devote his natural talents to the law, Lincoln confronts Palmer Cass with his guilt. Lincoln

takes the Almanac out of his top hat to show Cass the evidence
provided in this judicial setting by natural, not human, law
(Fig. 1.6). Justice done, the bar opens; now natural and social
space are connected, as when by the only partly obstructing gate-
poles Lincoln stood with Ann. Cass confesses, and is surrounded
on the near side of the bar by the public, which hems him in and
prevents his escape (Fig. 1.8). Visually and thematically the
moment is an echo and an undoing of the "escape" of Ann Rutledge
away from the fence, out of the frame, into life's contingencies,
and toward death, in that time before Lincoln entered and could
lead and emend that corruptible social world that could allow
it. Lincoln could then only turn to throw the stone of his
commitment into the stream of time (Fig. 1.9). But now, as the
lawyer Ann wanted him to be, he can preside over the fusion of
natural and social law that he had been powerless to effect when
he had been sensitive but powerless, a hatless boy.

After the decision at Ann's grave Lincoln wears a top hat
and becomes proficient in the social workings of the law. But
after Cass's confession Lincoln shows which law matters most.
As he stands in front of the judge and says "Your witness" to
Felder, Lincoln sets his hat decisively, rudely, on his head
(Fig. 1.10). Nature has been satisfied, and that quality of the
legal process that is worthy of respect has dissipated no matter
what formalities remain. It is as if here in the courtroom Ann
Rutledge's spirit returned for a moment and the tragedy of her
passing had been undone, as if there at the river she could have
reappeared from nature's side after Lincoln threw the stone.
It would not be the only time in Ford's films. In Pilgrimage
Jim Jessop throws a stone into a pool and the ripples spread and
clear to reveal Mary's image reflected in the water (Fig. 1.11)
before the camera tilts up to reveal her beyond the pool. And
in The Searchers, Ethan stoops, picks up and throws a stone
into a little river with just Lincoln's gesture (Fig. 1.12; cf.
Fig. 1.9). Debbie, the one who had been lost, appears "at the
top of the hill" beyond the water to run down and acknowledge
to Martin the primal kinship-no-kinship that is also Lincoln's
kinship to Ann (Fig. 1.13). In The Searchers Ethan the effector
resists and Martin inherits--but Ethan threw the stone.

To whom or to what one takes off one's hat is a touchstone
of Young Mr. Lincoln, whether Lincoln throws off his hat to
confront the lynch mob (like Dai Bando's tossing off his hat in
How Green Was My Valley as he prepares to teach a lesson to
another representative of effete and civilized perversions of
power) or, as at the very end, he merely tips his hat to Mary
Todd, then doffs it first to the people whose respect he accepts
and then to Mrs. Clay by the wagon, before he puts it back on
for the long walk forward, to "the top of the hill," into the
storms of history.

The quality emergent from this constant emphasis on hats,
here and elsewhere in Ford, is of a certain finely tuned
respectfulness for oneself and for the values to which the self-

respectful person pays homage.  One thinks of all the times that
are like the one in The Searchers--there is a scene of identical
structure, dialogue, and meaning in The Long Grey Line--when
Captain the Reverend Samuel Johnson Clayton responds to the
greenhorn Greenhill boy as he formally and eagerly reports on
the Indians outside but forgets where he is in the larger context
of society.  Clayton asks, "Your head cold, Son?," upon which
with a gulp the Lieutenant puts first things first and takes off
his hat with a dutiful "Beg pardon, Ma'am" to the woman of the
house in which the civilization he is concerned with protecting
is embodied.
    Young Mr. Lincoln is suffused with qualities of feeling
linked at every point to the meaning of hats.  There is something
offensive, as well as indefensible, in Cahiers's explanatory
and inferential interpretation, which claims that quite another
quality should be seen in the film when it is translated into
the meaning dictated by a certain theory.  But people who can
see an improbable levity in a Ford character's dealings with his
hat are capable of anything.


INTERPRETATION AND THE QUALITIES OF ART
    We have seen that aesthetic experience is provided occasion
by the qualities emergent from the structures and "worlds" of
aesthetic objects.  There remains a problem in understanding how
nonliving things like aesthetic objects can have qualities we
usually think of as belonging exclusively to living things.  And,
interestingly enough, Beardsley's solution to this problem also
illuminates his justification of the critical procedures that
are usually broadly called interpretive.  The first procedure
is explication, in which an element or small-scale complex is
explained in terms of its meaning within the context of the web
of meanings and implications that make up the design.  The second
is the process of elucidation, in which a crux concerning "parts
of the world of the work, such as character and motives, that
are not explicitly reported in it, given the events and states
of affairs that are reported plus relevant empirical
generalizations, that is, physical and psychological laws" is
resolved (p. 401).  And the third procedure is interpretation
proper, in which the relations among the work's implications about
its own world are connected to ideas about the real world through
analyses of themes and theses.  "A theme is something named by
an abstract noun or phrase:  the futility of war, the mutability
of joy; heroism, inhumanity," but it is not something that can
be said to be true or false (pp. 403-4).  A thesis is "something
about, or in, the work that can be called true or false, if
anything can" (p. 404).
    All these procedures involve accepting audience knowledge
as part of the web of meanings, suggestions, and implications
of the work--like the recognition of a Brahms passage as a melody
discussed earlier.  But if the objects of such knowledge come

from us, how can they be in the work to start? We may relate
this question to another: how a human quality can be said to
be in a nonhuman thing. The answer to both questions is simple:
"by metaphor." Beardsley's discussion of metaphor has two
purposes: 1) to give a model for all interpretation, since the
work is the metaphor writ large and "a metaphor is a miniature
poem" (p. 144); and 2) to justify the claim that works have as
qualities of their own what in part we must infer to be in them.
Aesthetic objects have, in effect, deeper structure than the
organization of surface relations among their elements and
complexes. They have relations among qualities and suggestions
that are linked to the connotations of their parts.

Beardsley's "controversion theory" takes metaphor as a
species of "Self-Controverting Discourse," in which "the speaker
or writer utters a statement explicitly but in such a way as to
show that he does not believe what he states, or is not primarily
interested in what he states, and thereby calls attention to
something else that he has not explicitly stated--'if he wins,
I'll eat my hat.'" The reader or hearer "looks about for a second
level of meaning on which something is being said" (p. 138),
since the surface level is obviously false or not credible. Here
are some examples from film of metaphor-like strategies. In
Boudu Saved from Drowning, there is no such person as Boudu
and we all know it, yet we are truly concerned with some "levels"
of meaning suggested by the false claim as to his existence and
its qualities. In Sunrise, when the camera suddenly takes off,
as if on its own, in another direction in the swamp from that
in which the Husband expects to meet the Woman from the City,
we look around for a level of suggestion commensurate with the
odd move, paying particular attention to the qualities of the
camera movement itself. In October, since nowhere in life do
Christs turn into Buddhas without warning, and these in turn
change into more primitive-seeming gods, we cast around for an
implication in the process that will explain its being shown to
us.[30]

That process of looking for what makes sense when we get
any signal that the primary implication is out of whack is the
process that underlies all of Beardsley's interpretive types.
Observing the process, we can say that the levels of meaning we
find are in the works themselves, since the works are "self-
controverting," false or misleading or stylized or distorted or
unnatural on the surface, precisely in order that the connotations
and suggestions by which we can make deeper sense of them can
come through.

The argument for metaphor is like that for the claim that
human qualities are in nonhuman objects. Beardsley disposes first
of the argument that the Matisse painting can't be cheerful
because a painting is "only a collection of electrons . . . and
obviously electrons can't be cheerful." Paintings aren't physical
objects, however, but perceptual ones with a physical basis.
So that argument is easily countered.

Then Beardsley posits a tougher interrogator who says that "only people can be cheerful, strictly speaking, and thus all statements attributing cheerfulness to something must be statements about people if they are not to be nonsense." But this, Beardsley counters, "would make metaphorical statements impossible," though admittedly "when I say that the Matisse painting is cheerful I cannot mean by the word 'cheerful' just what I mean when I say that a person is cheerful; it is a metaphorical extension of the term" (p. 36). It is a use of the term that calls attention to ways in which the attributes of the painting are similar to our attributes when we're cheerful, such as that its areas are bold and self-assured, bright, without tension but with vigor, related strongly yet not overassertively, and so on as far in the set of connotations of the notion "cheerful" as one can go and still remain within the facts of the painting.

But still problems remain. Even if we are signalled to import connotations and suggestions to a word or passage or color area or musical part, how can we say the ones we import are the work's and not ours? And second, even if we can grant connotations to words, so that metaphor proper is possible, how can we call such notions as boldness and brightness, which are only slightly less obviously self-controverting than cheerful as attributes of a painting, metaphorically true for forms of art other than literature? It is words that mean and connote. In painting and music, after all, as in the images of film, we have neither dictionary meanings nor connotations for the signs, if any, which make the elements of the arts, as we do for literature's elements, words. What is true for painting or music--or for film--on that level on which we are signalled by self-controversion to import connotations, that level on which "he is a lion in battle" means "he is a brave man"?

Beardsley answers the first problem simply and tellingly, and in a way similar to his treatment of the odd intervals in a Brahms melody. Connotations are "objective parts of the meanings of . . . terms as they belong to a certain speech-community, just as much as their dictionary meanings." Connotations of the words for objects "come from the way those objects appear in human experience. 'Desert' connotes unfruitfulness and death, whether a particular reader is aware of it or not; he can correct and improve his reading by recalling the real effects of deserts." Thus

if two people know the designation of "desert" and have all the relevant facts about the nature of deserts, and the current beliefs about them, and the past verbal contexts in which deserts have been spoken of . . . then they can, within narrow limits, agree on which characteristics are or are not connoted by the word. Moreover, maverick readings--"It reminds me of a pretty little sandpile I knew as a child"--can be spotted as such. (p. 133)

Metaphor, theme, and meaning seem possible, then, since
connotation and the related suggestion, which is to sentences
and assertions what connotation is to words (p. 123), belong to
the work and not to ourselves.
      But can we grant boldness or cheerfulness to other arts than
literature? The answer can be seen best in that art furthest
from literature, music. (If in music, then in nonrepresentational
and representational painting as well, and surely also in film.)
But the answer is not to claim that tones are like words in that
they both denote and connote. Beardsley refutes the
"Signification Theory," showing that it is a form of "Semiotic
Theory" and as such "tries to subsume music under a general theory
of semiosis, or sign-functioning" (pp. 333-34). Signification
theorists hold that "music does have a referential relation to
things outside itself" (p. 332), for which it is a sign. In
particular, musical passages are iconic signs of the sort that
are "similar to their significata." Music, according to this
theory, "is an iconic sign of psychological process. It
'articulates' or 'elucidates' the mental life of man, and it does
so by presenting auditory equivalents of some structural or
kinetic aspects of that life" (p. 333).
      Beardsley shows that there are two claims in this theory:
1) music can be iconic of a psychological process, which he argues
is true; and 2) by virtue of that iconicity, music is a sign of
that process, which he argues is false. Film students have become
accustomed to asssenting to the claim that there are three kinds
of sign, and these we tend to label, following the terminology
of C. S. Peirce, the symbolic, indexical, and iconic.[31] But
Beardsley claims convincingly that there are only two kinds of
sign, conventional ones, which Peirce would call symbolic, and
natural ones, which Peirce would call indexical. Similarity
between the sign and what it stands for is, in the organization
suggested by Peirce, the mark of an iconic sign, yet Beardsley
shows that

> it is clear in general that mere similarity, whether of
> quality or structure, is not sufficient to make an object
> a sign. If it were, we should have to say that the territory
> signifies the map, and that the mental process is a sign
> of the music, since similarity always goes both ways. One
> chair may be exactly like another, but that does not make
> it signify the other. (p. 335)

      Iconicity is, of course, a matter of resemblance. Max Black
objects to Beardsley's account of depiction in terms of
resemblance, which is that "'The design X depicts an object
Y' means 'X contains some area that is more similar to the
visual appearance of Y's than to objects of any other class'"
(p. 270). Black argues that there are difficulties in any claim
that "the look or appearance of the 'design' has to be 'more

similar' to the look of a tree than to the look of an ocean."
But suppose James J. Gibson is right that a picture presents in
its virtual objects just those formless and timeless invariants
that we observe in objects in the world. The light contains
information about these invariants, and so the picture is a record
of perception of objects imagined, known, or perceived. If that
were true, then the look of the given design would be more
similar to the look of the tree than to the look of the ocean
because that look, like a perception of either tree or ocean,
would be simply the design's presentation to us, its making
available to us, the one set of invariants rather than the
other.[32]
      The picture, we could say, resembles the tree. The design's
area that depicts the tree is more like its visual appearance
than that of objects of any other class, in the sense that the
design records some of the invariants of optical structure that
we notice when we notice trees: "Those features of a thing are
noticed which distinguish it from other things that it is not,"
and it resembles each thing that has those features. In the
context of the perception of aesthetic objects, we can say that
it is iconic of it. It is only when, like Black, you think that
you see not a thing but an optic array, that the problem of
"second-order looking at looks," in order to compare them, comes
up. If we see things, and notice their invariants of optical
structure, then those things that present many of the same
invariants resemble each other, and a picture that presents the
invariants that distinguish an object from other things that it
is not is a depiction of that object, and resembles it.[33]
      Concerning painting, Beardsley remarks that "a painting of
a nude, for example, is not exactly a sign of a nude" (p. 334),
though we can now understand how a painting may be said to
resemble a nude. And concerning music, "it is doubtful . . . if
we can find any good reason for saying that music is an iconic
sign, either conventional or natural, though it can be iconic"
(p. 336). For music is neither a conventional sign like a word,
except in the case of theme songs and leitmotifs and the like,
nor is it a natural sign of its composer's or performer's mental
state, like the song of a canary. Beardsley shows that there
is no reason to think music signifies anything, nor that it is
a special "'language of the emotions,' a discourse about the
tensions and torments of the mind" (p. 337). The alternative
to such a theory is convincing: that music, and other perceptible
objects that may well be iconic of mental and physical processes
because of their qualities, do not stand for anything else but
simply exist. As Beardsley puts it:

      To understand a piece of music is simply to hear it, in the
      fullest sense of this word, that is, to organize its sounds
      into wholes, to grasp its sequences of notes as melodic and
      rhythmic patterns, to perceive its kinetic qualities and,

finally, the subtle and pervasive human qualities that depend
on all the rest. When the music does not make sense to us
. . . it is not because we . . . are casting about for
something outside of it to connect or compare it with;
[rather] the elements or aspects of it that did take auditory
shape before us have not yet fitted together, as we hope
on further listening they will. (p. 337)

But that is not to say that music may not be iconic of
aspects of mental life. After all, both musical passages and
sequences of feeling and thought are processes; and "music and
mental life both have features that belong to process as such:
tempo, variations of intensity, impulsiveness, relaxation and
tension, crescendo and diminuendo." In fact, the patterns we
hear in music have their analogues in human experience: seeing
a joke, with sudden jolts of amusement dying down, is analogous,
Beardsley shows, to a passage in Beethoven with "increasingly
loud explosive bursts, jumping upward in pitch, followed by a
lightly tripping stepwise descent." Thus "when we say that the
passage is joyful, it is partly the kinetic parallelism that we
are relying upon for the metaphor" (p. 334). We need not think
only of psychological processes here, since "music is similar
to psychological processes partly by being similar to the
behavioral manifestations of those processes: the slow gait of
the depressed, the animated and ebullient movements of the happy"
(p. 336). But iconic of mental or physical processes, the music
is joyful like the Beethoven, or sad like the Debussy, because
it works in some respects in the way we work when we are joyful
or sad.

It is not only music that should be understood in terms of
the dynamics of designs that are iconic of mental or physical
processes. Rudolf Arnheim shows for visual design in general
how "'human' properties" may be parts of percepts if the percepts
have complex patterns of forces that are perceived as "organic."
Bernard Berenson, discussing painting, emphasizes the
"life-enhancing" capacities of "tactile values" felt when we
"realize" art objects: "We realize objects when we perfectly
translate them into terms of our own states, our own feelings."
Herbert Read uses the evidence of the sculpture of blind people
to show how "haptic sensations," "inner movements," often
correlate with the qualities of sculpture. E. H. Gombrich argues
that we even "interpret and code the perception of our fellow
creatures not so much in visual but in muscular terms."[34]

Considering the design of poetry and "that illusion of life
[which] is the primary illusion of all poetic art," Susanne Langer
shows that

all poetry is a creation of illusory events, even when it
looks like a statement of opinions, philosophical or
political or aesthetic. The occurrence of a thought is an
event in a thinker's personal history, and has as distinct

a qualitative character as an adventure, a sight, or a human
contact; it is not a proposition, but the entertainment of
one, which necessarily involves vital tensions, feelings,
the imminence of other thoughts, and the echo of past
thinking.

Thus "poetic reflections . . . create the semblance of
reasoning; of the seriousness, strain and progress, the sense
of growing knowledge, growing clearness, conviction and
acceptance--the whole experience of philosophical thinking," of
which, therefore, the poem is a "non-discursive presentational
form." And Marshall Edelson, deriving his case from Langer and
Noam Chomsky, argues that meaningful verbal design in poetry
results from any linguistic "operation, arrangement, or
selection" that "serves the construction of a presentation rather
than a representation." Thus "an identifiable sequence of
alterations in the arrangement of phonemes, words, or syntactic
categories might signify intensity, excitement, tension, or
relaxation" (though we would say "be iconic of" rather than
"signify").[35]
       For film, Sergei Eisenstein says of the episode on the ice
in Alexander Nevsky that it "passes through all the shades of
an experience of increasing terror, where approaching danger makes
the heart contract and the breathing irregular. The structure
of this 'leaping wedge' in Alexander Nevsky is, with variations,
exactly modeled on the inner process of such an experience."
Eisenstein is leading to his conclusion that "everywhere we see
as basic the same humanity and human psychology, nourishing
and shaping the most intricate compositional elements of form
exactly as it feeds and defines the content of the work."[36]
       All of these arguments provide reasons for recognizing
identical human qualities in different arts, qualities emergent
from aesthetic objects because of the iconicity of the dynamics
of their designs, of whatever sort, with mental and physical
processes. Beardsley says that the "iconicity of some music with
some mental processes, and perhaps of any music with some
conceivable mental processes, is admissible" (p. 334), and we
must generalize to all the arts, and agree with Arnheim
that "dynamics alone is responsible for expression and
meaning."[37]
       We understand music in its forms and qualities. There is
only one important difference in what must be said of our
understanding of the other arts. Since music represents nothing,
the process of attention to form and its qualities, as Beardsley
describes it, must be the only level on which we can experience
this art. When representations emerge from the complexes and
design of an object's visual or verbal elements and produce a
world of the work, that also may be attended to in this way.
Aesthetic experience of representational visual design, or
literature, or film, will be a double process, of attention to
presentational design, which we may refer to simply as design,

and to representational design, or subject. Beardsley asks,
"What is the connection between design and subject?" (p. 293),
and answers in terms of a "Fusion Theory": "the design [often]
contains presentational equivalents of its subject" (p. 299).
Understanding a film, then, is grasping the form and qualities
of its design, its subject, and the presentational equivalents
of each in the other. In all three aspects the essential feature
is the emergence of iconic qualities that we understand as
metaphors.

So we have solved our problem. The Matisse (Fig. 1.5) is
bold in the sense that a relation of major elements thrusting
forth in unambiguous assertiveness and simplicity from a dynamic
background is what we would call boldness if it were part of an
action of our own in a similar setting. And if we can call an
object bright or bold, then surely we can call it cheerful--and
the Matisse is not only bold but is also, perhaps most
significantly, cheerful, with its lively spring from the serene
but relaxed and squarish figured area on the left and behind to
the vibrant and jagged but easily curved and rhythmic figured
area on the right and in front. There is here the good cheer
of change, development, emergence that is in no sense rejection
of the roots from which it springs. We have less two women, one
playing and one listening, than the very incarnation of the
hovering muse--a cheerful event indeed!

We may conclude that the relations among the formal parts
of an aesthetic object, with their formal qualities, is always
metaphorically perceived in the light of our own experience.
Because we see their iconicity, we apply properly human words
to qualities that are in the objects, just as connotations are
parts of the words that connote them. But we properly describe
qualities metaphorically only by virtue of their presenting in
their objects the same processes that characterize our lives.
The qualities of objects and the mentality that perceives them
have the same processes, so we can fit them together and
understand the one in terms of the other.

Once we do, in fact, associate qualities with mental
processes, the problem of the comparability of aesthetic
qualities, which from the start seemed to pose such difficulties
and to lead into such swamps as the search for cinematic
specificity, simply dissolves. We now have a perfectly sensible
context, following Beardsley, in which to compare visual design
and music as Anne Hollander does in her discussion of the "poetic
possibilities of cloth" in Northern Renaissance painters:

> The drapery in the Crucifixions and Madonnas of Albrecht
> Dürer maintains a solid, unhysterical authority, despite
> its most extraordinary behavior. The oversized loincloth
> of the crucified Jesus may flap its unbelievable extra yards
> out into the air on both sides; but so perfectly reasonable
> seems every nervous twist of the fabric that the total
> composition has a cumulative solemnity and no flavor of
> emotional license. (This quality may be what makes it seem

appropriate to illustrate the music of Bach with Dürer
engravings, despite the disparity in dates; it is the same
inexhaustible linear invention, with the combined air of
inevitability and audacity.)[38]

We must, of course, know what the quality of confident and
reasonable yet nervous audacity is before we can report Dürer's
cloth or Bach's melody to have it, but the quality itself is in
the engraving and the music, and not in either our knowing it
or having the words to report it. The quality is solid and secure
there, yet inexhaustible, as is all metaphor, in its capacity
to evoke resonances to cultural and personal connotations because
of the dynamics of presented processes.


AESTHETICS AND FILM CRITICISM
    Again we see how Beardsley connects human experience and
the work itself, this time not as a part of evaluation, but rather
of description and interpretation. This emphasis lets us attend
to our responses to works like films, yet not imagine that we
are studying only ourselves. To study film is not to find, as
semiologists would have us believe, systems of signs to which
the elements of a film refer or on which they depend for their
meanings. The patterned elements in a film simply constitute
a set of relations that we perceive as part of the film's
structure. We comprehend their significance in terms of the
emergent human qualities of the regions of the film in which they
appear. We understand Lincoln's hat because we see how putting
on or taking off a hat is a grave matter, and how it is loaded
with the fierce assertiveness and dignified respect that qualify
the scenes where it goes decisively on or comes respectfully off.
This is not a grounding of these scenes in an external code of
hats, but rather a design feature so outstanding as to be a major
aspect of the composition. By its compositional importance, each
appearance of hat-play gains significance from each other
appearance, and the significance of the whole pattern is
comprehensible, like any metaphor, in terms of our own
experience. The Beardsleyan criticism, unlike the Cahiers
reading, stays within the film itself to observe the emergence
from its structure of the qualities for which we rightly
appreciate it.
    There are further consequences of this approach. Beardsley's
emphasis lets us reconcile traditions that are popularly, but
wrongly, believed to be in conflict. For V. F. Perkins, for
instance, the theory of formative film critics--Vachel Lindsay,
Arnheim, Eisenstein--is opposed to that of André Bazin. The
formative critics treasure the changes wrought by the image on
what its motif would look like if we were in its presence, but
Bazin treasures what he calls the objective transfer of reality
to an imprinted screen. How can both Arnheim and Bazin seem so
right in the reading, so responsive to and delighted by cinema
and, indeed, seem to feel that delight for the same reasons, when

their arguments are disparate? Is it because cinema has both
distortable images and a sense of realistic presence, and each
group of critics chooses to respond to a different one? No.
For Arnheim and Bazin the underlying criteria are the same,
though their beliefs and, hence, their arguments differ. And
we can say the same for Lindsay, Münsterberg, Eisenstein, and
Kracauer.

All these critics ground themselves in the aesthetic
experience of film, and focus on the elements that give cinema
its capacity to be complete and coherent and to render qualities.
For Lindsay, different types of film have qualities he finds in
different types of visual design; for Kracauer, all films have
a unique quality of suggesting the "redemption of physical
reality." Arnheim, Münsterberg, and Bazin emphasize the capacity
of film to render reality as if newly observed, stripped of
utility and of its ordinary implications of human bondage to laws
like gravity and point of view. Münsterberg emphasizes that film
frees us from attachments to things as we otherwise must
experience them, leaving us free to experience completeness and
wholeness in the film object itself. Bazin likewise emphasizes
how film "strips" from its object "that spiritual dust and grime
with which my eyes have covered it," and so "present[s] it in
all its virginal purity to my attention and consequently to my
love." Wholeness with strongly emergent qualities, whether
provided by film's addition of perspective to reality, or by the
imprinting of reality itself in the film, or by the embodiment
of nature's dialectic between chunks of reality and their
organizing principle as revealed in the montage process, or by
whatever means, is what this presemiotic group of critics prize.
And it is just the value of this wholeness-with-qualities for
which Beardsley shows us the reasons, in aesthetic objects in
general.[39]

Beardsley can thus remind us that aesthetic value lies in
the aesthetic experience to which the perceptual qualities of
artworks can give rise. The best classic critics always knew
this, and they are more alike than they appear. I think we can
get better criticism of films, and create a more intellectually
justifiable tradition of film criticism, by remembering it too.

                                                                W.C.


NOTES
1. Monroe C. Beardsley, Aesthetics: Problems in the Philosophy
   of Criticism (New York: Harcourt Brace & World, 1958), pp.
   18-29, 457-60. References to Beardsley's Aesthetics will
   be by page numbers in parentheses in the text hereafter.
   Except for quotations, I cite Beardsley by page only if the
   topic or term under discussion is not easily discoverable
   in his index or section headings.

2. Andrew Tudor, Theories of Film (New York:  Viking, 1974), p. 14.

3. Bill Nichols, Ideology and the Image (Bloomington:  Indiana Univ. Press, 1981), p. 12; E. H. Gombrich, Art and Illusion, 2nd ed. (Princeton:  Princeton Univ. Press, 1961), p. 298; James J. Gibson, The Ecological Approach to Visual Perception (Boston:  Houghton Mifflin, 1979), pp. 286, 282, 273, 286, 281.

4. Gombrich, Art and Illusion, pp. 181-287; James J. Gibson, Letter, Leonardo, 4 (1971):  198; see James J. Gibson, "The Information Available in Pictures," Leonardo, 4 (1971):  27-35; E. H. Gombrich, Letter, Leonardo, 4 (1971):  195-97; Rudolf Arnheim, Letter, Leonardo, 4 (1971):  197.

5. Rudolf Arnheim, Film as Art (1957; reprint, Berkeley:  Univ. of California Press, 1964), pp. 41, 17, 34, 35; Sergei Eisenstein, Film Form (New York:  Harcourt Brace, 1949), p. 48; F. E. Sparshott, "Basic Film Aesthetics," in Film Theory and Criticism:  Introductory Readings, eds., Gerald Mast and Marshall Cohen, 2nd ed. (New York:  Oxford Univ. Press, 1979), pp. 321, 328; André Bazin, What Is Cinema?, vol. 2 (Berkeley:  Univ. of California Press, 1971), pp. 98, 30-31; V. F. Perkins, Film as Film:  Understanding and Judging Movies (Baltimore:  Penguin, 1972), pp. 52, 61; Siegfried Kracauer, Theory of Film:  The Redemption of Physical Reality (1960; reprint, London:  Oxford Univ. Press, 1971), p. 28; Christian Metz, Language and Cinema (The Hague:  Mouton, 1974). I collect in a phrase here the terms Metz develops for cinema's "multiple specificity" p. 224, "iconic" p. 227, "mechanical" p. 228, "multiple" p. 231, "moving" p. 231.

6. Bazin, What Is Cinema?, vol. 2, p. 123; Christian Metz, Film Language:  A Semiotics of the Cinema (New York:  Oxford Univ. Press, 1974), p. 47.

7. Gombrich, Art and Illusion, p. 280; Gibson, The Ecological Approach, p. 283.

8. E. H. Gombrich, "Standards of Truth:  The Arrested Image and the Moving Eye," Critical Inquiry, 7 (1980):  260.

9. Rudolf Arnheim, Art and Visual Perception:  A Psychology of the Creative Eye:  The New Version (Berkeley:  Univ. of California Press, 1974), pp. 372-78.

10. Rhys Carpenter, Greek Sculpture (Chicago:  The Univ. of Chicago Press, 1960), p. 183.

11. Gibson, The Ecological View, p. 274.

12. For the opposing argument, see P. D. Juhl, "Do Computer Poems Show That an Author's Intention Is Irrelevant to the Meaning of a Literary Work?" Critical Inquiry, 5 (1979):  481-87.

13. Sparshott, "Basic Film Aesthetics," in Mast and Cohen, Film Theory and Criticism, pp. 323, 325.

14. Arnheim, Art and Visual Perception, p. 416.

15. Metz, Film Language, p. 47. See Arnheim, Art and Visual
    Perception, for examples of "induced structure" (p. 12)
    and for discussion of the actuality of "perceptual forces"
    (p. 16).
16. Umberto Eco, "Articulations of the Cinematic Code," in
    Movies and Methods, ed., Bill Nichols (Berkeley: Univ. of
    California Press, 1976), p. 593. See also Eco, A Theory
    of Semiotics (Bloomington: Indiana Univ. Press, 1976),
    pp. 178-261, and Bill Nichols, Ideology and the Image,
    Chapters 1-2.
17. Leonard Bernstein, The Unanswered Question (Cambridge:
    Harvard Univ. Press, 1976), pp. 17, 179.
18. Gibson, "The Information Available in Pictures," p. 31;
    Gibson, "On Information Available in Pictures," p. 198.
19. Gombrich, Art and Illusion, p. 298; Gombrich, "Standards
    of Truth," pp. 246, 258.
20. Noam Chomsky, Rules and Representations (New York:
    Columbia Univ. Press, 1980), pp. 134-40, 185-215.
21. George Dickie, Aesthetics: An Introduction (Indianapolis:
    Bobbs-Merrill, 1971), p. 68.
22. Jurij Lotman, Semiotics of Cinema, Michigan Slavic
    Contributions, no. 5 (Ann Arbor: Department of Slavic
    Language and Literature, Univ. of Michigan, 1976), p. 12.
23. For "the inherent value of art" see Beardsley, Aesthetics,
    pp. 587-89; Robert E. Lane, The Liberties of Wit: Humanism,
    Criticism, and the Civic Mind (New Haven: Yale Univ. Press,
    1961), pp. 106-36.
24. The Editors of Cahiers du Cinéma, "John Ford's Young Mr.
    Lincoln," Screen, 13, no. 3 (1972): 5-47; cited as
    Cahiers henceforth.
25. Cahiers, pp. 42, 36, 13.
26. Jacques Lacan, The Four Fundamental Concepts of Psycho-
    Analysis (New York: W. W. Norton, 1978), p. 62.
27. Cahiers, pp. 42, 43, 44.
28. Cahiers, p. 36.
29. Cahiers, p. 29.
30. Eisenstein, Film Form, p. 82.
31. Peter Wollen, Signs and Meaning in the Cinema, Enlarged
    ed. (Bloomington: Indiana Univ. Press, 1972), pp. 122-24,
    136-54.
32. Max Black, "How Do Pictures Represent?," in E. H. Gombrich,
    Julian Hochberg, Max Black, Art, Perception, and Reality
    (Baltimore: The Johns Hopkins Univ. Press, 1972), pp.
    118-19; Gibson, "The Information Available in Pictures,"
    p. 31.
33. Gibson, The Ecological Approach to Visual Perception, p.
    134; Black, "How Do Pictures Represent?," p. 118.
34. Arnheim, Art and Visual Perception, pp. 399-403; Bernard
    Berenson, Italian Painters of the Renaissance (1896;
    reprint, London: Phaidon, 1952), pp. 66, 73; Herbert Read,
    The Art of Sculpture, Bollingen Series, 35.3 (Princeton:

Princeton Univ. Press, 1956), pp. 30-31; E. H. Gombrich, "The Mask and the Face: The Perception of Physiognomic Likeness in Life and in Art," in Gombrich, Hochberg, Black, Art, Perception, and Reality, p. 36.

35. Susanne K. Langer, Feeling and Form (London: Routledge and Kegan Paul, 1953), pp. 213, 219, 211; Marshall Edelson, Language and Interpretation in Psychoanalysis (New Haven: Yale Univ. Press, 1975), pp. 82-83.

36. Eisenstein, Film Form, pp. 152, 159.

37. Arnheim, Art and Visual Perception, p. 108.

38. Anne Hollander, Seeing through Clothes (New York: Viking, 1978), p. 21.

39. Vachel Lindsay, The Art of the Moving Picture (1922; reprint, New York: Liveright, 1970), pp. 107-78; Kracauer, Theory of Film, pp. 300-11; Hugo Münsterberg, The Film: A Psychological Study (1916; reprint, New York: Dover, 1970), pp. 57-73; André Bazin, What Is Cinema? (Berkeley: Univ. of California Press, 1967), p. 15.

CHAPTER
2

# The Cleavage Plane
# of André Bazin

In his important essay, "The Evolution of Film Language,"
André Bazin argues that the great distinction to be made in the
study of film is not between the silent and the sound film. "The
arrival of sound was not an aesthetic watershed dividing two
radically different aspects of the medium. Some people saw that
sound was bringing a certain kind of cinema to an end; but this
was not at all the cinema. The true cleavage plane was
elsewhere; it was, and still is, cutting clean across thirty-five
years of the history of cinematic expression." The cleavage plane
lies between those "directors who believed in the image and those
who believed in reality" (p. 26). The cinema of the image makes
use of a "whole arsenal of devices with which it can impose its
own interpretation of a depicted event on the spectator" (p. 29).
But the cinema of reality, as in the case of Murnau, "adds nothing
to reality, it does not deform it; rather it strives to bring
out the deeper structure of reality, to reveal pre-existent
relationships which become the constituents of the drama" (p.
30). But this respect for the facts of the photographed scene
may be achieved either by the composition of Flaherty or Murnau
which "is not at all pictorial," or by the seemingly quite
different composition in depth of Welles and Wyler which seems
pictorial, which uses the resources of montage as it uses
close-ups and expressionist lighting, but which nonetheless
equally opposes the cinema of the image.[1]

One knows what Bazin means in calling Murnau an artist of
reality, and Brian Henderson analyzes it well in "The Long Take."
But there is a pictorial quality in many of Murnau's scenes in
Faust and Nosferatu and, especially, in Sunrise (think of
the happy family eating lunch under a tree, or of the wife
scattering grain to the chickens, as if in the style of Ford Madox
Brown) and a similar reservation can be expressed about Welles.[2]
Pauline Kael points out a certain oddity in Bazin's praise of
Welles for reinstituting realism after the artificialities of
thirties' classicism, noting that the contemporary response was
to see the portentousness and heavy lighting of Citizen Kane

39

as a return to Expressionism after a self-effacing naturalism
had dislocated it. She opposes Bazin's reading of Welles, for
she sees Citizen Kane's bravura, rather than its naturalistic
believability, as its main feature. But this was Bazin's genius,
to see that what Murnau and Welles were doing was realism, despite
appearances to the contrary, and that the unobtrusive style
replaced by Welles's practice represented not respect for reality,
but rather the replacement of the passion for observation with
subtly formative expressive conventions.[3]

Cinema of the image is represented by Eisenstein, Griffith,
and the Expressionists during the silent era. And it can be found
in the "classical" style of the 1930s, with its "invisible
editing" (p. 26), its "analytic" and "dramatic" montage (p. 35),
and its "discontinuous description" (p. 49) by which "the
classical narrative insidiously replaced . . . intellectual and
abstract time" with "the temporal truth of things, the actual
duration of an event" (p. 49). The directors who believe in the
image "do not show the event through their editing; they allude
to it" (p. 27) or analyze it "fragment by fragment" (p. 45).
But the cinema of reality showed the. event in "its physical unity"
(p. 45) and so seized "the secret of a cinematic style which was
capable of expressing everything without fragmenting the world,
of revealing the hidden meaning of human beings and their
environment without destroying their natural unity" (p. 48).

I think that something very like that is the distinction
to be made, though not merely with reference to the effects of
film styles or devices, but also to the nature of literature in
general and therefore of film in particular. But to see why the
distinction is right, it is important to understand why, as Bazin
handles it, the distinction is not good enough, in the sense that
the assumptions that lie for Bazin behind this true distinction
lead his application of it to falsehood of analysis and flaws
in taste. When Bazin intends to praise one attitude and thematic
point as opposed to another, he treats it as inhering in one style
as opposed to another. He has confused styles--which no doubt
display a sensibility and help to manifest a cinematic point--with
the sensibilities and the point themselves. Because he thinks
that cinematic significance is inherent in the sensibility that
style reveals, Bazin is put in the unfortunate position of having
to make the moral-critical point he intends to make in the form
of a technical-critical one. Yet such a point can be made without
losing the force of Bazin's discussion of style. The distinction
concerning means of suggesting and presenting points about the
real world is indeed appropriately drawn between assertive,
referential techniques of constructing meaning (such as montage)
and integrative, reflective techniques of discovering meaning
(such as depth of focus). Yet quite independently of means of
presentation (and freely varying with the different means), the
sensibilities or visions of auteurs, sequences of internal
fictions, oppositions of character, and other cinematic and
literary categories are likewise divided in essentially this way.

"Assertive" and "integrative" express a distinction that many people have said, using these or other terms, is entailed by the very nature of the relations between organisms embodying a teleological project and their world. It seems to me that art as a whole, and specific art objects, may well be knowable as such to us because, if they are well-formed formulas in the logic of art, they pattern their representations, value, designs, and structures in terms of it. To observe the manifestations of the distinction may therefore be to gain insight (in general) into the specifics of operation and content of what Dan Sperber calls the "Symbolic Mechanism," which evokes interpretations of the world's aspects which do not square with "encyclopedic knowledge," and (in particular) into the "grammaticality" of art objects as a subset of the products of this mechanism. (See Chapter 10 for discussion of Sperber in the context of cognitive psychology.)[4]

Some other sets of terms, in each case the central ones for those who use them, and in each case with the term for assertiveness first, for what I take to be the same distinction: Arthur Koestler distinguishes "self-assertive and integrative tendencies" for all "holons," the first the "dynamic expression" of the holon's "wholeness," the second of its "partness"; Gregory Bateson distinguishes "progressional and selective integration" of organisms into their environment; Susanne K. Langer argues "feeling" as of two types (depending on its origin at the "spinocerebral structures" or the organism's "periphery"), namely "emotivity" and "sensibility," in which respectively experience is "felt as action" or "felt as impact." She later claims that "the process of human experience" itself is the dialectic between "the subjectification of nature" into representations which carry projections of affect, and "the objectification of feeling" into representations of nature, the dual process manifested especially clearly in art objects. Jacques Monod sees a regularity in the artifacts of culture (e.g., religions, myths, art) deriving from the innate, biologically evolved structure of human thought, which makes people think they have a duty to themselves, to manipulate reality to their individual benefits (a notion of assertiveness), though people have also evolved to think that there is a purpose in the world to which they have a duty (a notion of integrality); Rudolf Arnheim sees "the human mind as an interplay of tension-heightening and tension-reducing strivings," with a "constructive tendency" creating a "structural theme" that, in each instance of mental activity, "constitutes what the mind is about, what it is after" (a notion of assertiveness), but this constructive tendency balanced by a "simplicity principle," which strives to "point out that everything fits nicely together" and hence enables us to "understand the rationale of completeness and incompleteness, whole and part, solidity and transparency, motion and standstill" (a notion of integrality).[5]

The distinction is clearly linked to the patternings Claude Lévi-Strauss finds in myths, e.g., the individual assertiveness

implied by autochthonous origins vs. the integrativeness of its
denial, or the assertiveness of underestimation of kinship ties
vs. the integrativeness of overestimation. Both pairs in this
pattern show what Sperber demonstrates as Lévi-Strauss's
insistence that myths reveal human focus on the paradoxes involved
in being human, each of us part and whole, all of us in nature
and culture at once. And the distinction, in a similar way,
yields the interplay of the "myths of freedom and concern," which
for Northrop Frye underlie the imaginative products of culture.
Indeed, it underlies the very distinction between "formative"
and "realistic" film theories, as well as the distinction within
film theories of such tendencies, and also such distinctions as
Jurij Lotman's between the world of signs and signs of the world,
between montage and plot texts; Christian Metz's between film's
language-likeness and its iconicity, between image discourse and
filmic discourse; Sergei Eisenstein's between "Being" and
"Synthesis" with all their synonyms and special aspects, the
assertiveness of the "Dynamism" of the constantly evolving
dialectic, vs. the integrativeness of the dialectic itself,
conceived as a product "arising from the opposition of thesis
and antithesis."[6]

All these sets of terms and ideas are versions and specific
applications of the distinction between what I simply call
"inside" and "outside" motives--versions of organization of the
world in light of plans, or in light of realities or illusions
to which plans, feelings, actions, and interpretations must adapt
themselves. In some way, everywhere we look we find a balance
of motives and opportunities in the world, and it is not
surprising to find a balance of these alternatives of emphasis
in every aspect of film or other art organization.

Thus, for instance, it is appropriate to think of an auteur
like Ford or Mizoguchi as implying, as making the point, that
the world is to be approached assertively and made to take the
shape it will take by human effort. Or of an auteur like Hawks
or Ozu as making the point that the world is to be approached
integratively, its lessons and implications submitted to with
a properly and decorously inferential and receptive air, an air
quite different from the arrogance of asserters--the world's shape
is to be discovered, and not imposed. Bazin intends to praise
a reverence for reality, which it is his perfect right to prefer
over manipulation or analysis. But he attaches that reverence
to a particular style; hence an excellent and pervasive
distinction is prematurely moralized and historicized. Broad
and deep as Bazin's notion of realism is, it is not broad and
deep enough to accommodate the full range of means by which it
may be achieved. Therefore, what might have been a superb
categorization system built from just such moral distinctions
as Bazin intended is, in fact, only a system for expressing
preferences solely on the basis of style and its implications.
Bazin's cleavage plane is far more extensively applicable than
he understood; it is indeed both technical and thematic, but the

relations between technique and theme are more subtle than Bazin's mistaken notion of film language can allow.

Of course, insofar as Bazin is arguing his case as a corrective to its predecessor, which took the silent film as the only art cinema and argued that the sound film could never be more than a miserable hybrid, he is exposing a quantum error. This earlier view is probably best associated with Rudolf Arnheim, who in a 1957 "Personal Note" prefixed to a reprinting of his influential Film As Art could remark that "the talking film is still a hybrid medium, which lives from whatever fragments of the visual language were salvageable and from the beauty of the creatures, things, and thoughts it reproduces." Richard Roud neatly gives Bazin's place in French film criticism, mentioning his debt to Leenhardt, and showing that before him there had been two views: the view that film is a mass art, held by Sadoul, and the view that only montage makes film an art, held by Brassilach, Auriol, Bradeche, and Moussinac, sound serving to add to the capability of film for montage effects.[7]

How indeed could people ever seriously have argued that a technical fact like sound could determine the value of films made using it? It would be like arguing after Homer's time that the discovery of writing would destroy literature, whose perfection could only be achieved in the direct confrontation of the improvising bard with his audience--or, closer to home, like arguing that, as Fritz Lang says in Godard's Contempt, CinemaScope is only appropriate for photographing snakes and funerals.

Bazin's case is designed to show the changing nature of the image available to the director's arsenal and the various effects of its qualities. He shows, for instance, that even in the silent era, Flaherty, Stroheim, and Murnau presented reality in such a way that the scene would make its own effect, rather than "expressing" what they had to say through devices, such as montage, "editing by attraction," and distortions of the image through lighting and scene design, which are extrinsic to the scene.

In their rejection of expressionistic devices in image and editing, Bazin sees these silent directors as more like Welles and Wyler than like Eisenstein or the Griffith of Intolerance. Similarly, he shows that the composition in depth with which Citizen Kane overwhelmed directors and the public follows that directorial principle of Stroheim to "look at the world from so close and with such insistence that it ends up by revealing its cruelty and its ugliness" (pp. 30-31). He argues that Lang's "editing by attraction" in Fury, by which gabbling women are followed by cackling hens, belongs to an earlier era not so much because it is in a sound film and hence as out of place as an aside to "dear reader" would be in a modern realistic novel, as because the richness of expression, the ambiguity of the image, and the respect for reality established as the dominant style by the very introduction of composition in depth made such

devices, like the earlier expressionistic forms of Eisenstein
and Griffith, seem thin and trivial (p. 36).[8]

Bazin builds his case by arguing for an objective appraisal
of the effects of specific film techniques on either side of his
cleavage plane. But he is really presenting a case for a
particular view of reality rather than for specification of the
laws that link filmic cause and effect. But he often speaks in
terms of the "carefully worked-out laws" that "govern" the "well-
tried genres" (p. 32). He argues that extended composition in
depth does exert as if mechanical control over the audience's
responses, which it is as easy, but no more accurate, to argue
is exerted by montage. In this view, then, audiences are
prisoners of the rules of film. Thus, in The Little Foxes,
"the placing of objects in relation to the characters is such
that their meaning cannot escape the spectator, a meaning which
editing would have built up in a series of successive shots" (pp.
39-40). Or, in The Best Years of Our Lives, in the scene
(beautifully analyzed by Bazin) where Homer shows Al how he can
play "Chopsticks" with his hooks while in the background Fred
telephones Marie to end his relationship with her, "the real
action is overlaid with the action of the mise-en-scène itself,
which consists of dividing the attention of the spectator against
his will, of guiding it in the right direction, and thus of making
him participate in his own right in the drama created by the
director" (p. 41).

But don't we all know how completely any viewer can refuse
that response the director "demanded"? The attentions of
spectators are very much in their own control. Even though Bazin
thinks he is talking about the laws of audience response, we can
see that what he is really doing is what most good critics have
always done: exposed and defended a certain view of the world
implied by the behavior of artists, and doing it by any means
necessary--including, of course, importations of contraband
lawfulness as a basis for argument. Thus we find that Bazin
speaks of "the secret of a cinematic style which was capable of
expressing everything without fragmenting the world, of revealing
the hidden meanings of human beings and their environment,
without destroying their natural unity" (p. 48). And we see that
the point is not so much the way the style works as it is the
ethical claim that the way to see things is to view them as
unfragmented, as having "hidden meaning," as possessing "natural
unity."[9]

But what Bazin means by "natural unity" is what Eisenstein
would consider illusionary, and what Eisenstein would consider
natural, Bazin would consider abstract and imposed on the world.
It is not that Eisenstein's montage will not "express everything,"
as Bazin would have us believe. It is that Eisenstein, as a
dialectical thinker, is interested not in expressing an essential
unity which he would deny as natural, but rather in expressing
the sense of the unity of opposites, in which the contradictions
in things are revealed by that analysis for which montage is such

an excellent rhetorical tool. He would never accept Bazin's terms
by which a "depicted object" can be "added to . . . by its being
depicted on the screen" (p. 26), but would instead say that the
depiction discovers the actuality of the object in its essential
contradictions. That style which Bazin praises is "capable of
expressing everything" it expresses, but just so montage permits
the expression of what it expresses. There is no development
here, no "evolution of film language," but rather a contrast of
world-views with a consequent and comprehensible difference in
aesthetic behavior.

Bazin argues, then, that "the arrival of sound proved fatal
to a certain aesthetic approach to film language, but this was
an approach that was leading it farthest away from its vocation
for realism" (pp. 48-49). Thus the praise of the Italian
neo-realists, of Wyler, of Flaherty, of Murnau, and the blame
of Griffith, the Expressionists, and Eisenstein, are to be seen
in relation to what Bazin sees as the proper development of a
"narrative [that] is again becoming capable of reintegrating the
temporal truth of things, the actual duration of an event which
the classical narrative insidiously replaced with intellectual
and abstract time" (p. 49). But the notions of "temporal truth,"
of "actual duration," of "insidiousness," of "intellectual and
abstract time," stand out not as expositions of nature, but as
persuasive phrases through the use of which it is intended that
we should accept, not only a cinema to be praised insofar as it
"believes in reality," but also Bazin's notion of the reality
in which cinema and its viewers should believe.

Bazin's argument comes down, then, to a quite proper and
much-needed plea for the conventions of the sound film as true
to life, as capable of rich and full exposition of reality by
auteurs from whom, finally, no technical device or film convention
is debarred:

> Far from eliminating the achievements of editing once and
> for all, modern filmmakers are giving them a relativity and
> a meaning. . . . The stylistic repertory of a director such
> as Hitchcock for example stretches from the powers of the
> documentary image to superimpositions and extreme close-ups.
> But Hitchcock's close-ups are not the same as those of Cecil
> B. DeMille in The Cheat. They are just one stylistic
> device among others. (p. 49)

Bazin claims "a total reconciliation of sound and image" such
as one finds in "an art that has attained a perfect balance, an
ideal form of expression," and there is no doubt that the standard
here is not merely technical, but also moral: "One admires
dramatic and moral themes which, although not entirely creations
of the cinema, were raised to a certain nobility, to an artistic
effectiveness that they would not have achieved without it" (p.
33).

In fact, Bazin's preference of Hitchcock to Eisenstein shows

both the strengths and the weaknesses of his case.  We can
understand why he likes Hitchcock so much.  Hitchcock's films
have a fine reserve, a searching and passive quality of being
experienced which is very appropriately praised in the way that
Bazin praises the other films he particularly likes--Nanook,
Le Jour se lève, Sunrise--and in the way that he praises the
presentational attitude of film itself, the feeling of the cinema.
As opposed to theater, which is anthropocentric, enrolling the
will of the audience, built on play and not on illusion, on the
text and not on spatial reality, cinema looks out through a window
on the world, finds a reality that always continues beyond the
limits of the frame, and demands passive adhesion rather than
individual consciousness, since "the mainspring of the action
is not in man but nature" (Gray, p. 102).  When a film treats
a novel, it should take an attitude toward it of excision and
inspection, as Bresson did in Diary of a Country Priest.  The
adapted film should move around in the reality of the novel in
the same way that the nonadapted film should move around in the
reality of ordinary life.
    Similarly, the cinema frame in Resnais's film Van Gogh
can wander in the paintings at will, since

    the outer edges of the screen are not, as the technical
    jargon would seem to imply, the frame of the film image.
    They are the edges of a piece of masking that shows only
    a portion of reality.  The picture frame polarizes space
    inwards.  On the contrary, what the screen shows us seems
    to be part of something prolonged indefinitely into the
    universe. . . . If we show a section of a painting on the
    screen, the space of the painting loses its orientation and
    its limits and is presented to the imagination as without
    any boundaries. (Gray, p. 166)

Resnais submits to the paintings of Van Gogh as Bresson does to
the novel of Bernanos, yet with no sacrifice of realism:  "The
activity of the filmmaker remains on the outside, realistic of
course, but--and this is the great discovery that should make
every painter happy--a realism once removed, following upon the
abstraction that is the painting" (Gray, pp. 167-68).
    The subject of Bresson is the novel of Bernanos, not what
Bernanos's subject is.  The subject of Resnais is the paintings
of Van Gogh, not what those paintings have as their subject.
The subject of Olivier's Henry V is Shakespeare's Henry V,
not what Shakespeare's subject is.  And Hitchcock's subject,
opposed to Eisenstein's, is, according to Bazin, life, not what
life's subject is--whatever that may be.  Bazin accuses
expressionist cinema in general and Eisenstein in particular of
emphasizing life in an essentially theatrical way, which is not
really in tune with the nature of cinema.
    Though Hitchcock uses any device he wants, he employs his
arsenal to put us inside the experience of characters who look

out at the world as if at something happening to them, something
they move around in as one moves a camera around a scene or as
Resnais moves around in the paintings of Van Gogh or in Hiroshima
mon amour. Think of the experience of Henry Fonda in The Wrong
Man, for instance, so vividly rendered not only in the coolly
detached sequences of identification in the grocery stores, but
also in the montage of bars and corridors and lights in jail.
Or think of the quite different, but equally involving, whirling
merry-go-round in Strangers on a Train, or the scenes on the
stage of the Albert Hall in Stage Fright, or the black-out going
through the tunnel in The Lady Vanishes, or the quiet
desperation of Father Michael Logan's experience in I Confess,
detachedly presented in quiet scenes of a Quebec as shabby and
hum-drum and ominous as the New York of The Wrong Man or the
motel of Psycho.

Surely no one could deny the force and power of these
expressions; their reserved and underplayed quality moves us
through an experience that might turn out badly or well. The
world goes on without regard for what we say of it; it is always
there outside the frame, on its own terms. Bazin's picture of
the presentational relation between film frame and reality is
mirrored in Hitchcock's presentation of the relation between man
and his world, and it is just this sense of tenuousness that we
also find so striking in Jules and Jim and This Man Must Die
and Vivre sa vie. Even when Hitchcock makes use of a montage
sequence, as in the tennis scene in Strangers on a Train, it
feels like a presentation of the experience of life as it impinges
on us, an expression of the quality of suspense appropriate to
that instant no less surely than the exaggeratedly quotidian
ferryboat of I Confess or Melanie Daniels's ostensibly quiet
trip by rowboat in The Birds. In this, Hitchcock is like
Bergman, whose montage sequences in Illicit Interlude, for
instance, strike us as radically odd intrusions on the film
surface, but are nonetheless justified since they show how we
feel Marie must respond to the objects of the montage as they
are presented--the oddly beckoning deck-hand and the elements
of wake and rail and funnel of her ferry, otherwise so different
from Father Logan's in I Confess. And Hitchcock's is like
Antonioni's montage sequence in Eclipse, which feels just like
what the film surface itself, its own rendered experience at that
moment, should feel like.

These montage sequences do not work in the least as those
of Eisenstein or of Buñuel work. Bazin does indeed have the right
"cleavage plane"--though its division is not between good and
bad or cinematic and uncinematic, but rather between rhetorical
points that can be made in a number of ways and that cannot be
attached simply to devices or styles. Thus, unlike the montage
sequences of Bergman and Hitchcock, those in Buñuel's Viridiana
of prayer at Angelus and workmen under Jorge's direction do not
look out from inside at a world going by. Rather, like Buñuel's
other characteristic devices--chickens, insects, udders, little

boxes of forbidding goodies, severed hands--montage sequences
in Viridiana do not render, but rather stand back from and
comment on, the feelings of the characters and the cumulative
feeling of the film surface. Like the montage style of
Eisenstein, Buñuel's imposes a meaning or interpretation on
reality to which one responds just as Bazin says one responds
to theater in and of itself because of the relation of audience
and actors across the footlights. It is a response of
understanding and appreciation, an act of the will that recognizes
something made out there rather than sharing something happening.

At the end of Viridiana the crown of thorns is taken
blazing from the fire by little Rita, who had pricked her finger
on it and tossed it in. At the end of The Exterminating Angel
a flock of sheep enters the church. No one, no character and
no consciousness of the film surface, looks out at the world there
as happens in Eclipse or Earth. The cinema frame is just
as centripetal as Bazin says the frame of a painting or the
footlights of a theater are; just as emphatic and full of
statement as Lang's closing lap dissolves in Metropolis, or
as the painted sets of Caligari, or as the painterly drapings
of Cherkassov around an imaginary painting's frame in Ivan the
Terrible. And this, too, is something cinema can do without
becoming theater: create an ironic, intellectual, witty awareness
of a universe charged with meaning, though not necessarily with
grace, a world that one makes sense of "out there" rather than
accepting almost passively "in here." It is a world that,
ironically enough, came to be what Godard put together from
Bazin's premises, which had seemed to point to such different
practice.

This distinction between "inside" and "outside," then,
whether applied to literature or its proper subset film, and with
the latter, whether applied to implied moral standard, point about
reality, or cinematic device, is the principal critical
distinction to make--it is the cleavage plane in any number of
dimensions. But why is what comes so passively from the world
to us properly called "in here"? Why is what one actively has
to put together by imagination or understanding properly called
"out there"? In part the answer is obvious, as soon as we point
out the falsity of the descriptions, which are of aesthetic
experience, but which use the language of alien psychological
fact. We do not in fact work harder, nor will our acts of
understanding and imagination in any more meaningful sense, in
understanding montage rather than moving camera. We do not submit
passively to an easy flow that we need not process, in
understanding deep focus. In fact, our minds work along making
perceptual and cognitive sense of things as minds always do, and
we should not be misled into guesses about the mind's operations
by the structure of aesthetic fact. So there is a point here,
but it is not psychological or a matter of what a medium or a
particular device within the style of a medium does to our minds

of itself, as Bazin suggests. What we are talking about in describing a putting together effect of montage or a submissive and receptive effect of deep focus or moving camera is the quality of the projective surface of the film, the tonal and emotive implications of its virtual world.

The film we watch is like an experiencing and acting entity-- either assertive or integrative, active or passive, processing and planning or receptive--both moment by moment and in general. When it emphasizes montage and theme and the meaning of the world, it is projecting assertions about the world's qualities and attributes. The film surface may be acting like an assertive person, but what it is projecting is the meaning of things "out there"; what we primarily attend to when a film has this assertive quality is what the film is saying, rather than its saying it. When, on the other hand, the surface emphasizes what happens in a piece of reality that it fluidly renders as moving by, or that ebbs and flows within a deeply focused scene, the film is projecting assertions as to the quality of experience-- what it feels like to be confronted by the world. The film surface here may be acting like a receptive or integrative person, but what it is projecting is what it feels like to be that way, what happens "in here," and thus the quality is of emphasis on the saying rather than the said.

When the film is like a rendering of our relatively untainted perceptions of reality, then we say that it has an inside quality, whether that effect is achieved by deep focus like Flaherty's and Welles's, or by montage like Ozu's, Dovzhenko's, and Antonioni's, or by moving camera like Murnau's in The Last Laugh or Resnais's in Hiroshima mon amour. A Lubitsch set of dissolves, such as those in Trouble in Paradise, is outside, statementy, but the dissolves of Borzage in History Is Made at Night are inside. Why? Because our understanding of the whole film lets us properly attend to the individual part when we come to it, and thus lets us properly interpret the attitudes implicit in a device as it is used where in fact it is.

When, on the other hand, the film is like an analytic exercise pointing out the nature of things and their connections, we can say that it has an outside quality, whether the quality is obtained by deep focus like Stroheim's or Hawks's, by montage like Eisenstein's or Buñuel's, or by moving camera like Godard's or Fellini's. The rolling camera passing over the faces of judges in Dreyer's Passion of Joan of Arc is inside, but the tracking back and forth of the camera in Vivre sa vie and Contempt is outside. When Hawks tracks across the battlefields of World War I in Sergeant York and The Road to Glory, we observe that war as surely as when Raoul Walsh drops Jimmy Cagney into a shell-hole with Bogart in Roaring Twenties, the montage sequences of which are classically outside. But when Kurosawa tracks with the woodcutter through the forest in Rashomon, or when Antonioni tracks up and across a pipe following Corrado's eye in the scene

with the Brazil-bound workers in Red Desert, we share the
feeling of the film surface, which inwardly accepts the world
with delight or empty despair.

Just why a particular device has the quality it has, and
just how we know that it has it, are difficult questions that
are not simply resolvable by statements to the effect that deep
focus does thus and such, but rather by appeals to the context
in the film, including the treatment in terms of sharpness of
focus, pacing, color values, accompanying sound, and relation
to other images. And if there is a science of the language of
film here, it is simply not going to be found by appealing to
the effects of aspects of film like montage or deep focus, but
rather by discovering the general and larger principles by which
films are put together. This is simply to say that Bazin has
a good grasp of one of those major principles but tries to see
it alone when it must be seen in its context, in which it looms
even larger than it seemed to in Bazin's analyses of style.

Bazin writes of his cleavage plane as if it were between
the precinematic and the truly cinematic, as if the involved mode
of deep focus, of passive adhesion, of "realism"--even as deeply
as he understands the term--were somehow better than and a
replacement of the detached mode of montage, of theatrical
comprehension, of expressionism. And this attitude of preference
shows through, even though he is capable of remarking cogently
that

> cinema has at its disposal means which favor a passive
> position or on the other hand, means which to a greater or
> lesser degree stimulate the consciousness of the spectator.
> . . . Thus theater and cinema will no longer be separated
> off by an unbridgeable aesthetic moat, they would simply
> tend to give rise to two attitudes of mind over which the
> direction maintains a wide control (Gray, p. 100).

For he can also claim that "montage which we are constantly being
told is the essence of cinema is, in this situation, the literary
and anticinematic process par 'excellence'. Essential cinema,
seen for once in its pure state, on the contrary, is to be found
in straightforward photographic respect for the unity of space"
(Gray, p. 46). And surely this is false; surely Hitchcock is
no more true to cinema or to the real world than Eisenstein.
Surely they are simply different.

The grounding of the distinction in the specific nature of
film itself must be as insecure as Bergman's claim that

> film has nothing to do with literature; the character and
> substance of the two art forms are usually in conflict.
> This probably has something to do with the receptive process
> of the mind. The written word is read and assimilated by
> a conscious act of the will in alliance with the intellect;
> little by little it affects the imagination and the emotions.

The process is different with a motion picture. When we
experience a film, we consciously prime ourselves for
illusion. Putting aside will and intellect, we make way
for it in our imagination. The sequence of pictures plays
directly on our feelings.[10]

The picture of mental functioning here, hopelessly at odds with
what is well known of the creative nature of all aspects of
perception, casts into doubt the conclusion built on it, that
the mental acts of understanding written literature and film are
different. What we have, rather, is a deep rhetorical division,
a difference in the forms of implication of various films that
may show up anywhere, in points to be gotten and effects to be
understood and devices to be explained. Bazin is simply mistaken
to argue one pole of this distinction as more truthful than the
other. Passages in films that manifest the qualities of the poles
simply mean, as we saw in looking at montage in Buñuel and
Bergman, what they mean in their contexts, in the films in which
they appear. They do not suggest any implicational attribute
of the film medium or of any device.

But there is still a problem in contrasting Hitchcock and
Eisenstein that emerges when we leave the implications of style
and consider the implications of vision. It is true that
Hitchcock's style does "believe in reality." But his point, the
emergent meaningfulness that comes from the fusion of the
qualities of his style with the structure and implications of
the world of his works, is not that the appearance of reality
is trustworthy. His films imply that the world in which we human
beings find ourselves reveals itself, as we learn to look closely
enough at it, as running quite differently from the way we infer
all too readily from our uninspected experience of it. The world
can only be known by deep and chastening and contemplation-
inspiring experience. Full awareness is realizing the human
chanciness of being at the mercy of things in a world not in any
obvious way made to our measure. The world of Hitchcock's works
always and surprisingly comes to seem alien and menacing to the
characters who suffer it. We watch them coming to wisdom from
a complacent superiority to such chanciness. What Bazin rightly
prizes is the Bresson tone, the Flaherty feeling, of people moving
within their worlds and unified with them, making their worlds'
purposes their own by creative and seamless adaptation. But
Hitchcock's films exactly deny that kind of adjustment, and
fiercely show people moved against their will, prisoners of what
happens and of their own inadequacies. Hitchcock's is a world
to whose mysteries, to whose otherness, people can only submit
and hope for the best, for the appearance of the grace which may
redeem them.

Hitchcock makes us feel the experience of coming to be
overwhelmed by that world, and to that extent is inside like Wyler
and like Bresson, as we have said. But throughout his career
the films emphasize not reality, but the image he projects of

it--the way the world is outside us, running by its own often
terrifying rules and surprising discoveries, and not to be joined
by the creative consciousness as are the worlds of Wyler and
Bresson. Hitchcock necessarily believes in Hitchcock's image,
not in Bazin's reality. He is more like Buñuel and Eisenstein
than Bazin could allow, for quite as much as Eisenstein he implies
the fragmentation between man and his world, the contradictions
that require an act of willed submission to resolve. Sylvia
Verloc in Sabotage, Charlie Newton in Shadow of a Doubt,
Anthony Keane in The Paradine Case, Eve Gill in Stage Fright,
Guy Haines in Strangers on a Train, Father Logan in I Confess,
Manny Balestrero in The Wrong Man, Margot Wendice in Dial M
for Murder, Scotty Ferguson in Vertigo, and preeminently
Melanie Daniels in The Birds and Blaney in Frenzy: these
characters, reduced to an often dumb awareness of how much more
than they at first thought lurks outside their egos, in the world
and in the depths of their hearts, have not come to be in harmony
with their worlds, but rather to understand their inevitable
ironic alienation from them. "Repent Ye and Believe" says a sign
Sylvia Verloc passes on the street after killing her husband,
and it implies exactly the Hitchcock point--a very Eisensteinian
assertion of the necessity for understanding the struggle of
opposites, of man's world and man's self.

It has been said that Hitchcock's continuing theme is man's
guilt. The notion of the sharing of guilt by one who looks the
innocent one of a pair is brilliantly stated by Claude Chabrol
in "Hitchcock Confronts Evil." For him Hitchcock's "main axis"
is "Man and the battle he must sustain" in the light of "a more
profound truth than that of moral laws." "The Catholic conception
of existence, which is Hitchcock's," has "the prize" as "Man's
salvation, for Man is considered in the last resort, to be
perfectly free. It is within him that the battle takes place; it
is up to him to sink or swim." The "necessity for confession,"
for "recognition of oneself," and a "will to accept not one's
destiny . . . but one's personality," are "the supreme exorcism
and the principal condition of Man's final triumph."[11] François
Truffaut, discussing Hitchcock's initial objection to this
interpretation ("How can you say a thing like that when in fact
we always have the theme of the innocent man who is constantly
in danger, although he isn't guilty?"), nearly makes Hitchcock
admit that "most of your work is strongly permeated by the concept
of original sin, and of man's guilt."[12]

It seems to us that, rather than emphasizing man's freedom
to confess, the quality of Hitchcock's films reminds us of the
need and the bare possibility of confession. We are reminded
that our living is dependent, that more is out there than meets
the eye, that we are vulnerable. The nature of man's struggle
is to accept his dependence, to confess to his own involvement
in a world from which he would like to remain aloof, to give up
to his "partness." In this, Hitchcock is different from
Antonioni, but similar to Hawks or Fellini. He is, in our terms,

an "outsider," and we can see the thrust of Chabrol or Bazin as
being the Catholic view of man's life, an "inside" view, which
focuses on man's freedom and not on his bondage to God's will,
whereas Hitchcock's view is exactly the opposite.

Bazin's marvelous interview with Hitchcock shows Bazin's
humor and delicacy as well as any piece of his. Confronted with
Hitchcock's usual insistence on his own exclusively rhetorical
and entertainment-oriented motives, Bazin (after insinuating by
means of an anecdote about William Wyler that directors often
don't know or admit to what they're up to) gets Hitchcock to agree
to the idea of transfer of personality, to his stylistic
"Jansenism," sober and austere, to the quality of his mise-en-
scène that amounts to an interior tension, an instability of the
image rendering a reality where all is in peril, in
disequilibrium. Thus Bazin leads Hitchcock to approve, yet as
if the case had been originated by Hitchcock, just what Bazin's
reading of him would be, and despite Hitchcock's patent intention
during the interview to admit to nothing of the kind. Hitchcock
saves his dignity, and Bazin saves his point.[13]

Bazin's reading of Hitchcock in this brief interview is close
to our own--far closer, we think, to Hitchcock's qualities than
are the readings by Chabrol and Truffaut in which it is often
implicated. As is evident throughout What Is Cinema?, vol. 2,
when simply interpreting films Bazin is marvelously responsive
to their subtlest qualities and their most finely discriminated
connotations. But in the article "The Evolution of Film
Language," where his intent is to generalize from film's qualities
to the relations between style and meaning, Bazin is led finally
to misread Hitchcock's mind through an accurate reading of his
style, since (as his basic ideas require that he should) Bazin
mistakes the part for the whole, the tone of the medium for the
point of the message. But the only appeals that can make any
plausible sense are to the interaction of elements in support
of the whole; no attempts to build a sense of the whole from
supposedly minimal elements like style or individual devices can
be successful. Even if they sometimes are accurate in terms other
than the ones suggested, they finally must be incorrect in their
implications about critical procedure and the analysis of truth
from facts.

But mistaken ideas did not prevent Bazin from being a superb
critic of those cases of film where his ideology did not lead
him wrong, or from being capable of expressing in excellent and
evocative readings the particular quality of the cinema's
expressive force in its varied sorts. Moreover, he saw and began
to express the proper cleavage plane for the elucidation of the
point of films: the proper abstractions to be made. Bazin found
the real differences in what auteurs make their film surfaces
imply but assigned them to the ways they imply them. He realized
that the great distinction is between a reality revealed and a
reality asserted, between showing and meaning, between "outside"
and "inside" motives in the creation of the film surface. But

that he thought this distinction should be at all historicized (and he does not historicize it much, what with his pointers between Dreyer and Bresson, Eisenstein and Duvivier) or that it should be assigned to style alone and not to the whole contemplatable interplay of the qualities of films, or to more abstract realities than images, is a sign of his structuralist times, and, indeed, a cause of much far worse criticism to follow him.

But can we finally be "Beardsleyan" and "Bazinian" at once, when Bazin is so insistent, especially in the more theoretical essays in What Is Cinema?, vol. 1, that we have been discussing here, on the physical basis of film as being what characterizes it, on the fact of the photographic transfer of reality which bears away our faith? It would certainly be gratifying to be able to feel that the sensitivity and truth in Bazin's readings of Neo-Realism, of Renoir, of Chaplin, of the Western, were not based on false ideas as, for example, Yeats's poetic truths are based on the looninesses in A Vision. I think we can be both Beardsleyan and Bazinian by noting that it is the aesthetics rather than the physics of Bazin's responsiveness to cinema that matters--it is clear from his practice that what his claim amounts to is that the cinema has for us the quality of the real, a capacity to present us with textures that are like the gradients of visual information presented us by the world. It is, then, simply a fact of cinema that in it the reallike and the structured play against each other as do fact and myth in the Red Balloon, like the copresence of Charles Spencer Chaplin and Charlie with the mass murderer in Monsieur Verdoux. Something very like this interplay is characteristic of all the arts--but the particular form of its presentation in cinema is what Bazin, fully translatably into our Beardsleyan terms, explained best.

W.C.


NOTES
1. The essay, "L'Evolution du Langage Cinématographique," is translated by Peter Graham from André Bazin's Qu'est-ce que le Cinéma?, I (Paris: Les Editions du Cerf, 1958), pp. 131-48, and is included in The New Wave, edited by Graham (Garden City: Doubleday, 1968), pp. 25-50, 31. The "Evolution" essay also appears in Hugh Gray's translation of Qu'est-ce que le Cinéma?, What Is Cinema? (Berkeley: Univ. of California Press, 1967), pp. 23-40. My parenthetical citations are to Graham's volume. When I quote from Gray, I use page numbers following his name in parenthetical reference.
2. Brian Henderson, A Critique of Film Theory (New York: E. P. Dutton, 1980), pp. 51-53.
3. Pauline Kael, "Raising Kane--II," The New Yorker, February 27, 1971, p. 46; for sensitive treatment of Welles's style

see Henderson, "The Long Take," pp. 58-61; Leland Poague, "'Reading' the Prince: Shakespeare, Welles, and Some Aspects of Chimes at Midnight," Iowa State Journal of Research 56 (1981).

4. Dan Sperber, Rethinking Symbolism (Cambridge: Cambridge Univ. Press, 1975), pp. 141-42.

5. Arthur Koestler, The Ghost in the Machine (New York: Macmillan, 1967), p. 56; Gregory Bateson, in Jurgen Ruesch and Gregory Bateson, Communication: The Social Matrix of Psychiatry (New York: W. W. Norton, 1951), pp. 183-86; Susanne K. Langer, Philosophical Sketches (1962; reprint, New York: Mentor-New American Library, 1964), pp. 18-20; Langer, Mind: An Essay in Human Feeling, I (Baltimore: Johns Hopkins Univ. Press, 1967), p. 241; Jacques Monod, Chance and Necessity (New York: Knopf, 1971), pp. 160-80; Rudolf Arnheim, Art and Visual Perception: A Psychology of the Creative Eye: The New Version (Berkeley: Univ. of California Press, 1974), pp. 410-12.

6. Claude Lévi-Strauss, "The Structural Study of Myth," in Richard T. De George and Fernande M. De George, The Structuralists (Garden City: Anchor-Doubleday, 1972), pp. 169-94; Northrop Frye, The Critical Path: An Essay in the Social Context of Literary Criticism (Bloomington: Indiana Univ. Press, 1971), pp. 36, 44; Jurij Lotman, Semiotics of Cinema, Michigan Slavic Contributions, no. 5 (Ann Arbor: Dept. of Slavic Languages and Literature, Univ. of Michigan, 1976), pp. 1-22, 65-76; Christian Metz, Film Language: A Semiotics of the Cinema (New York: Oxford Univ. Press, 1974), pp. 58-61; Sergei Eisenstein, "A Dialectical Approach to Film Form," in Eisenstein, Film Form (New York: Harcourt Brace, 1949), pp. 45-56.

7. Rudolf Arnheim, Film as Art (Berkeley: Univ. of California Press, 1957), p. 5; Richard Roud, "Face to Face: André Bazin," Sight and Sound, 28 (1959): 176-79. See J. Dudley Andrew, André Bazin (New York: Oxford Univ. Press, 1978).

8. Gray mistranslates femmes cancanant on p. 140 of Les Editions du Cerf edition, 1958, as "women dancing the can-can" (Gray, p. 32). He translates Bazin's misascription of the awakening lions in Potemkin to Pudovkin's The End of St. Petersburg correctly, though Bazin is mistaken (Gray, p. 32). Graham translates correctly, but silently corrects the misascription. Lang himself agreed that the women/hens joke was a mistake (Peter Bogdanovich, Fritz Lang in America [New York: Praeger, 1967], p. 28).

9. James Roy MacBean argues that Bazin's criticism, seemingly formal, in fact espouses what Marxists take to be a "religious" view of the world, a view that encourages passivity and argues that reality is something one suffers rather than creates ("Vent d'est or Godard and Rocha at the Crossroads," Sight and Sound, 40 [Summer, 1971]: 144-50). With the second volume of What Is Cinema?

available for English readers, it is easier to understand
how much more subtle Bazin's view is than it appeared to
be--for I would certainly not agree with Henderson's claim
that it is not so much subtle as incoherent; Critique of
Film Theory, pp. 32-47.

10.  Ingmar Bergman, Four Screenplays of Ingmar Bergman (New
     York:  Simon and Schuster, 1960), p. xvii.
11.  Claude Chabrol, "Hitchcock Confronts Evil," Cahiers du
     Cinéma in English, no. 2 (n.d. [1966]):  67, 68, 69.
12.  François Truffaut, Hitchcock (New York:  Simon and
     Schuster, 1967), p. 240.
13.  André Bazin, "Hitchcock versus Hitchcock," Cahiers du Cinéma
     in English, no. 2 (n.d. [1966]), pp. 51-59.  Further sources
     dealing with Hitchcock's image of the world include the
     comments of Truffaut immediately following Bazin's interview
     (pp. 60-66); see also Eric Rohmer and Claude Chabrol,
     Hitchcock:  The First Forty-Four Films (New York:
     Frederick Ungar, 1979).

# C H A P T E R
# 3

---

# The Problem
# of Film Genre

It is arguable that no concept in film study is more central
or more problematic than the concept of film genre. Stanley
Cavell, for example, refutes "essence of the medium" arguments
such as Panofsky's by remarking that the "medium" that matters
most in cinema is generic and formal rather than material. "The
first successful movies," says Cavell, "the first moving pictures
accepted as motion pictures--were not applications of a medium
that was defined by given possibilities, but the <u>creation of</u>
<u>a medium</u> by their giving significance to specific possibilities"
--by which Cavell means significance of the sort embodied by
character types ("types are exactly what carry the forms movies
have relied on") and genres ("for a cycle is a genre . . . and
a genre is a medium").[1]

Andrew Tudor, on the other hand, finds the notion of genre
problematic nearly to the point of uselessness, particularly as
regards its application to the practical task of film criticism.
Thus Tudor describes the scholarship of Jim Kitses and André Bazin
on the western as being caught by the "empiricist dilemma." That
is, "they are <u>defining</u> a 'Western' on the basis of analysing
a body of films which cannot possibly be said to be 'Westerns'
until after the analysis." Tudor goes on to argue that the genre
notion is only interesting when used to describe audience
expectations: genre has very little to do with objective
characteristics of films but rather it serves to describe
"conceptions held by certain groups about certain films."[2]

In "Genre and Movies" Douglas Pye counters Tudor's first
point by appealing to E. H. Gombrich and Wittgenstein, both of
whom argue a notion of "family resemblances" loose enough to be
flexible but conceptually specific enough to be useful. Thus,
while no single western will employ every convention or serve
as a perfect model for the genre, the generic term "western" will
remain valid for indicating that place where a group of specific
aesthetic conventions or conceptual categories intersect. That
such conventions exist for particular genres is empirically
verifiable (Pye writes at length on the tradition of the western

from Fenimore Cooper to Howard Hawks) and the system of such
conventions, as formalized by such as Northrop Frye and Tzvetan
Todorov, is powerful enough, Pye argues, to generate an almost
infinite range of meanings and associations without bursting the
conceptual bonds that hold the genre together.[3]

In the long run I believe that Cavell and Pye are the more
interesting theorists, but Tudor's second point, that genre refers
to audience expectations rather than to qualities intrinsic to
specific films, is worth exploring further, particularly as such
exploration will require a mentalistic approach to the problem
of film genre.


## LITERATURE--A MENTAL CATEGORY

I have argued elsewhere that "the 'literariness' of a text
is determined by reader expectation."[4] Some works, of course,
are more readily taken as literature than others, but it is
possible to understand almost any verbal or cinematic text as
a literary construct. In the present context we may rephrase
the contention: let us assume that there exists a mental category
that we shall term, for lack of a better word, "literature."
Such an assumption is warranted and the existence of the category
may be readily demonstrated. It is a standard and useful bit
of pedagogical trickery to take a sentence from, say, a history
book, or from the evening paper, and to rearrange it on the
blackboard into some sort of stanzaic or free verse form. Such
rearranging does nothing to the denotative value of the verbal
structure; but students (and readers generally) almost inevitably
respond to the language as if it were (and it now is) poetry.
They look for symbolic connections or for patterns of sound and
association. They show concern for "theme" where before they
showed concern for "fact." In which instance, to borrow
Wittgenstein's phrase, the "language-game" has changed.[5] A
new set of interpretive rules is in operation. And such rules
can only exist if a mental category "literature" exists:
otherwise the rules would never come into play.

The most important rule, the defining rule attending on the
category of literature, might be termed the "contextual
displacement rule." In the example of the rearranged newspaper
sentence such a displacement is quite obvious: what was once
an assertion becomes a mimesis of assertion. Such is also quite
obviously and necessarily the case with most cinematic works.
Consider the Mt. Rushmore sequence in Hitchcock's North by
Northwest. We are well aware that the images that we construe
as Eve Kendall and Roger Thornhill more properly "belong" to Eva
Marie Saint and Cary Grant. We are also aware that they do their
scrambling across studio mock-ups of the Mt. Rushmore faces rather
than across the faces themselves. Yet we choose, once again,
to "background" the "facts" for the sake of something else--for
the sake, we would argue, of vicarious or aesthetic experience.
We cannot ignore the facts altogether, or else we might very

well attempt to go to the aid of "Eve" and "Roger," but our mental process is one that devalues the literal for the sake of the literary.

The contextual displacement rule thus works vertically, as it were, shifting the entire import of the text up the specificity/generality scale. This can be true even with works of history or naturalistic fiction. When treated as literature, such works do not counsel attention to historical specifics. In most cases such specifics long ago ceased to be of any real consequence (it hardly matters to modern man who carried the day at Bosworth Field). What works of this sort argue is the general value of attending to specifics. Only in this context can films like Bicycle Thief and Umberto D. be of any interest to us--we cannot now solve the immediate problems of postwar Italy; Italy has new (if historically related) problems to attend to.

It is arguable, however, that such vertical shifts of import are impossible without the simultaneous operation of a second rule--which we may term, after E. D. Hirsch, the "rule of the generic hypothesis." Such a rule is necessary in verbal discourse, Hirsch contends, "because words follow one another sequentially, and because the words that will come later are not present to consciousness along with the words experienced here and now." Therefore, "the speaker or listener must have an anticipated sense of the whole by virtue of which the presently experienced words are understood in their capacity as parts functioning in a whole."[6]

Put another way, verbal meaning is "structure dependent." This is true even within sentences, where the rules of syntax provide the "anticipated sense of the whole." Thus "table" can be a noun or a verb depending upon its placement in a sentence; and we can know whether it is a noun or a verb before the sentence is completed by virtue of linguistic "conventions," i.e., by virtue of the fact that writer and reader share a common knowledge of the grammatical rules that constitute the language. Where "table" is preceded by an auxiliary (e.g., "will") we expect that the sentence is of a type in which "table" functions as a verb, and we understand the succeeding words accordingly. Conversely, where "table" is preceded by an article (e.g., "the") we expect that the sentence is of the type in which "table" functions as a noun and that expectation of the entire sentence governs our interpretation of it.

According to Hirsch, then, a similar set of "type conventions" must be at work across sentences as well as within sentences. Indeed, it is arguable that extrasentential relationships, being less clearly determined or circumscribed by syntax, are even more structure dependent than intrasentential relationships. In which case the "anticipated sense of the whole" becomes more crucial to our understanding of verbal texts. Without some "sense of the whole," without some hypothesis as to the nature of the relationships between sentences, we would be unable to read texts as anything other than randomly collected utterances. But of course we do read texts, we do "make sense" of them, and we do so by virtue of the fact that writers and readers share sets of expectations as to the likely intratextual or structural relationships that can be asserted and understood. Such expectations constitute the province of genre.

The argument for the necessity of generic expectations is equally applicable to cinematic as well as verbal texts--and for the same reason. Both verbal and cinematic texts are structured in time: we cannot properly interpret a given cinematic image (that image itself a complex symbolic entity) without some sense of the images that are likely to follow and the probable relationships among them. We must therefore posit a "type" of meaning structure from the beginning--and this "generic hypothesis" will guide our interpretation of succeeding images until such time as it is possible or necessary (as it often is) to refine or replace our initial intuitive generic guess. Thus, where the contextual displacement rule operates vertically, in conceptual space, the generic hypothesis rule operates horizontally, in conceptual time; and only when both rules are in operation is literature or cinema possible.


## GENRE AND AUDIENCE EXPECTATIONS

I have thus far argued that interpretive rules exist and have practical consequence. Without them there could be no community of artist and audience. Tudor is therefore right to assert that "genre" refers to audience expectations--it could hardly be otherwise. I have also noted that the existence of interpretive rules implies the existence of conceptual categories (literature, genre) that can be understood as "possible situations." That is, literature exists whenever a reader/viewer interprets a text as "literature"; a gangster film exists whenever a reader/viewer interprets a text as a "gangster film." In which case it is clear that the categories must preexist the situations, just as the existence of a language must precede the use of it. That is, generic expectations "must belong to a type of meaning rather than merely to a unique meaning, because otherwise the interpreter would have no way of expecting them."[7] Which is not to say that all texts are identical--no more than that all sentences are identical (sentences almost never are, nor are texts)--but it does say that the rules and conventions of interpreting sentences and texts are type-bound and sharable or else communication of any sort would be impossible. At which point we are faced once again with Tudor's "empiricist dilemma." How is it possible to know in advance, as in some sense we must, how to see a western as a "western"? How is it possible to know in advance, as in some sense we must, how to view a comedy as a "comedy"?

Tudor's manner of dealing with the issue, a manner he shares with other empirically oriented British social scientists, is primarily to side-step it. Tudor simply assumes that generic conventions are learned and lets it go at that. He does not even attempt to explain how such learning takes place.

Such an explanation is available to us, however, if we are willing to risk proposing it, an explanation involving a notion of "innateness" derived from Chomskian linguistics.

We may state the case for the innate character of linguistic knowledge as follows. Any reasonably competent description of the knowledge possessed by the native speaker of a language will reveal that knowledge to be of a very complex nature. Such knowledge amounts to a theory of language, "a theory of a highly intricate and abstract form that determines, ultimately, a connection between sound and meaning by generating structural descriptions of sentences . . . each with its phonetic, semantic, and syntactic aspects."[8] The abstract character of that knowledge is necessitated by the fact that sentences are seldom if ever repeated. Our knowledge of a language is therefore such that we can generate and understand an unlimited number of novel sentences, which means that linguistic knowledge is a knowledge of interpretive rules (e.g., nominalization) and conceptual categories (e.g., past, present), not merely a memory of sentences previously encountered or uttered. Furthermore, all native speakers, regardless of intelligence or motivation, acquire a complete knowledge of the rules and categories (though not the lexicon) at an early age (long before they could learn, say, physics) and on the basis of a minute sample of data, much of which is fragmentary and imperfect. The conclusion is therefore inescapable that language acquisition is radically unlike most other forms of learning and can best be accounted for by assuming the existence of a "language faculty," an inborn mental schema that constructs a grammar for any language within a child's hearing and does so on the basis of "linguistic universals"--e.g., mental categories like "sentence," "subject noun phrase," "predicate verb phrase." Thus as children we recognize sentences as "sentences" intuitively, no matter what the language, because we have an innate knowledge of what constitutes a sentence. In other words, we know what language is and how it works before we acquire any specific language.

By analogy, then, we can posit the innate knowledge of at least two general mental categories (and certain attendant interpretive rules) necessary to the existence of literary works: 1) literature and 2) genre. The more conservative, less speculative form of the assertion is that we have an innate and quite specific capacity unlike other learning capacities to recognize particular literary and generic categories and rules as they operate in actual discourse and to construct, on the basis of a very finite amount of data, a few works per genre, a "grammar" of such rules and conventions appropriate for the understanding and appreciation of the vast majority of the works that we subsequently encounter and/or create. Such a schema, in the more conservative version of the assertion, does not necessarily determine the genres that will actually exist--those being at least partially the result of historical and cultural circumstances outside the realm of aesthetics--but the schema will abstract and generate the generic hypotheses that make literature possible by making it understandable.

The more radical and speculative version of the assertion differs only to the degree that it posits further innate categories, subsets of the generic category, that are universal to literary discourse. In this light we might say, as I have said elsewhere, that specific generic forms are implicit in the order of literature and will find expression, in different guises, in nearly every era.[9] Comedy, for example, has a long, honorable, and surprisingly persistent history from Aristophanes to Woody Allen, and I would be perfectly willing to venture the guess that comedy will always be with us. But I can think of no mentalistically grounded logic that will permit the argument that there are only so many generic plots. Northrop Frye asserts that such is the case, and he demonstrates that certain plot structures are recurrent in literature, but he does so in a diachronic fashion which seems incapable of proving that case.

Fortunately, such a proof is unnecessary because the more conservative form of the argument is sufficient to account for our seemingly intuitive ability to arrive at an adequate understanding of most literary works, and to do so at a point prior to formal education or critical analysis. Furthermore, to say that there may be more than the four plots that Frye describes (i.e., romance, tragedy, comedy, and irony) has no effect whatsoever on the fact that Frye's four plots are the operative generic categories of drama, film, and prose fiction, in which case our "literary competency" will presumably include a fairly detailed knowledge of the various conventions of plot, character, and imagery that typify each of the various forms of imaginative and narrative literature.[10] The only question we cannot answer by the logic of innateness is how such a capacity for literary reading became innate. For the present it is enough to remark that the capacity for literature is evidently of genuine survival value to the species--perhaps for allowing us opportunity to exercise our faculties of intelligence and imagination.


THE CAPACITY TO LEARN

I have argued to this point that humans are innately endowed with a knowledge of mental categories--such as "sentence," "noun," "literature," "genre"--that enables them to master abstract mental systems and to perform complex mental operations without any necessarily conscious knowledge of their doing so. Without positing such categories it is impossible, given the present state of our knowledge, to account for the fact that children learn language and acquire a capacity to read literary works. A distinction must be made, however, having to do with the time

frame within which such learning takes place.  The capacity to
acquire a native speaker's competency in a language "shuts down"
during puberty (another argument for biological innateness):
thereafter languages can only be acquired with great effort.[11]
We may expand our active vocabulary, of course, but doing so
involves no new knowledge of the structure of the language.  With
literature and cinema, on the other hand, it is clearly the case
that acquisition is--or may be--a continuous and ongoing process.
As Northrop Frye puts it, "expanding images into conventional
archetypes of literature is a process that takes place
unconsciously in all our reading."[12]  Thus, while the category
"genre" may exist, it can only manifest itself in or operate on
generic forms that are within the realm of everyday literary
experience (we cannot learn a language we do not hear).
Accordingly, most people are capable of understanding the popular
literature of an era, and other forms of literature that employ
popular generic conventions, but they may initially be unable
to deal with literary or cinematic constructs that partake of
other, lesser known generic conventions.  Hence the frequent
rejection of avant-garde art:  "readers" simply do not have it
within their competencies to generate adequate generic hypotheses
that can make sense of avant-garde works.  Such generic constructs
exist, of course, or else avant-garde works would not exist:
they have been interpreted by artists in the process of creation.
And the fact of their existence evidences the fact of their
teachability.  But that they must be taught, usually in the
university, and are successfully taught there, attests to the
continuing capacity of human beings to acquire and make use of
new generic constructs.  Given adequate contact with less familiar
forms of literature readers can arrive at a satisfactory ability
to read a remarkably diverse variety of literary or cinematic
works.


AUTEURISM AS GENRE STUDY
     The significance of generic hypotheses to the study of cinema
is best evidenced by the history of auteurism.  As Raymond Durgnat
and Dudley Andrew (among others) point out, auteurism can be
understood as a form of genre study:  where a study of westerns
will be concerned with the system of shared conventions that makes
westerns intelligible as westerns (and as films) auteurism will
be concerned with the system of shared conventions that makes
Hawks movies intelligible as Hawks movies (and as films).[13]
     The two positions are by no means mutually exclusive.  Large
generic categories like the western are serviceable enough--
indeed, they are the operative categories at work in the minds
of most film viewers.  But the history of auteurism makes it
clear, however, that more specific generic paradigms, which exist
simultaneously with the larger categories while applying to
smaller groups of films (e.g., Rio Bravo is both a western and

a Hawks film), are far more powerful.  Put another way, to see
Rio Bravo as a western is to make it intelligible:  to see it
as a Hawks film is to increase its intelligibility by lending
significance to a greater number of details.  For example, as
Richard Jameson points out, Rio Bravo represents both in its
dialogue and action the ultimate Hawksian gloss on the concept
of "being good."[14]  Of course, the ability to survive on the
frontier is almost always at issue in westerns--but the specific
form that the concern takes in Rio Bravo has special
significance for Hawks.  Viewers unaware of this typically
Hawksian motif may assign no special value to the moment, early
in the film, when Pat Wheeler (Ward Bond) almost casually admits
to Dude (Dean Martin) that his "Spanish ain't too good."  But
no one familiar with The Big Sleep or Only Angels Have Wings
can fail to sit up and take notice.  Indeed, not being "good
enough" gets Wheeler killed very soon thereafter.

All of which accounts for the fact that auteurism initiated
an almost complete revision of the history of the Hollywood
cinema.  As Andrew Sarris points out, Hawks (for one) hardly
figures in Lewis Jacobs's The Rise of the American Cinema, Paul
Rotha's The Film Till Now, or Arthur Knight's The Liveliest
Art, all three standard accounts of the rise and fall of
Hollywood.  And yet it is generally conceded these days that Hawks
ranks as one of the overpowering figures of the Hollywood era.
It is easy to see how such a revision was possible (and
necessary).  Prior to the advent of auteurism the generic
hypotheses most favored by scholars and critics of Hollywood
derived primarily from the Soviet, the documentary, and the
expressionistic traditions--that is, from the European cinema.
Hollywood genres were therefore suspect:  not only were they
popular but they were provincial as well.  In other words, such
critics short-circuited their own generic competencies under the
pressures of intellectual politics.  It is hardly surprising,
then, that they had little of substance to say about the vast
majority of Hollywood films.

At the outset, however, auteurism side-stepped "les
politiques des genres" by proposing a new set of categories--
authorial rather than generic--that enabled auteur critics, armed
with a bit of foreign jargon, to speak eloquently and with genuine
seriousness about Hawks and Hitchcock and the rest.  We can now
see, however, that the auteurist gambit succeeded not by dumping
the then suspect concept of genre but by refining it.

As Hirsch points out, generic hypotheses function as
probability judgments.  They are guesses about the unknown (the
words and/or images to come) made on the basis of the known (the
words and/or images that have already been read, seen, or heard).
The fundamental assumption here involves the principle of "the
uniformity of the class."  The greater the similarity among the
known traits of the objects in the class, the greater the
probability that the unknown traits will be similar as well.

Hence it is that we can provide reasonable generic hypotheses on the basis of partial knowledge of given works. We compare what we know about the work in question at every level (thematic, stylistic) to the traits that are generic to specific categories of film or literature and, on the basis of the known, we arrive at an anticipated or probable sense of the as yet unknown whole. Accordingly, the more we know about a film the less improbable our generic hypothesis. Similarly, the more we know about the traits of the class the greater the probability that a given work will belong to that class (assuming that the known traits of the work in question correspond). The auteurist hypothesis is therefore more powerful for being more specific. A western may or may not be concerned with "professionalism." A Hawks western almost always is. The Hawks paradigm is therefore more powerful for providing more points of comparison. By the same token, however, the Hawks paradigm is less applicable for subsuming a smaller number of films.


PROBLEMS OF GENRE STUDY

Here, then, is the real dilemma of genre, one which has important practical ramifications for film study: the more powerful the genre the less general its applicability and the less likely that students will pick it up on their own. This explains why auteur studies are inevitably the most satisfying in terms of specific films. Clearly the auteurist paradigm is to be preferred where detailed film-by-film knowledge is the goal. And yet establishing the paradigm by seeing films enough to provide an adequate sense of so particular a generic construct is problematic, especially in the context of university film study programs where rental money and class time are at a premium.

To be sure, I have argued that viewers (and hence students) have an innate ability to construct generic grammars. But, paradoxically, the more readily acquired generic constructs (e.g., the western) are so adequate that students often feel little need to go beyond broad generic categories towards an auteuristic perception of films. I do not mean to imply anything negative about such categories: they are absolutely necessary and make a wide-based film-culture possible. The fact remains, however, that auteurism is the more powerful if less popular approach to cinema. Thus I find in the classroom context that it generally requires six or seven films to provide students with an adequate sense of a specific auteuristic genre. And if I can only cover two or three directors per term—and such is generally my practice—then it becomes very difficult to provide a strong sense of film history. I am forced to sacrifice history to methodology. As Robert Scholes puts it: "We cannot 'teach' enough individual works of literature to make our students as literate as we would like them to be."[15]

Fortunately, we do not have to teach them everything.

Viewers and readers already know a good deal more than most
critics would like to admit: otherwise, as I have argued, there
would be no such thing as literature or cinema to discuss. To
teach literacy, therefore, be it verbal or visual, does not
involve initiation into mysteries. It involves, rather, the
description of those competencies that are already possessed by
"native reader/viewers" and the extension of those competencies
by bringing students into contact with new generic paradigms.
Given the fact that literary/cinematic genres are coextensive
and hierarchical, however, some genres being less familiar and
more powerful than others, it is incumbent upon film scholars
to stake their claims and define their arguments in the most
specific generic terms possible (as Pye does in his discussion
of the western). We cannot toss the genre notion overboard, as
Tudor suggests we do, simply because it does not seem concise
enough to suit our passion for methodological precision. We can
only be as precise as reality allows. Ultimately, scholars must
appeal to the competency of their readers to place their work
in the larger perspective of literature and cinema. Like it or
not, we critics depend upon our audience. Were that not the case
literary scholarship in general and film scholarship in particular
would be far more fragmentary and frustrating than they already
are.


DECODING VS. INTERPRETATION (ADDENDUM)

In Chapter 4 William Cadbury draws a distinction between
a "strict" concept of grammar (wherein understanding entails
a kind of decoding) and the mental activity involved in the act
of interpretation: in the latter case understanding builds
from codes (via connotations, for instance) but is not
determined by them. Meaning, rather, arises from the
interplay of codes within texts. A film is not coded to the
same degree that a sentence might be (I make a similar point,
in the terms of the present chapter, on p. 59). To talk, as I
do here, of a "grammar" of narrative or literary forms is
therefore to use "grammar" as an analogy, though a suggestive
one. I agree that meaning in film is not decodable in the sense
that a more literal notion of grammar would imply: perhaps
"schema," as William Cadbury uses the term in our conclusion,
would be a better word.

However, my use of the grammar analogy here does not entail
a simple notion of decoding wherein meanings are read off of
surface elements alone as checked against a storehouse memory
(though memory plays a part). Rather, my concept of a grammar
of generic forms is precisely an attempt to account for the
acquisition of an "interpretive competency" in the face of what
Chomsky has called the "poverty of the stimulus."[16] How is
it that we know how to take artworks (including films) as
artworks with a minimum of prior exposure? And my usage of the

concept of genre entails no more than the two "rules" I explicitly propose: the contextual displacement rule and the rule of the generic hypothesis. Neither rule is "grammatical" in the strict sense--though both rules, I think, are "obligatory" to the aesthetic experience of literature or film. Indeed, the notion of generic hypotheses is completely in accord with Beardsley's theory of metaphor: to import a generic hypothesis to one's reading of a film is to entertain a set of possible connotations that may or may not prove appropriate. Such hypotheses or connotations remain indispensable, I am convinced, to our capacity to understand films. Our ability to provide and employ them is clear evidence that film viewing is far from a passive experience.

L.P.

NOTES
1. Stanley Cavell, The World Viewed: Reflections on the Ontology of Film, enlarged ed. (Cambridge: Harvard Univ. Press, 1979), pp. 32-36. Other recent discussions of genre include Robin Wood, "Ideology, Genre, Auteur," Film Comment, 13, no. 1 (1977): 46-51; Leo Braudy, The World in a Frame: What We See in Films (Garden City: Anchor Press/Doubleday, 1976); Barry K. Grant, ed., Film Genre: Theory and Criticism (Metuchen, N.J.: Scarecrow Press, 1977); Stephen Neale, Genre (London: British Film Institute, 1980); and Thomas Schatz, Hollywood Genres: Formulas, Filmmaking, and the Studio System (New York: Random House, 1981).
2. Andrew Tudor, Theories of Film (New York: Viking, 1974), p. 135, 147. See also his Image and Influence (New York: St. Martin's Press, 1975).
3. Douglas Pye, "Genre and Movies," Movie, no. 20 (1975), pp. 29-43. See also Northrop Frye, Anatomy of Criticism (Princeton: Princeton Univ. Press, 1957), and Tzvetan Todorov, The Fantastic: A Structural Approach to a Literary Genre, trans. Richard Howard (Ithaca: Cornell Univ. Press, 1975).
4. Leland A. Poague, "Explicating the Obvious: Five Propositions on the Problem of Value in Literary Studies," Journal of Aesthetic Education, 11, no. 4 (1977): 38.
5. Ludwig Wittgenstein, Philosophical Investigations, 3rd ed. (New York: Macmillan, 1973), p. 5.
6. E. D. Hirsch, Jr., Validity in Interpretation (New Haven: Yale Univ. Press, 1967), p. 82.
7. Hirsch, Validity, p. 80.
8. Noam Chomsky, Language and Mind, enlarged ed. (New York: Harcourt Brace Jovanovich, 1972), p. 170. See also his Rules and Representations (New York: Columbia Univ. Press, 1980).

9.  Leland Poague, The Cinema of Frank Capra (New York:   A. S. Barnes, 1975).
10. The notion of "literary competency" is proposed by Jonathan Culler in Structuralist Poetics (Ithaca:   Cornell Univ. Press, 1975), pp. 113-30.
11. Eric H. Lenneberg, "The Capacity for Language Acquisition," in Readings in Applied Transformational Grammar, ed. Mark Lester, 2nd ed. (New York:   Holt, Rinehart and Winston, 1973), pp. 46-80.
12. Frye, Anatomy of Criticism, p. 100.
13. J. Dudley Andrew, The Major Film Theories (New York: Oxford Univ. Press, 1976), particularly his section on "Christian Metz and the Semiology of the Cinema," pp. 212-41.  See also Raymond Durgnat, "Genre:  Populism and Social Realism," Film Comment, 11, no. 4 (1975):   23.
14. Richard T. Jameson, "Talking & Doing in Rio Bravo," The Velvet Light Trap, no. 12 (1974), pp. 26-30.
15. Robert Scholes, Structuralism in Literature (New Haven: Yale Univ. Press, 1974), p. 129.
16. Chomsky, Rules, p. 34.

CHAPTER

4

# Semiology, Human Nature, and John Ford

SEMIOLOGY
Chief among the drawbacks in the basic arguments of the
semiological enterprise is that extremely far-reaching conclusions
are made on the basis of a theory of structural linguistics that
in certain ways formed the foundation for modern linguistics,
but that is no longer taken seriously by linguists themselves
as a proposal about the nature of language or, by extension, of
human nature. Many of the conclusions derive from what N.
Troubetzkoy, Roman Jakobson, and others argued about the very
limited set of features that underlie the phonological
organizations of all languages. Phonology presents a picture
of a "complex pattern of paired functional differences."[1] And
this is the picture of language, la langue, as Ferdinand de
Saussure understood it: "a form and not a substance," where
"there are only differences without positive terms" (p. 28),
which go to make up a storehouse of items possessing syntagmatic
solidarity and a paradigmatic dimension permitting substitution
in the speech chain.[2]
The structure of this storehouse is the model for all
structure, and it is based on the primary operation of the human
mind.

The discernment of binary opposition is a child's "first
logical operation," and in that operation we see the primary
and distinctive intervention of culture into nature. There
are thus grounds for recognizing, in the capacity for the
creation and perception of binary or paired "opposites,"
and in the cognate activity of the creation and perception
of phonemic patterning at large, a fundamental and
characteristic operation of the human mind. (p. 24)

This is "what Lévi-Strauss has termed the 'socio-logic' of the
human mind, which structures nature in its own image, and thus
establishes the foundation for the system of totemic
'transformations' that overtly or covertly underpin our picture
of the world" (p. 88).

69

The first thing to notice about this picture of human nature is that it is based on what is taken to be evocative about the relations among features underlying phonology. Yet Noam Chomsky points out

> several reservations are necessary when structural linguistics is used as a model in [Lévi-Strauss's] way. For one thing, the structure of a phonological system is of very little interest as a formal object; there is nothing of significance to be said, from a formal point of view, about a set of forty-odd elements cross-classified in terms of eight or ten features. The significance of structuralist phonology . . . lies not in the formal properties of phonemic systems but in the fact that a fairly small number of features that can be specified in absolute, language-independent terms appear to provide the basis for the organization of all phonological systems. The achievement of structuralist phonology was to show that the phonological rules of a great variety of languages apply to classes of elements that can be simply characterized in terms of these features; that historical change affects such classes in a uniform way; and that the organization of features plays a basic role in the use and acquisition of language. This was a discovery of the greatest importance, and it provides the groundwork for much of contemporary linguistics. But if we abstract away from the specific universal set of features and the rule systems in which they function, little of any significance remains.[3]

Even if there were interest in the pattern, it couldn't be said to explain language in any interesting sense. A phonologylike system describes relations among items like sounds and words, but in no sense explains the fact that languages assign meaning to strings of sounds by means of grammars, which both link sounds and meanings and discriminate between well-formed and ill-formed, ungrammatical strings. Nor can it explain the mechanism of acquisition of these grammars by virtually all human beings at tender ages on the basis of limited, fragmentary, and often contradictory exposures to data. The relations among phonological features are taken as a privileged model for structuralist tenets about language acquisition, perception, knowledge, and human nature itself—yet they explain nothing very important about even language.

Our point here is the same as Dan Sperber's about Lévi-Strauss: the error of taking the pattern of phonemes as the characterizing aspect of language as a semiotic system leads to false inferences about culture's determinative effects on cognition. Once it is understood that such canons as myth, literature, and film are not semiotic at all but are symbolic systems, dependent on an entirely different, though probably also biologically innate, mechanism, then Lévi-Strauss's perception about the relation between the strategy of human categorizings and its products can be appreciated as an insight not into cultural, but rather into biological determination of symbolic systems. As Sperber says:

> The paradox that the fundamental contribution of Lévi-Strauss seemed to entail is resolved if it is considered in this perspective. Lévi-Strauss revealed as never before the universality of focalisation and the universal elements of the evocational field in cultural symbolism. But, wishing to explain his own discoveries in semiological terms, he has, on the contrary, rendered them incomprehensible. He has in fact described neither a language nor a semantic system. The universal properties he reveals certainly exist, but they are cognitive and not semiological.[4]

To us, it is exactly Lévi-Strauss's positive terms, with their relations to each other, that constitute the value of his analyses of myth, and not the method of his discovering them or the conclusions he drew. The positive terms amount to a very powerful set of connotations that apply to art objects. To acknowledge their existence in no way compromises our point about emergence.

Saussure himself claimed less than his followers. For Saussure, le langage (all there is to language as it is known and used) has two parts, language proper (la langue) and people speaking it (la parole). And he set the boundary of la langue to include only the level of the word or formalized phrase. Language for him does not include sentences, and he took it as perfectly natural that we should be able to construct sentences (that is, engage in la parole) by stringing the arbitrarily symbolic words of language together in the most natural way. For him, then, consciousness would have something other than language in it--it would contain whatever it is that could use language in its own way and construct meaningful discourse. But for the structuralists who follow him, consciousness has only language in it.

In Jacques Lacan's perverse version of Freud, for instance, what inaugurates and hence explains the child's passing beyond the stade du miroir, the "mirror stage," of Imaginary identifications, and enables him or her to participate in a world of Symbolic forms, is the perception of sexual difference. This perception, the entertainability of the idea of absence of the phallus, is generalized by means of the practice game of "Fort! Da!" Through the game the child masters the fear of lack and brings the differentiation between presence and absence into his or her own behavioral repertory. On this internalized capacity to differentiate, the rest of acculturated perception can be built, starting with the perception of phonemic difference. We see the world in the shape our minds let us. Starting from that point of generalized difference, our minds let us use the methods

of structuralist linguistics, establishing a network of
differences like that which characterizes la langue.[5]
    It follows that, as Heidigger said, "Language speaks, not
man" (p. 159), which is to say that our culture speaks through
us the way it wants to. From this perspective it is
understandable that, just as Lacan undermines Freud's generative
insights by conflating them with Saussure's descriptivism, so
Louis Althusser undermines what Michael Harrington shows are
Marx's generative insights about human freedom by absorbing them
into a Saussurian mechanism that is simply not, as Andrew Britton
has recently shown, commensurate with the claim for a "science"
that is able to make the epistemological leap beyond ideology.[6]
This case is Marxist if not like Marx: social being determines
consciousness; the structure of social being, of the Other, is
the structure of language; language determines consciousness.
    For Lacan and Althusser, consciousness has only language
in it. In fact, there is no consciousness, at least no Cartesian
"Subject," but only the Other.

> The human being can no longer be said to be the "cause" or
> "origin" of linguistic or cultural symbolism in the sense
> of creating this symbolism and reducing it to being a means
> for his projects as an absolute master. . . . [T]he young
> child submits to symbolism as a homogeneous and all-powerful
> mass into which he must insert himself. . . . One could,
> therefore, say that the human being is an effect of the
> signifier rather than its cause. Insertion into the
> symbolic world is a mimesis, a collage. It fashions a being
> of "representation" for us.[7]

So while it is not clear who we are as we do it, it is clear that
within the prison-house of language we move around among the cells
as we choose, never able to see the world outside but mechanically
bound, not to preestablished ideas, but rather to the very process
of demarcating differences. We assuage desire by establishing
pleasure as the differentiation from its neighbors of a given
erotogenic zone, so that sexual pleasure is only experienced at
and in the rim of the zone.[8] We thus achieve at best the
rapture of unintelligibility, jouissance in the Other. And
this is exactly Lacan's, though neither Freud's nor Saussure's,
picture of human maturity: to give up the Imaginary illusion
of access to reality and to exercise the Symbolic achievement
of seeing and putting things in chains of other terms in order
to live with and within that Other and to act always like
structuralist linguists. As has been said, to be human is to
be a structuralist.
    But it appears that, unlike Saussure, Althusser and Lacan
are urging something about consciousness as well as describing
it--they are urging that we be true to ourselves, that we be
more in "Science" and "the Symbolic" and less in "Ideology" and
"the Imaginary," more in that reality which is difference and

less in that illusion which is "presence." We seem to be free
to choose to be structuralists, as well as being imprisoned
in structuralism. There are imperatives here: Lévi-Strauss says
"be a structuralist and a good scientist"; Lacan says "grow into
the Symbolic"; Althusser says "break with Ideology." If one is
true to one's nature one can do better work, as Lévi-Strauss makes
plain in the "Overture" to The Raw and the Cooked, where he
indicates that if he does his analysis of myth by that method
he will thereby be in tune with, and accurate to the myths of,
the minds he is studying, savage and his (and our) own.
    Likewise for Althusser, for each of us it is the method of
science, of the operation of criticism and self-criticism, by
which the ahistorical ideology, always encouraging us by its
"Ideological State Apparatuses" to believe in the Subject so that
our relations to the relations of production will be reproduced
and those relations of production perpetuated, can be transcended.
Thus, the epistemological break is assured, so we can live as
concrete individuals in the actual reality of history, recognizing
that we are bound if we see ourselves as Subjects, or believe
in the reality we think we see, and free only if we see ourselves
as objects put in place by the process of what is outside
ourselves, by ideology and the realities of class struggle.[9]


HUMAN NATURE
    It follows from this picture of human nature--deluded by
the illusion of presence and in tune with reality only if able
to detect structuring absences through the operation of
différance, "deferment"--that an objectivist view of art objects
like books or films is going to be contaminated by ideology, and
that a structuralist view of human nature is going to entail a
structuralist criticism.[10] As to books and films, Roland
Barthes's S/Z, which is universally taken as the model of
structuralist method, applies this world-view to the concept of
criticism, and shows

        first that the text (and so all "realistic" texts) does not
        offer an accurate picture of an unchangingly "real" world,
        and second, that a reading of it is possible which can tear
        away the veil, reveal the signifier-signified connection
        as the un-innocent convention (however politically
        bolstered) it is, and offer a sense that reality remains
        genuinely ours to make and to remake as we please. (pp.
        120-21)

Thus Barthes rejects "'dishonest' criticism, based on the
supposition that the work criticized exists in some objective
concrete way before the critical act" (p. 155). The Symbolic
critical act, and not the dishonest Imaginary one, will be
faithful to the mind that performs it, and hence will be an act
of making the world over into an image of the structure of

language, into an image of structuralist method, since the prison-
house is one of process not of product, and since that process,
that method of différance, "deferment," is the exact and only
equivalent of human nature.

If there is no reality except that which we "make and remake
as we please"--and we have seen that that is exactly what
structuralism holds--then it is crucial to structuralist criticism
that there is no work itself, in the sense of the New Criticism,
which argued, as we have done above, that it is the work itself
that is the proper object of the critic's attention.  The closest
thing to it is the "process of becoming a text," which Cahiers
established as the outcome of its Barthesian critical method.
Hence the sense, on the one hand, that one is freed from the
stultifications of a spurious objectivism if one stops looking
directly for meaning, as we see when John Hess argues that
structuralist, semiological, and Marxist criticism avoid the
formalist errors of auteurism by primary attention not to films,
but rather to the conditions of their production.  "The
examination of a film's social context becomes more important
than the film itself," and so it should if the film itself is
an illusion and if that context defines and equals the human
nature that perceives it.[11]

But on the other hand, drawing attention away from the films
themselves feels at least as much like a defeat as a victory.
Andrew Sarris remarks correctly that Hess's attitude, far from
the new departure he thinks it, is simply the bad old days come
again, before the New Criticism, when somehow the work itself
was always, we were told, less important than some aspect of its
context, though the aspect was more likely to be history or
biography than the class struggle.[12]

In fact the whole structuralist argument is false at the
very root.  Even if Metz and others urge that a second semiology
based on Lacan rather than Saussure has managed the break from
Saussurian empiricism to poststructuralist materialism, it is
clear when you look at Lacan that, far from replacing Saussure
with Freud, he turns Freud Saussurian--"the unconscious is
structured like a language," after all, and, to Lacan, language
means exactly Saussure's langue.  And Saussure's langue and
all that depends on it by way of epistemology and the methodology
of establishing a network of differences are incorrect.
Saussurian linguistics and its derived world-view are refuted
by Chomsky's linguistics, which shows that language can actually
be understood as a set of principles that relate strings of sounds
and strings of meanings, and that we are not characterized
adequately by Jakobson's and Saussure's data-processing device
for the perception of a network of differences based loosely on
the data provided by the world around us, so that we end with
a completely different structure for each language.  The language
faculty, an aspect of human nature, is, rather, based on a richly
articulated, biologically given set of structures utilizing
positive abstract mental entities--rules, relations, abstract

representations, systems of recursive generations of strings and constraints on them.  According to Chomsky:

> Furthermore, to a greater and greater extent, current work in phonology is demonstrating that the real richness of phonological systems lies not in the structural patterns of phonemes but rather in the intricate systems of rules by which these patterns are formed, modified, and elaborated. The structural patterns that arise at various stages of derivation are a kind of epiphenomenon. . . . [T]he idea of a mathematical investigation of language structures, to which Lévi-Strauss occasionally alludes, becomes meaningful only when one considers systems of rules with infinite generative capacity. There is nothing to be said about the abstract structure of the various patterns that appear at various stages of derivation. If this is correct, then one cannot expect structuralist phonology, in itself, to provide a useful model for investigation of other cultural and social systems.[13]

The system of rules that governs a "cognitive domain" or "mental organ" like language is fleshed out by culture but in part at least clearly preexists it.[14]  In a very literal sense, we are born with language.  It is among those innate ideas we must postulate to account for aspects of human nature that culture operating on humans characterized by a data-processing device simply cannot be said to explain.

Language acquisition could not be achieved starting from Saussurian scratch or from "Fort! Da!"  Nor could other "mental organs" like "visual perception, formation of theories about the external world, whether those of common sense or of scientific research, etc.," which seem likely candidates for study as we study language.[15]  Hence, while we may leave the ultimate justice of the semiologists's contempt for notions of the real world up to the philosophers, we can certainly take from them any claims like Heidigger's that "language speaks, not man." It might not be the real world we see, but it demonstrably isn't a network of differences, either.

Let us conclude that différance isn't all there is, and that it is not sensible to deny that human beings can, because of their biological heritage, see and think about a common reality despite their differing languages.  But Hawkes is wrong in saying that we New Critics assume that a work of art "can ultimately be reduced to a univocal 'content' beyond which it is improper to go" (p. 155).  We can believe that human beings can be in touch with reality, yet not commit ourselves to "'univocal' content." The many connotations and suggestions in discourse supply aesthetic objects with "implicit meaning" that belongs to the work even though its context is in culture, and this meaning is probably not even exhaustible, much less "univocal."[16]

We can take this position by unabashedly asserting what the

structuralist would deny:  that the work itself is real, a
perceptible object with emergent qualities; that we can look at
it and see those qualities; and that its meaning looms large among
them.  An objectivist position like this is basically that when
we talk about the meaning of a film, we are talking, not about
ourselves, but about the work.  Works like films are metaphors
writ large.  A metaphor is an attribution in some sense contrary
to fact, but its very stretching calls attention to the way
there's a certain truth to it.  It is an evocative canting, and
the meaning of the whole work, made up of many evocatively canted
images, is the attitude implied by the ways the images fit
together.  The meaning is emergent from relations among parts.
Since it is a set of implications deriving from images fused
together and having meaning in the context they make, that meaning
is interpretable and not decodable as it would be if there were
an a priori message.  Meaning is a function of emergent
qualities, not of codes.
     But obviously the meaning doesn't emerge from the images
merely by magic.  There are suggestions and connotations in film
images--and in whole films, since as relations among images
accrete, they fuse into new wholes.  The suggestions and
connotations are in them simply because the images share, and
resonate with relations among, qualities possessed by what they
resemble in the world outside the work:  "'desert' connotes
unfruitfulness and death, whether a particular reader is aware
of it or not; he can correct and improve his reading by recalling
the real effects of deserts."[17]  Thus the work's implications
are, in fact, its pointers toward the meaning of objects,
culturally grounded expectations, and experience in the world.
All these account for the "certain truth to it" that metaphor
has.
     This view accounts for the phenomenon of inexhaustibility
of meaning, which is so striking about art.  It is worth noting
that the principle reason structuralists struggle so with that
idea is that, using the "functionalist" extension Roman Jakobson
made beyond Saussure, with its emphasis on speech acts and the
different functions of language--poetic, phatic, emotive,
referential, conative, metalingual--they are committed to an
assumption that meaning is linked to communication.  That is,
structuralists think there is a problem if we do not describe
meaning in terms of a relation between the message-producer's
intention (its embodiment as message in a code sent along a
channel in a medium) and its decipherment by an addressee.[18]
In describing New Criticism, apologists for structuralism like
John Hess seem to miss the basic and crucial New Critical attitude
that the artist's intention is unimportant to meaning.
Structuralists, perceiving that somehow meaning always outstrips
intention, try to account for multiple or implicit meaning by
allowing the critic to produce it.  We saw Barthes do this with
his idea that the work is ours to make and to remake as we please.
     Both Ben Brewster and Brian Henderson do it in their similar,
though antagonistic, attempts to explain Cahiers's Barthesian

reading of Young Mr. Lincoln. Brewster accounts for "the
capacity for the artistic text to accumulate information" by a
distinction between the producer's (and ideal reader's) codes
and those of the concrete reader whose "reading" imports both
the producer may not have shared, "with the proviso that the
'reading in' of codes is not arbitrary [because] governed by a
rule of pertinence." Henderson allows meaning to contain the
critic's process of "forcing the text," accomplishing a
"symptomatic reading," and locating the "structuring absences,"
which are, he seems to think, self-evidently not part of the text
exactly because they are absent from it.[19]

     But even though what is important to a text may not be
obviously present in it, we need not go to the length of saying
that meaning is somehow both the work's and our own, though that
is exactly what Cahiers, Brewster, and Henderson say of Young
Mr. Lincoln. They formulate a way to like the film without
having to praise it, for what we can say about it but not for
what it says on its own. But if "connotations [and suggestions]
are objective parts of the meanings of . . . terms [and sentences]
as they belong to a certain speech-community, just as much as
their dictionary meanings, though somewhat less obvious," then
it is simply the very quality of a work that "an important part
of the meaning is implicit," that is, "presented implicitly, by
suggestion and connotation," and this meaning is neither the
critic's nor "univocal," but the work's and perhaps limitlessly
expansive.[20]

     In sum, doubts about perception itself, derived from the
idea of ideology or the idea that language speaks, not man, need
not lead us to the belief that we must somehow ground our
criticism in some theory that is in fact a method supposedly akin
to the method of human mentation. We know only a few principles
of mind in the very limited area of human languages, and
principles for other aspects or "organs" of mind are a complete
mystery. If we can understand works as metaphoric designs with
emergent qualities, including meaning, then we need not seek to
replace our supposedly contaminated perception-systems with
"objective," "scientific" theories that purport to lead us to
a reality beyond ourselves.

     But that is not to say that there may not be considerable
heuristic value in appealing to notions and methods that are
unimpeachably aspects of culture, and hence part of the web of
connotations that may bear on works. These notions themselves
amount to metaphors with a certain truth to them in which various
aspects of human relations to nature are captured. By their
self-elaboration and development, they have turned into quite
powerful tools for alerting us to aspects of things we might
otherwise miss, even if they do not provide the all-purpose terms
of a science of human nature to which they aspire, as does
structuralism itself.

     In short, an emergent set of relations among connotations
in an aesthetic object might well be congruent with one or more
speculative pictures of reality. It would be a mistake to see

a particular set as determining what a reading of such a work
should be, though the devotees of particular theorists would urge
that we must always read everything in their terms. But the
relations would be in the work whether we had theory or not.
Of course, without the heuristic, we might miss them. If the
unfruitfulness of deserts may be in a work, then so may the
Oedipus complex, or the anima, or even the phallic mother.

S/Z works as compellingly as it does as a reading of
"Sarrasine," then, because Barthes, writing with his Lacan open
before him, can link the relations Balzac established to the terms
and descriptions of those same relations that Lacan has more
discursively provided. And Cahiers's reading of Young Mr.
Lincoln can copy S/Z copying Lacan, and benefit from that too,
since it is perfectly true that Balzac's, Ford's, Lacan's,
Barthes's, and Cahiers's readings all share a reflection of
certain important aspects of reality—for instance, that it is
striking and important that people tend to cling to their own
false (Imaginary) motive-dominated conclusions; people also find
it hard both to be free in process (in the Symbolic) and at the
same time to carry out their necessarily constrained purposes
(the Law). Perhaps we don't require such elaborate language,
but that we need the theories is at least hinted in the fact
that Barthes's and Cahiers's readings of "Sarrasine" and Young
Mr. Lincoln are a vast improvement over those of their
predecessors.

The way to handle the theories that permit such readings
in an objectivist criticism, then, is not to consider them as
proofs of claims about meaning, but as pictures of human nature
whose internal relations suggest truths about things of which
relations in artworks might well be iconic. Depth psychologies,
for instance, like the other theories considered here, claim that
human nature has a certain shape, so that the iconicity of
patterns in a perceptual object can be related to the patterns
of human nature and amount to interpretation. We can formulate
stories for depth psychologies, at least for those of Freud and
Jung, to use in making sense of films.

We note that for both Freud and Jung there is a distinction
between the conscious and the unconscious, between what a person
thinks he or she thinks and what he or she actually does think.
Both Freud and Jung feel the conscious can't ignore the
unconscious. If it is squelched, the unconscious will find a
way to make its presence felt, its shadow known. The situation
in both stories, then, is that something presses insistently upon
a world that would like to ignore it but can't.

Here Freud and Jung diverge. For Freud, the unconscious
tells us lies, but for Jung, it tells us truths. The Freudian
unconscious tells us that what matters most to us is winning over
old frustrations—for instance, achieving total gratification,
being able to get away with anything, being mother's only love.
But that's not what matters most, and we would not be happy if

we could make our unconscious fantasies come true. So the
Freudian success story is learning that these messages from the
unconscious are lies and that we don't need them: "Where id was,
there let ego be." A Freudian story will be one of people
creating some cover story with which to pretend they're not acting
under the sway of lies that, however, clearly move them. Being
confronted with evidence of bondage to those lies lets them become
free of them.

There's a Freudian failure story, too, in which we cling
to the lies and can't give them up. We resonate to what Northrop
Frye would call Freud's comic success stories, or to images that
connote them, with a feeling of pleased freedom. We resonate
to what Frye would call Freud's ironic failure stories with wry
recognition and more than a little guilty passion, since we want
to believe those lies.[21] Detour, for example, is a film in
which the protagonist never acknowledges his own creation of
his dilemma. Thus it is an occasion for recognition of what we
do ourselves. It's a forceful film because it's a straight look
at the absurdity of the cover story which it so anxiously and
intensely projects.

Hitchcock is clearly a Freudian filmmaker--his people believe
they're special, and so they must be confronted with proof that
a shadow version of themselves is loose upon the world. But it
isn't really them at all--Guy could be Bruno, Charlie could
be Uncle Charlie. Each is arrogant, and self-centered enough,
for this to be the case. But it doesn't have to be. Simply
turning against the shadow and moving away, chastened by the
recognition of similarity, can release them. Charlie's putting
on the victim's ring and dancing a train-door waltz with her uncle
amounts to, or connotes, a refusal of her initial delusion that
"we're twins."

Most of Hitchcock's films are suffused with the sense that
we can achieve freedom and that our troubles come from a willful
clinging to a kind of self-righteous complacency that we can and
should let slip. Since it's our doing that we get into such
trouble, there's a sense of good cheer to the films, a sense of
release, despite the gloomy implications of Hitchcock's projected
world. Freud's theory is that comedy saves psychic energy. When
you don't have to repress knowledge, libido is released as ready
cash; the feeling of that sudden wealth is experienced as
laughter. No wonder we're so cheerful after seeing a classic
Hitchcock film--we're richer than we thought!

Jung's world-view is based on a different analysis of human
experience. Its success and failure stories are different. In
one sense, all Jungian stories are failure stories, or
tragedies, except for those that are incomplete and can end
at their success phase. There is a literary parallel here:
romance is simply the rising curve of the tragic hero's whole
arc up and down again, and Jungian romances, with their dragon
slayings and sacred marriages and the like, are temporary

achievements, soon to be balanced by their opposites. For Freud,
there isn't any particular destiny: you are who you come to be.
The world confronts you, and you achieve freedom from the past
it builds in you, or you don't. But for Jung, there is destiny:
everything is in pairs; for any good there's bad, for every
cutting loose there's a sense in which it's also a forsaking,
for every act there's a shadow. There's no getting free, no ego
remotely capable of being where id was. Instead, there's always
the simultaneous presence in the world of the way up and the way
down. For each impulse there's an equal and opposite one to
redress what would otherwise become unbalanced. Thus the
progression toward individuation is a freeing from illusion (the
illusion that we can be free egos), accomplished by a willed
regression into bondage that is in tune with the world's very
nature. The victory of the hero is in a sense a repression of
his opposite. But, unlike Freud, for Jung that opposite is a
necessary part of the hero, and the unconscious will soon send
a message that the apparent victories of the ego are turning it
dry, cold, and rational, and in need of some emergence of the
disreputable double. In the Jungian story, the double turns up
with truths to tell, is sacrificed, but is finally memorialized
for having righted the balance. This is quite unlike what happens
with Uncle Charlie, but exactly what happens in Ford's The Whole
Town's Talking, when dark disreputable fascinating Killer Mannion
wakes the dreamer Jones from his romantic fantasies of Heloise
and Abelard, only to be sacrificed so that Jones, "the man who
looks like Mannion," may truly live.
      In the Jungian story, we must go up the serpent tree of
wisdom from matter to spirit, towards enlightenment and
Buddhahood. But the enlightened one at once feels compassion,
which returns him (or her) down from the ethereal and selfish
spirit world to the world of matter and illusion, to the pond
from the muddy bottom of which the lotus grows. From here,
however, the ascent to the clear light is again a sad detaching,
as well as a natural growth. Jungian stories are cautionary
tales, befitting a world-view where the unconscious tells us
truths beyond our logic, which we are likely to miss. A certain
reproach clings to them that is quite different from Hitchcock's
good cheer. They say "see how blind we always are," even if they
give images of success.
      Freud has a similar insight. Human nature has a darker part
that drives us, gives us the energy to do what we have to, but
that has to be tamed, if not rejected. But Freud emphasizes the
gain from realizing the actualities of the world and forsaking
our fantasies. Jung emphasizes the beneficent side of the energy
that must be cultivated and acknowledged for the source it is.
This energy takes on guilt but accomplishes the difficult and
temporary job of dragon-conquering, of freedom-achieving, of
struggling to enlightenment, which only comes with its own
ambiguous sacrifice. (Ethan Edwards is a model of this.)
      When a story like that resonates for us in a film, we are

responding as we do, not because we've read Jung, but because
of the truth Jung saw. The filmmaker renders an image for a
connoted pattern of general experience that the psychologist
discourses. But we have a problem here. If there is a generality
to the psychologist's stories, then there is a sort of a
priority to this kind of resonance, exactly as there is to the
fact that deserts connote unfruitfulness and death. This
resonance depends on no relations or emergence to be felt. One
might think the film's capacity for such resonance to be its
encoding of a message given by that reality to which Jung was
attuned and concerning which he had his insights, like the
filmmaker.

What then of emergence and the metaphor model, particularly
when both Freud's and Jung's stories themselves claim that what
does emerge must often be taken as a cover story for the hidden
experience that really applies? Should we allow resonance with
a depth psychological story priority over the film's own note,
so that its surface relations and their pattern of connotations
should be felt as cover story for the deeper coded truth? Or
does the resonating depth psychological story merely provide one
of the sets of connotations of the imagery that the film contains,
and that thus is subject to the same processes of fusion and
emergence as anything else? It will help with this to turn to
John Ford, a filmmaker as Jungian as Hitchcock is Freudian.


JOHN FORD

Ford's films show that the way to the higher is through the
lower, the way to civilization is through the disreputable.
Representatives of the disreputable provide vitality for more
decorous types, but are usually sacrificed. They pass the torch
but are debarred from entry into the promised land, like the New
Moses of Steamboat Round the Bend. There is usually
reevaluation, though: finally, the sacrificed one is known to
be the ground and source of value, a kind of reproachful presence
felt most often in the looks back of those who profited from the
sacrifice. If occasionally we get an unambiguous Jungian success
story like Judge Priest, where the disreputable simply overcomes
and floods the world with unity and wholeness, far more often
we get a story like The Sun Shines Bright, in which the now
pitiable outsider judge sacrifices his political career to assert
the worth of the disreputable whore who, he insists, must be
recognized as part of the town. His solitary funeral procession
draws the town together, but the somber postelection parade, so
different from the end of Judge Priest, is a valediction: Billy
Priest withdraws slowly into the depths of his house (of the
unconscious, Jung would surely say) as the young couple he frees
by his sacrifice watch him go, as Adam and his wife watch the
disreputable followers of the disreputable Frank Skeffington
retreat into his house, or as the couple saved with natural
medicine by Dr. Bull watch him retreat from the town which doesn't

deserve him. Likewise, in Tobacco Road, we watch Jeeter Lester
settle in on his porch, incorrigible but so in tune with his life
and his God that he seems to stand directly for the Jungian
unconscious itself.

Jeeter can only be matched in Ireland. Mary Kate Daniher
is chastened by a divinely ordered thunderstorm when she kisses
Sean Thornton in the churchyard, just as Jeeter's conscience is
roused by a thunderstorm in the matter of the turnips. Mary Kate
is shown as a nature spirit among her trees and fields much as
is Ellie May Lester who even raises her foot against the tree
of life, one hand on the tree and one by her loins (Fig. 4.1),
like the goddesses Joseph Campbell represents in The Mythic
Image.[22]

The disreputable one passes the torch to those who profit
by his sacrifice, and sometimes he sadly watches them go forward
into happiness--as do Citizen Hogan in Hangman's House and Ethan
Edwards--while he himself is banished to the desert. Whether
the disreputable is watcher or watched, the basic opposition in
Ford is between the warranting disreputables (linked in their
excesses to savages like Indians) and the proper civilization-
bearers who must be saved by them (and linked in their excesses
to vicious social prudes--"there's some things worse than
Apaches," as Stagecoach has it).

This has been Ford's pattern from the beginning. In
Straight Shooting, of 1917, Cheyenne Harry is a fine Ford drunk
and cut-up who has to get his bandit friends to rescue the easy-
going farmers. He bids the bandits a fond farewell as they
retreat to their stronghold in the rocks, since in that simpler
time Harry could change his ways and, unlike Ethan Edwards, have
for himself the girl he's saved. And the pattern holds to the
end, as disreputable Tom Doniphon sacrifices himself for Ransom
Stoddard in a way which ever after keeps that "pilgrim" in his
debt. The further Ranse goes along the route Tom won for him,
the greater his sense of the gap between his social ego and that
dark self upon which it depends.

Ranse's propriety, his rejection of the gun, is one of those
denials of the unconscious that Ford's Jungian stories show the
proper ones having to have beaten out of them. Repress the
unconscious, and a Liberty Valence-like shadow emerges, only to
be overcome by assimilation and awareness of one's unpayable debt
to the dark forces. Air Mail is a striking instance. Duke
Talbot seems a perfect heel in comparison to straight-arrow Mike
Miller, but Mike's inflexible rules release death on the mountain
from which Duke saves him with all the drunken bravado Mike has
tried to squelch. Mike is thus released for a more easy-going
and accepting life. Likewise, in The Quiet Man, Sean's
rejection of his brawling Irish self is linked to his guilt over
the death his fighting brought. His new propriety destroys his
social life and his sex life, at the same time that it releases
Red Will Daniher to be a bully and lout, a shadow version of what
Sean's acceptance of his own force lets Red Will become at the

end, a true brother and friend. The end of the film is a Judge Priest-like reemergence of a boisterous, drunken, rebellious selfhood that, far from killing, cures.

Mogambo displays the same iconic pairing of proper and disreputable. Blonde fragile Linda is so rigid that everywhere she goes the animals die, whereas brunette party girl Kelly is a female Duke Talbot, easily at home with animals and nature. Vic feels the attraction of Linda's culture and civilization, but fails to spot its prissiness and vindictiveness—Ford hates brittle blonde Grace Kelly for the evils decorum and Englishness bring, whereas Hitchcock loved her for the possibility of her salvation. Vic is saved only for his desert turned garden (where the gorilla family is the only Fordian group) by Kelly's quick and loving wit—like all Ford disreputables, she is more sensitive than she let on.

We can see that there are two versions of the Jungian story in Ford, appropriate to the directions of travel up and down the serpent tree of wisdom. In one, exemplified by The Searchers and The Whole Town's Talking, the world of matter is sacrificed for the heavenly city by the destruction of a representative of the dark forces. In the other, exemplified by Rio Grande and Mogambo, the dryness and coldness of the world of spirit, of propriety, can be reinvigorated by contact with the truths of matter. We can give up Bridesdale or Devonshire, and live in a desert of illusion. There our presence will be that of an enlightened ego accepting the depths of the self, like a Bodhisattva accepting the illusions of the world through pity. The desert then is transformed into a garden, as in Rio Grande, where the fort in the desert is fragile and barren, but trees shade the tents by the river and the band plays "Dixie" as the American flag is borne past us. But the films are all contemplations of the relations between the individuating but falsifying spirit and the fertilizing but self-absorbing capacities of nature, matter, and the unconscious.

But even though Jung's world-view is tragic, the Jungian story is a success story. Ego-consciousness tells lies of decorum, separation, and distinction; but as Campbell quotes Coomaraswamy,

> an expiation is provided in the sacrifice, where by the sacrificer's surrender of himself and the building up again of the dismembered deity, whole and complete, the multiple selves are reduced to their single principle. . . . Slayer and Dragon, sacrificer and victim are of one mind behind the scenes, where there is no polarity of contraries; but mortal enemies on the stage, where the everlasting war of the Gods and the Titans is displayed.[23]

As Jungian stories, resonating with what we have granted is an a priori coding of the Jungian world-view, films like The Man Who Shot Liberty Valence, The Last Hurrah, and Fort Apache

are tremendously up-beat. Their elegiac tone at the sacrifice
of heroes is simply a cover story.
     So we return to our central question of conflict of
readings. A film may resonate with a powerful story of which
it is iconic, as Seven Women resonates with the story of
sacrifice of the disreputable hero for a society in which her
inheritors get so much from her that it is as if she has part
in it and is resurrected in them like Osiris. But the film also
has emergent meaning from the relations of the images not only
to the story that underlies them, but also to the web of
connotations of the whole, its own world. To put it succinctly,
in Seven Women the desert clearly is not only, Jung fashion,
the garden under the veil of illusion, but also a real desert
connoting unfruitfulness and death. And Dr. Cartwright's story
is not only one of willing acceptance of her "feminine nature"
(symbolized by the Chinese robes that replace her masculine
dress), but also one of her miserable defeat. She is captured
by a world where the savages win, where the disreputable is an
insensitive brutality instead of a life-giving acceptance of the
unconscious, a world where everything Ford has tried to believe
is stood on its ear and rejected. The fight between Woody
Strode's Lean Warrior and Tunga Khan is a travesty of the fight
between Sean Thornton and Red Will Daniher.
     The disreputable Cartwright reveals the inadequacy and
concealed autocracy of proper Agatha Andrews, just as Kelly
reveals the hypocrisy of Linda in Mogambo. We can't miss how
similar her story feels to those of Ethan and Tom Doniphon. She
is aware of the unfairness of her lot and of her guilt, but she
is freed by this knowledge to select a life for others, freed
to pass the torch. But we also can't miss that Cartwright herself
simply loses.
     If there is a sense in which the film is a final version,
extending the aegis of Ford's personal myth over women as
Cheyenne Autumn did over Indians and Sergeant Rutledge did
over Blacks—that myth of the submission of the overreaching
individualism of the disreputable unconscious to the developing
needs of society, and to the conscious ego that nonetheless rests
on its base and owes it liberation from heedless savagery—there
is also a strong sense of the revision of that myth. If hero
and dragon are one behind the scenes, we feel uplifted by the
esoteric meaning of their actions: we have not been simple
cannibals to eat the body and drink the blood, but rather we have
partaken of the mystery of psychic divestiture and
reconstitution. But the emergent web of connotations in Seven
Women doesn't feel like that at all.
     The seven women who leave don't walk off hand in hand like
Dr. Bull and Janet or like the couple in The Sun Shines Bright.
They are simply led by the savages into the wasteland. Theirs
is a very tenuous and private kind of safety in a world denuded
of value. The world left behind is not rich and fertile like
Kelly's and Vic's in Mogambo: Cartwright and Tunga Khan are
a disreputable couple, too, but Tunga Khan is no Vic. In fact,

there is no Vic or Martin Pawley or Ransom Stoddard or Captain
Kirby Yorke in this film, no one for whom the sacrifice of the
hero can be a connection between the savage world and the
overcivilized one. There are simply the hassles of civilization
on the one hand, and a wasteland on the other.
    As for the hero, Cartwright herself sees her sacrifice coming
to nothing. In her completely ironic way, she plays the feminine
submissiveness that she had tried to avoid her whole life. In
one sense, Cartwright affirms what she has fought against, with
the acceptance that dooms her, like Ethan when he rescues Debbie
rather than carrying out his purpose to kill her. But in Seven
Women the sense of acceptance is completely ironic. "So long,
you bastard" is a disgusted acceptance of the defeat involved
in becoming woman to Tunga Khan's man. At least she can take
him with her, but when she changed her mind she lost, whereas
Ethan won when he changed his. Cartwright drinks, throws down
the poison cup, and sits with head bent, waiting for the death
that the film renders by pulling away and leaving her in the
dark. She doesn't fall, poleaxed like Tunga Khan, and in that
sense she maintains her resolve. We are left with an image of
it. But whereas Ethan closes himself to go on, with his Harry
Carey clasp of the arm, Cartwright throws down the cup and opens
herself to this world that kills her. She does not become
better for what she does.
    From the totality of Seven Women's connotations, then,
emerges a world below Northrop Frye's line of experience, a world
in which the tragic pattern serves the irony that is parallel
to it in the circle of forms and not the romance that lies next
to the tragedies of Ethan and Tom.[24] This world of ironic
tragedy is characterized by the necessity to sacrifice yourself
to roles imposed by a masculinity that is stupid and brutal rather
than pleasantly disreputable, and by the wandering in a wasteland
that is the only result of this sacrifice. The Jungian purpose
seems gone from Ford's universe, not to be reaffirmed in new and
extended terms.
    Now as I read and reread my argument about Seven Women,
I find myself being drawn, Jungianly enough, to its opposite,
to the claim that we do have here exactly Ethan Edwards, and
Judge Priest, and Duke Talbot. This is particularly pressing
when I imagine someone saying, "Yes, Ford changes late in his
career." At once, like Bazin imagining attacks upon auteurism
and feeling that he should leap to the defense of what he is
attacking himself, [25] I feel like saying, "No no, Ford is of
a piece throughout, the darkness and joy always chasing each
other's tails like the cosmic serpent." But this is simply to
say that the film is indeed a metaphor, that its connotations
work upon each other to yield a "counter-factuality," which yet
has a certain truth to it that is worth contemplating, rather
than a message that we might try to decode. The ambivalence of
Seven Women is unresolvable. Here is a world so bad that even
a good sacrifice seems not to avail, but the depth of personality
reached into for even this unavailing sacrifice overrides its

futility. From the whole film, then, emerges a quality of
contemplatability that depends equally on resonance with the
psychological story and with the connotations of the depicted
world of the work. Neither is privileged, and the whole film
both reasserts and deepens our sharing with the disreputable hero,
even as it emphasizes the virtually hopeless aspect of a world
desert almost impossible now to see as a veiled garden. The hero
with whom we share recedes from existential vividness to the
status of a hope, an "as if" case. Ford tells us as strongly
as ever what he would like to believe, but shows more clearly
than usual how hard it is to believe it. And this balance would
be completely obscured by any attempt to see in Seven Women
a dominant coding of the message of either aspect of the emergent
whole.

So we have our answer to the question of conflict of
readings. A film works just as Saussure wrongly thought language
does: the parts may be coded, just as we recognize the words
we hear in a language we know, and know the meanings attached
to them. But their combinations are not coded. Rather they
must be interpreted. The individual meanings fuse, as the
relations among their implications become apparent, to yield an
overall, many-faceted emergent meaning that may clash with any
individual set of coded meanings or implications among the parts.
This emergent meaning is understood by inspection of the relations
among the meanings of the constituting parts with each other,
an inspection guided by what Beardsley calls the Principles of
Plenitude and Congruence: plenitude, in that "all the
connotations that can be found to fit are to be attributed to
the poem: it means all it can mean"; congruence, in that "in
assembling, or feeling out, the admissible connotations of words
in a poem, we are guided by logical and physical possibilities"
as we come to see the emergent meaningfulness of an object which
as a whole may be entertained as having a certain truth to
it.[26]

This emergent meaningfulness is thus known by inspection
of the meanings of at least partly coded parts within the system
we are considering—language, literature, cinema—in the light
of the context for their mutual implications that is provided
by the knowledge of the world and ourselves. We have this
knowledge by virtue of the whole of our psychic apparatus,
with all its structurings and capacities to pick up
information.

Chomsky's analyses of "The ball was hit by the man" and "John
was persuaded to leave" were enough to demolish any notion that
the meaning of sentences is interpreted in any fashion like that—
we decode sentences by means of a grammar.[27] But we do not
decode but interpret discourse, and just so we interpret the
strings of images in films, whether manifestly iconic of some
set of physically determined appearances of the world or
"distorted" (in Beardsley's term) along some cultural and
semiotically ballasted line, whether naively naturalistic or
obviously built to carry some theoretical—Freudian, Jungian,

Lacanian, Marxian--freight. Just like the meaning of a sentence as Saussure understood it, or like the meaning of a discourse, the meaning of a film emerges from our inspection of the meanings of the parts, fusing in each other's lights. And we might note that this is the exact substance of what the New Criticism, of which so many recent film theorists speak with such ill-informed contempt, always understood.

W.C.

## NOTES

1. Terence Hawkes, Structuralism and Semiotics (Berkeley: Univ. of California Press, 1977), p. 24; hereafter cited by page number.
2. Philip W. Davis, Modern Theories of Language (Englewood Cliffs: Prentice-Hall, 1973), ch. 2, systematizes Saussure. On systems of difference, see Edmund Leach, Claude Lévi-Strauss (New York: Viking, 1970), ch. 2.
3. Noam Chomsky, Language and Mind, enlarged ed. (New York: Harcourt Brace Jovanovich, 1972), pp. 74-75.
4. Dan Sperber, Rethinking Symbolism (Cambridge: Cambridge Univ. Press, 1975), p. 140.
5. Jacques Lacan, The Language of the Self (Baltimore: Johns Hopkins Univ. Press, 1968); See also Richard Wollheim, "The Cabinet of Dr. Lacan," New York Review of Books, January 25, 1979, pp. 36-45.
6. Michael Harrington, Socialism (New York: Saturday Review Press, 1970), p. 41; Andrew Britton, "The Ideology of Screen," Movie, no. 26 (1978-79): 5.
7. Anika Lemaire, Jacques Lacan (London: Routledge & Kegan Paul, 1977), p. 68.
8. Wollheim, "The Cabinet of Dr. Lacan," p. 41.
9. Louis Althusser, "Ideology and Ideological State Apparatuses," in Lenin and Philosophy (London: NLB, 1971), pp. 121-73.
10. See Hawkes on Derrida for "illusion of presence" and "différance"; for "structuring absences" see the Editors of Cahiers du Cinéma, "John Ford's Young Mr. Lincoln," Screen, 13, no. 3 (1972): 5-47; Brian Henderson, A Critique of Film Theory (New York: E. P. Dutton, 1980), pp. 218-33.
11. John Hess, "Auteurism and After," Film Quarterly, 27, no. 2 (1973-74): 36.
12. Andrew Sarris, "Auteurism Is Alive and Well," Film Quarterly, 28, no. 1 (1974): 62.
13. Chomsky, Language and Mind, p. 75.
14. Noam Chomsky, Language and Responsibility (New York: Pantheon, 1979), p. 49.
15. Chomsky, Language and Responsibility, p. 45. See also William Cadbury, "Structuring Presences: Film Theory and the Language of Thought," forthcoming in 1982 Film Studies

Annual:   The Proceedings of the Sixth Annual Purdue
University Conference on Film.
16. For "implicit meaning" see Monroe C. Beardsley, Aesthetics
    (New York:   Harcourt Brace & World, 1958), pp. 126, 133.
17. Beardsley, Aesthetics, p. 133.
18. See Gianfranco Bettetini, The Language and Technique of
    the Film (The Hague:   Mouton, 1973), pp. 47-50; Umberto
    Eco, A Theory of Semiotics (Bloomington:   Indiana Univ.
    Press, 1976), pp. 40-43, 151, 261; Christian Metz, Film
    Language:   A Semiotics of the Cinema (New York:   Oxford
    Univ. Press, 1974), p. 40; Christian Metz, Language and
    Cinema (The Hague:   Mouton, 1974), p. 95.
19. Ben Brewster, "Notes on the Text 'John Ford's Young Mr.
    Lincoln' by the Editors of Cahiers du Cinéma," Screen,
    14, no. 3 (1973):   36; Henderson, Critique, pp. 224, 228.
20. Beardsley, Aesthetics, pp. 133, 126.
21. Northrop Frye, Anatomy of Criticism (Princeton:   Princeton
    Univ. Press, 1957), pp. 131-239.
22. Joseph Campbell, The Mythic Image (Princeton:   Princeton
    Univ. Press, 1974), pp. 260-75.
23. Campbell, Mythic Image, p. 479.
24. Frye, Anatomy.   Romance exists in the world of innocence,
    though its six phases move, like a romance itself, down
    towards the world of experience and disillusion before moving
    up again to firm possession of the "green world."   Irony
    exists in the world of experience, though its phases tend
    up toward innocence before returning to defeat and death.
    Tragedies move individually and as a sequence of phases from
    innocence to experience, and comedies from experience to
    innocence.   Here is a diagram by Prof. William C. Strange:

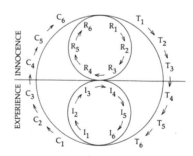

25. André Bazin, "La Politique des Auteurs," in The New Wave,
    ed. Peter Graham (Garden City:   Doubleday, 1968), p. 138.
26. Beardsley, Aesthetics, p. 144.
27. See Noam Chomsky, Syntactic Structures (The Hague:   Mouton,
    1957), esp. sections 5.4 and 5.5, pp. 42-44; Chomsky,
    Language and Mind, pp. 31-32, all ch. 2; John Lyons, Noam
    Chomsky (New York:   Viking, 1970), pp. 60-67.

PART

# II

# AUTHORSHIP, MEANING, AND INTERPRETATION

# 5

# Hitchcock and the
# Ethics of Vision

This section essays a double task. The first is a broad
thematic metareading of the cinema of Alfred Hitchcock aimed at
determining and describing the "deep structure" logic of the
Hitchcock cinema as it is revealed in plot, iconography, and
character. The second task, providing a theoretical context for
the first, is to consider certain of the premises underlying the
process of my reading: what are the terms and conditions of my
relationship to Hitchcock's films?[1]
    Three texts in particular serve as models or catalysts for
my own practice: the Cahiers du Cinéma reading of Young Mr.
Lincoln, Stephen Heath's two-part critique of Touch of Evil
in Screen, and Roland Barthes's reading of Balzac's "Sarrasine"
in S/Z.[2] I am certainly very much at odds with many of the
positions they take. I still believe in the efficacy of New
Criticism (in literary studies) and auteur criticism (in film
studies). But I seek here to submit those methodologies to an
extended, self-critical examination akin to those undertaken,
within other frameworks, by people like Heath and Barthes. To
be sure, I locate my argument by reference to the specific
theoretical problem of the relationship of spectator to text,
which means that I seldom refer directly to Cahiers, Heath,
or Barthes. But their essays provide the larger context within
which the essay ought to be read--as one metareading among
several.


THE PROBLEM SPECIFIED
    It attests to the complexity of the issue that film
scholarship has only recently addressed itself in any
thoroughgoing manner to the problem of "the spectator in the
text."[3] Realist film theory, while hardly silent on the matter
of spectator perception, side-steps the issue by subsuming the
viewer/screen relationship within the larger compass of the
spectator's relationship to the world as a whole. Thus André
Bazin, in the original version of his Orson Welles monograph and

in his essay on "The Evolution of the Language of Cinema," takes
the "analytical montage" of classical continuity editing to task
on the grounds that it "totally suppresses [the] reciprocal
freedom between us and the object" and substitutes "a forced
breaking down [of the scene] where the logic of the shots
controlled by the reporting of the action anesthetizes our
freedom" (my italics).[4] Of course, analytical montage may
precisely replicate our habitual (conventional) patterns of
attention: hence the "transparency" of analytical montage. But
in either case, in our perception of cinema or in our perception
of the world at large, habitual modes of attention falsify the
possibilities of perception and betray the ontology of cinema
and even of sight itself. That is, our attention to reality need
not nor ought to be guided by unseen hands or conventional habits.
Rather, we see the world whole, in depth, and are free to choose
our focal point. In contrast, the dramatic editing of the silent
era directed or authorized our attention along fairly simple
narrative/dramatic lines. For Bazin, then, the Hollywood cinema
is blatantly unrealistic, in terms of its technology and in the
ontology of viewer perception; and the alternative was Orson
Welles—whose use of extreme deep focus photography marked him
as the cinematic realist par excellence, in spite of his quite
obvious and baroque lighting schemes and in spite of his frequent
temporal/spatial disjunctions, because our perception of Welles's
deep focus sequences is so much more analogous to our perception
of the everyday world.

Auteurist film scholarship, on the other hand, seldom fell
into Bazin's ontological trap. There was never any question among
most of the first generation auteur critics that the "reality"
of a film was indeed "authorized," reflecting the filmmaker's
vision of the world as mediated by the filmmaker's own sense of
reality and ideology. Therefore one visual style can hardly be
preferred to another—as Bazin preferred that of Welles to, say,
Eisenstein—on ontological grounds. The point of most auteurist
scholarship is exactly to prove the presence of an authorial
vision by demonstrating how thoroughly self-contained and
self-expressive a filmmaker's world can be. And if the question
of the spectator's role comes up it is handled in terms that
accord by and large (and not illegitimately) with the
phenomenology of literature, where the temptation to praise
realism (in the literal sense) is far weaker and therefore less
problematic.

Recent developments in film theory have turned Bazin upside
down and have confirmed the essential wisdom of the auteurist
position. Readers familiar with recent articles in Film
Quarterly and Screen will recognize "system of the suture"
arguments as a Brechtian rehash of Bazin's position. That is,
critics like Daniel Dayan and Jean-Pierre Oudart are now arguing
that the Hollywood narrative film represents a sort of ontological
falsehood, for suggesting that "reality" is readily viewable,
that vision is not problematic or ideologically determined, that

the world "as it is" (or "as it is photographed") is unchangeable.[5] To a certain degree, of course, the position is the reverse of Bazin. For Dayan the Hollywood film is "too real," and is therefore false for being so deceptively illusory; while for Bazin the Hollywood film is not real enough. But both Dayan and Bazin argue their cases in terms of certain basic conventions and technologies and a dualist notion of the possible interplay among them.

The primary purpose of this essay is not to argue a full-blooded alternative description of the mind/screen relationship. My concern is to explore one specific set of such relationships, those obtaining between myself and certain films of Alfred Hitchcock, relationships that may be characterized both thematically (in terms of part-whole dramatic logic) and perceptually (in terms of the analogies that may be said to exist between Hitchcock's thematic points and our mode of attending to those points). In the former case I will deal with the theme of "reading," which I take to be a central Hitchcock concern, and will explore its expression through plot, iconography, and character relationships; and in the latter case I will extend the notion of "reading" to include the activity of the spectator.

My larger concern, however, is to demonstrate in very specific terms the falsity of the Dayan/Bazin position (hence my theoretical prologue). Never once does Hitchcock step outside the conventional technological bounds of the "classical narrative cinema"--and it is almost purely in terms of such conventions that Dayan and Bazin argue their cases--and yet to read Hitchcock's implications in their fullness is to confront the ethics of reading, as "modernism" would have us do, in a very direct way. In short, Hitchcock is a paradigm case of the filmmaker who bridges the gap which some critics have attempted to enforce between classical and modernist narratives, and by so doing Hitchcock calls the false dualism of Dayan and others into serious question.


## VOYEURISM AND REAR WINDOW

To date the mind/screen relationship in Hitchcock's films has been described largely in terms of "voyeurism" or "identification." The locus classicus here is Rear Window and the standard argument focuses on the implicit parallel between the voyeuristic tendencies of the film's central character and the viewer. Both are trapped in their seats, the viewer in a theater seat, Jefferies (James Stewart) in his wheel chair. And both use their entrapment, or so this line of reasoning has it, as an opportunity to indulge an irresponsible appetite for morbid, vicarious experience. Thus Jefferies peers out of his rear window to the windows across the courtyard and sees in each one some projection of his own worst fears and fantasies, the worst of which, his fear of marriage and his attendant desire to be rid of Lisa Fremont (Grace Kelly), governs his interpretation of the

actions of Lars Thorvald (Raymond Burr). When Thorvald murders
his wife it's as if Jefferies had willed it; and we share
Jefferies's guilt by seeing the film largely through his eyes
via Hitchcock's use of subjective camera.

All of which is true enough, as far as it goes, and Robin
Wood has demonstrated, in his seminal essay on the film, that
it does not go far enough. But the point to make in the present
context is that this largely negative description of the mind/
screen relationship in Hitchcock still has currency. One need
only look at Donald Spoto's recent book on Hitchcock to see how
temptingly simple and respectable the notion can be.[6] Spoto
never misses a chance to point out the voyeurism theme whenever
it (or something like it) crops up in Hitchcock, and he does so
without sufficiently accounting for Wood's altogether necessary
qualification. As Wood points out, a strict Jefferies-as-voyeur
reading of the film fails to explain the fact that Jefferies and
his neighborhood are both better for the experience. Ought he
not to be worse off if looking out his window were a vice per
se? Furthermore, and more significantly, isn't the logical
outcome of taking seriously the viewer-as-voyeur position some
species of blindness? Wouldn't the point of the film be that
we should not look at or through cinematic windows? Of course,
one could argue that Jefferies himself accepts just that sort
of myopia. At film's end he is asleep in his wheel chair with
his back to the window. But, in spite of the fact that his eyes
are closed, Jefferies's position in space is one that acknowledges
(and celebrates) the positive aspects of his voyeuristic
experience. He is facing toward Lisa rather than away from her,
thereby implicitly accepting the sort of sexual vulnerability
he had earlier rejected. And the obsessive sleeplessness that
characterizes his behavior throughout most of the film finally
gives way to an almost childlike sense of security. The cause-
effect logic is clear: only by accepting sexuality is emotional
security possible.

Such a rereading of the final scene of Rear Window fits
far better with my recollections of the film than Spoto's critical
description. Unfortunately, however, Rear Window only exists
for most of us as it has been described by such as Spoto and
Raymond Durgnat, and this may well account for the fact that
Hitchcock scholarship generally has not advanced much beyond the
judiciously qualified voyeur/identification model originally (and
most eloquently) outlined by Robin Wood in Hitchcock's Films.[7]
A central text was and is missing. So rather than rethink the
mind/screen relationship in Hitchcock, critics have by and large
and quite properly taken other approaches to his films. Having
studied and taught Hitchcock for several years, however, has
convinced me that we need not let the unavailability of Rear
Window stand in our way. If anything, the voyeurism thesis fits
the film almost too neatly. Perhaps it's just as well that we
are forced to reconsider the vision issue in Hitchcock without
special reference to Rear Window.

TO READ AND BE READ (NARRATIVE STRUCTURES)

One reason the voyeur/identification thesis fails to hold up is that it depends too heavily on a naive equation between technique (subjective camera in this instance) and theme (that of voyeurism). Of course, Hitchcock himself has repeatedly encouraged this sort of naiveté by his refusal to discuss the thematic and mimetic aspects of his films. He would much rather focus on exactly those visual grace notes which most overtly typify his style. But a critic's task is precisely to look at parts and wholes, to see, for example, the relationships which may exist between the plot-action of a particular film and its various visual and iconographic patterns. And to look at Hitchcock this way is to understand how thoroughly conventional he is in technological terms without thereby levelling the Dayan/ Bazin charge of simple-minded and therefore reactionary illusionism.

Looked at objectively, and purely in terms of shot construction or decoupage (and, again, it is in exactly such localized stylistic terms that Dayan and Bazin couch their charges), Hitchcock's stylistic repertoire is indistinguishable from that of Hollywood generally. His camera functions largely as an objective recorder of the profilmic spectacle, only occasionally (if tellingly) adopting a subjective point of view. His shot catalogue is likewise conventional, a mix of long shots, medium shots, and close-ups used in fairly conventional two-shot or three-shot or shot/reverse shot sequences. And even Hitchcock's more overtly expressionistic devices--his superimpositions, his occasional voice-overs, his expressive use of matte shots, his marvelous montage set pieces--all have conventional precedents in mainstream cinematic history. Thus, if one insists on trying to define the essential Hitchcock only and exclusively in terms of technology and the localized use of it one is bound to fail, either by overemphasizing the importance of specific stylistic devices (like subjective camera) or by condemning in a priori terms the whole of his technological repertoire.

We can best avoid the former error by beginning our discussion of the reading/vision metaphor in Hitchcock at its most general level--as it functions to motivate certain recurrent narrative patterns in Hitchcock's films. No doubt the most well known of these patterns involves the "wrong man" motif: one man is accused or suspected of a crime that another man has committed and this wrong man is inevitably forced to prove his own innocence. We may with equal accuracy term this the "misread man" figure. This may be taken quite literally in some cases: many of these films involve both newspaper accounts and news photographs of the crime and the "criminal." Thus the opening sequence of The Lodger is comprised of the discovery of a murder and a report of that murder, a report which we follow in an almost documentary fashion from the initial reporter's notes to the finished product as it is sold by street corner news boys.

Newspapers play an important part in The 39 Steps. Hannay
nervously reads newspaper accounts describing him as "The Portland
Place Murderer" while on the train to Scotland and in the
Crofter's cottage (Fig. 5.1); and it is news headlines that reveal
his true identity to the Crofter's wife. To Catch a Thief also
includes newspaper speculation on the guilt of John Robie; and
in North by Northwest we get both newspapers (the one that
Thornhill turns face down as he passes through the club car of
the Twentieth Century, for example) and newsphotos, specifically
the famous photo of an astonished Thornhill with a knife in his
hand standing over the freshly murdered corpse of the real Mr.
Townsend.

    Newspapers or not, however, the "wrong" or "misread man"
motif clearly involves a species of misreading. Clues are ignored
or misconstrued, conclusions are falsely jumped to, and in nearly
every case the assumption of guilt implies a corollary pleasure
in the perverse. In The 39 Steps, for example, the ladies'
underwear salesmen get a clear charge from speculating on the
Portland Place affair. In Young and Innocent the two girls
on the seashore misconstrue the product of the equation "dead
woman" + "running man" to read "man running away" despite the
equally reasonable "reading" that Robert himself suggests:
"innocent man running for help." The former is far juicier.
In Strangers on a Train both Ann and her younger sister assume
that Guy did indeed kill his wife. In I Confess Ruth reads
Father Logan's refusal to discuss the murder of the lawyer as
evidence that he still loves her (enough to kill for her?). In
The Wrong Man itself Manny is repeatedly "misread" by
"eyewitnesses" as police take him around to the various hold-up
sites; and the case against him hinges largely on his handwriting
and spelling, which the police misread as that of the real
criminal (Fig. 5.2). In North by Northwest Thornhill is
continually "read" as George Kaplan on the basis of the most
superficial yet ordinary evidence: dandruff, class photos, etc.
And Blaney in Frenzy is branded a murderer on the basis of a
half-overheard conversation (he is heard arguing with his ex-wife)
and planted evidence (Rusk hides the clothes of a murdered girl,
Blaney's barmaid girlfriend, in Blaney's valise).

    The opposite of the wrong man theme is the "right man" figure
--in which case the action's focal character is less a victim
of misreading than a perpetrator who encourages it. He is
guilty. We see this quite clearly as a subpattern in Stage
Fright in which the Richard Todd character "authorizes" the
famous misleading flashback in order to hide the truth of his
guilt. Dial M for Murder also involves elaborate attempts to
manipulate facts and evidence, in this instance to be rid of
someone rather than to escape a preexistent guilt. Torn
Curtain, particularly when read as a critique of the Paul Newman
character, can be seen to fit this pattern: Michael Armstrong
willingly endangers several lives (including that of his fiancée)
in order to further his own career and he does so by playing the

role of defector.  There is even a press conference at which he
publicly announces his "pacifistic" motives for switching sides.
     Already we can see the complementary nature of these
character/action categories.  To describe the first two as
opposites is accurate at one level--misread men generally attempt
through the course of the plot to establish the "legibility" of
their innocence while their opposites seek to "erase" evidence
of guilt; and it is also true that Hitchcock tends to focus
attention in particular movies on one or the other sort of
protagonist--but the two are frequently seen together.  Thus the
misread man is often the victim, not only of public hysteria and
rumor-mongoring, but of demonic playwrights as well.  In
Strangers on a Train Guy Haines is almost framed for murder
by the real murderer, Bruno Anthony.  In I Confess Father Logan
is framed by Otto Keller, whose coup de theatre involves
confessing his crime to the priest himself, thus preventing Logan
from making his own innocence public.  The Cary Grant character
in To Catch a Thief is likewise framed, and also by someone
who knows the trademarks of the victim's profession.  We see a
similar character alignment in North by Northwest: the misread
man is "wronged" by intelligence agents who refuse to clear up
the mystery of George Kaplan.  Perhaps the best example of a
character wronged by the theatricality of others is Scottie
Ferguson (James Stewart) in Vertigo:  Elster and Judy plot
murder and set Scottie up to take responsibility for "Madeleine's"
death.
     It is also worth remarking how alike both the "misread" and
the "misleading" can often be in their actions:  both spend most
of their time concealing their true identity.  For the misread
man, however, concealment is only a temporary survival tactic
that allows him time to "reread" the world, to break its codes
and uncover those signs or symbols that will verify his innocence.
It is also the case that the concealment of identity (often behind
glasses or sunglasses--again the sight metaphor) makes the
protagonist mortally and sexually vulnerable, requiring of him
exceptional courage and an exceptional willingness to trust in
others.  To seek the truth of identity in Hitchcock is thus
generally to undergo a process of growth and maturation.
Misleaders, on the other hand, tend to be arrested in their
development and their attempts to "rewrite" the world are often
predicated on the denial of vulnerability.  Thus Bruno Anthony
wants to be rid of his authoritarian father in Strangers on a
Train while Tony Wendice in Dial M for Murder seeks to be rid
of his cool, detached, and disregardful wife.  Likewise, Norman
Bates in Psycho "rewrites" the relationship between his mother
and her lover--and his motive is clearly security.
     A third narrative pattern in Hitchcock focuses not on the
misread or the misleading but on the "reader"--of which there
are basically two sorts.  The first is the Hitchcock "misreader,"
a character who chooses for basically selfish though often
unconscious or psychotic reasons to disregard evidence or to

misconstrue the actions or feelings of others. Mrs. Verloc in
Sabotage is an early example of this.[8] She marries her
husband for financial reasons, to provide for herself and her
brother, and she completely disregards or underestimates the depth
of her husband's affections. Mr. Verloc is thus put in a position
in which money is the language of love and he finds it necessary
to commit sabotage in order to get the necessary funds. Mrs.
Verloc's apparently unselfish concern for her brother thus
results, ironically, in his death when the bomb he carries for
Mr. Verloc explodes. A somewhat less malign version of the woman
who misreads is Lina in Suspicion. Lina, as Donald Spoto points
out, is the paradigm of the Hitchcock "reader": we first see
her with a book in her lap, and her reading glasses become a
dominant image through the course of the film. Equally
interesting is the self-reflective quality of the film's studio
settings. Lina's Wuthering Heights fantasies of murder on the
heath are marvelously embodied by Hitchcock's storybook gothic
backdrops; and it's the danger implicit in those fantasies that
the movie makes concrete and then rejects. That is, Lina's fear
of murder almost results in her death when she struggles with
Johnny as they drive along the sea-cliff: thus "misreading" her
husband's actions is almost fatal to them both, however satisfying
it might be in terms of Lina's persecution complex. It is
therefore appropriate that the film's last shot should be location
footage of the Aysgarth car turning around and driving away as
Lina stops cowering against the door and slides closer to her
husband. Reality thus replaces fantasy (as location footage
replaces studio footage) and this replacement serves to bring
Johnny and Lina more genuinely together than they had ever been
before.
     Notorious and The Paradine Case give us examples of men
who "misread."[9] In the former the Cary Grant character both
withholds affection from Ingrid Bergman and refuses to accept
his own vulnerability. Thus he repeatedly refuses to look Alicia
in the eye (if he looks at her at all it is accusingly, or with
his head turned sarcastically to the side, away from her) which
results in his more general and nearly fatal misreading of her
actions and motives. His "blindness" almost kills her—and does
result in the death (or so we assume) of Alex Sebastian. The
Paradine Case presents an interestingly complex variation on
this theme, looking forward, as Robin Wood points out, to
Vertigo. Anthony Keane (Gregory Peck) allows his attraction
to his client to pervert his reading of the facts. Thus he
ignores the guilt of Anna Paradine, who did indeed murder her
blind husband, and accuses her lover (Louis Jourdan) so
mercilessly that he eventually commits suicide. Once again,
"blindness" to the facts has death as its product.
     A second sort of Hitchcock "reader" serves to anchor a more
positive chain of narrative actions and events. Three examples
in particular stand out. The Joan Fontaine character in
Rebecca, unlike her counterpart in Suspicion, cannot be

described as psychotic, however much Mrs. Danvers would like her
to believe she is. The second Mrs. DeWinter is, rather, a genuine
Hitchcock innocent--whatever guilt she eventually incurs hinges
only on her wish that the dead Rebecca were really and finally
dead. Her primary activity in the film, the rightness of which
is eventually rewarded, involves the attempt to read her husband
and her circumstances. Thus she stages the Manderley party on
the mistaken assumption that Max's malaise results from longing
rather than guilt, and it backfires on her. The point, however,
is that she does her often naive best to see the truth, and that
truth eventually frees her from the spectre of Rebecca.

The action of Spellbound follows a similar pattern.[10]
Gregory Peck, as it turns out, is a "wrong man," falsely accused
of murder. But he is unable to "read" his own dilemma due to
a correlation between his present circumstances and a deeply
repressed childhood trauma. The film's ethical center is
therefore shifted to the psychiatrist played by Ingrid Bergman.
She is intuitively certain of Ballantine's innocence and she does
her analytical best to read the pattern of Ballantine's emotional
disturbances. It is worth remarking here that her ability to
help Ballantine is somewhat at odds with the detachment associated
with her profession:  hence the fact, as Spoto points out, that
"seeing" John correctly requires her to take off the glasses which
she wears at the film's beginning.

Far and away the best example of this "right-reader" motif
involves the Mark Rutland character in Marnie. Like Max in
Rebecca and Ballantine in Spellbound, Marnie Edgar is plagued
by a traumatic past--and Mark Rutland, like his predecessors,
opens himself up to the vulnerability and responsibility implicit
in learning to read the emotional pattern of another person's
life. Thus Rutland exercises his abilities as a reader (he runs
a publishing company and is frequently framed against bookcases)
and slowly assembles the clues--Marnie's fear of storms, her
reactions to the color red, her kleptomania, her fear of men,
her fear of tapping noises--which eventually become the
combination that allows him to unlock Marnie's past and set her
free. It is a dangerous course to follow. In the case of
Constance Petersen in Spellbound the effort to read John
Ballantine almost results in lifelong separation when John is
convicted, on evidence developed by Constance, of murder. And
in Mark Rutland's case there is the possibility of a prison term
for aiding and abetting. Furthermore, there is always the chance
that intuitive sympathy will backfire, as it does for young
Charlie in Shadow of a Doubt, as it does for Anthony Keane in
The Paradine Case. But it is generally true in Hitchcock that
assumptions of innocence are eventually rewarded. Even Eve Gill
in Stage Fright gains for her experience. At film's end she
finally appreciates the virtues of being ordinary--as they are
personified by Inspector "Smith."

One further narrative pattern is worth considering here that
may be understood as extending the implications of the

"wrong-reader/right-reader" pair. The films of this group might
be termed the "family" films, in that all are more explicitly
than elsewhere in Hitchcock concerned with multiple focal
characters.[11] Furthermore, all conceive of the process of
reading in terms not of individual subjects but more generally,
in terms of the world as a whole. Thus we find a connection
between family groups of one sort or another (actual families
in The Man Who Knew Too Much, The Wrong Man, The Birds,
and Topaz, an ad hoc "family of man" in The Lady Vanishes)
and social order or international politics: usually some
disharmony in the microcosm of the family, some "misreading" of
proper familial or sexual relationships, results in, calls forth,
or is paralleled by a similar or parody disharmony in the
macrocosm of society. Thus in The Man Who Knew Too Much (1934),
the Lawrence family is characterized by an almost fatal lack of
sexual decorum. The father jokes about his daughter, Betty,
"knocking [men] cold" before her time, while Mrs. Lawrence half
jokingly draws the conclusion, after losing a skeet shooting
contest with some help from her distracting young daughter, that
sportsmen ought not to have children. Indeed, only a few moments
later Jill Lawrence suggests that her husband take their daughter
to bed while she goes off with another man. In terms of the
film's ostensible intrigue, to be sure, things do not really get
under way until Jill Lawrence's parody paramour is shot, at which
point he whispers instructions to her regarding a state secret.
In the confusion the daughter is sent to bed alone, only to be
kidnapped by the terrorists who are responsible for the murder:
the Lawrences "know too much" and their daughter will be the
forfeit if they talk. The associative logic, however, is clear.
The Lawrences, like many Hitchcock parents, do not value their
daughter or her sexuality sufficiently and it takes her kidnapping
to bring them to their senses.

        But there is more to it than that. The British Foreign
Office knows that the terrorists are planning the assassination
of a foreign diplomat but they do not know when. The Lawrences
are therefore faced with an agonizing dilemma which forces them
to reread the world in two respects. To begin with, they fear
going to the police, so Bob Lawrence and his brother-in-law set
out on their own to break the code of the message Bob found in
the paramour's hotel room--in the hope that they will thus find
Betty. Secondly, however, it becomes intuitively imperative,
for Jill at least, to rethink her sense of social responsibility.
If the terrorists are not stopped a new world war might result.
Thus when she goes, at Bob's instruction, to Albert Hall, and
despite the warning she is given in the form of Betty's broach
not to interfere, Jill intuitively and spontaneously foils the
assassination attempt by shouting at the last minute, thus
spoiling the sharpshooter's aim.

        None of which is quite so neat in cause-and-effect dramatic
terms as the rereading undertaken by Mark Rutland in Marnie--but
it is a pattern seen frequently in Hitchcock, in both versions

of The Man Who Knew Too Much; in The Lady Vanishes, where
the secret to be uncovered is the whereabouts of the vanished
lady; in Notorious, where the secret, the uranium bottle in
Sebastian's cellar, is simultaneously sexual and political; in
The Birds, where the secret involves the logic of the bird
attacks themselves; and in Topaz, where two secrets are
involved: the extent of Russian military involvement in Cuba and
the identity of the French double agent. In both cases political
brinksmanship or double-dealing is paralleled, and commented on,
by illicit, extramarital sexual relations, Devereaux with Juanita
de Cordoba and Madame Devereaux with Jacques Granville
(newspapers, it should be pointed out, play a particularly
important thematic part in all of this). Thus in all of these
films we see the microcosm/macrocosm metaphor and in every case
the mystery to be "decoded" involves the survival of civilization.


THE PROBLEMATICS OF VISION
     Thus far I have suggested that a central metaphor, writ large
in the basic narrative patterns of the Hitchcock cinema, concerns
the act of reading. We can confirm the centrality of this
metaphor by attending to certain recurrent visual features in
Hitchcock, features which by themselves would not necessarily
serve to embody the vision issue, but which do when set within
the context of the reading metaphor which may be said to motivate
the majority of this films.
     The visual feature in Hitchcock most immediately relevant
to the reading theme involves subjective shots wherein the world
goes out of focus or is distorted in some way. The subjectivity
in question here is often that of an important or dramatically
central "misreader" and these misreadings are generally of two
sorts. The first involves literal visual or focal distortion.
Several instances come immediately to mind. During the Albert
Hall sequence in The Man Who Knew Too Much (1934), for example,
Jill's vision goes momentarily blurry, the blur correlating
exactly with her confused loyalties; and her vision snaps back
into focus when the assassin's gun barrel enters the frame in
close-up. The logic of Jill's visual and moral recovery is clear:
to attend closely to the immediacy of the situation is to resolve
her doubts. A man will die if she remains silent--and to her
credit she shouts the warning. We see a similar sort of visual
distortion early in Notorious. It's the morning after the night
before and Ingrid Bergman awakes to the sight of Cary Grant
standing in her bedroom door (Figs. 5.3, 5.4). The sequence
involves several cuts from objective (of Bergman watching Grant)
to subjective (Grant as seen by Bergman)--but the subjective shots
taken together amount to a single take, the camera panning and
twisting to follow Grant as he walks from the bedroom door to
Alicia's bedside. The shot is darkly lit, at first, Grant's face
indistinct in the shadows (both qualities corresponding to
Alicia's blurred sense of guilt, her disgust at her father's Nazi

sympathies running counter to her sense of daughterly loyalty); furthermore, its sustained subjectivity correlates with the film's general theme of entrapment:  because Alicia (the camera) maintains a fixed position, her view of Grant is constantly out of whack, as she (the camera) struggles to keep Grant in frame--at shot's end he is literally upside down.

This correlation between physical entrapment and distorted sense perceptions is also central to Psycho. In both Notorious and Psycho, close-ups correspond to the fact of entrapment by cutting characters off from each other and from the world around them. This entrapment motif is refined and extended in Psycho, however, by Hitchcock's systematic use of tight enclosures, small rooms and automobiles particularly (the trunk of Marion's car thus becomes her coffin). A corollary visual distortion is evidenced early in Psycho, as Marion drives away from Phoenix, and it results, like the distortion in Notorious, from spatial rigidity. Marion is driving along the highway, trapped both behind the wheel and by the road itself, and Hitchcock cuts between objective shots of Marion (shots which seem subjective because they are accompanied by subjective voice-overs) and truly subjective shots of the windshield and the road taken from Marion's point of view. Vision thus becomes problematic. Sight is distorted by a constant, seemingly hostile onrush of headlights from the darkness, and is distorted even more by the sheen of windshield water and the constant swing of the wiper blades. Marion literally can't see straight. And this lack of visual acuity corresponds to her lack of moral acuity, a lack further indicated by the paranoid "fine soft flesh" character of the voice-overs, which represent Marion's sense of the response her theft will elicit from her boss and her victim.

A second sort of subjective visual figure in Hitchcock, again corresponding in some sense with failures to read the world properly, involves hallucination sequences. An early one is found in The Lodger. The film's detective, Joe, seeks to "put the cuffs" on both the Avenger and on Daisy, Joe's girlfriend. Both concerns come together when Joe finds the Lodger (Drew) and Daisy out together on a Tuesday night, the night the Avenger always strikes. Joe tells Drew to keep his hands off Daisy; Daisy tells Joe to quit interfering; and Joe is left seated beneath a lamp post, his head in his hands. Joe looks out from under the brim of his hat at the departing couple, and then down at the ground where he sees the imprint of a man's shoe. We see the imprint subjectively, from Joe's point of view--and we see, superimposed within the "screen" provided by the shoe print, images projected by Joe's imagination:  the portraits of blonde women that Drew had ordered removed from his lodgings, Drew's black bag, Drew and Daisy embracing, the ceiling lamps in the room below the Lodger's--all of which serve, in Joe's imagination, to indict the Lodger for murder, but which serve equally, in retrospect, to indict Joe for false accusation, for "misreading."

Hallucination sequences also play a prominent role in
Sabotage. The first involves the pitiable Mr. Verloc and serves
to express his anguish at being ordered to plant a bomb in
Piccadilly Circus. As he stands alone in the London Aquarium
he "projects" an image of Piccadilly Circus onto the glass of
the fish tank and then watches the image "crumble," as if from
a bomb blast. More interesting in the present context, however,
are the hallucinations which Mrs. Verloc endures after learning
of her brother's death. Upon reading of his death in a newspaper
she faints. As a crowd gathers around her we get subjective
shots, from her point of view, of the faces staring down at her,
among which she sees her brother's face, appearing and
disappearing before her eyes. And later, after she stabs her
husband, as her detective/lover leads her away, down the street,
we again see subjective shots of the sidewalk crowd, within which
she again sees her brother's image. Such sequences may be read
in two ways. In dramatic cause-and-effect terms Mrs. Verloc's
hallucinations evidence a refusal to believe that her brother
is dead. In thematic terms, however, and in the context of the
film's general "viewing" theme (the Verlocs own and operate a
cinema; Stevie stops to "watch" a parade), the hallucinations
emphasize ironically Mrs. Verloc's failure to read the world with
sufficient care and attention. Not only does Stevie's image
appear; it disappears. She had married Verloc not for love but
to provide for and protect her brother; and by making money the
measure of affection she brings about the circumstances which
result in her brother's death.

Suspicion, as previously noted, is a paradigm case of the
misreader plot in Hitchcock. It also provides a striking example
of the hallucination figure. Lina, Johnny, and Beaky are playing
a word game, and Lina forms the words "murder" and "murderer"
in succession, "rewriting" the world to suit her own neurotic
conceptions--and the degree of her fearfulness is shown by the
sequence of shots which follow. We see a close-up of Johnny's
profile from her point of view (profiles are frequently correlated
in Hitchcock with "one-sided" readings or personalities as in
Shadow of a Doubt, Notorious, and The Wrong Man); another
close-up of Lina; a close-up of the word "murderer" after which
the camera tilts up and then zooms to a close-up of a seascape
photograph in a magazine which is held by Johnny; close-up of
Lina again, over which is superimposed a long shot of Johnny
pushing Beaky off the cliff; close-up of Lina; then another close-
up of Lina with the image of Beaky, falling to his death,
superimposed. Strictly speaking, of course, the "hallucinations"
here are not subjective. What we have, rather, are two
nonsubjective perspectives--objective shots of Lina combined with
objective shots of Johnny pushing Beaky off the cliff or of Beaky
falling. The cutting, however, authorizes the subjective reading
of the scene. The close-up of Lina isolates her from the game;
her glance at the magazine raises the reading issue, specifically

in terms of her reading of and about Johnny (he holds the
magazine--she has read about him in magazines before); and the
objective shots of the murder are obviously contradicted by the
context of the scene:   Johnny and Beaky are indoors playing
anagrams, not outdoors at the seacoast.

The red suffusions and the dream sequences in Marnie
represent Hitchcock's most elaborate use of the hallucination
figure, combining the subjective hallucinations characteristic
of films like The Lodger and Sabotage with the objective
hallucinations of Suspicion.  Most of the suffusion sequences
in Marnie follow a similar logic:   cut from a medium shot or
close-up of Marnie to a point-of-view close-up of some appropriate
red stimulus (flowers, a jockey's silks, red hunting jackets)
to a close-up of Marnie over which the suffusion itself is
superimposed.  The superimposition figure is similar to that used
in Suspicion but here it points backward, to Marnie's past,
rather than forward, to a future that Lina fears.  In both cases,
however, the combination of objective shots of the character and
subjective superimpositions mirrors the degree to which both women
"misread" the world (in neither case is the character's subjective
response authorized by the truth of the present) and also the
degree to which their misreadings are, in some meaningful way,
imposed upon them from outside--neurosis in both cases is
ultimately traceable to parental disregard.

Such is the general rule for the suffusions in Marnie--but
Hitchcock also works some significantly expressive variations
upon the pattern.  The first variation involves the first "dream"
sequence which takes place in Mrs. Edgar's Baltimore row house.
Here we do not cut from a point-of-view shot to a close-up of
Marnie because there is no visual stimulus to trigger the
suffusion.  Rather we have a single shot which begins with a
close-up of Marnie's window, where we see and, more importantly,
hear the knock of the window shade pull ring as it taps against
the glass; then we pan right to Marnie, still asleep, at which
point the suffusion is superimposed.  The second major variation
involves the scene in Mark's office when Marnie is frightened
by the thunderstorm.  The cutting of the sequence is fairly
complex, involving objective shots of Marnie, subjective point-of-
view shots from Marnie's perspective, as well as reaction shots
of Mark as he tries to read her actions.  The point to make again,
however, is that the stimulus which triggers Marnie's reaction
is as much aural (the thunder) as visual (the lightning);
furthermore, in this case the suffusion is not superimposed over
Marnie herself.  Rather, we see a long full shot of the floor-to-
ceiling window behind Mark's desk, taken from Marnie's point of
view, through which we see the lightning flashing--and it's the
flashing light which takes on the reddish tint (at which point
Marnie begs Mark to "stop the colors").

The third key exception "rhymes" with the first (both are
"dream" sequences) but with an added complication.  We see a
close-up of the adult Marnie in bed, but with rough bedclothes

and a sailor's pillow, over which is superimposed the red
suffusion. Then, as a mysterious hand knocks on a window behind
Marnie's bed we pull back and pan right--with no break in
continuity whatsoever--to a full shot of Marnie's room in the
Rutland mansion, and specifically of the door between her room
and Mark's through which he then enters. The final exceptional
suffusion scene, Marnie's reliving of her mother's "accident,"
is also the initial suffusion scene. Here we return to the
general pattern of the other suffusion scenes but again there
are some significant, this time temporal, variations. That is,
the first shot (Fig. 5.5) is in the past (Marnie as a young girl),
the point-of-view shot (of the dead sailor's bloody shirt [Fig.
5.6]) is also in the past and is further complicated by using
the zoom motif (thus enforcing a parallel between this scene,
having to do with sex, and the final "robbery" scene which had
to do with money); furthermore, the suffusion is superimposed
over the point-of-view shot rather than Marnie herself; and
the final shot is of Marnie, but of Marnie in the present (Fig.
5.7).

We can see a clear progression to these exceptional suffusion
sequences. Each of them "externalizes" Marnie's subjectivity,
either for us or for Mark, though for us first, allowing us not
only to read her but to read Mark reading her. Thus we are given
the aural clues to Marnie's situation (knocking, thunder); but
we get as well the only truly subjective suffusions--those seen
literally through Marnie's eyes--the "reddish" lightning and the
suffusion over the sailor's shirt. The implication, I think,
is clear: to be truly "objective" in our reading of other people
requires an imaginative involvement in their subjectivity. Thus
we become both the misreader (as we see the storm through Marnie's
eyes) and the right-reader (as we see Marnie through Mark's); and
we are both almost simultaneously.

The curative potential of this sort of imaginative
involvement with others is also evidenced by the mirror image
construction of the two dream sequences. The first starts with
the stimulus and then includes Marnie by panning right, as if
the camera were "imposing" the illness upon her. The second,
however, begins with Marnie in a limbo state, half in childhood
(the bed), half in adulthood (it is Tippi Hedren), half in dream
(the childhood set), half in reality (the Rutland house)--and
the explicit character of this confusion can be read positively,
as if Marnie were getting ready to break out of her psychosis.
Thus the camera pans away from Marnie, as if to remove her
illness, and the agent of that removal, the reader who cracks
the code, enters at the end of the shot. All of which finds its
logical visual and thematic pay-off in the final suffusion scene,
wherein the symbol of the suffusion is reunited with its proper
emotional referent. Thus the past/present split in Marnie's
personality is openly acknowledged, by cutting back and forth
between two actresses of different ages playing the same
character, and the suffusion is linked quite explicitly to the

gaze of the child Marnie as she looks directly at the blood on
the sailor's shirt--which is where the suffusion then stays.
That is, by going back to the past Marnie "places" the suffusions
in their proper emotional context at which point she can finally
leave them behind.

Most of the hallucinations or distortions thus far considered
have been, at least in their immediate genesis, internally
motivated. Marnie's "suffusions" thus "belong" to her, even if,
in mimetic fact, her general psychosis can ultimately be traced
back to her mother's actions and values, both before and after
the "accident." A related species of Hitchcock hallucination
requires brief comment here--that of "induced hallucinations."
We see an early example of this in The Man Who Knew Too Much
(1934) when Betty's Uncle Clive is put under hypnosis by Abbot's
Nurse in her role as a bogus priestess of the Tabernacle of the
Sun. The sequence is shot largely in alternating close-ups as
the Nurse invokes the "first degree of the seven-fold way" and
holds a glass talisman between herself and Uncle Clive. Clive
slowly goes under and his increasing subservience to the trance
is emblematized by a prismlike subjective point-of-view shot of
the priestess as Clive sees her through the glass: the world
literally "fragments" around her and the result of this
fragmentation is the surrender of Clive's consciousness.

A central sequence in The Wrong Man, wherein Manny
Balestrero (Henry Fonda) is booked and locked up, evidences a
similar surrender of consciousness. The mise-en-scene as Manny
is shut up in his cell is restricted to medium and close shots,
alternating between objective and subjective points of view.
Hitchcock employs moving camera, furthermore, both to follow Manny
as he paces and to replicate the nervous pattern of his gaze as
Manny views his confinement. Hitchcock cuts away briefly to a
scene involving Manny's family as they are informed of Manny's
arrest (cutting away has the effect of eliding time, thus to
stretch out the duration of Manny's agony) and then Hitchcock
returns us to the cell where Manny's pacing accelerates. Manny
then stops moving, his back now to the wall, his eyes closed,
and the camera starts to trace an accelerating clockwise circle
such that Manny's face seems to bounce around the edges of the
frame until the shot fades to black. Properly speaking, of
course, the shot is not a point-of-view shot; and yet the
encircling camera does seem to reflect Manny's internal state,
his subjective sense that the world has gone off its axis. It
is as if Manny had imparted his own anxious energy to the wall
and the cell in such a way as to set them in motion, thus
impugning the moral and visual stability of a world which has,
quite literally and brutally, "framed" him.

A similar threat to consciousness, embodied by a similar
fragmentation or distortion of vision, can be seen as late as
North by Northwest. In an early sequence Roger Thornhill (Cary
Grant) is forced to drink an overdose of bourbon prior to being
put in a car and pushed (or such is the plan) over a cliff.

Thornhill is an experienced drinker, however, and he manages to
take control of the car and flee for his life. The subjective
shots in question thus represent his view of the road as distorted
by alcohol, the distortion in this case being a multiplication
of images: Thornhill sees two roads, two sets of yellow lines
diverging into opposite corners of the frame, and his problem
is thus, quite literally, to read his own hallucination. The
point to make in all three cases, however, is that the
hallucination or distortion is imposed immediately and fairly
directly from the outside. It is not a matter, as it was in
Suspicion and Marnie, of a character's psychic past distorting
his or her view of the present. Rather, some external influence,
generally personified by spies or international terrorists, is
aggressively involved in rewriting the world or a character's
view of it, often by means of or for the purpose of murder. Thus
the Nurse is part of a conspiracy to murder a European diplomat;
thus Alicia in Notorious is poisoned by her husband and mother-
in-law for being an American intelligence agent; and thus
Thornhill's life is threatened in North by Northwest on the
assumption that he is George Kaplan, another American agent.

Another important image in Hitchcock of vision run amok is
less a matter of subjective vision than dramatic context. To
this point we have been concerned with visually attributable
confusions of sight: vision is obscured because some particular
character misreads the world, either voluntarily or under some
form of duress (psychic or chemical). Such images are generally
to be found in films which focus on misreaders. In films (or
filmic subtexts) which focus on "misleaders" or the "misread,"
however, the iconographic consequence is more frequently for some
physical object to assume an importance, both moral and graphic,
far out of proportion to that which it would have in everyday
existence.

Three remarkable examples come immediately to mind. The
first is found in The Lady Vanishes when Dr. Hartz tries to
eliminate the threat to his scheme to make the old lady vanish
by "doctoring" (or so he thinks) the brandy. While waiting for
Iris and Gilbert to down their drinks, Dr. Hartz chats with them
across a dining car table--and Hitchcock shoots the scene so as
to emphasize the brandy glasses in the foreground. Indeed, he
uses oversize glasses at one point, along with repeated close-ups,
to achieve the effect. Rhetorically speaking, this amounts to
a fairly direct sort of dramatic underscoring; but in graphic
terms the oversize glasses bespeak a world on the verge of
obliteration (they rest on the bottom of the frame and threaten
to fill it altogether). A similar and equally famous example
of graphic distortion or foreshortening is found in Notorious.
Once Sebastian and his mother learn of Alicia's identity as an
American agent, they begin to poison her with daily doses in her
coffee. There are three such episodes of Alicia drinking the
doctored coffee, the last of which culminates in an extended
example of the "induced hallucination" figure as Alicia realizes

what is happening and tries to escape, only to black out (quite
literally at certain moments). This is preceded, however, by
several shots which serve as emblems for Alicia's situation.
We thus see her sitting in a wing-backed chair, chatting about
the poor state of her health with Alex, his mother, and Dr.
Anderson, one of Sebastian's Nazi cohorts. The cutting breaks
down on conversation but the sequence is tied together by the
coffee cup motif (we see Alex's mother pour it and hand it to
Alicia; we watch Alicia drink). The logical outcome of the
scene's action is that the drugged coffee will eventually
"overwhelm" Alicia. And in graphic terms this is exactly what
happens: the camera repeatedly returns to up-angle medium two-
shots of Alicia (screen left) and Dr. Anderson (screen right),
but the foreground, and therefore the shot itself, is dominated
by Alicia's coffee cup (Fig. 5.8). In two dimensions, indeed,
it is larger than Alicia herself and threatens to push her out
of the frame (and out of existence) altogether. In any reasonably
ordered world coffee cups would not assume such proportions.
But until the Nazis can be controlled there is little chance that
the world will be reasonably ordered.

A less obvious but equally interesting use of this motif
can be found in Strangers on a Train. In The Lady Vanishes
and Notorious the disproportion figure comes well into the
intrigue of the film and involves an overt disjunction of
dimensions: people are overtly and graphically overshadowed by
ordinarily small-scale physical objects. The central object in
Strangers on a Train is Guy's cigarette lighter, and at times,
towards the film's conclusion, it does indeed grow in size and
significance beyond ordinary measure. Thus, during the famous
crosscutting sequence, Guy playing tennis while Bruno reaches
into the storm drain to retrieve Guy's lighter (which he intends
to plant as evidence of Guy's guilt), the lighter comes almost
to fill the screen. Indeed, we cut directly from Guy to the
lighter as Bruno finally takes hold of it, almost as if the
lighter were going to push Guy out of the frame for good. The
juxtaposition here is temporal rather than spatial per se, but
it has much the same effect.

That this use of the lighter is of the same order as
Hitchcock's use of the glasses in The Lady Vanishes and the
cup in Notorious is confirmed, however, by the role the lighter
plays earlier in the film. We see it initially during the first
conversation scene between Guy and Bruno, in the dining car of
the train, where Hitchcock underlines its significance by a
close-up of it and by references to it in the dialogue. We next
see it in the following scene, when Guy and Bruno have lunch
together in Bruno's compartment. Already we associate the lighter
with Guy's vulnerability: he is married, the lighter is a present
from another woman--an association further underlined by an
implicit visual parallel with another piece of personalized
jewelry, Bruno's name-plate tie pin, a gift from his mother (which
we also see in close-up during the first conversation scene [Fig.

5.9]).  The scene in Bruno's compartment thus recalls the earlier
conversation scenes in The Lady Vanishes and Notorious.  In
every case the superficial orderliness of the dialogue is undercut
and qualified by the presence of an object on a table in the
foreground, an object emblematic of one character's vulnerability
and another character's desire to rewrite the world through the
exercise of power (Fig. 5.10).  Of course, the literal size of
the object, relative to character size, is nowhere near so
distorted as in the corresponding scenes in the earlier films--but
the placement, significance, and thematic effects in all three
examples are clearly of a piece.  The lighter draws our attention
far more than it should; and that by itself amounts to a form
of visual distortion.

These three examples hardly begin to catalogue Hitchcock's
use of the distortion figure.  Indeed, as the previous examples
suggest, there is a range of such figures in Hitchcock, a range
whose parameters are defined both spatially and dramatically.
At one extreme we find gross distortions of spatial relationships
wherein small objects literally overshadow larger objects.  Think
of the little finger of Professor Jordon in The 39 Steps, the
razor blade and the pistol, respectively, in crucial scenes of
Spellbound, the stuffed birds in Psycho, the bird cages in
the opening scene of The Birds, the pistol in Marnie.  A
special case involves diagetically acknowledged distortions such
as we see with the gigantic dentures in The Man Who Knew Who
Too Much (1934), the giant heads in Blackmail and North by
Northwest, and the Statue of Liberty in Saboteur.  At the other
extreme we have small-scale objects, like the lighter in
Strangers on a Train, which assume an overload of dramatic
significance and therefore demand foregrounding, either literally,
as evidenced in The Lady Vanishes, Notorious, or Strangers
on a Train, or by repeated use of leitmotif close-ups.  Such
objects include kitchen knives (The 39 Steps, Sabotage),
personal jewelry (Betty's broach in The Man Who Knew Too Much,
the incriminating ring in Shadow of a Doubt, Rusk's stick
pin in Frenzy), lamps (The Wrong Man, Vertigo, Marnie),
photographs (The Lodger, Shadow of a Doubt), tea cups (The
Birds), money (Psycho, Marnie), purses (Suspicion,
Marnie), keys (Notorious, The Wrong Man, Marnie), wine
bottles (Notorious), and beverage glasses (Suspicion,
Notorious, Topaz).

One final special case is worth remarking upon.  In
Notorious we see an instance where an inanimate object grows
in size to threaten an on-screen character.  Also in Notorious
we see a thematic correlation between expensive gem-stone jewelry,
which Alicia borrows from the agency to wear to dinner at
Sebastian's, and dehumanization (we see this also in Family
Plot).  Thus Devlin refuses to help her put on the diamond
necklace, because he understands the implicit significance of
the gesture.  These two motifs, one thematic, the other visual,
are brought together in the party sequence of To Catch a Thief.

The film begins with a thematic correlation between dehumanization, evidenced by the grotesque close-up of a screaming woman, and jewelry: stolen jewels are the cause, the scream the effect. There is also a running verbal subtext setting jewels against people (Jesse Stevens complains, for example, that she cannot "snuggle up" to her jewels). But this thematic motif has an interesting visual/iconographic correlative. The party sequence begins with a series of ritual entrances, as guests in Louis .XIV regalia glide down a receiving line, between two ranks of costumed on-lookers, directly toward the camera. As the guests come into close-up the camera focuses on the jewelry at the necks of the women: and the visual effect of the attention to wealth is to "decapitate" the women who wear the jewelry (Fig. 5.11). Their faces matter so little that the camera can ignore their humanness altogether. But it is not completely the camera's fault. Rather, this is how the women wish to be seen. They invite this sort of visual beheading--and the visuals only serve to reflect their own "wrong headedness."

In summary, then, we can say that a clear associative relationship exists in Hitchcock between certain recurrent narrative-dramatic structures, wherein characters find their normal sense of themselves and their world (their habitual manner of interpreting self/other relationships) called into question by events, and specific and recurrent graphic patterns, wherein normal proportions or expectations of clarity go awry or unrewarded: each seems a function of the other. It remains to specify the exact nature of that relationship: what is the causal logic underlying this association of action and imagery?


ISOLATION AND ITS ICONOGRAPHY

I have suggested, in connection with Psycho and Notorious, that a correlation exists in Hitchcock between fixity or enclosure (spatial, emotional, both) and a lack of visual/moral acuity. We can extend this generalization in two directions. In terms of "deep structure" dramatic logic we can say that moral and visual disorder in Hitchcock generally follows from some denial of life's wholeness, a retreat from its responsibilities and attachments. The two primary contexts for conflict in the world of Alfred Hitchcock--the family and international politics-- both raise the issue.

The primary sexual/familial sin is desertion, either in fact (various sorts of familial or sexual desertion are evidenced, for example, in Young and Innocent, Mr. and Mrs. Smith, Stage Fright, I Confess, Topaz, and Family Plot, to name only a few) or in emotional fantasy (as in Rebecca, Psycho, The Birds, and Marnie); and both sorts of desertion tend to set in motion a similar sequence of emotional events. That is, desertion or the fear of it tends to drive characters, literally in some cases, into emotional corners where they cannot respond openly to the world. They either retreat into psychoses or

obsessions of one sort or another (cf. The Lodger, Rebecca,
Suspicion, Spellbound, I Confess, The Wrong Man, Marnie)
or they lash out in anger, anger that usually takes the form of
murder (Shadow of a Doubt, Rope, Strangers on a Train, Dial
M for Murder, Psycho, Family Plot). Vertigo, for one,
shows us how closely aligned obsession and murder can be:
Scottie's obsession with Madeleine/Judy leads ultimately to her
death.

Likewise, the primary political sin in Hitchcock almost
always involves attempts by one country or group to gain some
sort of advantage over another. Thus the saboteurs in The 39
Steps, Sabotage, and The Lady Vanishes all have England as
their target, although in every case, including The Man Who Knew
Too Much, the ultimate aim seems to be to spark international
conflict through which the saboteurs or their party hope to
profit. Similarly, in Hitchcock's Hollywood films, America
becomes the target, as in Notorious, North by Northwest, and
Topaz. But in these cases too there is an international
component at work. The Nazis in Notorious threaten world peace
generally, while in Topaz the plot intrigue involves a leak
in NATO security. The point to make, however, is how seldom
Hitchcock makes a positive case for national patriotism. The
patriotic component is usually present for being implicit in the
spy-thriller genre; but Hitchcock usually works to subvert it,
particularly in Torn Curtain. Hence the fact that we seldom
know whom the saboteurs represent--it doesn't much matter in
Hitchcock. The positive case in these films is seldom argued
in political terms at all. The positive case is argued, rather,
in sexual terms. The political plots in Hitchcock move to deny
the bonds of humanity which tie people together by strengthening
the hand of one party or country over another. The sexual plots,
however, move to reassert the bonds of love which connect people,
in spite of the political climate which would deny such
interconnectedness. Hence the correlation in Hitchcock's "family
films" between sexual or familial disorder and international
disorder: the former is a primary and microcosmic version of
the latter. Only in Topaz, which I find one of Hitchcock's
most pessimistic films, do sexual relationships fail to embody
a thematically powerful antidote to political cynicism.

To deny the wholeness of life is thus the cardinal Hitchcock
sin: retreating from one's family responsibilities or from one's
responsibilities to the larger family of man are its two primary
forms, although variants clearly exist. Social class, for
example, can be seen as a form of nationalism which denies the
wholeness of mankind. Thus The Lodger, as a matter of
subconscious class prerogative, takes his mother's injunction
to bring the Avenger to justice (an injunction which in itself
carries implications of class) as a license to kill: hence the
gun he carries in his bag. Religion is also a form of nationalism
in Hitchcock, for denying the connectedness of mankind: hence
his generally satiric treatment of it in The Man Who Knew Too

Much, The 39 Steps, The Lady Vanishes, Shadow of a
Doubt, and Family Plot.  Even I Confess and The Wrong Man,
purportedly Hitchcock's two most positively "religious" films,
lack any sort of religious warmth.  Montgomery Clift is no Bing
Crosby.  Rather, religion in both films serves as an emotional
retreat.  Thus Father Logan retreats retroactively from his
experiences in the war by entering the priesthood; and thus Manny
Balestrero retreats from his own uncertainty by conjuring up his
own "wrong man," someone who can take his place in the cycle of
accusations that the film embodies.
    Such are the primary psychological retreats in Hitchcock:
obsession with the past, anger at the present, nationalism,
sexism, social class, and religion.  In terms of dramatic logic,
characters become isolated in one or more of these retreats and
accordingly lose their ability to read the world in its wholeness
and immediacy.  The causal chain in Marnie demonstrates how
complex this can be.  Bernice Edgar was impoverished as a child
(class), turned to prostitution as a consequence (sexism), became
so obsessed with the past that she denied its existence, and
turned to religion to justify her denial.  Marnie, in her turn,
thus becomes subconsciously obsessed with the past, and this
obsession finds conscious expression in a form of class warfare
(Marnie's thievery) which has sex as its primary weapon.  No
wonder Marnie is so troubled.
    We have been concerned in the last several pages with the
thematic correlation between "psychological enclosure" or
"psychological fixity" and the lack of moral and visual acuity.
We can refine this observation by attending to iconography, here
the iconography of causes where earlier we were concerned with
the iconography of visual effects.  Many of these, of course,
we have already touched upon in other contexts.  Bruno's tie clip
in Strangers on a Train, for example, is emblematic of the
Oedipal matrix which cuts him off from ordinary experience.  As
such the clip is an icon of causality.  But Hitchcock's visual
treatment, the close-up in the first conversation scene which
connects it by means of visual rhyme to Guy's cigarette lighter,
transforms it into an icon of effect as well.  Such
visual/thematic economy is one characteristic of the Hitchcock
style, a characteristic which reminds us that our critical
categories must remain flexible.  Nevertheless, and with this
qualification in mind, it is possible to locate several symbol
systems which bear particularly on the themes of retreat and
denial as those themes relate to the larger issue of reading and
misreading.
    The first of these involves clothing, including jewelry as
a subset, which serves by and large as a class-marker, indicating
how people of wealth and status generally (and mistakenly) wish
to be seen.  Thus the protagonist in The Lodger is defined in
class terms by his elegant wardrobe (e.g., his smoking jacket);
while the general movement of the film, with its theatrical and
fashion model subtexts, is concerned precisely with the illusory

significance of outward appearances.  In The 39 Steps Hannay's
basic resiliency and responsiveness to events is evidenced by
his ability to manipulate appearances via costume changes (he
poses as a milkman; he is saved by the hymnal in the pocket of
the Crofter's coat) or by self-dramatization (at the political
meeting and the hotel).  In Sabotage the class issue comes up
again.  On the one hand Mrs. Verloc complains of financial ruin
should she be forced to give refunds to the cinema patrons when
the power goes out; but on the other hand she doesn't hesitate
to order tailor-made clothes.  To Catch a Thief is analogous
to The 39 Steps in this regard; the whole movement of the film
is toward underscoring the arbitrariness of appearances and the
fancy dress ball provides Hitchcock a marvelous opportunity to
undercut the clothing code.  North by Northwest is also
concerned with the superficiality of classism and sexism and it's
significant that Thornhill's elegant blue suit (Leonard: "He's
a well-tailored one, isn't he?") is disheveled and eventually
discarded by film's conclusion.  A similar devaluation of clothing
marks the changes in the Tippi Hedren character of The Birds.
Even Marion Crane in Psycho undergoes this process of
"undressing"; and while she dies nude it is less her nudity which
is called into question, we see in retrospect, than the false
costume of her murderer.
     A special case of the clothing motif, special not for the
functioning of the motif but for the clothing involved, is found
in I Confess, where the thematic correlation involves religion
rather than class.  Father Logan's cassock is nevertheless
emblematic of his retreat from experience, and it is therefore
appropriate that the cassock should be the strongest evidence
in the murder case against him.
     One final article of clothing remains to be mentioned:
eyeglasses.  Donald Spoto writes on this motif at length in The
Art of Alfred Hitchcock, noting the high correlation in Hitchcock
between characters who wear eyeglasses and characters who evidence
some sort of denial of human relationships, notably Pamela in
The 39 Steps (she is reading when Hannay first sees her),
the judge in The Paradine Case, Guy's wife in Strangers on
a Train, Thorvald in Rear Window, the Professor in North by
Northwest, the highway cop in Psycho, and Strutt in Marnie.
One must be careful, however, not to overgeneralize.  Certain
characters who wear eyeglasses are more victims than perpetrators:
one thinks of Lina in Suspicion and Professor Lindt in Torn
Curtain.  The point in every case, however, involves the
problematics of vision, which is the crucial element for our
discussion.
     Another iconographic system relevant to the reading theme
involves furniture, generally chairs of the wing-backed variety,
couches, and/or beds.  These may best be thought of as "sites
of isolation."  Characters may retreat into them of their own
volition—Lina in Suspicion repeatedly hides in her high-backed
chair, as does Ruth in I Confess, and Lina eventually retreats

into her lavish bed and into the corner of the front seat of the
car as she and Johnny drive along the cliff; Shadow of a Doubt
begins with Uncle Charlie in bed and continues, in the first Santa
Rosa sequence, to show Young Charlie in the same position. Or
characters may be forced into isolation: Erica in Young and
Innocent is ordered to her bedroom by her father, and Alicia
in Notorious is made a prisoner of her bed and bedroom. The
point in both sets of circumstances, a point having obvious visual
consequences, is that such isolation cuts people off from each
other. Backs are turned. Faces are hidden. Feelings are
repressed. People cannot see or be seen if they get stuck in
such physical circumstances.

An obvious elaboration of this correlation between physical
isolation and visual/moral distortion involves architecture
generally. Perhaps the most common use of the architectural motif
is the "naturalistic" correlation between the upper class and
its architectural context. Hitchcock's films routinely take place
in high-class hotel rooms or flats (The Man Who Knew Too Much,
The 39 Steps, Rebecca, Rope, To Catch a Thief, North
by Northwest), mansions (The 39 Steps, Rebecca, Suspicion,
Spellbound, Notorious, Strangers on a Train, To Catch
a Thief, North by Northwest, Marnie), or townhouses (The
Lodger, Strangers on a Train, Topaz, Family Plot). It
is usually the Hitchcock case that upper-class characters are
called into question by their complacency--and their marvelously
elegant living quarters are clearly a factor in this. In strict
visual terms, the high ceilings and elegant moldings and columns
and bookcases create an almost excessively ordered graphic
context; and in nearly every case something very unorderly and
extraordinary takes place within it.

Another special architectural characteristic associated with
upper-class living quarters in Hitchcock is the staircase.
Hitchcock's staircases are famous--both Spoto and Maurice Yacowar
(in Hitchcock's British Films) deal with their expressive
possibilities at some length--but a few observations are in order
here. First of all, staircases tend to segregate space as well
as connect it: at the head of the staircase one generally finds
the "living" quarters. This in and of itself is ominous, for
isolating sexuality from sociality. Furthermore, those rich
enough to have staircases are usually rich enough to afford
separate sleeping quarters for husband and wife, as we see
in Rebecca and Marnie (in Notorious we see twin beds, while
in Suspicion Lina eventually chooses to sleep alone in the
double bed). If love is going to flourish under such
circumstances it is usually necessary to get out of the house,
so as to overcome the isolation implicit in the domestic
architecture. Thus in Rebecca, for example, it takes the night
in the beach house to set things straight, while the resolution
of Marnie takes place in the Baltimore row house of Marnie's
mother. And similarly in Suspicion and Notorious: both films
conclude, like Marnie, with the central characters (the couple)
driving away from the camera (though the final troubling image

in Notorious is of Sebastian walking back up the front steps
into the mansion).

A less class-bound architectural setting in Hitchcock
involves back rooms or basements, both of which are associated
with isolation or dissimulation and hence with the reading theme.
One early Hitchcock basement is found in The Lodger. Daisy's
parents spend most of their time in their below-street-level
kitchen, where Daisy's father eagerly reads newspaper accounts
of the Avenger's latest exploits; and their willingness to misread
Drew is partly a class matter. They see themselves as lower
class, a status reflected in their choice of living quarters,
and hence their readiness to think ill of those "above" them.
The wine cellar in Notorious is another sort of basement and
it also reflects issues of class and sex. That it is a wine
cellar marks it as an index of class; that it contains Sebastian's
secret, a secret that he refuses to share with his wife, marks
it as an index of sexuality (or the lack of it); and that the
secret is ultimately connected with the technology of mass murder
marks it as an index of detachment and denial (we have already
seen one murder connected with "wine" from that cellar). A less
malign version of the Hitchcock basement crops up briefly in To
Catch a Thief. After Robie has conferred with his ex-resistance
colleague Bertani, he ducks out to avoid the police, departing
through the restaurant's wine cellar to a boat tied up below; and
again we see the correlation of architecture and class. Bertani
himself, Foussard (the wine steward), and Foussard's daughter,
Danielle, conspire to make their own fortune and let Robie take
the rap for their thievery (Danielle's motives are more sexual
than financial, it should be noted). The point to make, however,
is that the false sense of deprivation which drives them to crime
is reflected by the wine cellar setting: Foussard and Bertani
feel themselves to be "too low"; yet their basement is full of
expensive wines. Other such basements, reflecting similar issues,
are to be found in Psycho (the "fruit cellar" of the Bates house
where Norman keeps his mother's stuffed corpse) and Family Plot
(the secret basement room where Adamson hides his kidnap victims
and where he and his wife are themselves eventually trapped).
Both are discussed at length by Spoto.

Back rooms in Hitchcock, as opposed to basements, serve to
put the focus more on dissimulation, more on the contrast between
fact and facade, than on the contrast between upper and lower
social strata. Thus in The Lodger we see several "backstage"
sequences in which girls take off costumes and wigs (usually
blonde) and then put on street clothes, another sort of costume.
Some of them even don brunette curls as camouflage. In The Man
Who Knew Too Much the terrorists who kidnap Betty Lawrence keep
her in a secret apartment suite, the only entrance to which is
hidden behind the walls of the vestry of the Temple of the Sun.
In Sabotage the "front" of the Verloc place is the Bijou Cinema,
which functions for Mrs. Verloc as financial salvation (hence
the irony that Stevie should be killed while delivering a film
tin), while the "back" is the living quarters. The point here,

I think, is less that someone is trying to obscure sight (as the
terrorists do in The Man Who Knew Too Much) than that Mrs.
Verloc's sense of priorities, her moral sight, is out of
alignment. She quite literally puts money first (we first see
her in the ticket cage [Fig. 5.12]); and accordingly "living,"
specified here as involving her sexual relationship to her husband
and thereafter to Ted, takes the "back" seat. A similar analogy
between back rooms and perverted sexuality can be seen in
Psycho. At the film's beginning Sam refuses to marry Marion
because, among other reasons, he cannot see the two of them living
in the back room of the hardware store he inherited from his debt-
ridden father. As a result Marion steals $40,000 and winds up
at the Bates Motel, where she sees two back rooms--the office
behind the motel desk, an office decorated with Norman's stuffed
birds (emblematic of his relationship with his mother--and her
corpse), and the bathroom of her motel room. The bathroom is
the last room she ever sees, although the fault is not so
much hers as it is Sam's and Norman's. Both men confuse the
fact of love with the appearance of it and both suffer for their
sins.

Two special case uses of architectural motifs relevant to
the reading issue deserve brief mention here. A variant of the
back room motif is the glass-enclosed office. We see this briefly
in the newspaper sequence of The Lodger: there are glass
partitions in the London newsroom that we see. But the earliest
expressive use of the glass-room figure, in my experience, is
in The Man Who Knew Too Much (1934). While Bob Lawrence is
searching the murdered agent's room, looking for the message in
the shaving brush, Jill Lawrence, who was dancing with the agent
at the moment the fatal shot was fired, is taken to the office
of the hotel manager for interrogation, as we discover when Bob
himself is brought down to await interrogation in his turn. Bob
is forced to cool his heels in a glass-walled outer office; and
we only hear snatches of Jill's interrogation as the glass door
to the office proper is repeatedly opened and closed. This is
played almost comically at first. Bob tries his best schoolbook
French and German in an attempt to get word to the British
Consul; and his attempts to get in to see Jill are constantly
frustrated. Suddenly, however, he is handed a note informing
him of the kidnapping of his daughter and warning him not to
talk--at which point he barges through that door and, on a
pretext, gives Jill the note. The thematic implications of all
this are fairly clear: glass cuts off communication and thereby
threatens the life of Betty Lawrence. As a result it is necessary
for Bob to "crash" the glass-wall barrier. (The film's final
shootout escalates the breaking of glass.) Similar correlations
of glassed-in offices with executive (class) isolation,
problematic communications, and the endangerment of life are seen
in To Catch a Thief, Psycho, Marnie, and Topaz. In the
first the office is Bertani's, adjoining the kitchen of his
restaurant, and it is within the glass walls of his office that
Bertani dissemblingly promises to help John Robie track down his

double.  In Psycho the glass office is that of Marion's boss;
and while it is Marion who dissembles in this case, her deception
is prompted, at least in part, by the crassness and dishonesty
of her boss's high-spending client.  Cassidy places himself both
above Marion (as he leans on her desk) and apart from her (as
he goes into her boss's air-conditioned office).  The glass room
in Topaz recalls that of The Man Who Knew Too Much in that
the glass doors of the florist's walk-in refrigerator, behind
which Dubois and Devereaux scheme to photograph Cuban military
documents, block out sound--a motif which is extended in the
following sequence at the Hotel Teresa.  To be sure, one could
argue that glass encourages rather than hinders vision; but in
To Catch a Thief, Psycho, and Marnie, at least, the glass
is in some sense opaque.  Thus we get the egg splattering across
the glass in Thief (Fig. 5.13); the glass wall of the Psycho
office is tinted (which associates it with the dark glasses of
the cop whom we see later in the film); and executive offices
in Marnie, both Strutt's and Ward's office at Rutland & Co.,
feature pebbled glass doors and/or partitions.
     In general, then, we can say that glass in Hitchcock
represents a tenuous and ultimately false sort of orderliness
or emotional security--false for being predicated on the erection
and maintenance of barriers between people:  barriers to sight,
to sound, barriers ultimately to the communication and
comprehension necessary to seeing the world whole.  Care must
be taken, though, not to overgeneralize.  In The Birds there
are moments when glass serves a more positive but related
function.  Specifically, there are two instances in The Birds
when Melanie Daniels risks her life, quite intuitively and
immediately, to go to the aid of others (during the bird attack
on the school and, only moments later, during the attack on the
restaurant and service station).  In both instances glass
enclosures appear (the white station wagon by the side of the
road, the phone booth), as if out of nowhere, to provide her
momentary shelter.  The shelter in both cases, however, is
temporary and fragile, and both need to be left behind before
the film concludes.
     At which point we have already touched upon the second
special case architectural motif:  automobiles and trains.  As
enclosures, cars and trains in Hitchcock carry ominous
implications.  Thus a recurrent scene in Hitchcock involves a
car driving at high speeds on a coastal or mountain road
(Suspicion, Notorious, To Catch a Thief, North by
Northwest, The Birds, Family Plot).  Sometimes the high
speeds evidence naiveté (as in To Catch a Thief when Grace Kelly
drives), sometimes cynicism (as in Notorious when an inebriated
Ingrid Bergman is behind the wheel).  In Family Plot the speed
sequence is initiated by external influence:  Maloney drains the
brake fluid from Lumley's car.  But in nearly every case excessive
speeds are correlated with visual distortion and/or subjectivity
(the montage tends to accelerate into close-ups and point-of-view
shots) and potential death (we repeatedly see automobile tires

careening along the edge of a cliff). Trains represent a similar
sort of danger. Train passengers, like car passengers, are often
trapped in their vehicles. In The Lady Vanishes Iris and
Gilbert et al. become sitting ducks when their railroad car is
sidetracked and assaulted. In both The 39 Steps and North
by Northwest the protagonists are pursued by police and only
ingenuity allows them to escape capture despite the constricted
hallways and sleeping compartments. And in Strangers on a Train
Guy allows the constraints of train travel to further his
relationship with Bruno: the dining car is full so Guy dines
with Bruno in the latter's compartment.

All of which said, trains and cars are also vehicles, capable
of movement, and it's by taking that possibility to heart that
Hitchcock protagonists are often enabled to recover their
identity. Thus both Hannay and Roger Thornhill use trains as
a means of discovery as well as escape. Rather than flee from
they travel to someplace, in search of knowledge. Cars can
also function positively. A recurrent Hitchcock ending has hero
and heroine driving off together and their togetherness is
significant. Barriers to personal warmth have been overcome (as
in Suspicion, Notorious, Marnie, and The Birds) and a
unity of decorous movement replaces the disunified close-up
decoupage of the speed sequences.

One final iconographic system can be related to the
isolation/fixation theme (and hence to the reading theme) in
Hitchcock: that of geography. This can be complicated. To begin
with, we are discussing a sort of large-scale iconography.
Geography generally provides a background, almost constantly
present and significant, but not obviously dominant. Only on
set occasions are we shown a long establishing shot which can
foreground geography. And in some films, Suspicion
particularly, relevant geographical factors are less shown than
alluded to (we know that Lina was raised in the provinces but
the mise-en-scène is constrained and stylized: we never get a
long establishing shot of her country village). Secondly, the
significance of geographic motifs is often a reflection of the
dramatic development of the characters who occupy the space.
Consequently a recurrent Hitchcock opening or credit sequence
will feature long shot views of a city, via moving camera and
dissolves, and in most cases the implications are negative.
Cities can dehumanize and disfigure, as is evidenced in the
opening sequences of Shadow of a Doubt, Notorious, I
Confess, Strangers on a Train, The Wrong Man, To Catch
a Thief, North by Northwest, Psycho, The Birds, and
Frenzy: in every case long shot city-scape mise-en-scène is
immediately correlated with sexual deviance, familial disunity,
or the objectification of human beings. So we seldom see faces
(they are either too distant or absent from the frame altogether)
or the faces we do see are generally cold and grim (e.g., the
corpse-like visage of Uncle Charlie in Shadow of a Doubt, the
marching soldiers in Topaz). In other words, cities can isolate
people from one another and the isolation has its visual referent

in the countless box-like buildings or windows so frequently seen
in these sequences.
Another geographical motif, likewise raising the isolation
issue, involves country houses or mansions, often seen as solitary
dwellings in otherwise empty landscapes. Early examples of this,
reflecting also on issues of religion and class, are the Crofter's
cottage and Professor Jordon's country house in The 39 Steps.
Mansions similar to the Jordon mansion, and occupied by equally
elegant yet duplicitous characters, are to be found in
Spellbound (the "Green Manors" sanitorium for the sake of which
Dr. Murchison commits murder), Notorious (Sebastian's mansion),
North by Northwest (Vandamm's glass-walled country house), and
Topaz (the "safe" house occupied by the Russian defector).
Other mansions, though occupied by less reprehensible characters,
are seen in Rebecca (Manderley) and To Catch a Thief. And
we see less sumptuous but no less isolated dwellings in Psycho
(the Bates house) and The Birds (the Brenner house). In every
case geographic isolation both results from and reflects an
inability or unwillingness to see the world whole; and in most
such instances (Topaz, again, being the exception) characters
are forced by ultimately benevolent circumstances to leave their
isolation, however temptingly secure that isolation might seem.
Thus Manderley finally burns down in Rebecca. Thus Ingrid
Bergman leaves Green Manors to marry Gregory Peck in
Spellbound; and in Notorious she leaves Sebastian's house
with Cary Grant. Thus Cary Grant is forced to come down off his
mountain top in To Catch a Thief and at film's end he returns
but followed by his wife- and mother-in-law-to-be. He is not
the "lone wolf" he thought he was. The benevolence in Psycho
is less personal (in that no specific character in the film is
better for it) but it is real nevertheless and attends upon the
fact that Norman is finally forced out of his mansion and back
into society where he can be locked up. He will no longer be
able to "stuff" any "birds" and the basic justice of the universe
is evidenced by the fact that "birds," specifically Marion and
Lila "Crane" of "Phoenix," are the primary agents of his downfall.
A similarly problematic benevolence is at work in The
Birds. The standard view of the film is that the bird attacks
are ultimately senseless and unmotivated and represent the basic
absurdity underlying human existence. Ultimately, however, the
absurdist view hinges on three incidents: the attack on the
farmer, the second attack on the school children, and the attack
which kills Annie Hayworth. All other attacks can be correlated
with specific instances of human coldness or superficiality.
There are, we should remark, only three deaths in the film, and
the second, that of the loudmouthed salesman, represents no
problem: he blows himself up for not paying close enough
attention to the world around him. And ultimately the same can
be said for the only other two victims, Dan Fawcett and Annie
Hayworth. Both live alone and both are in some sense isolated
from their communities, Fawcett in his farmhouse (which we see
in extreme long shot), Annie Hayworth in her cottage, which

is generally hidden from view by the schoolhouse which stands
between her place and the town.  In both cases, furthermore, death
is associated with sexlessness.  Fawcett sleeps alone in a double
bed and Annie's presence in Bodega Bay is predicated on
maintaining a sexless relationship with Mitch, her former lover.
We can thus see her pupils as surrogate children and the most
fruitful action she can take is to die saving Cathy.

   Ultimately, then, the interpretive crux in The Birds comes
down to the attack on the schoolhouse; and here the iconography
points towards a sounder reading.  The school, as Hitchcock frames
it (the camera almost always pointing away from the town so as
to isolate the building against the hills, thus obliterating our
view of Annie's house) is a visual double of the Bates house in
Psycho:  both are associated with children, isolation, and
perversity.  The perversity in The Birds is of a lesser order;
but it is evidenced by the nonsense song sung by the children
and by their real and oddly unanimous unwillingness to leave
school when Annie tells them they are going home for the day.
One senses that their home lives are unpleasant and lonely (as
Cathy Brenner's is evidently lonely:  hence her eagerness that
Melanie stay for the party) and the effect of the attack is to
drive the children out of the school and back to the town where
the issue of parent/child relationships (a central concern
throughout the film, particularly in respect to Mitch and Melanie)
can be dealt with (Fig. 5.14).  A similar logic can be seen to
underlie the last bird attack, on the Brenner house.  Mitch does
his best to read the pattern of the attacks and decides, wrongly
it turns out, to board up the house and wait it out.  The birds
then attack in waves, the second of which finds Melanie isolated
and endangered in Cathy's bedroom (that it is a little girl's
room is itself ultimately hopeful:  Melanie in some sense returns
to her girlhood and then finds a new mother, Lydia, to replace
the one who deserted her).  Finally, the point sinks in:  for
Melanie's sake and for the sake of everyone, Mitch decides to
leave, to go back to the city, back to civilization which
ultimately provides the proper context in Hitchcock for human
relationships--despite the fact that cities are themselves
difficult places to live in.  The problem of reading is a
quintessentially human problem for Hitchcock, and a problem which
therefore requires a human context for its genuine solution.

   A variant of the isolated house is the isolated (provincial)
town or city.  In some instances this involves vacation spots
(a Swiss ski resort in The Man Who Knew Too Much, a Tyrolean
resort in The Lady Vanishes, the French Riviera in To Catch
a Thief--we might even include the small-town amusement park
of Strangers on a Train here) and vacationers in Hitchcock are
usually trying to avoid something, often having to do with
sexuality.  More commonly, the provincial city is the character's
home town and serves to reflect the character's almost willful
ignorance of the world outside.  The best example of this, of
course, is found in Shadow of a Doubt and the movement of the
film, both in its general plot action and in its mise-en-scène,

is to call provinciality, particularly as manifested in sexual
relationships, into question.  Of course, provinciality is not
the only attitude undercut in the film; the city seen in the
opening sequence is equally as dead and disspirited as Santa
Rosa.  The film's general fable thus becomes a fall from innocence
to experience but the fall is nearly overwhelming: hence the
ironic conclusion with Charlie and Jack, the film's couple,
standing on the steps of the church while the pastor inside
preaches a glowing funeral oration for Charlie's murderous same-
name uncle.

I Confess presents a special case of the provincial town
which serves as a large scale icon of isolation.  At one level,
certainly, Quebec is a city like any other Hitchcock city.  If
anything, the opening sequence emphasizes its "cityness" by slowly
tracking in, behind the credits, from extreme long shot to long
shot, with our focus kept constantly on a fortresslike castle
which overlooks and dominates the city-scape.  The correlation
between cityness and isolation of people from each other is made
remarkably explicit midway through the film when Ruth and Father
Logan meet aboard a ferryboat to discuss their relationship.
Ruth pleads on behalf of their love affair and Logan assures her
of the sincerity of his vocation; and as he pulls away from her,
shifting his stance at the rail, the fortress from the credit
sequence appears directly between them, as if it were the barrier
keeping them apart.  The fortress is further equated with Father
Logan's cold single-mindedness by an association of Logan with
church architecture (we first see him framed in the glass door
of the rectory) and by the provincial synonomy of Quebec
architecture generally:  thus Logan = architecture = fortress.
In other words, the church is his fortress, within which the
ex-soldier retreats from the world at large.  Nevertheless,
Quebec's insular status, as a French-speaking city in an English-
speaking continent (Hitchcock plays a good deal on the class/
language correlation), reinforces the closed-in, small-town
quality which Hitchcock's treatment generally accords it.  Logan
is no less entrapped by his prejudices than are the members of
the courtroom mob who demand that he be stripped of his collar:
both associate righteousness with sexlessness.

One final small town deserves comment:  Bodega Bay.  Most
critics of The Birds treat the town as a neutral if not bucolic
setting, different from San Francisco in kind rather than degree.
But this rings false for reasons both extrinsic and intrinsic
to the film.  In the context of this discussion we can see how
completely uncharacteristic it would be for Hitchcock to treat
Bodega Bay differently from any of his other provincial townships.
Accordingly, it becomes a critical imperative to look carefully
at Bodega Bay, as a "function" in The Birds, to see if Hitchcock
runs true to form in his treatment of it and whether we should
follow form in the significance which we might therefore import
to it.  And run true to form he does.

I have already discussed the questionable relationship
between the town and its school.  There are two other factors,

one embedded in iconography, the other expressed largely through
dialogue, which support an alternative reading. The first
involves the "cage" motif which dominates the opening sequence--
both in the visuals (the San Francisco pet shop full of cages)
and the dialogue (Mitch, a lawyer, talks about putting Melanie
in a cage). This cage motif is picked up in the Bodega Bay
general store where Melanie asks for directions. The storekeeper
stands behind a cage, in the post office corner of the room, and
behind him are post office boxes, cages of another sort.
Furthermore, when he stands with Melanie on the porch, to point
out the Brenner place across the bay, we see the half-glassed
door to the store which features a wanted poster (again, the
equation of people and cages) next to a notice about dog licenses
(Fig. 5.15).

I take this correlation of people, cages, and animals to
be ominous on the face of it--even if at this early point in the
film we cannot tie this ominousness specifically to Bodega Bay
as a whole. But it takes Hitchcock only a few more minutes of
screen time to tie the thematic knot. Thus Melanie and the
storekeeper go back into the store where Melanie asks the name
of Mitch's sister. The storekeeper is unsure, quarrels with a
disembodied voice emanating from behind a row of boxed goods,
and then suggests "Alice." Melanie presses him--she needs the
exact name--and he suggests that Melanie go ask the school
teacher. When she talks to Annie Hayworth only a few moments
later, however, she is informed that Mitch's sister's name is
Cathy. And Annie explains the storekeeper's confusion by
reference to the fact that the mail never gets delivered to the
right place: as postmaster and storekeeper he may be the most
frequently visited man in town, quite literally the center of
the community, but he doesn't know who lives where. It all adds
up. Bodega Bay may look like (may want to look like) a town of
friendly neighbors, but that is not the state of affairs. Most
of the people we see (other than children) are transients
(including Melanie and, to a degree, Mitch) and the few natives
we do see are self-serving provincials: the bar keeper is worried
about law suits, the ornithologist spouts ornithology in the face
of the facts, the boat skipper refuses to help Mitch mobilize
the town, and the local policeman is laughable in his skepticism.
The irony is clear. The birds flock together when, by natural
instinct, they shouldn't; and the people refuse to "flock" in
any positive sense (some few cower together at the rear of the
restaurant) though by all ethical standards "flocking" ought to
be a natural state of human affairs. Thus Hitchcock, via his
special effect birds, makes them get together, almost in spite
of themselves. It is therefore necessary that Melanie and the
Brenners leave Bodega Bay behind; and hence the appropriateness
of the film's concluding image, which has them leaving that Bodega
Bay house and driving into the bird dominated distance (Fig.
5.16). Bodega Bay is still visible on the horizon (as a final
reminder of the danger of isolation) but by accepting

vulnerability (to each other and to the birds) Melanie and the
Brenners embrace an essential quality of civilization.
     One further geographical motif remains to be considered in
connection with the vision issue, and the concluding image
of The Birds is an instance of it:   persons or people isolated
in nature or space.  In beginning this discussion of geographical
iconography and significance I pointed out the necessity for
keeping in mind the relationship of character to environment in
determining the thematic value of geography in Hitchcock.  Thus
it is possible for opening city shots to be negative in their
connotations, for being associated with characters who sag
into big-city facelessness; while concluding city shots, as
in Sabotage and Marnie, can be positive, for showing us
characters who accept the vulnerability of human existence.
     A similar sort of fine tuning is necessary in discussing
the "isolation in nature" motif.  To be too isolated in nature,
to be settled into it by means of a domicile or mansion, is either
to deny one's own vulnerability or to attempt to increase the
vulnerability of others (as when the isolated character is one
like Jordon in The 39 Steps or Vandamm in North by Northwest
who works as an agent of a foreign power).  And yet a recurrent
scene in Hitchcock has a central character (or characters) at
hazard in an open landscape or, in special cases, on roof tops.
The classic examples here involve the two chase-on-the-heath
scenes in The 39 Steps and the crop-dusting and Mt. Rushmore
scenes in North by Northwest.  Both Hannay and Roger Thornhill
initially represent a trivial, sexually cynical, city-bound
lifestyle (though Hannay, a Canadian rancher, is only temporarily
a city dweller) and to a certain extent their exile to nature
is an appropriate comeuppance.  Yet in both cases the character
willingly takes fortune into his own hands, assumes some real
measure of responsibility, for himself if not for others, and
this acceptance of vulnerability finds visual expression in long
shots of characters (Hannay on the heath; Thornhill in the
cornfield) against the background of barren geography.  This
acceptance of vulnerability, a specifically visual vulnerability
(both can be seen), pays off in each case.  Hannay's pursuers
have difficulty negotiating the landscape (as if the landscape
were on Hannay's side) and Thornhill is saved by the petrol truck
which appears, as if out of nowhere, to cover him like a
protective parent.  Furthermore, acceptance of legal/political
vulnerability results in (and foreshadows) a corollary acceptance
of sexual vulnerability.  Thus Hannay and Thornhill each finds
himself at hazard in nature a second time and both are accompanied
on the second occasion by a woman.  In the earlier film the woman
is reluctant at first (for being married to a politician); but
in both cases male/female teamwork eventually has positive
emotional and political results.  Pamela thus helps Hannay to
unmask Mr. Memory.  And while the entertainer dies as a result
(a death Hitchcock invests with genuine dignity) the defense
secrets he carries are not allowed to leave the country and

endanger peace. Likewise, it's teamwork between Eve and Roger which prevents Vandamm from taking another batch of secrets, hidden in a piece of statuary, out of another country. And this willingness to take political risks has its pay-off when Thornhill pulls Eve up off the cliff and into their nuptial railway berth.

A similar willingness to accept vulnerability and responsibility can be seen to motivate isolation in nature or isolation in space sequences in Spellbound, To Catch a Thief, and Marnie. The Spellbound sequence ties the vulnerability theme and the reading theme neatly together. In order to break the code of John Ballantine's amnesia, Constance Petersen insists that they return to the scene of Dr. Edwardes's murder, a Vermont ski slope. They then ski the same slope, straight toward the edge of a cliff, and the alternating long shot/close-up decoupage simultaneously emphasizes vulnerability in space (as they approach cliff's edge) and the psychic vulnerability which attends upon their attempt to relive and reread Ballantine's past. Significantly, it is John's psychic breakthrough, his "reseeing" of the childhood accident, which then allows him to pull Constance and himself off their skis before they go over the edge. In To Catch a Thief the isolation motif is architectural as well as geographical—but, like the corresponding scene in Spellbound, it involves an implicit acknowledgement of sexual dependency (Robie needs the help of Francie, and that of her mother and Hughson as well, to distract the attention of the police while he waits for his double on the roof of the mansion) and a corollary willingness to take physical and visual risks in space (when he chases Danielle he is caught in police spotlights [Fig. 5.17]). The isolation sequence in Marnie likewise involves the correlation of psychic and spatial vulnerability. During the hunt sequence Marnie's fear of blood is triggered by the death of the fox and by the red hunting jackets. Her response is to spur Forio to a gallop and set out pell-mell through the fields. To be sure, Marnie does not voluntarily choose to isolate herself from the other hunters in the way that Robie chooses to hunt down his double across the mansion roof. But her willingness to stay at the Rutland mansion and participate in the hunt, to act out her role as Mark's wife despite her desire to flee, is analogous to John Ballantine's willingness to return to the ski slope. Both would rather avoid reality and are to be praised for accepting the vulnerability imaged by their placement in the landscape.

To summarize: "reading" is a central metaphor in Hitchcock, writ large in recurrent patterns of narrative action and further specified in and through an iconography of visual distortion and disorder. Looking at causality in narrative terms, we can say that misreading in Hitchcock results from some form of interpersonal isolation: characters isolate themselves by their denial of human relationships and in their denial they isolate others—and this opposition applies equally well to personal and political motives or circumstances. In iconographic terms

causality finds expression in several complementary sets of
symbolic associations:  isolation can be correlated with clothing,
with furnishings, with architecture, and with geography, though
in each case the iconography is such that characters can deny
or reverse its negative implications.  Image and theme are thus
fused in a complex economy of expression which bodies forth
Hitchcock's dynamic vision of both the dangers and the
possibilities of human existence.


THE DOUBLE FIGURE
     As generally employed in Hitchcock criticism, the "wrong
man" motif involves an implicit corollary which has both narrative
and iconographic consequences.  This corollary motif is the
"double" or "mirror" figure, by which characters are encouraged
to "read" or "reread" themselves in or through their opposites.
     I have already referred to one species of this character/
narrative trope in remarking upon the similarity of action
evidenced by misread and misleading characters:  to a certain
degree they are "mirror" images of each other.  Classical examples
of this character parallelism are the two Charlies in Shadow
of a Doubt and Guy and Bruno in Strangers on a Train.  Indeed,
Hitchcock usually suggests such a parallelism by means of mise-en-
scène or decoupage long before it becomes explicit in dialogue
or plot action.  Thus in Strangers on a Train we begin with
parallel sequences, of Guy and Bruno's feet respectively, as each
departs his taxi and boards the train, and the parallelism of
activity is further stressed by crosscutting.  Once the two have
met (their feet touch beneath a table [Fig. 5.18]), their
interconnectedness is further reinforced by jewelry (both carry
icons of questionable sexual relationships), by use of the shot/
reverse shot figure, by means of "rhyming" shadows, and by means
of profile two shots with the men facing--mirroring--each other
across a table.  And implicit in all this, at least as critics
have usually characterized the implication, is a "transference
of guilt" from the apparently evil character to the conventionally
innocent one:  hence the frequent critical discussions of the
original sin theme in Hitchcock and hence as well his reputation
as ironist and prankster.  If guilt can be transferred between
characters it can also be transferred to audiences who seem to
revel in a complicity which they never overtly acknowledge.  The
thematic pay-off, then, for viewers who get the point of the film,
is the chastening acceptance of their own capacity for evil as
it is mirrored in the activity of Hitchcock's characters.
     I do not wish to suggest that the "complicity" theme is
nonexistent or unimportant in Hitchcock--but it is clearly less
central than some would have us believe.  For example, the
acceptance of guilt is generally a first step rather than the
last.  It is a predicate of action (as in Spellbound and
Marnie) rather than a product.  And often explicit
acknowledgements of guilt on the part of focal characters are

lacking altogether. Rather, it is frequently the case that
characters take actions which are consonant with an increased
sense of personal and social responsibility without ever finding
it necessary to accept direct culpability for actual, already
committed sins. Strangers on a Train is a case in point. Guy
never acknowledges or accepts the proposition that his guilt in
the matter of Miriam's death is equal to Bruno's. He rather
accepts the fact that he appears more guilty than Bruno and
therefore endeavors to establish the legibility of his innocence.
And there is no necessity within the film that he accept the
accusation. If the film questions anything it is precisely the
ready attribution of guilt. Bruno attributes to Guy a desire
to kill his own wife (Guy's sin here is that he does not reject
the exchange-of-murders proposition explicitly enough: because
he doesn't take Bruno or life as seriously as he should); and
Ann and her sister each attribute the murder to Guy in a way which
dehumanizes them both (Barbara gets her comeuppance at the party
sequence when Bruno "strangles" her). More significantly, it
is the willingness to accompany attribution with punishment that
allows the police to shoot into the amusement park crowd and kill
the merry-go-round operator. As a result, the ride spins out
of control and eventually off its axis, injuring a great many
people, when the little old man tries to put on the brakes.

Indeed, we are given opportunity ourselves to attribute false
motives to Guy when he goes to the Anthony mansion to tell Bruno's
father about his mad son. The treatment of Guy's entering the
Anthony house is sufficiently ambiguous--Guy sneaks in with a
flashlight and Bruno's map--to allow the attribution. But in
retrospect he does nothing inconsistent with his eventually
professed intention to tell the truth about Bruno. His sneaking
into the house can be credited to caution: in case he's being
followed (he wouldn't want to ring doorbells or call attention
to the house by having the lights turned on) or in case Bruno
hadn't left (a reasonable fear, as it turns out, for Bruno hadn't
left as Guy had asked him to: Bruno rather waits for Guy in his
father's bed). And the moment when Guy stops outside the bedroom
door to shift the gun, Bruno's gun, from one pocket to another
can be directly related to his intention to expose Bruno. The
gun, like his own lighter, is an icon of guilt which Guy can
present as evidence of the truth of his story. It is reasonable
that he would check his evidence before going in to lay out his
case (just as Manny Balestrero checks the insurance policy in
his coat pocket before entering the offices of Associated Life
in The Wrong Man). The point of Strangers on a Train, at
least as far as Guy is concerned, has little to do with whether
or not Guy accepts guilt for killing Miriam. It is whether or
not he takes Bruno, and the chaos which Bruno represents,
seriously and acts in responsible accord with that seriousness,
as he does when he tries to tell Mr. Anthony of Bruno's illness;
as he does when he turns his back on Bruno and walks away, despite
the fact that Bruno holds a gun on him; as he does during the

final fight sequence when he again accepts vulnerability by turning his back on Bruno--this time in order to rescue the little boy.

None of which prevents us from comprehending the parallels of action and character which Hitchcock establishes in Strangers on a Train. But to see the degree to which Guy and Bruno mirror each other in their capacity for irresponsible, self-serving behavior, a capacity verging on madness in Bruno's case, is to provide the very context in which Guy's actions gain positive significance. To be sure, Guy's actions are self-serving, to the extent that he is trying to clear himself of a murder charge. But, as is often the case when one of Hitchcock's central characters assumes a responsible human stance, service to self and service to others become one and the same. To establish his own innocence it becomes necessary for Guy to establish Bruno's guilt, something which the police are unable or unwilling to do. Maintaining social order thus becomes a personal responsibility (it is the refusal to take it personally that condemns the judge we see at the Senator's party). If Guy doesn't stop him Bruno will no doubt kill again (like Norman in Psycho or Rusk in Frenzy).

The irony, however, is that so many people have to die or suffer injury before Bruno can be stopped. And the film provides little evidence that the society within it has benefited from Guy's experience. The police treat the whole thing as just one more bit of work to be cleared up and they let it go at that. So what the film lacks is less a "transference of guilt" than a "transference of responsibility." Indeed, the film's conclusion, Guy and Ann on a train, denying a human relationship when they get up and walk away from another "stranger," evidences how easy it is to fall back into old habits. Nevertheless, the point to make here is simply that the transference of guilt formula only represents one potentiality of the double motif in Hitchcock. To look for it at the expense of other such potentialities is only to invite disappointment.

The significance of doubles in Hitchcock, both positive and negative, can be better understood by reference to the several varieties of the double figure which we find in Hitchcock's films. The most benign and hopeful sort of doubling in Hitchcock is sexual, the pairing of male and female.[12] Such pairings are so obvious and seem so obligatorily conventional that we tend to overlook the significance which Hitchcock assigns to them. Very seldom does Hitchcock rely solely on convention to motivate sexual relationships in his movies. Rather, it is generally the case that the central male and female characters are both variations on a similar theme--they are alike in some crucial and thematically relevant way.

In The 39 Steps, to take an early example, the central male and female characters share a crucial trait, an unwillingness to believe the crazy story about the 39 steps. Thus Hannay refuses, in a mildly sarcastic manner, to grant credit to the

woman he brought home from the Music Hall when she tells him she's
a spy. His first impression, indeed, is that she is an actress
(= prostitute?). Only when, at her urging, he looks down at the
street below to see the men who followed her to his flat does
he believe her story. The pattern then repeats itself with
Pamela. She refuses to believe Hannay, on two different
occasions, and again a sexual motive is involved (his first move
is to kiss her, so as to hide his face from the police, which
she, being married, resents). And it is only when she "looks
down" from the second floor landing in the hotel where she and
Hannay spend the night as "newlyweds," to see (and hear) Jordon's
henchmen reporting in, that she believes Hannay's story in her
turn. A common belief in imminent danger shakes them both out
of complacency and binds them more strongly together than the
handcuffs which had literally made them one being during the chase
sequence (and which Hannay still wears in the final shot).

A similar pairing, raising similar issues of sexuality and
cynicism, is at the thematic heart of Notorious. Cary Grant
and Ingrid Bergman spend the whole film both adoring and
distrusting each other, neither willing to take full
responsibility for their love affair, although Devlin seems even
less willing than Alicia. In neither case, however, is it a
matter of pure cynicism: both have been hurt in love before,
Devlin with other women, Alicia with her father, and it is not
until Devlin is on the verge of taking another assignment that
he finally comes to his senses and rereads Alicia's malaise as
something other than a mere hangover. In fact, he had believed
in her all along, had defended her repeatedly when she was not
present to hear him, had refused as much as possible to
collaborate in the scheme to prostitute her to Sebastian (hence
his request for the transfer), but he had simply lacked the
courage to openly acknowledge his feelings for her until it was
almost too late. Indeed, his distrust is almost as deadly to
Alicia as the poisoned coffee Sebastian provides her. It is
therefore appropriate that Devlin's love should be the necessary
antidote. He tells her that he "couldn't see straight" and looks
repeatedly into her eyes as he helps her out of her bedroom and
down the stairs. Similar sexual pairings are to be found in Rear
Window, To Catch a Thief, North by Northwest, The Birds,
and Marnie.

Another version of the sexual pair in Hitchcock involves
characters who complement each other by being in some sense
opposites. An early example of this is the Daisy/Drew pair in
The Lodger: he is dark, upper class, and secretive while she
is blonde, lower class, and entirely open in her dealings with
people. As a fashion model she is well aware that appearance
does not necessarily match up to reality and hence her ability
to see through the circumstantial evidence against Drew. A
similar upper class/lower class pairing can be seen in Rebecca.
Lina and Johnny in Suspicion are also opposites of a sort.
He's the playboy, she's the spinster. And yet each represents

for the other an essential quality that is missing from life. She wants to be sexual and he wants to be emotionally honest. As opposites they thus mirror and complement each other. The central pair in Torn Curtain is an interesting special case. Paul Newman's loyalty to himself and his career is so great that he will risk destroying his relationship with the Julie Andrews character, risking the lives of the members of an East German underground group along the way, in order to get information that will enable him to regain his position as a government research scientist. Anything rather than be a university teacher. Sarah, on the other hand, refuses to look out for herself. Thus she follows Michael Armstrong to East Germany and agrees to work with him for the Communist government; it's only when she is asked to divulge defense secrets that she refuses to go along with Michael's defection. Again, she puts others first. That she should go to such lengths for Michael is one reason that the film seems cold and centerless: he doesn't really seem worth it.

Far less common than the sexual pairings in Hitchcock are the pairings of the criminal and his double. The number of Hitchcock films which key fairly exclusively on this character alignment are relatively few. The Lodger uses this theme (among several); and it can be seen at work in varying degrees of centrality in Young and Innocent, Spellbound, I Confess, Rear Window, To Catch a Thief, The Wrong Man, and North by Northwest. But only in Shadow of a Doubt, Rope, Strangers on a Train, Psycho, Frenzy, and Family Plot is this the dominant configuration. Most of the misread man films are similar, to be sure, but in many of those the parallelism of criminal to victim is weak because the real criminal plays only a peripheral role in the film. Such is the case in The Lodger (we never see The Avenger), in Young and Innocent (the murderer is only seen at beginning and end), in Spellbound (we don't know that Murchison killed Edwardes until the final minutes), in To Catch a Thief (we don't know that Danielle is Robie's double till the very end), and in The Wrong Man (we are never sure whether the second man committed the crimes for which Manny was arrested [Fig. 5.19]). Furthermore, direct transference of guilt is fairly limited even in those films which play most thoroughly on this sort of character parallelism. Rope probably represents the purest example of the transference of guilt pattern: the two (homosexual) students act out the Nietzschean theories of their professor--but the film is unavailable for viewing and can therefore play little role here. In Shadow of a Doubt the attribution of guilt is far less certain. Charlie longs for a savior who will shake things up in Santa Rosa and her uncle seems the answer to her prayer. But she never theorizes about killing people, as Cadell does in Rope. It is her father who plans the perfect murder. Yet for Mr. Newton it is clearly a Hitchcockian pastime. Young Charlie's guilt, such as it is, hinges less on her desires per se (though

her desires are called into question) than on her reaction to
her uncle once she realizes (a realization which comes from
reading newspapers in the town library) what he's done. She hates
him, wants him to leave, and threatens to kill him if he doesn't
go. In this she seems even more culpable than Guy in Strangers
on a Train. Charlie clearly means what she says, and eventually
carries out the threat though she does so in self-defense. Guy,
on the other hand, while avowing that he "could strangle" Miriam
does so in the heat of anger and out of Miriam's presence. In
neither case do we get a complete and self-acknowledged
transference or acceptance of guilt; and, as is true of Strangers
on a Train, the transference of guilt is less important to both
films than a "transference" of knowledge.

Psycho and Family Plot also involve parallel characters
(or sets of characters) yet in neither case do we get a classic
transference of guilt. The key to Psycho is the relationship
between Marion Crane and Norman Bates. Both are associated with
enclosures and entrapment (Marion's flat is nearly identical to
the room she eventually takes at the Bates Motel); both are
influenced by the emotional legacy of dead mothers (Marion longs
for sexual respectability; the "Mrs. Bates" fantasized by Norman
to replace the mother he killed out of jealousy likewise insists
on a rigorously puritan sexual morality); and both are associated
with birds (Marion is a "Crane"; Norman stuffs birds as a hobby).
But in spite of the similarities we never associate Marion's guilt
with Norman's. She is in no sense responsible for the death of
Norman's mother. Rather, Marion sees Norman as a mirror of sorts,
both visually (the "mirror image" two shots, often with a mirror
or reflecting glass between them) and dramatically. As they talk
in Norman's bird decorated office, and she sees the fantasy of
her longed for "private island" made real in Norman's oppressive
solitude, she comes to the understanding that her own problems,
both sexual (vis-à-vis Sam) and social (vis-à-vis the money she's
stolen) have to be faced up to: she cannot run away from either
without losing her identity. Thus she decides to return to
Phoenix and she uses her own name when saying goodnight to Norman.

It is important to remark on what happens here. Marion
"identifies" with Norman only to the extent that she recognizes
an analogy between his situation and her own. And by recognizing
that aspect of herself in him she gains the knowledge necessary
to lessen the degree of their similarity by changing her
situation.[13] She will not be like Norman if she can help
it. Madness lies exactly in the opposite direction, in the
overidentification of one personality with another; and it's that
madness, incarnate in Norman/Mrs. Bates, that finally does Marion
in. As viewers, however, we are kept--by means of editing and
the visual obstruction provided by the plastic shower
curtain--from recognizing "Mother" as Norman. Through the rest
of the film, then, we sympathize with Norman and his attempts
to cover up for his mother--and only in retrospect does this
"identification" carry an implication of complicity. Furthermore,

to feel sympathy for Norman is not to desire the death of
Arbogast or Lila. What is really horrifying about Psycho is
not the magnitude of events nor our complicity in them, but the
commonplace nature of their origins. The Bates house is far less
bizarre than we might have imagined and Norman's madness is rooted
in nothing more unusual than a frightened boy's love for his
mother.

Family Plot displays a similar pattern of action and
implication. Like Norman Bates, Arthur Adamson (né Rainbird)
is "deserted" by his mother before the film begins (Norman's
mother takes a lover; Adamson's mother gives him up for adoption
to protect the family name) and the result in both cases is
violence (Norman kills his mother, her lover, and others; Adamson
kills his foster parents) and the confusion of identity (Norman
dresses up like Mother; Adamson "buries" his childhood self, Eddie
Shoebridge, while Blanche and Lumley try to uncover the Rainbird
heir--who is Adamson). The point is, however, that Blanche, who
functions as Adamson's double in the film, is not at all
implicated in Adamson's original act of violence. If anything,
Blanche almost becomes (like Marion in Psycho) a victim of
violence. Adamson fears that Blanche and Lumley are on to his
kidnapping racket and is willing to kill to eliminate the threat.
Once again we have the double figure, then, but without a
transference of guilt. The figure functions, rather, to raise
issues of similarity and likeness, to set forth a continuum of
actions and motives (as in Psycho) and the figure does its job
if we come to understand those traits shared by Adamson and
Blanche (and by the two couples generally) and those traits, like
the willingness to kill, which they don't share. It is far
more a matter of knowledge than guilt.

No doubt Frenzy, among Hitchcock's later films, best
embodies the transference of guilt pattern.[14] Richard Blaney
(R. B.) and Bob Rusk (B. R.) are close friends, one divorced,
the other never-married. More importantly, both are "frenetic"
vis-à-vis sexuality, and they share the same sexual partners:
Blaney's ex-wife (whom Rusk rapes/murders) and Babs, Blaney's
bar-maid girl friend (who also falls victim to Rusk's apparent
gentility). Blaney's "frenzy," however, involves publicly
expressed anger towards his ex-wife's sexual cynicism (she runs
a matrimonial bureau); and it seems clear that his habit of
expressing his anger serves as a safety valve. It is only when
denied the freedom to be publicly angry (as when he is convicted
of the necktie murders and shut away) that he finally allows that
anger to get out of hand: he escapes from custody and "kills"
Rusk with a jack handle. It is only a Hitchcockian benevolence
that the "Rusk" he kills is already dead, is in fact Rusk's latest
victim. Rusk himself, on the other hand, exhibits a behavior
pattern exactly opposite to that of Blaney. Where Blaney is
"public" in expressing his "frenzy," Rusk is "private." Once
again we see the correlation between privacy and perversity (hence
the ominousness of that long tracking shot from Rusk's door, down

the stairway and out of the building--the camera seems "sinful"
for withdrawing).  And to the extent that Blaney becomes private
in the same sense (the last scene takes place in Rusk's flat)
we do have a "transference of guilt."

Even here, however, there is a mediating factor which short
circuits the transference of guilt, if not from Rusk to Blaney,
at least from Blaney to the audience.  That factor is Inspector
Oxford--who increasingly occupies the focal position in the film.
Oxford thus becomes a third term in the film's thematic matrix.
Like Blaney and Rusk he is associated with food or appetite
(Blaney is a bartender; Rusk is a fruit wholesaler; Oxford's wife
is a gourmet cook); and also like the other two men he is
associated with some sort of sexual disfunction:  Mrs. Oxford
complains that he cannot stay awake at night.  Oxford differs
from the other two men, however, in maintaining an appropriate
balance of public and private (we alternatively see him in his
office and at his flat) and it's that balance, specifically his
ability to correlate his own humanity with his public
responsibility, that enables him to read Rusk's guilt and thereby
prevent further murders (beyond that of the dead girl found in
Rusk's bed in the final scene.)  The larger point of the film,
then, which incorporates but is not exhausted by the transference
of guilt between Blaney and Rusk, involves an understanding of
the relationship (and difference) between the capacity for private
sinfulness on the one hand and its enactment on the other.  It
is precisely that understanding which enables Oxford to reach
the conclusion that Blaney did not kill his wife.  That is, Oxford
recognizes a similarity between Blaney and himself (both men are
in some sense estranged from their wives, though Blaney more so
than he) and that recognition causes him to doubt the legitimacy
of Blaney's conviction:  estrangement does not necessarily entail
homicide.

None of which is intended to argue that the character trope
of the criminal-and-his-double is unimportant to Hitchcock or
to Hitchcock criticism.  I suggested the contrary in connection
with Strangers on a Train.  But accuracy to fact requires that
we place it in context.  This particular species of the double
figure in Hitchcock is less common than the sexual double.
Furthermore, the significance of the criminal-and-his-double trope
is generally less directly pointed vis-à-vis the spectator than
critics often describe it.  As viewers we do not become "guilty"
by any metaphor of transference.  Rather, at its most emphatic,
we become "implicated" via a recognition of likeness.  Even in
Family Plot, where direct transference is at its weakest, we
find this implication structure at work.  The primary locus of
our empathetic attention is the Blanche/Lumley couple.  We sense,
I believe, a measure of similarity between Blanche and Lumley
and ourselves (this assumption of similarity ought probably to
be understood as a convention of reading which is generic to
narrative cinema).  Through the course of the film we are then
forced to extend our recognition to include Fran and Adamson,

who thus come to represent a possibility inherent in our own
behavior. We could be like them. And recognizing that lends
moral force to the moment toward the end of the film when Lumley
shuts the door which ensnares the Adamsons in their own secret
room. We threaten ourselves by allowing our capacity for
selfishness and isolation free play. But only by recognizing
that capacity can we place it in a necessary framework or
perspective.

One final double figure demands attention, both for itself
and for the interplay which it introduces into certain Hitchcock
films. Thus far the double tropes we describe have consisted
of two characters: male/female or criminal/victim. In
Hitchcock's political films we see another sort of doubling--the
pairing of conflicting spy or intelligence organizations. The
most remarkable component of this pairing, above and beyond the
fact that each term in the pair consists of multiple characters
(which allows for possible subset variations on the double figure,
particularly in Topaz), involves a precise lack of
differentiation. Partly this results from Hitchcock's tendency
not to identify the other side except as the "other" side:
it is a mirror or opposite of "our" side. Furthermore, it is
frequently the case that Hitchcock credits members of the other
side with far more emotional substance than their our-side
counterparts. In The Man Who Knew Too Much (1934), for example,
we reach an unexpected depth of emotion when Peter Lorre, during
the final shoot out with the police, turns to find that his nurse
has been shot: he embraces her tenderly, cradles her in his arms,
then returns to the firing line with an intensity of purpose
previously lacking in his expressions. This is particularly
striking in the context provided by the police who storm Lorre's
stronghold. Some drink tea and steal candy while others crack
cynical, sexist jokes.

Notorious employs a similar parallel of espionage groups
and once again the other side, though this time explicitly
identified as Nazis-in-exile, is granted a measure of emotional
reality far in excess of that shown by the chief representatives
of our side. Prescott, the head of the Rio office of U.S.
Intelligence, is portrayed as a callously self-confident pimp
(complete with slicked-back hair and a pencil moustache) while
Alex Sebastian, the ostensible ring-leader of the Nazi group,
is humanized, via his relationship to his mother and his genuine
affection for Alicia, and comes to seem, thereby, a pathetic
victim of his own (and Prescott's) scheming. In this context,
indeed, Devlin's refusal to allow Sebastian to escape underscores
the degree to which political corruption in a "notorious" world
infects even the most hopeful relationships.

The James Mason character in North by Northwest is also
humanized. He is genuinely hurt and enraged when he discovers
that Eve Kendall is, like Alicia in Notorious, a double agent.
By contrast, the Professor (Leo G. Carroll) seems altogether too
cool and collected and Thornhill rightly berates him for his

attitude ("If you fellows can't like the Vandamms of this world without asking girls like her to bed down with them and fly away with them and probably never come back alive, maybe you better start learning to lose a few cold wars!"). This cold-war cold-bloodedness also finds vivid expression in Topaz where the film's most moving scenes all involve some species of denial: Madame Devereaux refuses to see her husband off on his trip to Cuba, while Rico Parra can only express his love for Juanita de Cordoba by shooting her to death to save her from torture.

I suggested, in discussing the isolation theme in Hitchcock, that his attitude toward nationalism is largely negative. Thus it is generally the case in his spy thrillers that couples--the most positive double figures in the Hitchcock lexicon--carry the weight of affirmation. The same interplay of doubles is also at work in those films which employ the criminal/victim trope. Such films usually begin with a male character who is misread as his criminal double. The criminal/victim trope is thus initiatory (as is the transferred guilt implicit in the figure). The action of the film then requires the misread man to establish the evidence of his innocence, often by establishing the guilt of his criminal or espionage double. In most cases it is impossible for the misread man to establish his "legibility" without the help of an outsider and that outsider is generally female. In associative terms we can therefore say that "innocence" in Hitchcock requires the acceptance of sexuality and responsibility. In terms more familiar to Hitchcock criticism, innocence depends upon acceptance of "original sin" which in Hitchcock takes the form of sexuality. Once this responsibility and vulnerability is accepted, a second double figure is thereby established, that of male and female, which replaces and stands in thematic opposition to the initiatory double figure.

The contrast of doubles can therefore be read as follows: in films where there is something like a genuine transference of guilt the initiatory double generally involves two males. In such films (e.g., Rope, Strangers on a Train, Topaz, Frenzy) there is often a strong homosexual sub-text. For Hitchcock such characters are too alike, and the movement of the film is toward establishing some thematically relevant and usually sexual difference. Shadow of a Doubt represents a special case but again the criminal/victim pair involves sexual deviance based on too great an identity: the two Charlies are uncle and niece. A similar logic is at work in the spy films. Spy organizations on both sides are generally male dominated. Women within them are either maternal and possessive (the Nurse in The Man Who Knew Too Much, Mrs. Sebastian in Notorious) or they serve as ideological prostitutes (Eve in North by Northwest). Furthermore, there is often a hint of impotence (Sebastian is too short for Alicia in Notorious) or homosexuality (Martin Landau talks about his "woman's intuition" in North by Northwest). Spy organizations are also, then, too

alike; and overmuch likeness is a negative circumstance in
Hitchcock (as we see in Psycho when Norman becomes his mother).
The alternative to both sorts of debilitating likeness is the
simultaneous similarity/dissimilarity which characterizes male/
female pairings in Hitchcock. Such men and women share an
essential complementarity, for sharing certain traits or for
mirroring each other's desires, and yet there is also an essential
and ultimately healthy difference evidenced by the very fact of
their sexuality.

In terms of the sight metaphor, then, we can say that doubles
in Hitchcock serve as a perspective device, permitting or
requiring a necessary correction or expansion of vision, both
ocular (as argued through the iconography of distorted sight and
perspective) and moral (as evidenced through Hitchcock's fables
of isolation and detachment). Which is not to say that characters
necessarily see themselves reflected in some direct manner in
their double. For certain characters this is impossible precisely
because the images are identical--they cannot recognize their
reflection as a reflection because they do not recognize its
otherness (this applies primarily to spies or intelligence
agents). In certain other instances, such as The Lodger, The
Man Who Knew Too Much, and Strangers on a Train, the mirror
effect works obliquely. The logic of the films is such that the
initial double throws the world of the character out of balance
(hence the frequent odd angle shots in The 39 Steps, Shadow
of a Doubt, Strangers on a Train, I Confess, and The Wrong
Man) and in attempting to right that balance, by rereading the
world--or by insisting that others do so--it is necessary to
accept vulnerability, in space, in society, and in sexuality.
Indeed the world cannot be read without accepting such risks.

In the majority of Hitchcock's films, however, the double
figure does indeed give rise to genuine self-reflection precisely
via a recognition both of otherness and likeness. In some cases
this involves a literal rereading of the self through
recollection, often with the assistance of a right-reader
double (Rebecca, Spellbound, Marnie). In other cases self-
reflection attends upon a character's recognition that he or she
has been misreading others (e.g., Suspicion, Shadow of a
Doubt, I Confess, Frenzy) in which case the double is often
a victim of misreading (in some of these cases the double
intentionally misleads, as in Stage Fright). And furthermore,
in most cases the reading works in both directions. John Robie's
attempt to read the identity of the criminal who doubles for him
in To Catch a Thief requires that he reread his own sense of
independence and requires further that he reread Francie Stevens
as well. Likewise, Francie has to reread her sexual motives and
accept the responsibility which attends upon her commitment to
John. She cannot run sexual interference for her mother
indefinitely. In The Birds Mitch Brenner tends to misread
Melanie Daniels, for reasons having to do with class and
profession; and he is forced to reread her under the pressure

of the bird attacks.  Melanie, similarly, commits errors of a
like sort, evidenced primarily by the mixed motives behind her
trip to Bodega Bay; and she too is tested and changed by the bird
attacks.  Specifically, she comes to reread her relationship to
her mother, and the fact that her mother deserted her, a rereading
which she accomplishes by reading Lydia:  hence the repeated shots
of Melanie paying close attention to Lydia's movements or
actions.  Mark Rutland's rereading of Marnie also requires
rereading himself and his motives, as he helps Marnie to reread
hers.  And the ultimate effect of all this is generally to put
the world of the character, visually, sexually, and socially,
back together again--to make it whole by making them whole.  Hence
the fact that Hitchcock so often ends his films on long shots
or group shots.  Things are thus put back in focus after a period
of distortion and disorientation; and it is the act of reading
that restores visual and moral order.


THE PLAY OF SPECTATION
        It was suggested early on in this essay that the mind/screen
relationship relative to the films of Alfred Hitchcock could be
characterized in at least two ways:  thematically (in terms of
part-whole dramatic logic) and perceptually (in terms of the
experiential analogies which may be said to exist between
Hitchcock's thematic points and our mode of attending to those
points).  It will be noted that I give thematics a certain pride
of place.  This is justified for several reasons.
        To begin with, to discuss the thematics of a film, the
structure of its implications, its "ideology" or "idealogic,"
is to discuss one of several possible mind/screen constructs.
Importing a "theme" to a film, via the act of reading, is to make
a connection, in the mind of the spectator, between the world
within the film, a world the existence of which we read
metaphorically, and the world outside the film, a world which
includes the spectator.  Such and such a pattern of action and
imagery thus has aesthetic and cinematic significance precisely
to the extent that  1) we purposefully misconstrue (without
ignoring) the literal denotation of the images (our knowledge
that a certain visual pattern corresponds to, more properly
"belongs" to, Cary Grant) in favor of narrative or symbolic
connotation (which attends upon our responding to that same
pattern "as if" it denoted "Roger Thornhill"); and also to the
extent that  2) we recognize some general pattern behind those
misconstrued specifics, without which they would be nothing but
misconstrued specifics; and a pattern, furthermore, that may be
said to embody some humanly relevant assertion of value or
attitude.[15]  We might say of Eisenstein's October, for
example, that it celebrates a disciplined, self-aware sort of
revolutionary energy, an energy which finds its most perfect and
appropriate expression in the manipulation of history, reality,
and language for revolutionary ends.  We might say a good deal

more. We might say something altogether different or
contradictory. We do not need to say anything on particular
occasions if we choose not to play the role of critic. We need
not even believe that such statements exhaust every aspect of
a work (experience indicates just the contrary: that works cannot
be so exhausted). But the likelihood that we can make such
a statement if called upon, can generalize significance in such
a way that we might assert the film's values (however we may
describe them) as our own, is one precondition of criticism.
That is, as E. D. Hirsch points out, significance is always
significance for someone.[16] To find the theme of the work,
the logic of values (sociological, authorial) which may be said
to "motivate" it, is therefore one way of asserting a relationship
of significance between mind and screen. It implies a cognitive
discourse (we speak of the "argument" of October) and a
cognitive subject (someone who "understands" that argument).

There are those, certainly, who would disallow validity or
significance to thematic analysis, on the grounds that analysis
is a product of criticism rather than reading and effectively
forecloses the work of the text by imposing an interpretation
upon it. This attitude is frequently though inconsistently that
of Roland Barthes. In certain contexts he allows a positive role
to criticism for embodying or for replaying the "voices" of the
text.[17] And clearly through the course of S/Z Barthes
fulfills in no uncertain terms the traditional role of the critic,
assigning each signifier a signified within larger patterns of
significance ("Sarrasine, who was not devout, broke into
laughter.* SEM. Impiety."[18]) and in accord with an explicitly
acknowledged and ideologically grounded methodology (his five
codes). But at the same time Barthes clearly fears that the
ultimate effect of criticism is to deny the "play" of the text
and the reader by assigning the text a global, over-arching,
univocal interpretation. Thus in "From Work to Text" he talks
of critics who "execute" texts, who "kill" them, by "the reduction
of reading to a consumption." In "Writers, Intellectuals,
Teachers" he points to the school exercise of "réduction de
texte" as a paradigm of the critical activity which substitutes
a summary of the message of the text for the text itself. "The
summary," he says, "is a disavowal of writing."[19] And in S/Z
he reverts to Freudian terminology to suggest that the critical
act of "tieing up" the "threads" of the text is to castrate it:
"Freud, considering the origin of weaving, saw it as the labor
of a woman braiding her pubic hairs to form the absent penis.
The text, in short, is a fetish; and to reduce it to the unity
of meaning, by a deceptively univocal reading, is to cut the
braid, to sketch the castrating gesture."[20]

For Stephen Heath, on the other hand, this foreclosure is
less a matter of castration than containment, but he sees it as
having much the same effect. The reader-subject's search for
a position of significance shuts down when the text recoups its
excesses and makes narrative sense. The "play" of the text, which

is predicated on the violation of expectation, is eliminated when
the expectation of closure is fulfilled.  Furthermore, the effect
of narrative closure, as Heath has it, is to elide or efface the
terms of narrative process (though not necessarily the fact of
the process itself):  narrative proceeds by contradiction but
concludes in resolution, and effectively denies, under the rubric
of "realism" or "representation," the "other scene" of its
production.  Thus "narration is to be held on the narrated, the
enunciation on the enounced," and the process of signification
is eventually, ultimately subsumed by the process of the
signified--all of which recalls in its vocabulary and logic the
Daniel Dayan scenario of viewer perception.[21]

We must agree that criticism can be reductive after this
manner.  But it is clearly wrong to suggest, as Barthes does in
S/Z and as Coward and Ellis suggest in Language and
Materialism, that this is necessarily the case in conventional
literary or film criticism.[22]  One criterion of validity in
New Criticism has always been the ability of specific readings
to enrich our experience of the text under analysis by bringing
to consciousness an awareness of signification, connotation, and
structuration.  To be sure, critical articles of this sort often
conclude with an attempt at characterizing the thematic component
of the work in question, but such characterizations are exactly
an attempt to deal with matters of value and ideology as those
values arise from the hierarchical play of signifiers.  In
addition, thematic characterizations are always subject to
verification or refutation at the hands of other critics and
readers, and verification inevitably takes us back to the text.
Indeed, one could readily assert that Anglo-American New Criticism
had exactly the effect of questioning the signification process,
where previously it had been subsumed under a simple minded notion
of authorial intention or historical determinism.  We need only
point to the unprecedented productivity of New Criticism, and
to the countless and often acrimonious debates within it, to
support the contention.  It will not do, then, to say that
criticism, thematic or otherwise, cuts off the work of the text.
Critical statements are always provisional in fact if not in their
rhetoric, and the effect of such statements is generally to
encourage textual play rather than deny it.

Furthermore, one can argue in reference to Barthes and Heath
that aesthetic texts have the capacity to be something more
than discourse.  They have discursive qualities, certainly, and
to attend to thematics is in part to attend to those qualities,
but such texts are different from informative discourse in one
crucial respect:  they are repeatable.  Exhaustibility is a
characteristic of informative texts.  Once I learn the procedure
for adjusting the valves on my VW bus I have no reason to reread
the appropriate section of The Idiot's Guide to Volkswagen
Repair.  To understand the meaning of the text in this case is
to shut down my desire to play with its signifiers.  Only if I
have forgotten or misinterpreted the text will I feel the need

to reread it. Exhaustibility may thus be correlated with utility or use-value.

Aesthetic texts, however, may have no use-value in the same direct sense. We go to them primarily for their own sake and their use-value is more cultural than personal, more oblique than direct, cumulative rather than immediate. Our experience of those texts may be direct, personal, and immediate. We may even learn something from them. But the use-value or truth-value of such texts is always "on hold." As fictions they are not necessarily subject to truth tests of the sort applicable to informative or historical discourse. And even when considered thematically there is no particular obligation for the reader or critic to endorse or approve the ideology of the work in question. If anything, it is precisely this lack of obligation, denying any pragmatic context requiring action or belief, which makes it possible for us to enter into the play and pleasure of the text.

Which is not necessarily to say that our experience of aesthetic objects is mere play or pastime. No doubt it can be, though I am not sure that such play amounts to the misuse of such objects. But criticism differs from reading precisely to the extent that it seeks, among other things, to comprehend the range and character of the significance that such play may have for human beings. To talk of use-value (or the lack of it) is therefore to talk about a condition of reading. Aesthetic objects do not have use-value of the sort associated with informative discourse. Accordingly, they are not necessarily exhausted when they are understood, however much Barthes and Heath may be misled by their use of the "discourse" analogy into believing that they are. I do not have to forget or misinterpret Rio Bravo to be eager to see it again. I may have other reasons for not wanting to see Rio Bravo next week but the fact that I have seen it previously will be a minor consideration. No doubt for some people, however, it would be a major consideration—and perhaps it is these people that Barthes has in mind when he speaks of criticism cutting off the play of the text. But in that case the objection is misdirected. Truly casual readers or viewers never read criticism. Criticism cannot affect them one way or the other. Those who do read criticism, on the other hand, are precisely those who are most likely to enter into the play of the text—by rereading the text itself and by reading texts about the text.

Criticism, therefore, is a kind of textual play, a means of entering into relation with the text. The history of criticism, furthermore, teaches us the same lesson that we learned from considering the difference between informative and aesthetic discourse: aesthetic objects are simultaneously discursive and ritualistic. They embody value systems and ideologies which are in some sense signified by the texts and over which we may differ and debate. But aesthetic objects also entail a ritualistic, experiential component which allows us to renew our experience

of them--both through repeated viewings (in the case of films)
and through rethinking those texts in criticism.

At which point we can see a very positive relationship
between reading and criticism. If we define "reading" as the
moment by moment perception of a text, a simultaneous
"performance" and "reperformance" of it, we can see how such
performances are of necessity inexhaustive (though not
incomplete). Even with informative discourse the reading process
is one which structures the flow of information into hierarchies
which enable key or salient points to pass through short term
memory into long term memory. Thus I will remember the procedure
for adjusting the valves on my bus though I will not remember
the exact words that were used to describe the procedure. And
something similar can be said in regard to the reading of
aesthetic texts. Hence the fact, as Metz points out in Film
Language, that the most readily remembered aspect of a narrative
film is its plot, something which we never see but which we rather
abstract from the moment to moment flow of information; while
the least memorable aspect of a film is precisely such specific
details as its cutting and camera movement.[23] To a certain
extent, then, the transparency of classical film texts is less
a matter of ideology per se than of information processing and
memory retention. We quite literally cannot remember everything
in a film and so will remember those aspects which are
foregrounded (with foregrounding to be understood as a matter
of style and hence of ideology) and which can be arranged into
some hierarchy of salience. Reading, that is, works both
horizontally, from image to image and sound to sound, and
vertically, as it arranges those images and sounds into structures
of pertinence. We therefore retain all and only such information
as can be processed into some larger structure of significance.

Criticism, then, can be seen as a retrospective extension
of the reading process itself which fulfills a double function.
To begin with it generates upper-level abstractions (e.g., plot,
theme). Thus the films of Alfred Hitchcock may ultimately be
understood as reflections upon the ethics of reading. The
statement by itself is very abstract and might be thought
reductive--and would be were it not for the fact that upper-level
generalizations effectively stretch out and thus expand the
framework of pertinences. The more abstract my characterization
of the thematic of a given film, the greater the conceptual
distance between my statement and the film in question, the
greater the opportunity and responsibility I have for laying out
the data of the film along the hierarchy of comprehension and
recollection. Put another way, the more abstract my abstraction,
the greater the detail which can be elucidated beneath it.
Secondly, then, and as a consequence, the effect of thematic
reading, at least in potential, is exactly the reverse of that
foreseen by Barthes. Rather than close down the text it opens
the text up, brings it alive, by assigning significance to a far
greater number of details. Subsequent experiences of the text

or texts in question will thus be all the more ritualistic and celebratory as readers become more attentive to the play of signifiers and signifieds.

Furthermore, this play of spectation, when seen in its ritualistic aspect, can readily be extended to include the perceptual circumstances obtaining between subject and screen. The traditional account of the mind/screen relationship in Hitchcock, however negatively framed by the metaphor of voyeurism, was founded, correctly I think, on the supposition that it is possible for directors to suggest analogies between the actions and circumstances of characters and the actions and circumstances of the members of the film audience.[24] This is seldom a matter of absolute point-of-view identification of character and viewer over the entire length of a film. No matter how thoroughly the analogy is developed it remains an analogy. Nevertheless, I would not want to take issue with the proposition that character/viewer analogies can be employed to lend a certain ethical/experiential resonance to the act of film viewing. Where I have taken issue with traditional descriptions of the Hitchcock cinema I have done so for the purpose of offering a more accurate account of the films which should lead in turn to a more accurate description of the resonances which may exist between subject and screen.

I have argued in general that Hitchcock's films are about the "ethics of reading." This is evidenced at various levels of the text or texts in question. In narrative terms the plot actions of Hitchcock's films focus on characters who reread the world, who misread the world, or who are themselves read or misread. At the level of iconography the reading issue manifests itself in symptomatic distortions or obstructions of sight, many of which we see via subjective point-of-view sequences. At the level of causality we come to understand how various actions (desertion, denial, detachment) and circumstances (physical, architectural, social, geographical) can lead to visual and moral distortion. In terms of the logic of narrative resolution, we come to see how character alignment, embodied specifically by variations on the double figure, allows characters to put themselves and their world back together again. By seeing themselves in their opposites they are enabled to reread and hence to rewrite their relationship to others and to the world: thus change replaces fixation, openness replaces isolation, vulnerability replaces paranoia, and sexuality replaces sterility.

The reading theme, then, which serves to motivate the structural and iconographic logic of the majority of Hitchcock's films, can be said to imply a viewer-subject position which ultimately encourages us to reflect upon the dynamics and ethics of our own process of reading. Negatively, Hitchcock allows us the freedom to read poorly. It is this possibility that the voyeurism metaphor perfectly captures. We can become fixed, isolated, paranoid, and sterile in our responses to Hitchcock's films and characters. To a certain degree the circumstances within which we view the films are reinforcing factors. There

is a measure of fixity and paranoia implicit in the popular
generic conventions which Hitchcock employs.  If anything,
Hitchcock's public persona encourages misreading.  His walk-ons,
his television shows, his various pulp publishing enterprises,
and particularly his statements to interviewers:  all seem
positively calculated to throw our readings off track by prompting
us to view the films as macabre entertainments.  One might even
suggest that Hitchcock's dedication to the notion of pure cinema
and to the tradition of montage requires him to adopt this
tactic:  by cutting the world up into little pieces Hitchcock
effectively challenges us to put it back together again.

In spite of all of this, however, misreading in Hitchcock
almost always involves a certain willfulness.  We see this
especially in connection with characters, like the young girls
on the beach in Young and Innocent or Ann in Strangers on a
Train, who attribute false and often sexually loaded motives
to others.  But we can cite here, as an emblem of willful
misreading, the sequence in The 39 Steps when the Crofter gets
up from the dinner table and leaves the cottage.  He has seen
the exchange of glances between his wife and Hannay, he interprets
it (we learn from the subsequent course of events) as evidence
of infidelity, and he withdraws from the scene, taking up a
position in the shadows outside the house so that he can peer
in at his wife and Hannay (Figs. 5.20, 5.21).  The latter two
are thus doubly "framed," graphically, by the glass and the window
frame, and dramatically, by the Crofter's self-servingly false
expectations:  it's the "rear window" syndrome all over again.
The point, however, is that the Crofter chooses to take up the
position and it is precisely this perverse willingness to be
isolated and detached that the film calls into question.

It is thus possible to misread the films of Alfred
Hitchcock.  But it is neither necessary nor particularly
appropriate.  It is rather the case that the films themselves
raise the reading issue very directly and explicitly and suggest
an alternative conception of the viewer-subject position.  We
need not cower in the darkness like the Crofter.  We need not
detach ourselves from the film's action by the imposition of false
readings.  Rather, we are free to take seriously the analogy
between our own process of reading and that reading process
undertaken, however partially or imperfectly in some cases, by
Hitchcock's characters.

The most powerfully resonant component of the analogy
involves the correlation, both in the films and in our viewing
of them, of 1) "active" reading, 2) the assertion of positive
human relationships, and 3) the restoration of visual and moral
order.  To paraphrase the last line of Shadow of a Doubt, the
world of Alfred Hitchcock goes crazy when it is not watched
carefully enough.  And the converse is also true:  to watch the
world carefully is to maintain sanity, one's own, and the world's.
To read actively is thus to be openly attentive, to be willingly
vulnerable to the possibility of change.  Reading is therefore

a process of activity more than a goal:  hence the correlation
between reading and maturation.  Maturity in Hitchcock is defined
precisely as the ability to read new situations as creatively
and responsively as possible.  To read actively is also to read
oneself "into" (or "in terms of") patterns of human relationship
which do simultaneous duty both to similarity and difference.
To read another person requires an acceptance of their otherness
(otherwise they would not exist to be read); but it also entails
a willingness to be involved in their subjectivity, to try to
see things from their point of view (as Mark does in <u>Marnie</u>).
Hence the appropriateness of the sexual double figure, which
serves in Hitchcock as a paradigm of properly balanced, properly
read and readable, human relationships.  And the result of
achieving this balance, through an equal acceptance of guilt,
of vulnerability, and of the necessity to continue the process
of reading and growing, is to restore a proper sense of proportion
and significance to the visual universe.

All of which applies equally well to reading <u>in</u> the films
and readings <u>of</u> the films.  Characters who read actively, who
see the world as a social whole which transcends boundaries of
class, religion, and nationality, thus establish positive
relationships with others and with society and thereby reestablish
some sense of visual and moral order.  Likewise, viewers who read
actively, who see the world of the film as a whole that bears
a metaphorical relationship to the world beyond the film, are
also in the process of establishing positive relationships between
themselves and others--whether those others include the characters
in the film, the "character" behind the film (i.e., Hitchcock),
or the other members of the film audience--and by so doing they
too may contribute in some sense to a reestablishment of visual
and moral order.  To be sure, the film will run through the gate
at a set rate and order regardless of the stance we as viewers
may assume.  We must not confuse the film itself with our
perception of it.  But within these parameters we are free to
take seriously and thus to activate the hopeful implications which
attend upon Hitchcock's fables of sin and redemption.

To read the films well, therefore, to take their implications
as personally and as completely as possible, is effectively to
celebrate in our own lives and actions the very qualities of
ethics and activity which the films themselves may be said to
advance.  At this level, the level of "action," the play of
criticism and the play of spectation can thus be seen to come
into perfect alignment:  each gains in resonance and significance
for being juxtaposed with the other.  It is no wonder, then, that
our ultimate response to a Hitchcock film is typically one of
genuine, well-earned elation.  We do not peer voyeuristically
<u>at</u> the characters.  We read along <u>with</u> them.

Hence the fact that the point-of-view figure, wherein our
vision is most thoroughly analogous to that of Hitchcock's
characters, is far more likely to involve some species of reading
or misreading than some type of voyeurism.  If anything, voyeurism

is to be seen as a subset of the reading motif in that it
represents a particularly wrong headed and self-destructive sort
of visual behavior. It is precisely that sort of wrong headedness
that Hitchcock's characters typically overcome, however, and we
overcome it along with them. Their success thus becomes our
success. The ultimate orderliness of their visual field thus
becomes an orderliness of our visual field. In both cases the
act of reading well becomes in some sense its own reward.

It is possible, furthermore, to extend the application of
this analogy to cover certain specific aspects of the viewing
experience. The voyeurism theme activates certain of these
aspects, as we have seen in our discussion of Rear Window.
Thus the theater seat is equated with Jefferies's wheel chair;
while the screen is equated with the windows across the courtyard
from Jefferies's apartment. The general movement of the film,
however, is toward asserting the inaccuracy of this particular
version of the viewer/character analogy as that analogy
determines, at least initially, Jefferies's behavior. That is,
unlike the film spectator, as that spectator is characterized
by the voyeurism metaphor, Jefferies is not safely "screened off"
from the action he observes. He can thus send Lisa into
Thorvald's apartment, "onto" the screen or field of action; and,
more ominously, Thorvald can reverse the movement by leaving the
"screen" opposite Jefferies and reappearing behind him, thus
invading Jefferies's space, the space of the spectator. A
different characterization of the viewer/character analogy,
particularly of its spatial co-ordinates, is therefore necessary.

The reading theme suggests an alternative conception of the
analogy between screen space and theater space. Earlier I
suggested a causal relationship between various forms of
psychological and physical isolation or fixity on the one hand
and misreading on the other. Isolation is consequently the
primary cause of moral and visual disorder, and the tendency
toward isolation is both reflected in and reinforced by physical
circumstances. It appears, however, that the circumstances within
which we generally view Hitchcock's films mediate against
isolation. To begin with, to go to the cinema is implicitly to
accept a sort of social and spatial vulnerability akin to that
so frequently and so positively accepted by Hitchcock's
characters. One thinks of all the theater or theaterlike scenes
in Hitchcock (in The Man Who Knew Too Much, The 39 Steps,
Sabotage, Young and Innocent, Saboteur, Stagefright, I
Confess, Torn Curtain, and Topaz) wherein characters put
themselves at hazard within and often for the sake of society.
Such scenes provide a counter-emblem for the viewer/character
analogy and are found far more frequently in Hitchcock than scenes
of voyeurism. In other words, to go to the cinema is to be public
rather than private, is to be seen, is to be social, is to
establish the very sort of communal bonds which the films
themselves so often celebrate. In this respect Hitchcock is,
like his fellow Catholics Ford, Capra, and McCarey, an ultimately

comic director who values sexuality and community above all
else.
     Two objections may be raised to this characterization of
the spatial co-ordinates of the viewer/character analogy as thus
far sketched out: that it is not constant, in the sense that
the co-ordinates differ greatly depending upon whether one views
the film in a theater or at home on television; and that the
openness of the theater space is effectively closed down by the
darkness necessary to projection (i.e., one could argue that
darkness once again fixes us in an isolation like to that of the
Crofter in The 39 Steps).
     The former objection is less crucial but more interesting
because answering it helps to confirm the logic underlying what
has heretofore been a fairly common subjective impression, that
Hitchcock's films are somehow better when one sees them with an
audience. There are valid theoretical grounds for asserting that
a theatrical feature film retains its "theatricality," and by
implication its "audience," regardless of the means of
transmission. In this regard it is clear that the "subject
position" is an implied feature of the text and is therefore as
much a construct of a film's rhetoric as an implied narrator would
be. We may construct our own subject position, of course, which
may or may not correspond to that which is implicit in the
rhetoric of the text (which is nothing more than to say that some
viewers are better "readers" than others). But most texts
"fictionalize" their audience in some demonstrable way and that
fictionalization, depending as it does upon some measure of reader
co-operation, may very well remain relatively constant.[25] That
is, we can imagine ourselves as part of a film audience even if
that audience does not exist for a particular performance of a
specific text. Thus it is quite possible for us to watch To
Catch a Thief, say, on television and still celebrate in some
perceptual sense the sociality encouraged by the text: we don't
need an audience to feel ourselves a part of one. Nevertheless,
it remains true that the real presence of an audience can lend
an extra measure of sociality to the viewing experience, an extra
resonance of circumstance and implication. We don't have to
overcome the inertia of solitude when we view films with other
people; and thus it is far easier to enter into the state of
social wholeness and elation which Hitchcock's films invite.
     The objection that the darkness of the theater reinstitutes
solitude by fixing our attention on the screen is closely related
to the voyeurism model of the mind/screen relationship and suffers
from the same insufficiency. Both assume that a relatively
constant angle of view correlates rather directly with a
restricted field of vision. This is plausible in the case of
Rear Window, where Jefferies's field of vision is delimited
by the tenement courtyard and the windows opposite his own, though
even here there are a good many things to look at, far more than
one might expect of a typical city tenement. But Rear Window
is quite atypical in this respect, belonging, as it does, with

films like Lifeboat, Rope, and The Wrong Man which play
particularly upon the dangers of fixation and enclosure.
   Most Hitchcock films, however, are nowhere near so limited
or restricted in their field of vision, either socially or
spatially. Particularly when seen as a group, Hitchcock's films
evidence a surprising range of social settings in spite of the
fact that his protagonists generally belong to the bourgeoisie
or the upper middle classes. We see destitute lower class or
working class characters or neighborhoods repeatedly (in The
Lodger, The Man Who Knew Too Much, The 39 Steps, Sabotage,
Young and Innocent, Shadow of a Doubt, Strangers on
a Train, The Wrong Man, Psycho, Marnie, Torn Curtain,
Topaz, Frenzy, and Family Plot). It's as if Hitchcock felt
obliged to show us the whole of the social world, an obligation
corresponding to the responsibility which his characters accept
to see the world whole, to read themselves as part of the whole.
Likewise, in spatial terms, Hitchcock's films typically cover
a great deal of territory and a variety of locales. One minute
we are in London, the next in Scotland; or we move from New York
to Chicago to South Dakota. Thus, in spite of the fact that our
literal vantage point remains constant, fixed in our theater seat,
the fictive vantage point which we assume in attending to the
films is precisely such that we do not become fixed. Or if
we do it is something ominous and threatening, as is the case
in Rear Window and Psycho. As we have seen, however, it is
Hitchcock's tendency to urge his characters, for ultimately
benevolent ends, out of their isolation, just as he urges us to
leave the isolation of our everyday lives for the sociality of
the Hitchcock cinema.
   I concluded my thematic reading of the cinema of Alfred
Hitchcock with a discussion of the double figure. We may conclude
this discussion of spectator play on a like note. I have already
suggested that doubling in Hitchcock has less to do with guilt
than with knowledge, the knowledge, specifically, of a correlation
which binds the act of reading, the assertion of positive human
relationships, and the restoration of visual and moral order
together as components of a single ethical or ideological
gestalt. Implicit in this is a somewhat abstract yet powerfully
resonant analogy between the actions of characters and the actions
of viewers. We might be tempted, then, to suggest that viewers
are ultimately to be seen as doubles of Hitchcock's protagonists.
We must be careful here. This particular double notion is not
very far removed, in certain respects, from the old voyeurism/
identification model of the subject position; and, as we have
seen, the identification metaphor tends to emphasize likeness
at the expense of otherness.
   We can avoid this error by switching metaphors for the
moment. Rather than conceive of viewers as doubles of the
characters, or vice versa, we can see viewers and characters,
as I suggested earlier, as parts of a single continuum of actions
and consequences. Thus we may be "like" characters, in that we

are on the continuum, are implicated in their motives and
movements; yet we are "other" than those characters for
occupying a different point on the continuum, a difference which
is defined primarily by degrees of knowledgeability.

It is often the Hitchcock case, for example, that we will
know far more about the plot circumstances of a particular film
than will many of the characters. On occasion Hitchcock will
open a film by divulging a secret against which we read the
rest of the movie, as is the case in Sabotage, Young and
Innocent, Shadow of a Doubt, Rope, Strangers on a Train,
I Confess, and Family Plot. More frequently we are let in
on some essential secret, or some aspect of it, in advance of
the central characters, though not necessarily in the film's
opening sequence. We see this in Notorious, where we are aware
that Alicia is being poisoned in advance of Alicia herself and
Devlin, and in Vertigo as well, where we are made aware of
Judy's masquerade as "Madeleine" far in advance of Scottie
himself. This is also the case in North by Northwest, where
we see the Professor long before Thornhill ever meets him, and
where we are also made aware of Eve Kendall's ambiguous connection
with Vandamm before Thornhill learns of it. Likewise, we are
clued into Marnie's neurosis long before Mark Rutland becomes
aware of its full ramifications. Frenzy too fits this pattern,
in that we are aware of Rusk's guilt far in advance of Blaney
or Inspector Oxford. Equally common are plot sequences, often
of the "misread man" variety, wherein our state of knowledge
generally matches that of the focal character or characters.
This is clearly the case in The 39 Steps, The Lady Vanishes,
To Catch a Thief, The Wrong Man, and Topaz; and even in
these films the state of our knowledge exceeds that of most
characters, in that we understand that the wrong man is indeed
innocent, or that the protagonists are correct to believe that
a plot is afoot. Only in a select few films is our knowledge
less than that of the protagonists--one thinks of The Lodger,
Suspicion, and Psycho particularly--and even in these
instances our ignorance does not equal that of most of the film's
characters. We see enough of Drew in The Lodger to doubt the
clues pointing to his guilt; in Suspicion we are almost as
suspicious of Lina's perceptions as we are of Johnny's motives;
and in Psycho we know a good deal more about Norman Bates than
any of those who investigate Marion Crane's disappearance, even
if we do not know that he actually killed Marion while dressed
in dime store drag.

Furthermore, those viewers acquainted with the iconography
of Alfred Hitchcock gain knowledge of another sort, a knowledge
which is generally unavailable to the characters themselves.
Thus our first view of Devlin in Notorious focuses on the back
of his head, on his facelessness, and it is only at film's end
that he too comes to understand the degree of his own
dehumanization. Likewise, in To Catch a Thief we see marvelous
helicopter shots of Robie's car as it races along the cliffside

roadway.  Robie isn't _in_ the car (his housekeeper is at the
wheel--as _les flics_ eventually discover); and even if he were
at the controls he could not be seeing what we see, an alternating
pattern of roadside towns, their houses hunched together on the
mountain face, and bare stretches of roadway.  But the contrast
between isolation and congregation provides a context which calls
Robie's mountain-top solitude into question.  Similar observations
on the interplay of iconography and character can be made
regarding almost every shot in the cinema of Alfred Hitchcock.
The point to make, in every case, is that Hitchcock's use of
settings and symbols provides a background to the actions of his
characters, a background the significance of which they often
disregard or fail to take into account, yet it is a background
which we can read for clues as to the nature of the problems they
face.
     In general, then, we can say that viewer knowledgeability
is almost always greater to some degree than that of the
characters in the films.  One really has to work at it if one
wants to misinterpret Hitchcock's movies.  On the other hand,
however, and here is where the continuum metaphor is particularly
appropriate, the gap of knowledgeability separating the viewer
from the characters can be said to imply a measure of humility
on our own part rather than hubris.  If our position on the
continuum is, say, in the center, with that of the less knowing
characters on one side, who is to say that the continuum does
not also extend in the opposite direction, such that we may be
less knowing in our turn than some other person or character?
All of which is speculative--but it has the advantage of
accounting for certain intuitive responses to Hitchcock's films,
the simultaneous sense we get at film's end of elation (for having
read well) and gratitude (for being _able_ to read well).
     In terms of the viewer/character analogy, then, the double
notion is accurate but only within limits that are determined
by the fact that our state of knowledge generally exceeds that
of the characters in the films.  Thinking of the double less as
a figure than as a function, however, allows us to specify in
somewhat more accurate terms the sense in which we as viewers
may be said to encounter _our_ double during the viewing
experience.  I have suggested that the double serves a catalytic
function vis-à-vis its opposite.  The double is a perspective
device which encourages characters to reread themselves and their
world.  In some cases this requires self-reflection.  Thus
characters will see some aspect of themselves reflected in the
actions or circumstances of another character and will often
though not always explicitly acknowledge that similarity by
asserting some distinction between themselves and their opposites.
In other cases self-reflection per se is less important than the
adoption of a course of action running implicitly counter to that
which the character had previously followed.  In every case,
however, the change is brought about by the intrusion of something
new or foreign into the world, into the visual field, of the

character or characters; and their subsequent actions represent
an attempt to incorporate the implication of that new element
into the ethical and visual patterns of their own lives and
activities.
    In order for the double figure to legitimately apply to or
incorporate the viewer, then, we must shift our focus somewhat.
What enters into our field of vision is not merely another
character but rather the film itself.  To draw analogies at the
level of action and circumstances between viewers and characters
is thus permissible and illuminating--because there are
characters in the films who do take action and whose actions take
place within particular temporal and physical circumstances.
But it is the whole package of those characters, actions, and
circumstances which occupies our attention.  In which case the
ultimate double figure is not that of viewer and character alone
but that of mind and screen, of the viewer and the viewed.[26]
It is the definitive perceptual circumstance which neither
criticism nor reading can avoid without ceasing altogether.
    The point to make, in any case, whether we make it in
thematic terms or experiential terms, is that the films of Alfred
Hitchcock put us face to face with the screen, with the cinema,
and therefore with our own "cinematic practice."  The films are
the catalysts which allow for the play of spectation, but
ultimately we are responsible for how well and upon which terms
we will read the films.  Some viewing strategies will be more
successful and more truly satisfying than others, for responding
more thoroughly and positively to the possibilities provided by
the films.  I have described one such strategy here.  But we are
the ones who activate those possibilities within the range of
our abilities to do so.  Thus we are "like" the films in certain
respects--in terms of the character/viewer analogy, for example--
but ultimately we are "other," and are responsible for the
readings we undertake.  Hitchcock can do no more than suggest
that what we choose to see and how we choose to see it are matters
of ethical consequence.  It's something to think seriously about,
and serious thinking is a hallmark of aesthetic experience.


CONCLUSIONS
    This study hardly lacks for conclusions even to this point.
I have offered alternative solutions to a variety of cruxes in
Hitchcock criticism for example; and I have also taken issue with
the idea that the effect of criticism is to "kill" its objects.
Aesthetic objects are not "killable" to begin with; their life
does not depend on our ignorance but rather upon our willingness
to attend to them.  If anything, criticism is a higher form of
attention which allows a more intense and fruitful play of
spectation than that enjoyed by naive reader/viewers.
Nevertheless, there are several debts of patience that need
repayment and I feel obliged to discharge those debts in this
final section.

More specifically, I suggested earlier that my discussion of Hitchcock's films would eventually call into question a certain tendency in film aesthetics which mistakenly equates specific, localized stylistic devices or conventions with far more general aesthetic and sociological consequences. In Bazin's case the stylistic device or figure is that of "analytical montage" and the effect is a denial of our freedom of reading and the anesthetization of our sensitivities to cinema and to the world at large. In the case of Daniel Dayan the device or convention is the shot/reverse shot (really the point-of-view figure) and the effect is one that masks the ideological functioning of the film by implying that the film is or contains its own cause.[27] Our perception of any single shot raises the question of origin (Who is taking this picture? Who is ordering these images?) but the reverse shot "claims" this causality, or so argues Dayan, by occupying the space of the "absent-one" (the camera). In Dayan's own words: "The absent-one is masked, replaced by a character, hence the real origin of the image--the conditions of its production represented by the absent-one--is replaced with a false origin and this false origin is situated inside the fiction. The cinematographic level fools the spectator by connecting him to the fictional level rather than to the filmic level."[28]

The similarity of the two positions is remarkably self-evident: in both scenarios "the receptive freedom of the spectator," to use Dayan's phrase, "is reduced to a minimum" and the oppressive "tyranny" of the filmmaker (whether that "maker" is conceived of as an individual or as a class) is correspondingly maximized.[29] To be sure, Bazin and Dayan prescribe different remedies (Welles vs. Godard) and they obviously operate out of remarkably dissimilar frames of reference--but their descriptions of the illness and its effects are indistinguishable. In essence, both are attacking continuity cutting for denying the freedom of the spectator and they do so in fairly absolute terms, as if "entrapment" were an inevitable consequence of classical cinematic practice.

My view of Hitchcock allows for the possibility of entrapment. And no doubt those who misread Hitchcock's films are unlikely to acknowledge the ideological or thematic implications of their readings. But it is not Hitchcock who entraps them, nor is it the classical narrative cinema. They trap themselves. Indeed, the fact of their entrapment argues the falsity of the Bazin/Dayan scenario. Only by leaving us free to read as we will does Hitchcock allow the possibility that we will read poorly. However, by leaving us free Hitchcock also establishes a cinematic circumstance which rewards reading well. Our freedom is not anesthetized in the least. Rather, it is put at hazard so that the act of reading carries genuine ethical consequence.

Of course, it is possible to agree with my reading of Alfred Hitchcock and with my description of this particular variety of mind/screen relationship without thereby discrediting the general

accuracy of the Bazin/Dayan position. One need only deny that
Hitchcock is typical of classical cinematic practice and one
denies the general applicability of my findings. Yes, Hitchcock's
films urge us to consider the ethics and practice of reading,
but most films do not. I would agree in part with this position.
Many Hollywood films are not overtly concerned with "reading"
as that concept is used here. Thus, if the ethical or aesthetic
validity of a film depends upon the degree to which it questions
the reading process, few films of any sort are likely to pass
muster.

Yet I believe that my findings are defensible and significant
in the study of the classical narrative cinema. The "typicality"
issue remains something of a weak link; but the weakness
characterizes the arguments of Bazin and Dayan as well as my
own. If anything, given the sweepingly inclusive nature of
their charges, the burden of proof belongs to those who uphold
the Bazin/Dayan position. Thus, while it is difficult to
prove that Hitchcock is typical it is just as difficult to
prove that he isn't--unless, of course, one begs the historical
issue by defining typicality a priori in terms of
"readability."

Furthermore, Hitchcock clearly is typical to the extent that
typicality really matters to Bazin and Dayan. Both, it must be
noted, seldom if ever talk of films in arguing their theoretical
cases. They talk rather of shots or sequences. That is, they
talk in localized terms and with little if any regard for context
or function. Thus Hitchcock's films provide us with textbook
examples of "analytical montage"; and Bazin's position,
particularly in the Welles monograph and in his own essays on
Hitchcock, leaves us little choice but to describe Hitchcock as
a "tyrannical" director.[30] By the same token, Hitchcock's films
never show us the absent-one (the camera), even if they do show
us Hitchcock on occasion; and the shot/reverse shot and
point-of-view figures in his films are indistinguishable from
those described and condemned by Dayan--so once again we have
little choice, within the terms of the argument presented to us,
but to describe Hitchcock as typical of the classical narrative
cinema.

In which case, then, my own argument is sufficient
refutation of the Bazin/Dayan line of reasoning--at least to the
extent that that argument makes absolute claims about the
necessary relationship between specific cinematic techniques
and specific viewer responses. If it were absolutely true that
analytical montage or shot/reverse shot or point-of-view sequences
deny my freedom to see cinematic images as parts of a filmic whole
and require me to accept without question or consideration the
self-evidently natural truth of the ideology of the narrative,
as if that narrative were not a product of ideological
determination, then I could not have written this essay which
is very much concerned with ideology and causality. If, on the
other hand, Bazin and Dayan are not speaking in absolutes but
only of the general tendencies of particular audiences at specific

moments in history, then the question of mind/screen relations remains totally open. In which case we will have to continue doing our best to read each and every film as carefully as possible on the premise that we can evolve a discipline of film studies, a descriptive discipline that will provide the sort of knowledge necessary to the development of a valid film aesthetic and an accurate film history.

Fortunately, the discipline I have described exists to a large and important degree under the rubric of the auteur theory. It is demonstrable, I believe, that auteurism, more than any other theory of textual criticism, accords with the basic mental procedures of connotation, hypothesis, and testing by which we comprehend cinematic and aesthetic objects. Thus it is less likely than many other modes of criticism, and particularly of that suggested by the Dayan/Bazin scenario of spectator activity, to reduce the data of the text to some a priori model. The Bazin and Dayan positions both posit a macro-class of texts which is defined by a minimal number of traits. The applicability of their results is therefore tenuous in the extreme. The auteurist approach reverses priorities, however, by positing a micro-class of texts defined by a maximum number of traits. The effect of auteurism is therefore to increase our attentiveness rather than to decrease it. Equally important, however, is the fact that auteurism legitimately provides exactly that sense of causality which Dayan and Heath declare to be lacking.

Clearly the most questionable assumption in the Dayan scenario of spectator perception involves that moment when the reverse shot retroactively claims the causality of the preceding shot, thus answering the question "Who is ordering these images?" with the image of a character within the fiction--at which point the film becomes its own cause, and becomes, therefore, reality. The obvious auteurist rejoinder, of course, is to answer that question with the name of the director--at which point the film's "reality" becomes primarily an effect of rhetoric rather than sleight of hand. Neither answer to the causality question is absolutely necessary. It is difficult to imagine any spectator so naive as to take cinematic images as literal reality. Indeed, it is logically demonstrable that the "reality effect" depends upon the spectator's concurrent knowledge, however subconscious, that the images are merely images. In a world full of Instamatics it is far more likely that the answer to the "Who?" question will always be "a man with a movie camera" (to paraphrase Dziga Vertov). But the next question--"Which man or woman?"--quite legitimately invites an auteurist answer: Alfred Hitchcock.

To give that answer is not to imply that Hitchcock worked alone; nor is it in any way to deny the determining effects of history or ideology. It is a powerful acknowledgement, however, of the fact that films are made, are caused, and that they are not mere transcriptions of reality. Furthermore, to acknowledge causality (of any sort) encourages us to attend carefully to aesthetic relationships, both within and across shots. The whole

signifier/signified relationship is thus thrown into utmost
relief:  to perceive a teleology of the signifier automatically
implies a corollary teleology of the signified that the viewer
"generates" in the process of reading.  Therein lies the true
realm of textual pleasure--in the act of "narrativity," as Robert
Scholes has termed it; and pleasure so perceived and experienced
is unlikely to enslave or deaden our sensibilities.[31]  New
Criticism has long been aware of this; auteurism has known it
intuitively if sporadically; and the work of structuralist and
poststructuralist critics serves in the present context to repeat
and confirm (sometimes by negative example) the wisdom of this
textually centered view of criticism, however much our
poststructuralist colleagues might protest their disagreement.

L.P.


NOTES
1.  In this latter respect the essay owes much to readings and
    discussions undertaken while participating in a National
    Endowment for the Humanities Seminar on "The Classical
    Narrative Cinema and Modernist Alternatives" directed by David
    Bordwell at the University of Wisconsin-Madison, Summer 1978.
2.  The Editors of Cahiers du Cinéma, "John Ford's Young Mr.
    Lincoln," Screen, 13, no. 3 (1972):  5-44; Stephen Heath,
    "Film and System:  Terms of Analysis," Screen, 16, no. 1
    (1975):  7-77, and no. 2 (1975):  91-113; and Roland Barthes,
    S/Z, trans. Richard Miller (New York:  Hill and Wang, 1974).
3.  See, for example, Nick Browne, "The Spectator-in-the-Text:
    The Rhetoric of Stagecoach," Film Quarterly, 29, no. 2
    (1976):  26-38; and "Narrative Point of View:  The Rhetoric
    of Au Hasard, Balthazar," Film Quarterly, 31, no. 1
    (1977):  19-31.
4.  André Bazin and Jean Cocteau, Orson Welles (Paris:  Editions
    du Chavanne, 1950), p. 58, cited in J. Dudley Andrew, The
    Major Film Theories (New York:  Oxford Univ. Press, 1976).
    See Andrew's note, p. 258, for a history of the revisions
    in Bazin's Welles book.  Also see Bazin's "The Evolution
    of the Language of Cinema," in What Is Cinema?, vol. 1
    (Berkeley:  Univ. of California Press, 1967), pp. 23-40.
5.  See Daniel Dayan, "The Tutor-Code of Classical Cinema," Film
    Quarterly, 28, no. 1 (1974):  22-31; Jean-Louis Baudry,
    "Ideological Effects of the Basic Cinematographic Apparatus,"
    Film Quarterly, 28, no. 2 (1975):  39-47; and Jean-Pierre
    Oudart, "Cinema and Suture," Screen, 18, no. 4 (1978):
    35-47.
6.  Donald Spoto, The Art of Alfred Hitchcock (New York:
    Hopkinson and Blake, 1976).  See also Peter Wollen,
    "Hitchcock's Vision," Cinema (Cambridge), no. 3 (1969),
    pp. 2-4, and Laura Mulvey, "Visual Pleasure and Narrative
    Cinema," Screen, 16, no. 3 (1975):  6-18.

7. Robin Wood, Hitchcock's Films, 3rd ed. (New York:  A. S. Barnes & Co., 1977); and Raymond Durgnat, The Strange Case of Alfred Hitchcock (Cambridge:  The MIT Press, 1974).

8. On Sabotage see Leland A. Poague, "The Detective in Hitchcock's Frenzy:  His Ancestors and Significance," Journal of Popular Film, 2, no. 1 (1973):  47-59.

9. On Notorious see articles, identically titled "Alfred Hitchcock's Notorious," by David Bordwell, Film Heritage, 5, no. 3 (1969):  6-10, 22; and William Rothman, Georgia Review, 29, no. 4 (1975):  884-927.

10. On Spellbound see Thomas Hyde, "The Moral Universe of Hitchcock's Spellbound," Cinemonkey, no. 15 (1978): 30-34.

11. This "family film" notion is derived from Maurice Yacowar's discussion of The Lady Vanishes in Hitchcock's British Films (Hamden, Conn.:  Shoe String Press, 1977).

12. Roger Greenspun points out the importance of couples in Hitchcock in "Plots and Patterns," Film Comment, 12, no. 3 (1976):  20-22. I agree with his basic assertion, that Hitchcock's is "one of the great normative visions in the history of world cinema. To an astounding degree, men and women still have the option of loving one another and living together in sanity--under the aegis of Alfred Hitchcock" (p. 20).

13. William Cadbury discusses the Freudian implications of this ability of Hitchcock characters to "turn against the shadow and move away" in "Semiology, Human Nature, and John Ford."

14. See Poague, "Detective in Hitchcock's Frenzy," for elaboration.

15. On the relation of fictional specifics to thematic generalities see John M. Ellis, The Theory of Literary Criticism:  A Logical Analysis (Berkeley:  Univ. of California Press, 1974).

16. See E. D. Hirsch, Jr., The Aims of Interpretation (Chicago:  Univ. of Chicago Press, 1976). Hirsch's distinction between meaning and significance is crucial, though difficult to work out in terms of film. The point is that significance must be understood as a relation between text and context (p. 2). See Chapter 9 for further discussion.

17. Barthes, S/Z, p. 15.

18. Barthes, S/Z, p. 155.

19. Roland Barthes, Image/Music/Text (New York:  Hill and Wang, 1977), pp. 163, 193.

20. Barthes, S/Z, p. 160.

21. Stephen Heath, "Narrative Space," Screen, 17, no. 3 (1976):  90.

22. Rosalind Coward and John Ellis, Language and Materialism (London:  Routledge & Kegan Paul, 1977).

23. Christian Metz, Film Language:  A Semiotics of the Cinema (New York:  Oxford Univ. Press, 1974), p. 46.

24. For example see the discussion of Marnie in V. F. Perkins, Film as Film (Baltimore: Penguin Books, 1972), pp. 151-54.

25. On the "fictionality" of the reader/viewer see Walter J. Ong, "The Writer's Audience Is Always a Fiction," PMLA, 90 (1975): 9-21; and Robert T. Eberwein, "Spectator-Viewer," Wide Angle, 2, no. 2 (1978): 4-9.

26. Support for this conception of the viewer/film relationship is provided by Jack Foley in "Doubleness in Hitchcock: Seeing the Family Plot," Bright Lights, no. 7 (1978), pp. 15-28, 31.

27. See William Rothman, "Against 'The System of the Suture,'" Film Quarterly 29, no. 1 (1975): 45-50, for critique of Dayan's terminology.

28. Dayan, "Tutor-Code," p. 31.

29. Dayan, "Tutor-Code," p. 27.

30. Bazin, it should be noted, was never very comfortable with the unquestioning enthusiasm of "la jeune critique 'hitchcocko-hawksienne,'" and that discomfort, revealed in his essays on Hitchcock collected in Le Cinéma de La Cruauté (Paris: Flammarion, 1975), clearly derived from the conviction that Hitchcock's style was typical of Hollywood. As he puts it at one point (my translation): "The continuity cutting ('découpage continu') of Hitchcock in fact restores classical decoupage. Each time that we are struck by his efficiency, it is because he has succeeded, at the cost of overcoming a thousand difficulties, at using shot/reverse shot or the close-up where it would have been easy, as it is for everyone else, to employ some truly unusual shot. His moving camera mise-en-scène is nothing but a perpetual succession of recenterings, and is completely unlike the fixed frame ('plan fixé') of Wyler or of Welles, who succeed at integrating countless moments of virtual montage into a single frame" (pp. 133-34).

31. Robert Scholes, "Narration and Narrativity in Film," Quarterly Review of Film Studies, 1 (1976): 283-96.

# 6

# Auteurism:
# Theory as against Policy

## AUTEUR POLICY

An "auteur policy," as Andrew Sarris has renamed "la politique des auteurs," is the study of film history in terms of the canons of directors. It might well yield treatment of films like the following analysis of the two strands of the Fritz Lang canon.[1]

In Lang's Destiny the heroine gets from Death a series of chances to restore her lover to life by rescuing him, in various incarnations, from malevolent authority figures. They are too strong. She loses and the lover dies every time. But Death gives her another chance. She need only find one life to be given up for her lover's, and he will be returned to her. She finds a baby in a burning building to hand over to Death. Exactly what she wanted is in her grasp—but she cannot take it. She lowers the baby to safety, turns, and goes herself with Death, to die and meet her lover elsewhere. And just so are Joe Wilson in Fury, Jeremy Fox in Moonfleet, Sonja in Spies, Frank in The Return of Frank James, Dave Bannion in The Big Heat, and Tom Kent in The Testament of Dr. Mabuse tempted to immoral self-assertion, but turn at the last from revenge or safety and act morally.

But in other Lang films there is no such return. Sometimes the characters see the errors of their ways too late. They may repent at leisure, as Countess Told does in Dr. Mabuse, during her imprisonment by Mabuse when she longs for the husband she earlier despised as she heedlessly sought "sensation." More often, the characters are driven by social or personal injustice into catastrophic action. The action is often justified, yet it dooms them to death or madness. This happens to all three major characters of Rancho Notorious, Eddie and Joan Taylor in You Only Live Once, Brunhild and Kriemhild in Die Nibelungen, Vance Shaw in Western Union, and, despite the tacked-on happy ending, Alan Thorndike in Manhunt.

Sometimes, finally, the characters are driven from the start by inner fury or torment, for reasons that have little to do with response to oppression or loss. They are carried to their destruction by their own singleness of purpose. This happens to Becker in M, Haghi in Spies, and Mabuse, Professor Baum, and Professor Jordan in the three Mabuse films. Joh Fredersen, in Metropolis, allows himself to stir his own world to cataclysm by means of Rotwang, an evil projection of himself. He is saved only by his moral projection, Freder, who turns to moral action as Fredersen himself cannot. Like Mabuse's, Joh Fredersen's hair turns white at the climax.

Yet there is an underlying similarity among the issues and attitudes of films so different in outcome. Lang investigates various aspects of a situation central to his vision. Lang's people are pressed by something--regimentation, weakness in the fabric of society, deep personal loss--that tempts them unbearably towards a rejection of the morality which at the same time it demands. Individuals have a tendency to become other than moral in revenge or hope or desire. The inner force explodes upon the outer rot in cataclysms of fire and flood. The characters act with a crystalline morality of self-sacrifice or with a passionate self-destructiveness, depending on what aspect of the tension-bearing issue is emphasized in the individual film.

Even within a single film there may be virtual balance of the conflicts. We are certain that Becker, the child molester in M, should, like Mabuse, be caught. Yet we know that Mabuse was tempted by an unequivocally decadent society, and that Becker is both driven from within and terribly alienated from others who might give him support. We are drawn into sharing the manhunt for Becker, but we see that cops and crooks alike find him simply an obstacle to business-as-usual, and this attitude we cannot share. It is clear that their harrying of him is a social projection of lusts and drives like Becker's own. A plague is on both houses. It is terrible to be driven by personal demons, but organizations are as heedless of Becker's humanity as he is of the humanity of the girls he murders. The cops and crooks and beggars and bourgeoisie are terrible, too.

The auteur policy that permits analysis like this is adopted in order to discover the characterizing vision of a director by inspection of all his or her films. It is therefore a policy of unabashed induction. Its appeal, as Sarris has always said, is to the whole body of a director's work. From the simultaneous mental inspection of the films of a canon, he argues, the evidence of the informing authorial sensibility will stand forth. Likewise, the argument for a particular reading of a given film must always appeal to the whole canon. We cannot comprehend a film's place in film history, its aesthetic worth, or even its meaning, unless we understand how it takes its place in its natural context--that is, how it deals with problems of aesthetic choice, thematic implication, and accommodation to convention and fashion, in ways fathomably related to its neighbors in the canon. Under an auteur policy we can show resemblances of aspects of films, and even rightly claim that the whole sweep of film

Fig. 1.1 Wagon and rocks echo each other. John Ford's *Wagon Master.*

Fig. 1.2. Elegant tensions of the "Myronic moment" in silhouette. *Diskobolos,* by Myron. Marble copy of a bronze original. Rome, National Museum. Courtesy of Hirmer Verlag, Munich.

Fig. 1.3. Feet, hands, knees, shoulders — implicit movement through torsion. *Bronze Seated Hermes* from Herculaneum. Naples, National Archeological Museum. Courtesy of Hirmer Verlag, Munich.

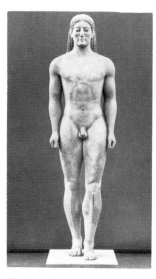

Fig. 1.4. Vigorous, foursquare dignity. *Kouros* from Anavysos. Athens, National Museum. Courtesy of Hirmer Verlag, Munich.

Fig. 1.5. "The Matisse painting is cheerful." *La Musique* by Henri Matisse. Courtesy of Albright-Knox Art Gallery, Buffalo, New York.

[Fig. 1.6–10.] John Ford's *Young Mr. Lincoln.*

Fig. 1.6. No magician, Lincoln uses
what he has kept under his hat.

Fig. 1.7. Ann is lost from the space
of truth.

Fig. 1.8. Palmer Cass does not
escape. Visual design as metaphor.

g. 1.9., Fig. 1.12.]  *A rock is thrown in the stream.*

Fig. 1.9.

Fig. 1.12.  John Ford's *The Searchers.*

Fig. 1.10.  "Your witness," and the hat decisively, rudely on.

ig. 1.11, Fig. 1.13]  *The woman appears beyond the water.*

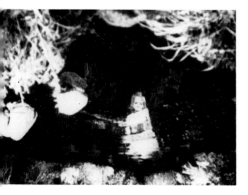

Fig. 1.11  Mary's reflection appears in the ripples. John Ford's *Pilgrimage.*

Fig. 1.13.  *The Searchers.* Debbie appears beyond the river.

Fig. 4.1. Ellie May Lester as tree
goddess.

## HITCHCOCK AND THE ETHICS OF VISION / TO READ AND BE READ

Fig. 5.1 *The 39 Steps:* The reader in
the text.

Fig. 5.2. Misreading in *The Wrong
Man.*

## THE PROBLEMATICS OF VISION

Fig. 5.3. *Notorious:* The seeing and . . .

Fig. 5.4. . . . the seen.

[Fig. 5.5–7.] *Marnie:* The final hallucination sequence.

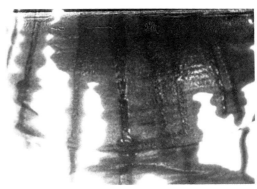

Fig. 5.6.   The sailor's shirt.

Fig. 5.5.   The young Marnie.

Fig. 5.7.   The return to the present.

Fig. 5.8.   Disproportion in *Notorious.*

Fig. 5.9.   *Strangers on a Train:*
Bruno's tie clip.

Fig. 5.10.   *Strangers on a Train:*
Bruno with Guy's lighter.

Fig. 5.11.   *To Catch a Thief:*
Distortion and class.

Fig. 5.12. *Sabotage:* Architecture and entrapment.

Fig. 5.13. Opacity in *To Catch a Thief.*

Fig. 5.14. The school on the hill in *The Birds.*

Fig. 5.15. At the door of the general store in *The Birds.*

Fig. 5.16. Accepting vulnerability in *The Birds.*

Fig. 5.17. *To Catch a Thief:* At hazard in space.

Fig. 5.18.   Paired feet in *Strangers on a Train*.

Fig. 5.19.   Manny and his "Double" in *The Wrong Man*.

Fig. 5.20.   *The 39 Steps:* Framed in the dark.

Fig. 5.21.   *The 39 Steps:* The temptation of voyeurism.

[Fig. 9.1–2.]   Alternatives in the hospital.

Fig. 9.1.   Champagne.                Fig. 9.2.   Slaps.

[Fig. 9.3–4.]   Alternatives in the architecture.

Fig. 9.3.   The first shot.          Fig. 9.4.   Milan and its reflection in
                                     the Pirelli building.

[Fig. 9.5–6.]   A hostile environment.

Fig. 9.5.   A shovel falls in the street.     Fig. 9.6.   A man sees Lidia watching.

Fig. 9.7.　The band at dawn. A checkered cloth.

Fig. 9.8.　Roberto steps between Lidia and the revelers. A checkered lawn.

Fig. 9.9.　Giovanni's reflection sees Valentina's game. A checkered floor.

Fig. 9.10.　Double reflections.

Fig. 9.11.　Lidia sees a kiss by trees.

Fig. 9.12.　Pan from Fig. 9.9. No longer reflected, but Valentina separated by trees.

Fig. 9.13.　After the kiss, separated and truncated.

Fig. 9.14.　Divided by posts.

[Fig. 9.15–20.]   Lidia, Giovanni, and trees.

Fig. 9.15.   A tree, not a game. See
Fig. 9.9.

Fig. 9.16.   The couple approach three
trees.

Fig. 9.17.   The couple as couple.
Which tree with which person?

Fig. 9.18.   The question answered.
Straight with straight.

Fig. 9.19.   And bent with bent.

Fig. 9.20.   Lidia on her own, not as
part of the couple.

Fig. 9.21. The norm.

Fig. 9.22. Giovanni listens.

Fig. 9.23. Closer.

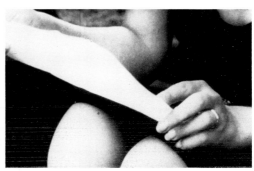

Fig. 9.24. Closer yet.

Fig. 9.25. A sad remembering.

Fig. 9.26. Trees and the couple at the end.

Fig. 9.27. Valentina turns out the light.

Fig. 9.28. From one window of Roberto's. Shrubbery.

Fig. 9.29. Happy under trees with Piero.

Fig. 9.30. At the construction site. A full frame of blowing foliage.

Fig. 9.31. Etched sprays in Piero's gloomy house.

Fig. 9.32. From Roberto's other window. A concrete reduction of the tree shape.

Fig. 9.33. Vittoria brings home a fossilized reduction of the tree shape.

Fig. 9.34. Trees and the valued building site.

Fig. 9.35. Eclipse of the natural. The tree curve emerges from trees.

Fig. 9.36.   A picture of Kenya.

Fig. 9.37.   Vittoria has fun.

Fig. 9.38.   Dwarfed by flagpoles.

Fig. 9.39.   Rebars barely protrude.

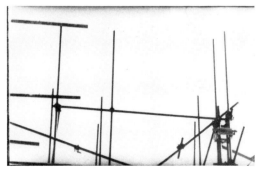

Fig. 9.40.   At the site the last time, a new shot. Spears no more.

Fig. 9.41. Piero leaves "the Beast."

Fig. 9.42. Vittoria leaves Piero.

[Fig. 9.43–50.] The beginning of the love affair, and its affectionate parody.

Fig. 9.43. "I'll kiss you on the other side."

Fig. 9.44. A stranger walks where the couple lingered.

Fig. 9.45. Kissing through glass.

Fig. 9.46. Vittoria mimes it, and comes after Piero.

Fig. 9.47.   Piero presses.

Fig. 9.48.   Vittoria gets a headlock.

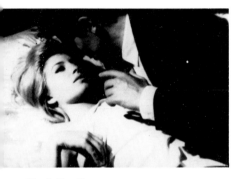

Fig. 9.49.   Piero pounces.

Fig. 9.50.   Vittoria pounces.

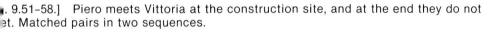

. 9.51–58.]   Piero meets Vittoria at the construction site, and at the end they do not
et. Matched pairs in two sequences.

Fig. 9.51.   Vittoria walks behind the
masonry.

Fig. 9.52.   Masonry again, without
Vittoria.

Fig. 9.53. Vittoria waits by the crosswalk.

Fig. 9.54. Crosswalk again, no Vittoria.

Fig. 9.55. Piero approaches, sulky behind.

Fig. 9.56. Sulky, no Piero.

Fig. 9.57. Vittoria touches matchbook and stick, for remembrance.

Fig. 9.58. Matchbook only, and the water about to drain.

history demonstrates that the resemblances of films arranged by
"directional bundles" are the most rewarding for aesthetic
analysis.[2]

But there are limits to the claims we can make under such
an appeal. Under the auteur policy, we cannot actually analyze
an individual film, whether we know its author or not. An
inductive policy's chain of inference pulls in the wrong
direction. From the qualities in a set of films we can infer
a pattern of resemblances among them, and argue for the value
of treating the films as a bundle on the basis of the qualities
of the whole set. But we cannot infer from the pattern the
determinative force of the qualities emphasized by the pattern
in the individual instance. After all, the film's form may be
dependent on structural relations that appear nowhere else in
the canon, even though some hallmark images or sequences do.
We might find exactly those relations in the single film that
we find in the bundle--but where in our policy are we licensed
to say that those relations which recur must be the ones under
which we ought to organize the reading of the single film?

Surely we ought to read a film as _it_ deserves to be read,
not as its context encourages us to read it. With a policy of
induction we can "prove" authorship of a bundle of films. But
without a theory of the significance of such qualities as we find
in directional bundles to the individual films from which we
inferred them, we cannot "prove" that a film should itself be
analyzed as we are suggesting, and hence we cannot finally make
the claims we want to make about the authorial vision. For even
if we noted a striking pattern of resemblances and permutations,
we would still have to admit that each film of the group might
be organized, in those key ways which give it its own aesthetic
value, entirely on its own and without any crucial similarity
to the other films with which it might share what antiauteurists
are so scornful of, "directorial touches."

Lacking proof that the resemblances in a bundle are crucial,
we can be comfortable neither with our analysis of the individual
film nor with our synthesis of the qualities of the bundle. We
may have spotted a pattern that holds it together. We may feel
that the pattern is the one that counts, and that our exposition
of it may be an ostensive proof that it is the right one--"See,
here's the pattern, now deny that I've got it right." But we
haven't supported our exposition in a rational framework that
could stand up to the charges of Cartesian subjectivism and
imprisonment in imaginary illusions that are being brought against
auteurists by the neo-semiologists.

But we need not be embarrassed by Descartes. Chomsky isn't,
and it is his influence, rather belatedly received, that has
caused the current awkward shift from Saussurian to Lacanian
semiology. And I think something can be said for an "auteur
theory"--taking theory in a sufficiently colloquial sense--
grounded in outright acceptance of the Cartesian Subject. Under
such a theory an individual film would have a proper analysis

in terms of rationally grounded theory, in addition to offering
a set of attributes to be processed inductively as evidence
bearing on the nature of an authorial bundle. An auteur theory
would say that certain things count for authorship because they
are the things that count for meaningfulness of the individual
film.

Authorship refers to the vision manifested in a work, rather
than to control of the work's production. If a work doesn't have
the minimum balance among the three canonical attributes--unity,
complexity, and intensity of human qualities--that enables it
to provide aesthetic experience, then the question of authorship
never comes up, since authorship concerns aesthetic objects.
Asking "Who is responsible for this?" in a schoolmasterly tone
is a historical question, and not a critical one. When the
question of authorship does arise, it can only be answered by
analysis of the unique shaping imagination, and not by appeal
to an unrecoverable historical record.[3]

Analysis of individual films in the terms an auteur theory
prescribed would yield a set of qualities that we could use, with
other analyses, to constitute the characterizing pattern of
resemblances in a canon in terms of the theory. With that set
established, we would be justified in inferring, when we found
a member of that set of qualities to be determinative in an
individual case, that the case was in fact one of this vision
and not of some other, even though the author with that other
vision might be responsible for certain aspects of the film in
question. And this would be possible because the theory, as a
theory, asserts a specific relationship between the authorial
vision and the qualities of specific films. It is the
relationship of being described in the same principled terms,
the terms of the theory. But an auteur policy, as a policy of
induction, can only assert that inspection of a director's canon
will yield a pattern of resemblances among qualities of member
films.

A perfect opportunity to test a film for authorship by means
of a theory is Desire, directed by Frank Borzage and produced
by Ernst Lubitsch. Because Borzage and Lubitsch are auteurs with
strong visions that we can specify and compare in terms of a
theory, a description of Desire in the same terms should give
clear indication of which vision may be understood to underlie
it. We will turn to this after discussing the plausibility and
the outline of an "auteur theory" with which we can make our case.


AUTEUR THEORY

We may generalize our point that there is an underlying
similarity among Lang's films despite their different patterns
and implications of plot. What we seek primarily in an author's
canon is neither repetition of elements nor specific thematic
implications, nor even continuities of style. Rather we seek
an attitude toward issues of people's relations to their own

purposes and to their worlds, which attitude charges and informs
each film's implicational logic and style.  Such an attitude is
the consequence of an authorial vision.  An authorial vision is
a particular set of relations constituting a view, on the one
hand, of what people are like in their drives, plans, capacities,
and limitations, and, on the other, of what the world is like
in its opportunities and restrictions, its nourishment of and
resistance to the fulfillment of human hopes.  An individual art
work raises, develops, and resolves an issue concerning attitudes
to particular interactions between people and their worlds that
stand out as important under the vision.

The point is not restricted to realistic or even to
representational works.  Deren's Meshes of the Afternoon,
Légers's Ballet Mécanique, even "structuralist" works like Paul
Sharits's Ray Gun Virus, resonate with such interactions, though
by means different from imitation of life.  Ballet Mécanique,
for instance, develops an attitude of approval of the mechanical,
by moving from a conventional treatment of human habitation of
space and nature to a presentation of human processes intimately
and pleasingly linked with what we are likely to think to be
antihuman and merely mechanical.

We should be clear about what is meant by issues and
attitudes, though there is nothing technical here, nothing
incompatible with ordinary usage.  If, as in Lang's vision, the
world itself brings forth people's capacity for manic intensity,
then how should we feel when a justifiable goal is contaminated
by the mania caused by reaching for it?  That is the kind of
question indicated by our use of "issue."  Answers to such
questions are provided by the very implicational structure of
the whole film itself, the fused interrelationship of all its
implications and meaning and value.  The particular interactions
in the film, inseparable from the images by which we know them,
amount to demonstrations of an attitude toward such issues.  What
an image connotes, suggests, and entails (as well as what both
society in general and art works in particular have said and
thought about both similar images and what they represent) is
part of it.  For someone who has been to the movies before,
and knows their conventions, and is paying attention, seeing the
image is seeing what it means.  So such contemplatable, attitude-
bearing images (up to and including that of the whole film) are
themselves virtually Beardsleyan "theses" that suggest what
attitude could be taken when the film's issues appear in the real
world.  We might call them "aesthetic statements," remembering
only that unlike ordinary statements they are not asserted but
merely presented for contemplation.[4]

Each aesthetic statement may well be different in the
different films of an auteur, but each is commensurate with the
set of relations constituting the authorial vision, and with only
that one.  In fact, to see that it is commensurate is what we
mean by "knowing" the auteur, having that set of relations so
carefully discriminated that only the aesthetic statements that

fit this set and no other will seem to belong together under the
theory, to be characteristic of this authorial vision. "The way
the film goes, it couldn't be anybody else's," is the way we
usually put such knowledge. It is not, of course, that we know
the author as we know our friends, and it would make no difference
to us if we found that Shakespeare was really Bacon after all.
It is that we know the range of attitudes that can be in the films
of an auteur.

So the individual film renders an attitude that is its own
but is among those compatible with the attitude discernible in
the authorial vision. If we get the point of the film, we
understand its attitude because the particular issues developed
by the totality of its style and action illustrate for us certain
relations among our drives and hindrances, and the contexts that
impede or support them. We grasp the facts of the film surface--
the plot, characterization, style, setting, elements of mise-en-
scène--in terms of these relations. Thus we understand the
film because it is grounded, like the vision itself, in a set
of attitudes about issues of relations between people and their
worlds.

We know such issues when we see them--they are important
to us--and we know attitudes toward them, though we need not agree
with the attitude presented by the film. We know, moreover, how
various actions and their outcomes could count toward expressing
an attitude toward such issues. We can see, for example, how
the quest for sensation in a rotten world might be comprehensible
and even forgiveable. But we can also see how what happens to
Countess Told in Dr. Mabuse can amount only to an ·expression
of a statement. In the very film that asks us to sympathize with
her, there is shown a terrible drawback to her plan.

Films' attitudes, and the attitudes implicit in authorial
visions, are rich and complex and different from each other, like
the attitudes which a sensitive observer can take to life. Our
argument here is that the sequences and images, which is to say
the parts and the whole of both cinematic surface and its
projected world, are in fact organized in the logic of aesthetic
statements. Two qualities become plain in any film that will
count as well-formed for us, that will seem coherent and
meaningful, and bear contemplation. These two qualities we call
"the vision of the good" (or simply "the good") in the work, and
the vision of what it is set against, "the hindrance." The issue
of feeling, of the interactions between people and their worlds,
that underlies the work's particular sequences and allows them
to image forth an aesthetic statement, is properly analyzed in
terms of the struggle of the good both against its own weaknesses
or "drawbacks" (to make a technical term of it) and against the
hindrances brought against it from the depths of character or
from the world outside. The presentation of that struggle amounts
to a proposition in the logic of the imagination, a particular
aesthetic statement as to the desirable vs. the fearful, their
interplay, and its consequences. This assertion is itself one

of the derivable shapes of the imagination and may be considered
the equivalent of the auteur's vision as it is manifested in a
particular film.
      The good and the hindrance are always clear--that is, it
is only when they are clear for us that we will find the film
coherent.  We know what we must value as desirable, within the
film's design and subject, if we are to participate in its flow
and not work against its grain.  We know also what it is that
is getting in the way of the good.  In trivial films that may
be all we know.  Such films may not do much more than appeal
to stock responses to ensure our knowing it.  Much may be said
for getting the girl or killing the villain, much may be made
of the impediments and intrigues, but little may be said on the
other side--what a prudent person fears by way of an aftermath
for the couple, or what we may become as we do the justifiable
killing.  But living in the world as we do, and knowing that there
are imaginable goods and hindrances in it, as well as knowing
that the goods are liable to such overextensions and under-
realizations as to amount to drawbacks assignable to the goods
themselves, we know that what may seem purely hindrances have
a good side, as goods have a bad.  We know, in effect, that as
goods have drawbacks, so hindrances have what we might call
"hedges," sets of qualities lending good possibilities to the
apparently worst directions.  A good film knows it too, as does
a good vision informing a set of films.
      In fact, the better a film or vision knows the relations
of goods and hindrances, the richer, the fuller, the more
evocative, the more humane, in fact, the better the film or
vision is.  And this is simply because aesthetic value is the
capacity in an aesthetic object to induce aesthetic experience
of some magnitude in an observer prepared to see what is going
on in a design and the world it projects.  Aesthetic experience
amounts in large part to the observation and contemplation of
a set of relations among parts that in their human aspect are
contemplatable exactly because they suggest all sides of the
attitude we can take.  It is obvious that a balanced work must
be the work that is best suited to aesthetic experience.
      So not only does the theory presented here let us name
visions, it lets us name them in the way we care about most, the
way that will encourage us to judge among them and the films that
manifest them, and to appreciate them for their aesthetic value.
Such a judgment must be implicit in any specification of an
author's vision, simply because its definition is couched in the
terms that are also the terms for its capacity to induce aesthetic
experience--the terms for aesthetic value.  It is notable, too,
that in the work of those who take this approach the question
of evaluation very seldom comes up.  When the critical work is
careful, and the specification of film meaning and form of vision
appropriately finely tuned, by the time the terms of the vision
are spelled out its value has become obvious.
      To summarize:  to know a film or vision under an auteur

theory is to perceive that it organizes a set of issues in terms
of a set of implications about what in the particular metaphoric
world of the work or vision in question is desirable or
undesirable in human experience.  What is wanted or feared is
presented in such a way as to induce audiences to contemplate
the nature of things as seen under just this organization, and
to share the attitude rendered, whether an attitude of delight
in possibilities or anguish at their absence.  We see a film in
its own terms.  Hence we see and think about the world in those
terms through the film that suggests them.  To know the film is
to know what those terms are.  And, as well as knowing the author
as the hypothetical imagination that can have organized the film
in those terms, we can, using the theory, also hypothesize whether
a given film should be seen as belonging in the canon of a
particular auteur.  This is a side effect of the theory that is
not possible for a mere policy, which does infer visions from
regularities of elements, but never asks whether to include some
new, questionable balance of elements in what it seeks to
regularize.

    Let us turn to Desire, both to explicate the theory and
to prove its worth in establishing attribution by seeing how the
film's aesthetic statement marches with the visions of the two
strong auteurs who had a hand in the film's production, Borzage
and Lubitsch.  The film's presentational surface is full of
"Lubitsch touches" of cleverness, elegance, surprise, and comedy.
For example, the pan, from the door of Duval's jewelry store to
the peephole from which he watches his customers, deflates the
snooty elegance of the shop.  The pantomime conversation behind
glass doors--it echoes Trouble in Paradise-- between Carlos,
Madeline's "uncle," and Tom Bradley, Madeline's savior, American
rube, and salesman of Bronson 8's, distances us a bit from the
comic complications we know we will savor.  The constant routines
involving cigarettes render the fun and play of human
interaction.  And there is a wonderful insouciance to such lines
as the one spoken by Tom, who, when having kicked Carlos's gun
out of his hand and into a serving dish, instructs the cook to
"Take this to the kitchen and disarm the fricassee."

    The lightness of touch here and in many other scenes is
distinctly Lubitsch-like.  But there are scenes that Lubitsch
would have shot differently.  For instance, Tom reports how he
has slapped and spanked Madeline for thievery.  While he tells
it, she seems to approve and to adore him for the chastisement.
There is a certain almost aberrant coarseness to Borzage--think
of Chico's holding Nana over the open sewer and laughing at her
terror in Seventh Heaven, or of Gilly Johnson in Moonrise
acting the grand Southern lady in order to reduce the sexual
tension that she intends to release and also to relish.  Lubitsch
would not indulge in a frisson about the possibility of rape.
Borzage's romanticism is partly a sexism that Lubitsch escapes.

    That coarseness might distinguish Borzage from Lubitsch and

show why Lubitsch belongs in the Pantheon and Borzage on the steps
of the temple.  But we would not wish to define Borzage merely
through his deficiencies.  Nor do we have to.  The distancing
Lubitsch-like touches are the dominating tonal devices only in
the beginning of Desire.  After that, the film emphasizes a
more intimate matter--the achievement of a relationship between
Madeline and Tom that will redeem Madeline from the nastiness
of Carlos, Olga, and her previous life.  As the film develops,
individuality becomes transcendent through the commitment of
love--and with that transcendence the characters are empowered
to act in a conventionally moral way.

     The feeling attending conventional moral action, however,
is not conventional.  Olga argues that Madeline could never love
Tom because she could never flee the law or escape her past.
But the argument is denied in the attitude the film projects.
The sincerity of Madeline's appeal to Duval, of her assurance
that "I have changed my life" as she returns the stolen pearls
and asks that he not prosecute, constitutes the substance and
proof of her escaping her past, of being freed from domination
by mere circumstance.

     In Borzage, the conventional is made luminous with selfhood.
Madeline's assurance to Duval renders the same rich mixture of
tones as those which, in Moonrise, attach to the scene when
Danny comes back to his friend Sheriff Clem who will arrest him,
to his hound-friend Daisy Belle who has tracked him down, to his
black friend Mose who approves his surrender, and to his girl
friend, Gilly, with whom he walks off toward prison in the
sunrise.  We accept our accountability and are, in some sense,
imprisoned--yet at the same time we can achieve a transfiguration
that makes the submission inconsequential.  In Three Comrades
the characters walk off together at the end even though two of
them are shades.

     In the phrase of the Boss in Sturges's The Great McGinty,
the Borzage characters are "at the mercy"--exactly where the love
is.  It would not fit Lubitsch's delicately ironic respect for
his characters' autonomy to emphasize, as Borzage does, the
adoration with which Madeline looks at Tom over breakfast or over
dinner, while he commiserates with her for her red hands which
he has slapped.  And Lubitsch would certainly never have
portrayed, as does Borzage, the way Madeline and Tom come together
to discover their love.  Tom is an utterly American rube to
Madeline's totally decadent European sophisticate as he tells
her about Detroit, smoke, and work.  But Madeline says, as she
relishes him, that "The Spanish moon is very becoming to you,
I never saw you in this light before."  As they kiss we see, first
over her shoulder to him and then in a high shot past him to her,
a delirious rendition of sexuality of a sort we never find in
Lubitsch.

     But this is where Borzage lives.  We see it very clearly
in a contrast with Murnau.  Murnau directs Janet Gaynor,

reconciled with her husband in Sunrise, as playful, sweet, and
winning, but hardly as sexual.  But in Seventh Heaven, Borzage
directs her, in the role of Diane, as a very paradigm of open
sexuality.  When Diane and Chico admit they love each other, she
leans against him, kisses his ear and neck, and sags against him
in a sexual abandon like Madeline's in Tom's arms.  Again we see
this in a sudden high shot.  It is unusually intimate, not only
in its explicit sexuality, but also in the way sex, as it so
seldom is in the movies, is perfectly attuned to strong feelings
of mutuality.  In contrast, when Murnau does treat open sexuality
in Sunrise, it is by having the Woman from the City bite the
husband on the neck like Nosferatu.

Borzage makes it plain that the people who experience the
kisses he shows are never the same again.  No matter how many
Lubitsch-like touches there are in Desire, the way Tom and
Madeline look at each other later reminds us that their kiss was
what counted.  And we must remember that those kisses are the
kind of thing a director literally has in his control.  There
is no disputing their evidence; they render the quality of
intimate intensity that is the central aspect of Borzage's image
of the good.

The achievement of that quality is accomplished again and
again through camera placement.  We saw, in both Desire and
in Seventh Heaven, sudden surprising high shots attending the
key kisses.  In Moonrise, as Danny and Gilly begin to dance
together in the ruins of the Blackwater mansion, the camera swoops
back and up to bring into the foreground a cobwebbed chandelier,
while the couple dances in the background.  The camera comes down
and toward the couple as they move toward a tattered harp.
Finally the camera comes to rest in a curtained window, with a
close two-shot of the pair in silhouette, saying "It's never been
like this before," and kissing.  This is another magic Borzage
moment.

Thus in one sense, the shape of Borzage's imagination is
visual—it can be expressed as "from far away to close two-shot."
In Three Comrades, a sudden high shot introduces the ending
sequence.  The opening theme from Tristan begins as, in the
high shot, Pat gets out of bed to stagger to the window to die.
Erich sees her from below, again in long shot, as she pirouettes
and collapses.  Then he rushes to her, to share, in close two-shot
and to the accompaniment of the Liebestod, the ecstatic moments
of her death.

In History Is Made at Night after the ship has struck the
iceberg, we enter a sequence with a long shot of the fog-shrouded
ship, a track towards it, a dissolve to Paul and Irene sitting
on a companionway in the mist, and finally a cut to the close
two-shot in which, while strange shrieks and moans surround them,
they speak of their early lives.  They enrich their experience
of each other, and fill their minds with all that matters to them
at that moment despite their plight—with talk of Irene's braces

and Paul's eyes, of her young shyness and his truancy. Again
we see a transfiguration within an imprisonment which the
transfiguration makes inconsequential.
    Borzage gives the same treatment to an earlier sequence in
the film. Beginning in a street scene, he pans to the carriage
and horses in which Paul and Irene are riding, then cuts inside
to where Irene rests her head on Paul's shoulder, and finally
dissolves to that close two-shot, in which they kiss. "Oh," says
Irene. They kiss again, and "Oh again"; and they kiss again,
"And Oh forever."
    Borzage's style presents his vision and valuation of the
good in human relations most directly in shots like these which
render the symbolic shared experiences and transcendental
attitudes of his characters in very direct visual images. The
characters form a world of their own in the intimacy of these
two-shots that makes everything else irrelevant, until, like Paul
and Irene, Gilly and Danny, they have to bring the lesson of those
moments into the moral dawn again.
    But we might still argue that Desire is a film by Lubitsch
despite the Borzagian elements, unless we could claim that it
was incommensurate with Lubitsch's vision as well as commensurate
with Borzage's. For instance, Desire is a clearly different
film from Trouble in Paradise, in that the jewel thieves in
Desire are not sophisticates who reject bourgeois security,
but rather immoral outcasts who should be caught if they do not
reform and who are transfigured if they do. We might argue for
Lubitsch's authorship by pointing out that Desire is a later
film. Perhaps we might see it as a film on the road to
Ninotchka and The Shop around the Corner. In Desire, as
in Ninotchka, after all, a woman is brought to change her ways
by the force of a man's love. She moves toward salvation from
a maladaptive commitment in which she was imprisoned. But the
difference in visions of the good between the two films outweighs
their similarity in plot. Ninotchka is truly committed to her
Soviet ideology and morals, silly as the troika of Iranoff,
Buljanoff, and Kopalski make them seem. The love life she will
lead with Leon is clearly a bittersweet acceptance of the pressure
of laughter and civility. Madeline, on the other hand, learns
that what she thought she could only dream of is possible after
all.
    Similarly, Leon redeems Ninotchka with his sophistication
as Tom redeems Madeline with his innocent directness. But Leon
changes too, away from what he was like with Swana and towards
what Ninotchka herself is like. Tom, on the other hand, does
not change at all. He is a silly rube like Ninotchka, but
rubishness in Borzage needs no qualifying. The good in Desire
is ecstatic American directness opposed to European
sophistication, but in Ninotchka, it is a very European mixture
of values by which one settles from extremes into laughing sense.
While it might seem as if Ninotchka is more Borzagian than is

Trouble in Paradise, the same relations among attitudes hold
for Lubitsch under the more softened later conventions as under
the brighter ones of a decade earlier.

Garbo's contribution to Ninotchka might be said to obscure
a comparison of that film with Desire. The Shop around the
Corner might support a better argument--that Desire is a
Lubitsch film halfway to the forties. Indeed Kralik has the same
sort of saving effect as Tom when he helps Klara get over her
snobbishness about culture and jobs. But Tom is an unequivocally
romantic hero, a wondrous lover disguised as a car salesman.
Kralik, on the other hand, is a mixed character who continues
to the end with a quality of delightfully mercenary and seedy
clerkishness, which is exactly what Klara learns to appreciate.
Similarly, Klara is as mistaken in her aims as Ninotchka. But
at the same time she is appealing and corrigible for her mistakes
in pursuing her aims without moderation. Madeline, however, is
not a partly approvable prisoner of her own bad goals, but a
prisoner absolute, whether when she is a willing vamp or when
she is in despair after learning of an alternative that she thinks
cannot be hers. The underlying relation between people and their
worlds in Lubitsch is one in which errors of exaggeration are
corrected by laughter and the middle way. But in Desire, the
miserable sophisticate longs for reclamation by love, and achieves
it.

The contrast between these relations illustrates the truth
of Northrop Frye's remark that there is a difference that is more
than a distinction between comic romance and romantic comedy.[5]
Borzage's romances are often funny, but they turn on the emergence
of force in a rescuing hero. They approve the feelings of release
and command that attend the victory of our simplest plans over
the apparently constraining qualifications and complexities with
which the world surrounds us--and in the presence of which we
feel like naive rubes. Lubitsch's comedies are often romantic,
but they approve the feelings of satisfied awareness that go with
the realization that there are no romantic simplicities to which
we could leap, but rather that the world is as it is, in all its
mixedness and irony, and still the best source of satisfaction.

The interactions between people and their worlds that
Lubitsch presents illustrate his image of value, as Borzage's
presented interactions illustrate his. Gaston is tempted to
simplify his life and goals by becoming the rich husband of Mme
Colet. Ninotchka tries to cling to an absolutist view. Kralik
and Klara wish to leave the shop in which they work and enter
a world of poetry and rhetorical bliss. Gilda, in Design for
Living, thinks she will be more secure with Max than with her
merry wastrels. Lady Windermere wants to give up all for love.
Danilo, in The Merry Widow, would remain free and ecstatic with
his Maxim's girls. Danilo's satisfactory prison wedding can stand
for the retreat to the mixed, funny, middle life of all these
comedies. Whereas Borzage's romances assert the ecstasy of
forceful simplicity, Lubitsch's comedies assert the graceful irony

of  acceptance.   The  conclusion  is  plain:   _Desire_  is  by  Borzage,
not  by  Lubitsch.

We  can  distinguish  Borzage  from  Lubitsch,  then,  largely
through  comparison  of  their  visions  of  the  good.   But  our  goal
was  to  _specify_  Borzage  rather  than  merely  distinguish  him.
Our  theory  says  that  any  imagination  must  possess  an  attitude
toward  what  it  sees  as  the  _hindrance_  to  its  image  of  the  good.
And  Borzage  has  a  very  clear  image  of  what  acts  as  hindrance  to
his  lovers'  transcendence.   In  Borzage  the  universe  is  not
composed  solely  of  those  who  have  not  reached  the  lovers'  ecstasy,
but  also  of  positive  oppressors.   The  analysis  of  the  interplay
between  visions  of  the  good  and  the  bad,  the  auteur  theory  says,
is  the  goal  of  the  shaping  imagination.   As  we  contrasted
Borzage's  image  of  the  good  with  Lubitsch's  because  it  is  similar
yet  discriminable,  so  we  can  contrast  Borzage's  image  of  the  bad
with  another's  to  show  that  auteur  analysis  is  indeed  governed
by  theory  and  not  merely  by  the  policy  of  discovering
continuities.

In  many  ways  the  characteristic  couple  of  Nicholas  Ray,  the
bearers  of  his  vision  of  the  good  like  Bowie  and  Keechie  of  _They_
_Live  by  Night_  or  Tom  and  Vicki  of  _Party  Girl_  or  Walt  and  Naomi
of  _Wind  across  the  Everglades_,  is  like  a  Borzage  couple,  though
Ray  is  more  coltish  and  exuberant  in  his  image  than  Borzage,  who
is  more  monolithically  sexual.   Ray's  Inuk  and  Asiak  play  childish
pushing  games  in  _The  Savage  Innocents_,  and  Judy  and  Jim  romp
in  fine  young  fettle  in  _Rebel  without  a  Cause_.

More  important,  for  Ray  the  central  couple  is  surrounded
by  paired  opponents,  by  gangsters  on  one  side  and  by  nasty
bourgeois  respectables  on  the  other.   Cottonmouth's  wild  gang
in  _Wind  across  the  Everglades_  is  opposed  to  the  cold  real  estate
promoters.   Rico's  gang  in  _Party  Girl_  is  opposed  to  the  bourgeois  lawyers  of  Chicago.   Chicamaw  and  T-Dub  in  _They  Live  by_
_Night_  are  opposed  to  all  the  others,  who  are  "thieves  like  us"
but  won't  admit  it.   The  Dancin'  Kid's  gang  in  _Johnny  Guitar_
is  opposed  to  Emma  Small's  horrible  townsfolk.   Buzz  and  his  gang
are  opposed  to  the  parental  generation  in  _Rebel  without  a_
_Cause_.   And  the  same  characteristic  weighted  structure  in  these
films  holds  for  _Bigger  Than  Life_,  _Knock  on  Any  Door_,  _The_
_True  Story  of  Jesse  James_,  and  _On  Dangerous  Ground_.   It  is
only  in  _The  Savage  Innocents_,  an  overt  fantasy,  that  we  find
respectable  exploiters  like  the  Troupers  and  other  white  people
without  parallel  gangsters.

These  paired  opponents  provide  alternatives  for  the  central
couple.   The  gangsters  are,  by  and  large,  the  more  sympathetic,
but  the  point  is  always  that  the  couple  must  try  to  escape  from
them  and  their  heedless  self-destructiveness  into  a  kind  of
domesticity,  a  freedom  within  the  microcosm  of  the  couple,  which
will  allow  them  to  escape  the  oversocialized,  overintegrative
loss  of  self  within  bourgeois  society,  as  well  as  the
undersocialized,  overassertive  exaggeration  of  self  within  the
gangsters'  mirror-image  of  it.   So  Ray  always  implies  a  kinship

with the gangster motive, though always recognizing how that motive, unchecked, carries us too far--we must become a part of one of his unique couples to avoid both the gangster's mania, the delusion of being bigger than life, and the submissive, integrative slide into coldness, acceptance of social constraint, anxious uncertainty, and death from that nameless disease that only a tempered dose of psychic cortisone, despite its implosive-explosive dangers, can hold in check.

The Borzage imagination does not see the lovers surrounded by these pairs, but rather as imprisoned in a world of uniform hostility from which they must escape as a couple. Rather than half admiring those whose extremes must be avoided, Borzage entirely despises the evil and always-pressing controllers of the lovers who would reduce them to subservience to the social structure, would grind them down. So for good Diane there are evil Nana and Brissac. For Chico there is the war machine itself, as well as his friend Gobin the streetwasher, who is entirely too accepting of authority--and whose hoses bear entirely too close a resemblance to the flamethrower that blinds Chico. So for Madeline there is Carlos and for Tom there is embarrassment and a sense of reduced possibilities in being a postman's child. So for Irene there is Bruce, her millionaire husband, while for Paul there is the embarrassment of being a headwaiter, even though he is the best in the world. And for Danny Hawkins, the hillbilly, there is the oppression of Jerry Sykes, the banker's son, while for Gilly, the country girl, there is the insidious pressure to rise in social class and not run with the likes of Danny at all.

The oppressors are a nasty lot. Carlos is an evil and strangely perverse man, someone to be feared. Nana is evil incarnate and overblown. Bruce combines class hauteur with simple obsession in the jealousy that sends Irene to Paul. And Jerry Sykes taunts Danny with his father's execution to earn himself a largely justified murder--which Sheriff Clem understands so well that he can assure Gilly that Danny will have most of his life before him when he gets out of jail. So, whereas some of the oppressors self-destruct like Bruce and Jerry, it is clear in Borzage that the couple transcends pressure through the sort of fidelity that saves Diane from Brissac, and also that it is perfectly impossible for a nontranscendent person to resist pressure. In History Is Made at Night, for instance, the Commodore, knowing from the water temperature that they are in iceberg waters, nonetheless obeys ship-owner Bruce's radioed commands for more speed. These commands are literally intended to result in the deaths of Irene and Paul, but the Commodore cannot resist them. His submission presents the alternative to the lovers' freedom within the self-regulation of their own plans. And we observe, through the Commodore, how it is possible that an apparently obsequious headwaiter actually may be self-determining in a way that an apparently high official may not be.

The Commodore's catatonic obedience, his willingness to do

what he is ordered to do and his emotional dissociation from his
own acts, make up a Borzage image of the world when our acts are
not guided by love.  This image informs the whole film and
provides us with a sense of a structure of possibility that the
lovers must transcend.  This clearly contrasts with Ray, for whom
the point is not to go too far toward a craziness that is in part
a natural reaction against the class system.  For Borzage the
point is to escape from the surrounding deadness in the only way
possible, by the kind of lover's transcendence that is his image
of the good and that replaces for the lovers the class system
altogether.  We see from this that the Borzage image of the
hindrance is and must be as explicit as is his image of the good.
We can only really understand a quality if we understand
thoroughly how it is not its alternative.

The auteur theory must specify the full shape of the
imagination, including its image of the hindrance as well as its
image of the good.  When we have a clear picture of the images
of someone like Borzage, we see they are all varieties of deadness
of spirit imposed by a world of class dominance and by an
associated psychological mania.  When we see how this differs
from Ray's picture of a polar evil--an explosion into madness
like that of the red exploding planetarium star in Rebel without
a Cause or the emptiness and ineffectuality of the schoolteachers
of Bigger Than Life--we can describe the imaginations of the
two very directly.  We can say that Ray's picture of the good
is of something lying between extremes, which is to say that we
can see him as a moralist cautioning against the dangers of what
he sees as a quite natural kind of satisfaction.  But we can say
that Borzage's picture of the good is of something that is
extreme, the all-consuming power that directly opposes that
hindering extreme of deadness.  Ray tells us to watch for
deadness, but Borzage tells us to transcend it.

We come to a precise discrimination among different authorial
visions under our theory.  We have not been impressionistic in
reporting on similarities or differences that strike us as
important.  It is this precision that antiauteurists have felt
the lack of in studies under an auteur policy.  That lack has
sent them to seek alternatives that they thought were better
related to solid knowledge.  We can sympathize, but we realize,
too, that solid knowledge is never either easy to come by or
obvious.  But the solid comparisons under a simple yet defensible
set of principled terms, such as our theory provides, are
extendable both into specific analysis of individual films and
into illuminating and forceful comparisons among auteurs.  This
is the kind of work that the auteur theory is fully theoretically
justified in doing, and, perhaps, uniquely capable of providing.
As a theory of the imagination, the auteur theory demands that
we discover the total shape of imagination in its vision of good
and hindrance, rather than settling easily into any component
image, even such a striking one as a Borzage kiss.

                                                                    W.C.

NOTES
1. Andrew Sarris, in interview in <u>Film Heritage</u>, 8, no. 4
   (1973):   30; Andrew Sarris, "Notes on the Auteur Theory in
   1970," <u>The Primal Screen</u> (New York:   Simon and Schuster,
   1973), pp. 55, 58.
2. Andrew Sarris, "The Auteur Theory and the Perils of Pauline,"
   <u>Film Quarterly</u>, 16, no. 4 (1963):   28; for "directional
   bundles" see Sarris, "Note on the Auteur Theory in 1962,"
   <u>Film Quarterly</u>, 28, no. 1 (1974):   63.
3. For excellent and underrated debate on the question of
   authorship see Alan Lovell, "Robin Wood:   A Dissenting View,"
   <u>Screen</u>, 10, no. 2 (1969):   42-55; Robin Wood, "Ghostly
   Paradigm and H.C.F.:   An Answer to Alan Lovell," <u>Screen</u>,
   10, no. 3 (1969):   35-48; Alan Lovell, "The Common Pursuit
   of True Judgment," <u>Screen</u>, 11, no. 4-5 (1970):   76-88; John
   C. Murray, "Robin Wood and the Structural Critics," <u>Screen</u>,
   12, no. 3 (1971):   101-10; Robin Wood, "Hawks De-Wollenized,"
   <u>Personal Views</u> (London:   Gordon Fraser, 1976), pp. 191-206.
4. Monroe C. Beardsley, <u>Aesthetics</u> (New York:   Harcourt Brace
   & World, 1958), pp. 419-37, esp. pp. 422-23.
5. Northrop Frye, <u>Anatomy of Criticism</u> (Princeton:   Princeton
   Univ. Press, 1957), p. 177.

# 7

# Intentionality, Authorship, and Film Criticism

DEBATE OVER AUTEURISM

It is probably mistaken to speak of "the discipline of film criticism." Quite clearly there are several such disciplines and a good deal of theoretical confusion results from the fact that the differences among them are seldom fully acknowledged. This confusion is most serious in cases where general differences in critical purpose are argued at the more specific level of critical categories. The ongoing debate over auteurism is a good case in point.

The category has fallen into disrepute, as I read the situation, not because of any inherent or internal weakness but because particular critics have come to disagree with the critical purpose generally served by auteurism. Auteur criticism, that is, concerns itself primarily (though not exclusively) with the significance that specific texts might have for contemporary viewers: why watch The Big Sleep now? To be sure, the methodology for determining significance is intertextual and generic in focus. One proceeds by setting one Hawks film, say, next to another in order to discern their similarities. But it is an unstated though implicit premise of auteur theory that those traits held in common by the films of a given director are likely to be exactly those traits which the most rigorously intrinsic criticism would choose to focus on in discussing those films. Hence the fact that auteur studies have typically been constituted as collections of essays on specific films rather than as biographies using films as a source of evidence. Put another way, auteurism in practice is a textually centered theory of criticism the purpose of which is generally to demonstrate the kind of life that a film text might have in the community of viewers, past, present, and future.

Much poststructuralist criticism, on the other hand, for all of the attention it devotes to system and text, is not textually centered in purpose. The goal of most materialist critics is to establish the relationship between films on the one hand and the structures of society on the other. The premise is that society in some sense causes films, and, conversely, that films in some sense cause society; and the implicit hope is that discovering exactly how this is true will enable us to recast society by changing the films that we make and see. In other words, the goal of materialist film criticism is "supratextual." If an individual film comes under analysis it is not for the sake of the text itself but to illustrate some larger concept--the symptoms or effects of bourgeois style, say, or the methodology of deconstructive criticism. Hence the fact that materialist film criticism has little patience with textual analysis per se; and hence as well the fact that materialist film criticism finds little use for the auteurist paradigm. It is not that auteurism does not do the job but that the job it does is irrelevant to materialist film critics.

Whether the structuralist/materialist concept of the purpose of film criticism is adequate, however, is also open to question. I do not doubt, for example, that films are reflective of, and in part are determined by, genetic circumstances. It Happened One Night, for instance, is clearly a Depression era Hollywood film (note the hungry boy on the bus or the hoboes that Gable waves to while waiting at a railroad crossing). And critics whose primary interest is to resurrect the social context of the early 1930s--or even the more general context of "bourgeois ideology" (itself an historical category)--are perfectly entitled to cite or refer to the film in the course of their work. But doing so amounts to film criticism, in my view, if and only if the statements that are made regarding It Happened One Night are of some help in describing the intrinsic qualities of the film itself, which is not the same thing as explaining its historical or ideological genesis. To explain why It Happened One Night was made within a particular culture at a certain point in history tells us next to nothing of the significance that the film might bear for audiences (rather than social historians) in the future, audiences whose members are likely to know even less about the specifics of life in the 1930s than we do. Put another way: if genetic knowledge were crucial or necessary to the comprehension or appreciation of works of art, how then do we account for our ability to understand the vast majority of the art works we come into contact with when in most cases our knowledge of genetic circumstances (social, authorial) is only of the most general sort and is likely to be derived almost exclusively from our experience of other art works? (Of course, one could argue that most people do not understand or appreciate works of art at all--but then the notion that art in some sense "causes" society becomes suspect: people will do what they will with films and no investigation of the films themselves is likely to explain their behavior.)

None of which is likely to convince the members of the Screen editorial board of the philosophical errors of their way. Such is not particularly my purpose here. Rather, I am concerned with one specific aspect of the auteurist debate--the

problem of intentionality--as that problem is raised by recent
critics of auteurism and authorship. I hope to show that
auteurism (of a sort) can withstand both intentionalist and
antiintentionalist objections. This lengthy prologue is
necessary, however, so as to "place" my own remarks. In defending
auteurism I accept the general view of criticism which I take
it to imply. My argument proper, however, will be addressed to
a more specific problem of critical vocabulary and usage.

## AUTEURISM AND AUTHORIAL INTENTION

*The intentional Fallacy* [handwritten annotation]

Much of the criticism of auteur theory keys on the matter
of authorial intention: whether it is discoverable or
attributable; whether it is conscious or unconscious; whether
or not it ought to be a criterion of criticism. Antiauteurists
will not all provide the same answers to these questions but most
assume that auteur criticism depends upon intentionality for its
legitimacy.

The issue of attributability is in many respects the most
complicated of the objections to auteur criticism for it asks
questions that are difficult if not impossible to answer,
particularly if they are answered, as they are asked, in empirical
terms. Thus someone like Graham Petrie might contest the
proposition that "the final scene of The Grapes of Wrath
expresses the world view of John Ford" on the empirical ground
that Zanuck proposed (and shot?) the scene.[1] The objection
is less conclusive than it might seem. There is nothing inherent
in the fact of Zanuck's collaboration that prevents the
attribution of expressivity to Ford. He was free to protest the
inclusion of the scene. Moreover, it is arguable that Ma Joad's
final speech fits perfectly into the structure of the film, as
if Zanuck, having grasped the film's logic, were merely filling
out Ford's thematic design. Nevertheless, some measure of
attributability is necessary for auteurism to function. Thus,
even if the empirical issue is less clear cut than it might seem
at first, we must explore it further.

Knowledge of genetic (as opposed to aesthetic) circumstances
cannot be necessary, I have argued, to the interpretation
of aesthetic texts. We know next to nothing of the particular
genetic circumstances that attend upon the creation of most works
and yet we have little difficulty discussing their qualities or
their values. Such is the case with anonymous authors like Homer
and the Pearl Poet, and will become increasingly the case in film
criticism as the last of the pioneers pass on. Nevertheless,
some knowledge of genetic circumstances can be helpful--and this
is the auteurist claim. The kind of knowledge necessary to
auteurism, however, has very little to do with intention, and
the data to confirm attribution derive primarily from the text
itself.

We have already remarked upon the logic of auteurism: auteur
criticism operates on the hypothesis that the qualities shared

[handwritten margin note: Are genetics actually necessary tho?]

by the films of a given director are likely to be precisely those
qualities which a rigorously intrinsic reading of those films
would discover. The auteurist method thus continually tests its
own validity (a strength, in my view, rather than a weakness).
It begins with the hypothesis that the director of record, as
evidenced in the screen credits, was indeed the efficient cause
of the text at hand; and it concludes with a determination of
the degree to which the auteurist paradigm has indeed been useful.
In cases in which the directorial paradigm teaches us next to
nothing about the text, we doubt the initial guess and seek out
another probable paradigm (of screenwriter, actor, producer,
studio). In cases in which it teaches us a great deal, however,
we can reasonably enough take this to confirm the initial
attribution. As far as interpretation is concerned, this sort
of confirmation is all that is required. It is only in cases
in which reputations are at stake or being argued that more
definitive evidence is necessary.

     In most cases, however, such evidence is almost impossible
to come by. How are we to know, from scene to scene, which member
of a production team exercised the authorial function? In most
cases we can never know for sure. The best guess, hardly
inconsistent with an historical approach, is the director. And
even in cases in which the attribution is eventually discounted,
the directorial guess still has the advantage of foregrounding
the text itself. To see a John Wayne film as a "John Wayne film"
is generally to attend to Wayne and the nuances of his persona
and performance: we can see Wayne. But we can only see a
director by implication. To look for the director in a film is
to look at the whole film because there is no place else to look.
The empiricist objection to auteurism is not an argument over
critical method, then, but over the goal of criticism. If the
end of criticism is value judgments of authorial worth rather
than of the work itself, then auteurism will not do the job with
the finality and certainty desired by those who pronounce value
judgments. If the goal of criticism is description and
interpretation of the work and its qualities, however, auteurism
is completely adequate (though not absolutely necessary) to the
task.

## INTENTION AND CONSCIOUSNESS

     A second frequent objection to auteurism has to do with
intention and consciousness--on the premise that conscious
intention on the director's part must exist prior to the creation
of a given text and prior to any subsequent auteuristic
discussions of his works and the values they celebrate. As Edward
Buscombe put it in Screen: "The themes of transferred guilt
in Hitchcock, of home, and the desert/garden antithesis in Ford
. . . are almost entirely unconscious, making it inappropriate
to speak, as so much auteur criticism does, about a director's
world view."[2] It takes little effort to demonstrate the flaw
in this argument.

[Handwritten marginalia: Can film auteurism exist? There are so many artist making of a film!]

Clearly, when one now screens Psycho there is no question
that Hitchcock is not present and is not presently intending the
film. Any intentions implied by or evidenced in the film could
only have existed during production. The intentionalist argument
is thus a special case of the genetic argument. Both suffer from
the same insufficiency. That is, if it is difficult to know with
certainty who fulfilled the authorial function at any point in
time, how much more difficult will it be to determine that
author's state of mind (conscious or unconscious) during
production? The best evidence we have of authorial intention
is the text itself; and even that evidence is indirect and
inconclusive. Texts may "evidence" intention. They may have
been "intended." But they are not "intentions." They are texts.
To discuss intention is therefore to discuss an implication of
the work, one of many such implications, and not the whole of
the work itself. Thus, even when someone like Hitchcock
apparently reveals conscious intentions to interviewers, such
revelations are of little consequence to criticism the concern
of which is works and texts and not the circumstances that gave
birth to them. That is, we are not concerned with what Hitchcock
did in 1959 but what we do now when we watch and think about
Psycho. To the extent that Psycho realizes Hitchcock's
intentions, to talk about Psycho is to talk about intention
to the degree that it is relevant. To talk about intentions not
evidenced in or by the text is simply not to talk about the
text.


BARTHES'S OBJECTION
A third objection to auteurism, the last to be dealt with
here, might be termed the Roland Barthes objection, though it
can be seen clearly enough in the film scholarship of Peter Wollen
and Paul Willemen.[3] The first two objections to auteur
criticism, from Petrie and Buscombe, imply in different ways that
knowledge of intention is possible but problematic: if we ever
could be certain about directorial intention (conscious--or not),
then auteurism would be a reasonably valid philosophy of
criticism. The Barthes objection argues just the contrary.
According to Barthes, criticism has no trouble discerning
something akin to authorial intention. The problem is that
criticism effectively substitutes intention for the text:

> To give a text an Author is to impose a limit on that text,
> to furnish it with a final signified, to close the writing.
> Such a conception suits criticism very well, the latter then
> allotting itself the important task of discovering the Author
> (or its hypostases: society, history, psyché, liberty)
> beneath the work: when the Author has been found, the text
> is "explained"--victory to the critic.[4]

It can be demonstrated (see Chapter 5, "Hitchcock and the
Ethics of Vision") that Barthes drastically overestimates the

power of criticism and underestimates or misrepresents the power
and status of aesthetic objects:   the effect of criticism, in
my experience, is exactly the reverse of that foreseen by Barthes,
in that genuine criticism brings texts alive for readers by
generating frameworks of pertinence.  One can have little sense
of a signifier without perceiving a signified.  Nevertheless,
the Barthes objection to authorship is interesting because it
reinforces two points that I would make:   1) that arguments based
primarily on intention are illegitimate and reduce works of art
by limiting their significance to the private context of authorial
psychology; and 2) that the proper and only necessary context
for interpretation is the linguistic or semiotic context.
     To invoke Barthes on these two points is not to call for
the death of the author, but the contrary.  Auteurism does not
depend upon intention and never really has.  Intentionality
language can be very easily translated out of most auteurist
criticism without destroying the logic or validity of its results.
Accordingly, we can perfectly well continue to employ the
auteurist paradigm as long as our goal is to interpret the text
and to describe its particular use of linguistic and aesthetic
conventions.  The knowledge necessary to doing so, furthermore,
is not knowledge of genetic circumstances primarily but of
aesthetic circumstances.  That is, we must know the language and
conventions of reading appropriate to a given text, which
knowledge we acquire primarily through previous contact with
literary or aesthetic objects, not through historical or
biographical research.  The auteurist paradigm works on this
principle:   every Hawks film we see teaches us how to see
succeeding Hawks films by teaching us the "language" of the
Hawksian cinema.  Auteurism cannot guarantee in specific instances
that there is such a language to discover—so auteurism cannot
claim to be equally useful in every case.  But such a discovery
is the best evidence we can have of authorial causality and it
is certainly evidence enough to warrant a continued allegiance
to the general methods and goals of auteur criticism.


THE POSITION CLARIFIED
     I wish to point out that I lay no special claim to the logic
of the argument here presented.  The intentionality debate has
a long history in literary studies and aesthetics.  I agree with
Barthes and Wollen that intentionalist arguments do violence to
the life of the text—but Monroe Beardsley and W. K. Wimsatt made
that point in 1946.[5]  Thus there is nothing particularly
"modern" in the antiintentionalist position.  The debate goes
on, however, for the very reason that aesthetic texts lead
multiple lives.  People can use aesthetic objects in a variety
of ways:   as historical evidence, as biographical evidence, as
works of art.  What a text "is" thus depends upon the use that
is made of it, even in cases where such uses seem completely
inappropriate to the qualities of the text at hand.  Ultimately,
then, the geneticism debate (and the auteur controversy as a

localized version of it) cannot be settled apart from the larger
question of critical objectives. The best I can hope to show
here is not that the goal of criticism as I practice it is
superior to that proposed by materialist film critics (though
I clearly believe it is) but rather that a version of auteurism
is completely consistent with a textually centered variety of
film criticism. In so doing I believe I have cleared up some
confusions. The fewer of those the better.

L.P.

NOTES
1. Graham Petrie, "Alternatives to Auteurs," Film Quarterly,
   26, no. 3 (1973), 27-35. Petrie doesn't use Ford as his
   example (he uses Welles) but the objection is typical of his
   approach. My information on The Grapes of Wrath comes from
   Mel Gussow, Don't Say Yes Until I Finish Talking: A
   Biography of Darryl F. Zanuck (Garden City: Doubleday,
   1971).
2. Edward Buscombe, "Ideas of Authorship," Screen, 14, no. 3
   (1973): 83.
3. See Peter Wollen, Signs and Meaning in the Cinema, enlarged
   ed. (Bloomington: Indiana Univ. Press, 1972); and Paul
   Willemen, "Notes on Subjectivity: On Reading Edward
   Branigan's 'Subjectivity under Siege,'" Screen, 19, no. 1
   (1978): 41-69.
4. Roland Barthes, "The Death of the Author," in Image/Music/
   Text (New York: Hill and Wang, 1977), p. 147.
5. Monroe C. Beardsley and W. K. Wimsatt, Jr., "The Intentional
   Fallacy," Sewanee Review, 54 (1946); in W. K. Wimsatt, Jr.,
   The Verbal Icon (Lexington: Univ. of Kentucky Press, 1954).

CHAPTER
# 8

---

# History/Cinema/Criticism

I have in mind a question bearing upon the theory of interpretation: to what degree is a film critic obliged to read a film within or against the background of the historical period or forces which may be said to have determined it? I also have in mind an answer which, with certain important qualifications, I would wish to defend: that the obligation is on principle very weak. Indeed, one can argue that there is a strong obligation not to read a text--filmic or otherwise--primarily or exclusively in the context of its genesis. None of which is intended to deny the historicity of cinema or of criticism. To the contrary, I believe that reading a text primarily against the social context of its genesis is profoundly unhistorical in certain crucial respects (though it may well be the case among Marxist critics that the denial of history--of any further role in history for certain kinds of films--is exactly the point).[1]

One additional question immediately presents itself: can we understand a film apart from the history of its genesis? Clearly in one respect we want to answer this question no, if by "genetic context" we refer to every aspect of the culture wherein the work was produced. To be totally ignorant of Renaissance culture would make interpretation of Renaissance painting, for example, impossible. But there are degrees of pertinence and knowledge. An understanding of the Catholic doctrine of damnation, for instance, is clearly essential for an understanding of Michelangelo's Last Judgment. But then again much that we might wish to know about a Catholic conception of damnation may be acquired by studying the Last Judgment--so that the painting may be said to embody aspects of the knowledge we need for its interpretation. And clearly some knowledge about the Renaissance, say a knowledge of sixteenth century sailmaking, aids interpretation very little. Also of little interpretive help, I would assert, is knowledge of causality--if by "causality" we refer to those factors (authorial, social) which initially generated the work. Let us summarize the case for the moment as follows: in order to interpret the Last Judgment one needs

181

to know something about the conventions and categories of
Renaissance painting (and hence of painting in general) and also
something about the more general state of Renaissance culture;
i.e., one must have some access to the body of knowledge, of
classical mythology and literature, say, and also of "history,"
common to those members of the culture who were then (and are
now) capable of reading the painting.

Note, however, that we are speaking here of a relatively
general and readily acquired sort of knowledge, analogous in
several respects, as John M. Ellis would argue, to language.
As Ellis puts it, in the case of literature:  "To understand
Goethe, I must learn German, with all that means:  I must become
conversant with the language and conventions of the German
speaking community.  The crucial theoretical point here is that
this process must be represented not as ascertaining the local
circumstances of the composition of the work, but as being
initiated into the community within which the literary text is
literature."[2]  Likewise, to understand the Last Judgment one
must "become conversant" with the "language" of Renaissance
painting, "with all that means."  Neither sort of knowledge,
however, is historical knowledge in the "particular" sense--no
more so on principle than a knowledge of Spanish would be for
a nonspeaker wishing to read Lorca.[3]  And this sort of
linguistic or semiotic knowledge is significantly different from
a knowledge of authorial biography or from a detailed knowledge
of Renaissance economics--though it does require us to accept
a weak form of historicism.  What we are really dealing with,
however, is a generalized history; and, more crucially, with
history seen as "total synchrony"--as a set of aesthetic
possibilities encompassing the potentially inexhaustible range
of choices, attributions, and connotations (including "history"
itself) available to the painter as artist and to ourselves as
interpreters.

At least two counter-positions common to film criticism
suggest themselves.  For example, someone versed in Lacanian
semiotics (or Skinnerean behavior theory, for that matter) might
well question whether or not linguistic knowledge of the sort
I have mentioned properly amounts to "knowledge" at all--and
whether or not it would enable one to do any more than rehearse
the subject position already inscribed within the
(inter)textuality of the work in question.  I would answer yes
in both cases--and would cite Cadbury's critique of Lacan in this
volume to support the contentions.

A more interesting counter-position is the conventional
Marxist argument that the goal of criticism, hence of
interpretation, is to expose the relationships of determination,
of ideology, which bind any given work to the material context
of its genesis.  To be sure, Marxist theory is a subject in
considerable flux at present; but two elements of Marxist cultural
theory are common enough to be definitive, such that without them
any theory would cease to be a version of Marxism at all:  1)

a conviction, however complex we take the infrastructure/
superstructure relationship to be, that "in the last instance,"
to use Althusser's phrase, it is "mode of production" which is
"determining"; and 2) a "dialectic" or "diachronic" view of
history.[4]  Both assumptions raise significant issues in the
theory of criticism.
     The former premise is clearly a necessary reduction, as are
all such idealizations, and its validity is less a function of
verification per se than of productivity:  is the idealization
appropriate to the phenomenon it seeks to posit and to explain
and are its explanations illuminating of our experience?  Both
questions are far from settled, it seems to me.  In the present
context, however, the point to be made involves what I take to
be an implicit (though not perhaps irresolvable) tension between
Marxist explanations and more general interpretive procedures.[5]
As John Ellis points out, an important aspect of language use
is that meaning derives, at least in part, from systematic
contrasts; "any expression derives its meaning from the choice
of that expression rather than others which contrast with it in
a variety of ways."[6]  And the problem with much Marxist
interpretation is that, within the paradigm of "history-as-
language," it privileges a limited range of "possible" meanings
(those which are congruent with particular scenarios for the
ideological or psychological functioning of film, for example)
and accordingly downplays others that tend in the analysis of
particular works to be read off as cover stories or evasions.
The danger here is the elementary aesthetic error of taking a
part--of the work in question or of the entire "semantic
field"--for the whole (as a "totalizing instance"); and the likely
result is distortion beyond the limits of interpretive validity--
as in the case of the Cahiers critics' interpretation of Young
Mr. Lincoln.[7]
     The objection that Marxist criticism tends to distort the
system of contrasts wherein we generate our readings is on
principle an objection to a particular and limiting view of
synchronicity.  More crucial to the present discussion is the
tendency among Marxist film critics to limit their view of the
diachronic relationships of artworks to history--to see that
relationship primarily in terms of a causality of production,
of cause-and-effect.  In the words of Cahiers editors Jean-Louis
Comolli and Jean Narboni, the function of Marxist film criticism
"must be a rigidly factual analysis of what governs the production
of a film (economic circumstances, ideology, demand and response)
and the meanings and forms appearing in it, which are equally
tangible."[8]  Indeed, in the Cahiers analysis of Young Mr.
Lincoln "reading" is defined as the ability to "distinguish
the historicity of [the] inscription" of the film in question.[9]
     One objection to such a view of the critical task involves
the logic of understanding--the assumption that understanding
the cause of something amounts to or is crucial for understanding
the thing itself.  To be sure, if the object of inquiry is the

cause/effect relationship, then there is no problem--it must be discussed. But the tendency among historicist critics, Marxist and otherwise, is to suggest that understanding the genetic cause of a work of art or film is all there is to understanding the work itself. The assumption is clearly false. In art and literature there are countless works by anonymous authors and of uncertain dating--but we have no trouble describing the structure of such works or interpreting their meaning in terms that have much to do with the emergent qualities of the particular works they are, and little to do (aside from their function, an important one, of providing connotations in the text) with the historically and socially determined "codings" which interact so that such qualities emerge. If anything, the logic of explanation pulls in the opposite direction, not leading from facts of history to the explanation of the work's qualities, but rather leading from the facts of the work's qualities to the explanation of history. Again, I cite John Ellis: "Genetic questions depend on prior results of structural analysis, and therefore . . . the former are always dependent on the latter."[10]

A far more powerful objection to the practice of many Marxist film critics involves the logic of aesthetic categories and the historical reality of their application. In the case of literature, for example, and the case of film is in every crucial respect analogous, one cannot define it solely by reference to the objective properties of the members of the class (though members of the class are, we have argued, capable of owning their own properties--hence the possibility of interpretive "validity"). Neither particular features nor modes of organization are sufficiently common to allow for such a referential definition of literature--and intentionalist definitions (involving an author's intention to create a literary work) always leave unanswered the question of whether the intention has been fulfilled. Rather, what makes a particular text literary is the way it is used. In Jonathan Culler's words, a piece of language is a literary work "because it is read in a particular way, because . . . potential properties [structure, meaning], latent in the object itself, are actualized by the theory of discourse applied in the act of reading."[11] And one may therefore define the class of literary works as those which the members of particular societies or communities agree to use as literature.

Two aspects of such a definition of literature are immediately relevant to the issue of historicity. To begin with, under such a theory of literature neither causality nor function are fixed. A given work may function as literature for one person or community and not for another, may function as literature at one point in time but not at others. This is true because causality does not depend upon genetic context but rather upon the context of "reading"--an action that takes place typically at some often great remove in time from the moment of original

composition. The issue is less clear in film only because its
history is so brief--though I would cite the history of auteurism
as a case in point: suddenly whole classes of texts were shifted
from the category of non-art into the category of art (see "The
Problem of Film Genre"). The tendency among many Marxist film
critics, however, especially under the influence of Althusser
and Lacan, is to deny this radically diachronic view of cause
and function. What we often see, in fact, is what Tony Bennett
has called a "metaphysic of the text," the "assumption that the
text has a once-and-for-all existence, a once-and-for-all
relationship to other texts which is marked and determined by
the circumstances of its origin."[12] The notion of "The
Classical Narrative Cinema" is a paradigm case of this--as can
be seen, for example, in Laura Mulvey's explicitly Lacanian
argument that narrative cinema inevitably involves particular
visual and psychological formations and therefore necessarily
evokes very specific and essentially negative (i.e., psychotic)
viewer responses. It is in this respect that much ostensibly
"historical" film criticism is not historical enough by half.

The history at issue in interpretation, however, is not the
history of the text but of its reading. Indeed, the second aspect
of a use-based definition of literary (and cinematic) texts which
bears directly on the question of historicity is exactly the
"particular way" in which such texts are used. There is
significant agreement among many American literary theorists--
especially those influenced by speech-act theory--that "the
characteristic use of texts as literary is one that lifts them
out of the context of their origin and no longer assumes that
they are part of the practical give and take of any particular
context."[13] Such a definition has the advantage of avoiding
the fiction/non-fiction dichotomy (to read a text "out" of its
genetic context is exactly to "fictionalize" it or, in Beardsleyan
terms, to make of it a metaphor) and the definition by itself
entails no a priori value judgments of the high art/low art sort:
proof of value is in the using. And to use a text, under such
a theory, is precisely a matter of "interpretation." That is,
by "detaching" or "decentering" a text from its original context
the reader opens up a conceptual space within which significance
may be generated or attributed to as great an extent as text and
reader can bear in accord with what Beardsley has called the
Principle of Plenitude--and this rather than limit the text
to the significance it might have had for its initial audience
or may have now in reference to that audience.[14] As Barbara
Herrnstein Smith has put it: "What we mean when we speak of
interpreting a poem is, in large measure, precisely this process
of inference, conjecture, and indeed creation of contexts"--which
come, then, to occupy the space created when the work is
abstracted from the context of its genesis.[15] To read a text
back into its context of origin, accordingly, is not simply
a matter of adopting one interpretive strategy as opposed to
another. Rather, such a reading effectively removes

its object from the category of literature (or of art in general) altogether--hence the strong obligation, where our interest is in the "literariness" of a text, not to succumb to the fallacy of geneticism. Indeed, it is only by detaching or decentering filmic texts from the pragmatic context of release, exhibition, and consumption that we may hope to "foreground" their status as constructs and thereby actualize their value as artworks.

One may thus argue a necessity for doubting the wisdom and logic of much historicist criticism, especially as that criticism functions in the area of film studies. In closing, however, it may be well to consider the general issue of motive: why have so many critics felt compelled to maintain the view that literary or cinematic texts need to be understood in the context of their genesis? At heart, I would suggest, such arguments are grounded in the legitimate though unfocused belief that artworks as a class (including films) matter, but the contention is often crippled by the mistaken assumption that a work of art cannot matter apart from (or, conversely, matters most in) its initial historical context. It is arguable, however, that binding a text to the context of its genesis has exactly the reverse effect--to urge historical significance is to close the space wherein we find or create the general significance which alone makes the text relevant in and to the context of the reader. By the same logic, cutting a text off from the pragmatic context of its genesis has the effect of upping the ethical ante by making individual readers and particular communities responsible for the use they make of the text in question. Only under such a theory can criticism matter, in Beardsley's phrase, as a "principled activity."[16]

Put another way, we can readily agree with Marxist scholars like Tony Bennett who insist that criticism is an essentially political act which ought not to be concerned with how a text has functioned but rather with how it can be made to function.[17] For Marxists, accordingly, aesthetic and filmic texts often function (not always consciously) as "pretexts" for an ongoing (and much needed) intervention into history and ideology. The tradition of philosophical aesthetics, however, is equally concerned with a kind of intervention into history-- though under a different set of presuppositions, as to the nature of language, for example. Briefly put, many aesthetic philosophers (Beardsley especially) have consistently urged the value of aesthetic experience--as distinguished from other and often more popular modes of audience response--because the act of carefully attending to works of art including films is itself productive of (in the sense of "reinforcing") behaviors and cognitive skills which are worth promoting (attentiveness, sensitivity, self-consciousness, creativity, the appreciation of form) and which may themselves, indeed, be prerequisites for an understanding of more concretely historical, political, and ideological realities.[18] Indeed, bringing works from the past into the present requires even greater facility in these skills if aesthetic experience is to take place, especially in cases where the work in question is remarkably "other" and resists our initial schematizations. In this one respect, indeed, there may be little to choose between Marxist and more traditional modes of interpretation--however much their critical vocabularies and interpretive procedures may seem to differ--because all interpretations are inevitably historical acts which seek to change how people see and think about the works which, taken together, constitute the aesthetic aspect of their culture.[19]

L.P.

NOTES

1. See, for instance, Laura Mulvey, "Visual Pleasure and Narrative Cinema," Screen, 16, no. 3 (1975): 6-18. See also a counter argument by William Cadbury, "Story, Pleasure, and Meaning in The Scarlet Empress," in Narrative Strategies, ed. Syndy M. Conger and Janice R. Welsch (Macomb: Western Illinois Univ. Press, 1980), pp. 115-27.
2. John M. Ellis, The Theory of Literary Criticism (Berkeley: Univ. of California Press, 1974), pp. 145-46.
3. See Terry Eagleton, Marxism and Literary Criticism (Berkeley: Univ. of California Press, 1976): The aim of Marxist criticism "is to explain the literary work more fully; and this means a sensitive attention to its forms, styles and meanings. But it also means grasping those forms, styles and meanings as the products of a particular history" (p. 3; my italics on "particular").
4. Louis Althusser, For Marx (London: NLB, 1977), p. 111. For a commentary on Althusser's Marxism see Terry Lovell, Pictures of Reality: Aesthetics, Politics, and Pleasure (London: British Film Institute, 1980).
5. See Tony Bennett, Formalism and Marxism (New York: Methuen, 1979): "Instead of 'Marxism and aesthetics', the real concern should be with 'Marxism versus aesthetics'" (p. 104).
6. Ellis, Theory, p. 122.
7. See Robert Scholes, "Language, Narrative, and Anti-Narrative," Critical Inquiry, 7 (1980): 207, and Michael Rosenthal, "Ideology, Determinism, and Relative Autonomy," Jump Cut, no. 17 (1978), p. 21.
8. Jean-Louis Comolli and Jean Narboni, "Cinema/Ideology/Criticism," in Movies and Methods, ed. Bill Nichols (Berkeley: Univ. of California Press, 1976), p. 28.
9. The Editors of Cahiers du Cinéma, "John Ford's Young Mr. Lincoln," Screen, 13, no. 3 (1972): 5-6.
10. Ellis, Theory, p. 119-20.
11. Jonathan Culler, Structuralist Poetics (Ithaca: Cornell Univ. Press, 1975), p. 113.
12. Bennett, Formalism, p. 69.

13. Ellis, <u>Theory</u>, p. 44.
14. The terms, if not my usage of them, are Althusser's: see <u>Lenin and Philosophy</u> (London: NLB, 1971), p. 204, and <u>For Marx</u>, pp. 144-45; on the Principle of Plenitude see Monroe Beardsley, <u>Aesthetics</u> (New York: Harcourt Brace & World, 1958), pp. 144-47.
15. Barbara Herrnstein Smith, <u>On the Margins of Discourse</u> (Chicago: Univ. of Chicago Press, 1978), p. 33. In addition to Herrnstein Smith, Culler, and Ellis, see Mary Louise Pratt, <u>Toward a Speech Act Theory of Literary Discourse</u> (Bloomington: Indiana Univ. Press, 1977) and Louise M. Rosenblatt, <u>The Reader/the Text/the Poem</u> (Carbondale: Southern Illinois Univ. Press, 1978).
16. Monroe Beardsley, <u>The Possibility of Criticism</u> (Detroit: Wayne State Univ. Press, 1970), pp. 11-12.
17. Bennett, <u>Formalism</u>, p. 141.
18. Hilde Hein, "Aesthetic Consciousness: The Ground of Political Experience," <u>Journal of Aesthetics and Art Criticism</u>, 35 (1976): 143-52.
19. For further elaboration of my general position on the text/ context relationship, especially as contrasted with the Althusserian arguments of Pierre Macherey's <u>A Theory of Literary Production</u> (London: Routledge & Kegan Paul, 1978), see "History/Cinema/Criticism (2)," <u>Film Studies: Proceedings of the Purdue University Sixth Annual Conference on Film, April 1-4, 1982</u> (West Lafayette: Purdue Office of Publications, forthcoming).

# 9

---

# Film Interpretation:
# Theory and Practice

QUASI DISCOURSE:  THE CASE FOR MEANING IN FILM
    Sometimes  the  remarks  of  nonspecialists  can  reveal  the
structure of issues that specialized debate within a discipline
may have obscured.  Roger Shattuck argues that how to rescue
literature is in part through oral interpretation, which grounds
the audience in actualizations of relations among sender, message,
and  addressee.   But Shattuck cites Susanne Langer's opposed
opinion that in a novel, for instance, "the creation of virtual
personalities" (of implicit speaker as well as of characters)
"suffers, when read aloud, by the peripheral presence of the
reader."  Shattuck acknowledges that there is something to
Langer's point, saying that "it is closely related to a debate
in film criticism about the relative virtues of a novel and a
film version of it," in which debate, he says, the nature of film
gives support to Langer's view:

> Since words only signify and suggest, and do not in any way
> embody a world, a written text projects a virtual or implied
> space which the reader's imagination must actively fill out
> of its own experiences and associations.  By contrast, in
> performance or in a film, this space is filled in by the
> speaker's or director's imagination.  The ambiguities and
> mysteries in the printed text are channeled into a limited
> range of rhetorical and dramatic effects.[1]

    Clearly film is here a whipping boy, an exemplary instance
of reduced meaning that contrasts with the rich evocativeness
of literature.  The point is not completely unfamiliar within
film criticism, but in a form in which it is used not to denigrate
film, but rather to establish film's autonomy.  Ingmar Bergman,
for instance, has argued that "the written word is read and
assimilated by a conscious act of the will in alliance with the
intellect," but "when we experience a film, we consciously prime
ourselves for illusion.  Putting aside will and intellect, we
make way for it in our imagination.  The sequence of pictures
plays directly on our feelings."[2]

The "second semiology," as the body of semiotic work inspired by Lacanian psychoanalysis is sometimes called, takes film as an imaginary signifier, which is to be understood as playing on feelings in a special way. But we note that Bergman's point is also Christian Metz's during the period of the "first semiology." Emphasizing always that the film image is to "express" rather than "signify," Metz urges in Film Language that "'meaning' is naturally derived from the signifier as a whole, without resorting to a code," and "that is why literature is an art of heterogeneous connotation (expressive connotation added to nonexpressive denotation), while the cinema is an art of homogeneous connotation (expressive connotation added to expressive denotation)." Film images have the expressiveness of objects in the world (or of the sound of the Wagnerian oboe). If we are to find meaning in film of the sort that, like the meaning of language, comes from culture, it "must be sought on other levels" than that of the image, sought in "the codes peculiar to connotation . . . or the codes of denotation-connotation related to the discursive organization of image groups," for instance, in Metz's "grande syntagmatique." Bergman's "will and intellect" and Shattuck's "experiences and associations" are required in order to understand film as film--what Metz calls its "filmic discourse"--just as they are required in order to understand literature as literature. But the specificity of cinema is that, whereas they are also required (under a linguistics of memory such as Ferdinand de Saussure's) to understand literature as language, they are not required to understand film as "image discourse." Film images, Metz concedes, give us the world "naturally."[3]

These claims and concessions, then, are taken to amount to the same thing, that film is incapable of being as contemplatable as literature. Rather than meaning, film is. And like things that are, but not like things that mean, film can make "rhetorical and dramatic effects," but cannot enter the space of "ambiguities and mysteries" that follow from the autonomy caused by distance between signifier and signified, what Stephen Heath nicely phrases as the "fixed virtualities of langue."[4]

These virtualities have the curious quality, the ambiguity and mystery, of being comprehensible only in terms of all the differences that hold between the virtuality we are considering and every other virtuality in what Saussure calls the "storehouse" of the language, so that meaning itself is finally a property attributable only to language, where alone there are no positives but only differences, only the process of being led along an endless chain of signifiers as "one sign gives birth to another," as C. S. Peirce describes. For words to "signify and suggest," in Shattuck's phrase, or for us to use the "will and intellect," in Bergman's, is to follow that track, to place the discourse composed by its words in the web of all the discourses it isn't and hence to find its meaning.[5]

The Web, the Rock, and the Rose

Is the term "meaning" so inapplicable to film?  Must we see the image discourse of film as a vulgar positive rather than a sophisticated web of differences?  One way to answer is that film images give us not the world, but the arbitrariness of culture. In a series of footnotes in Film Language, and throughout Language and Cinema, Metz emends his position and argues that film images are not "naturally expressive" but that their expressiveness is guaranteed "without recourse to a special and explicit code.  But not without recourse to vast and complex sociocultural organizations, which are represented by other forms of codification" that nevertheless "extend . . . beyond the cinema" so that Metz can discount them in seeking cinematic specificity.[6]

But this draws Metz further from contemplation of film meaning, not closer to it.  His argument fits semiology's consistent view that meaning is in every respect something drawn from some sort of culturally established storehouse, as under the Saussurian model of language, whether a storehouse of potential representations of the world, or of meaningful elements of filmic discourse, or of types of identification with the visual image established for the individual in the socialization process, or of representations created by the contradictions in objective situations for an individual hailed into existence by ideology itself.  Chomsky's linguistics removes the credibility of thinking of the meaning of discourses as being drawn from any storehouse at all, and hence undercuts all such models.  If there is meaning in the image discourse of film, it must be viewed as the result of a far more complex set of processings than are explicable by any notion of recognition of cultural codes, any matchings of signifiers with signifieds.

But the problem may be approached another way.  The same sort of question concerning meaning may be posed about painting. Monroe C. Beardsley's discussion of the differences between literary and visual design can help answer it.  Literature, being a structure of words that signify, is among other things a discourse in which "something is being said by somebody about something."  Most important, Beardsley says that the "referential capacity of sentences--their semantical aspect--is . . . based upon, and in the last analysis explainable in terms of, the capacity of a sentence to formulate beliefs," and that "to understand the sentence is to know what beliefs it could formulate" (p. 117).  Thus the discourse that sentences compose presents "theses" and other predications, matters of the work's meaning, whether explicit or implicit, where "meaning" equals "cognitive purport," or the utterance's "capacity to convey information about the speaker's beliefs."[7]  Literature itself, in fact, is defined by Beardsley in terms of language, with the claim that literature is that which is "distinctly above the norm in ratio of implicit . . . to explicit meaning."[8]

Painting is not like that, says Beardsley. Whereas literature presents (though it does not assert) statements that may be true or false, a representational painting, or any of its parts, not "constitut[ing] a proposition-vehicle [,] simply offers a subject" about which we can make a statement that "may be true or false, but it is a statement about the picture, not in it."[9] We mean different things when we talk about the meaning of a painting and the meaning of a novel: as we read a novel's sentences and comprehend their discourse, we trace the facts of, development of, and relations among, the implicit speaker's beliefs, which are a point-source of the novel's meaning. About the painting, we report on the qualities of the design and its subject, which belong to and emerge from that design without any implication that there is a point-source for them such as is entailed by the very fact of language.

Cases for such point-sources of meaning in painting are not convincing. The "ways of seeing" argued by John Berger constitute such point-sources, such ways of taking painting as discourse. Berger criticizes the terms of art historian Seymour Slive's praise of Frans Hals's The Governors of the Almshouse and Lady Regents of the Almshouse. Berger calls them "art appreciation" terms, language of "mystification." Slive's terms are of composition and qualities--"harmonious fusion," "breadth and strength," "rhythmical arrangement"--and Slive's summary is undeniably purple: "Hals's unwavering commitment to his personal vision . . . heightens our awe for the ever-increasing power of the mighty impulses that enabled him to give us a close view of life's vital forces."

One can see, with the help of Berger's instructive reproductions of details, that indeed Slive "evades" the human qualities of the Regents and Regentesses, who are a terrifying lot, indeed. While Berger acknowledges that "it is reasonable to consider a painting's composition," still to do so, he says, "transfer[s] the emotion provoked by the image from the plane of lived experience, to that of disinterested 'art appreciation.' All conflict disappears." We are taken away "from the only confrontation which matters. . . . In this confrontation the Regents and Regentesses stare at Hals, a destitute old painter who has lost his reputation and lives off public charity; he examines them through the eyes of a pauper who must nevertheless try to be objective, i.e., must try to surmount the way he sees them as a pauper." The painting presents a "way of seeing" that fulfills the formula that "an image [becomes] a record of how X had seen Y."

Yet that Slive ignores the ominousness of the designs--faces and hands floating in a void, a rhythm of hand gestures that resembles a film strip freezing stages of blows and rejections-- and the coldly judgmental characters of the sitters, does not show that the "drama of these paintings" is the confrontation between sitters and painter, or even between what is seen and the way of seeing it, a point-source for the "drama of an 'unforgettable contrast.'" Rather, it is within the designs themselves. The conflict is between the fragmentation of these floating figures and the unity that they compose through their rhythmical relations and through the uniform solidity of the fragments. Slive ignores that these people are horrible, making him fair game for Berger, but the paintings have as well as contempt some other qualities, too--sympathy, a kind of sadness for what it is like to be these people in their uniformity but alienation, and an admiration for their solidity in being what they are.

Each painting is chilling, but not because it presents the discourse of the implicit viewer, the pauper painter Hals, but because of the multiple ironies that emerge from its design, especially those that simply set the extraordinary power of certain human qualities of individuation and strength in the associated context of bleakness, coldness, and alienation. The "mighty impulses that enabled [Hals] to give us a close view of life's vital forces" are phrased intentionalistically, and the phrasing is purple. But they seem in fact to be in the paintings, not to be "mystification," as we can tell when we consider fusion of the qualities of design and subject rather than each painting's status as "record of how X had seen Y."[10]

It is the difference between the ways we properly talk about literature and visual design that leads Beardsley to place discussion of the meaning both of the discourse and of the world of the literary work, which that discourse creates, under the category of its description, and to place discussion of the meaning of a painting's representation under the category of its interpretation. A painting's design, what is to be described about it, is unconnected with the notion of meaning except in that extended (though applicable) sense in which meaning amounts to meaningfulness and is an emergent regional quality of the design. It is meaningful, surely, that a design is cheerful, or forbidding, or serene. But literary meaning is a more narrow notion, depending on its relation to language. It is clear that explication of a poem's meaning (passage by passage, as the word "explication" implies) is an aspect of its description, but equally clear that it would be a stretch of "explication" to say that to describe a visual design was to explicate it. A painting's meaning, then, is more like its significance in appropriate contexts than like its sense--that is, more a matter of interpretation (as when we interpret the theme of a literary work after and depending on the meaning of its discourse) than description.

There is thus good sense in Metz's usage:  a painting expresses and a film does too, since, although it has many images and sounds and their sequence and interplay can build a discourselike set of connections as do literature's, still there is no way to trace an implicit speaker's beliefs in the

succession of images. But a literary work first signifies. Its
sentences stand for a meaning attached to them by the rules of
language and extendable among them by rules of discourse.
     This, not the usually emphasized implication about film's
vocation for realism, is the treasurable truth in André Bazin's
wonderful image of the "stepping stones," which he applies to
Neo-Realist film, but which actually applies to film (and other
nonverbal arts) in general. A poem, we have said, does its own
telling, its words primarily signify and go to make discourse.
But _we_ talk about the film or the painting:  "It is not the
essence of a stone to allow people to cross rivers without wetting
their feet any more than the divisions of a melon exist to allow
the head of a family to divide it equally."  Rather, "the big
rocks that lie scattered in a ford are now and ever will be no
more than mere rocks. Their reality as rocks is not affected
when, leaping from one to another, I use them to cross the river."
Images have their quality on their own, we attend to them, we
submit to _their_ discipline rather than to the discipline of
that arbitrary system by which rules establish what they stand
for, and though we use many codes to interpret them and understand
their connotations, we do not use a code to find their primary
meaning.[11]
     So while we will eventually wish to accept a sense in which
it is well within the range of common and desirable usage to speak
of a film's or a painting's meaning, it is important not to ignore
the slight, but significant, sense of strain of doing so.  Simply
because something is meaningful doesn't mean that it has a meaning
in the way verbal discourses do.  We resist the very idea that
in artworks, as such, we are seeking to find the messages sent
by the discourses composed by their parts, the sets of relations
outside themselves of which they are signifiers.  One can readily
understand the metaphor in which it can be said that the way the
aspects of an art object fit together send a message about that
way--but one must also remember that it is a metaphor, not plain
truth.  As Frank B. Ebersole points out, the rose just _is_ red,
it doesn't tell us it is or send us the message of its red-
ness.[12]
     But the plain truth about meaning as expression may easily
be put in terms that have nothing to do with codes or with
point-sources of messages.  Beardsley makes plain that when we
have understood a piece of music, for example, its aspects have
"fitted together" for us in terms of their own internal relations,
including the relations of their qualities. As Leonard Bernstein
puts it, "when a piece of music 'means' something to me, it is
a meaning conveyed by the sounding notes themselves." And, "these
intrinsic musical meanings are generated by a constant stream
of metaphors, all of which are forms of poetic transformations."
These transformations--deletions, repetition, inversion--are
metaphoric in the sense that they provide a pattern of
expectations, fulfillments, and denials that are iconic of (so
that in some sense they substitute for, though they do not

signify) some aspect of "our interior lives, our psychic landscapes and actions," just as for Beardsley the human qualities of music derive from "iconicity . . . of any music with some conceivable mental processes [like] variations of intensity, impulsiveness, relaxation and tension" and so on. Musical semantics is thus entirely "intrinsic to music," but "expressive" of the mental landscape of which the pattern of musical transformations is metaphor. Bernstein extends the principles of Chomsky's linguistics into aesthetic analysis by relying on relations between underlying representations and surface structures as the source of aesthetic meaning, and by emphasizing transformation as the source of metaphor. Just so we can claim metaphor for film, which like music is nonlinguistic and would seem thus to resist interpretation in terms of rhetorical figures. And it is by this argument, too, that we can commit ourselves to a connection of film with reality—the reality of the mental landscape—without succumbing to any naive notion of realism.[13]

## The Quality of Meaning Is Not Strained

Of course, semiologists have long recognized the problem that the rose simply is red. Dealing with it has been their principal undertaking. Roland Barthes acknowledges, in Elements of Semiology, that "many semiological systems (objects, gestures, pictorial images) have a substance of expression whose essence is not to signify," but he claims that the "function" in these systems "becomes pervaded with meaning" in a "universal semantization of the usages." "There is no reality except when it is intelligible"; even if things aren't signs first, as socialized humans we must take them that way. And the connection is plain here with the Marxist analysis of the transformation of objects from use value to exchange value, and with the Lacanian analysis of the transformation of our modes of engaging the world from fantasies of plenitude to imaginary identifications, and from those identifications to symbolic alienations whereby we perceive only what we can engage with the discourse of the other.[14]

But, although Barthes at first distinguished between denotation and connotation, he came to see that the underlying logic of the argument in Elements of Semiology undercuts that distinction. In Elements, he stresses a double movement, a "tendency (each aspect being complementary to the other) to naturalize the unmotivated and to intellectualize the motivated (that is to say, to culturalize it)." This is a double movement of coming to see as natural, as the world, what culture makes us see that way, and of adding a sense of relevance within culture to what we do know to be natural. Thus we are in part deluded into thinking that what is cultural is natural, but in part we know full well that there is the natural, even though we also know that it can hardly be known without the cultural connotations that infuse it.[15]

But it became more and more difficult for Barthes to sustain
the idea of direct denotations of any signs at all, even motivated
ones, or to argue that we are perceiving something natural even
in a partial aspect of a sign. The end to which Elements of
Semiology pointed, that all signs are connotative, is reached
in S/Z. Manuel Alvarado summarizes the two stages of Barthes's
treatment of semiological signs:  the first in which Barthes
"retains the classic distinction between appearance and
construction in his opposition denotation/connotation. Denotation
he defines as a non-coded iconic message, a literal message
possessing a trace of the real; connotation, in contrast, is a
coded iconic message, a symbolic message representing the layers
of cultural accretions surrounding the depiction"; but after
S/Z, "denotation is no longer seen as the trace of reality
(appearance) but rather as the final effect of all the
connotations at play. (Differences in individual readings,
therefore, would relate not to the more or less accurate
apprehension of the reality denoted, but to the range of
ideologically determined connotations brought into play by the
viewer.)" Semiological signs are now generally thought to be
entirely pervaded by culture, just like linguistic ones.[16]

The connotations at play are the meaning of the
semiological discourse. This formulation resolves the problem
in the earlier distinction between denotation and connotation--the
problem that as we have argued images cannot be said to denote
because they cannot be said to signify--by abolishing denotation.
But it still presumes that there is a discourse in which
connotations at play signify and send a message, and hence it
presumes a meaning distinct from, somehow beyond, the signifiers
that send it. It argues that a semiological discourse, composed
of nonarbitrary signs like Bazin's stepping stones, can retain
that feature of a linguistic discourse by which "something is
being said by somebody about something." The first semiology
quite generally found no problem in assuming the same sort of
point-source assignability of meaning to linguistic and
semiological discourses. Jurij Lotman is simply more explicit
than most: "Language is an ordered communicative (serving to
transmit information) sign system"; "this rather broad conception
of language embraces the entire area of communicative systems
in human society"; "no one doubts" that "cinema [is] a
communicative system"; "all those who create films--directors,
actors, scenario writers--wish to tell us something through their
works. Their ribbon of film is a kind of letter, a correspondence
addressed to the audience."[17] We should note, just because
the misapprehension is so pervasive, that Chomsky has often
refuted the idea that "the function of language is communication,
that its 'essential purpose' is to enable people to communicate
with one another," and other ideas that language primarily
"achieve[s] certain instrumental ends, to satisfy needs, and so
on." "Surely," he goes on, "language can be used for such
purposes--or for others. . . . The functions of language are
various."[18]

But even for the first semiology there were troubled stirrings about whether what could be said semiologically about literature and language could be said about semiological systems like film.  Ben Brewster, reviewing the book The Structuralist Controversy for the audience of Screen, which was early receptive to structuralist ideas, argued the inapplicability of the discourse-model to film on grounds that, whatever else may be languagelike in film, a film "discourse" will lack those "shifters" that it is the essence of language to provide.  Those words--"I," "here," "now"--are in the symbolic web of la langue and hence share in the meaning established by the web of differences of language, but have a profound indexical connection to the speech act, the parole, of which they are part.  We know what here means as a word in language, yet we also know (unlike what we know of other sorts of words) that it means in a given discourse what this use of it entails; we know where here is at a given time.  Likewise, when someone says he we know what that means.  We can put ourselves in the place of the speaker as if we ourselves had said he.  Hence, in effect, we can share, we can look out from the point-source of the sentence in which he appears, and know both what that sentence means and that it is not we who mean it, because we have shifted into the speaking position of the other.  We can look from the stated or implicit "I" toward the "he" of whom the "I" speaks.  Shifters thus enable sentences to speak for others, for "somebody," rather than restricting them to the capacity of offering us specimens of behavior as if they were gestures to be perceived and inferred from and observed for qualities and significance in a context, but not to be joined as point-sources, or addressers, of messages.[19]

This is clearly not the case in film or painting.  It is raining is a sentence that can be a vehicle for the proposition that it is raining.  A picture, however, of raining is not and cannot be.  A picture could as properly propose, if it proposed anything, that light sparkles thus on water or that shadows are softened thus in the rain as it does simply that it is raining.  There is no way--over-the-shoulder shots, a system of suture, emphatic close-ups, or camera movements--for us to be forced or permitted to join the image, to find in it one proposition rather than another, to feel that what it images implies anything proposed or anyone proposing it, in the way we commonly join the sentence through shifters and feel its capacity to say something and to be said.  We look at the image and see what it's up to, rather than listen to what it has to say.  We can, of course, see that a single image's significance in the total flow of images is deeply and profoundly influenced by conventions, so we can speak with assurance of the connotations of the image in an ordinary language sense that is perfectly congruent with semiological usage.  But there is no way for the image itself to signify those connotations.  It has them.

Hence the distinction between image discourse and filmic discourse in no way alters our point.  Because the parts that

make it cannot be proposition-vehicles, film must have that
ambiguity about meaning--about who is saying what about what--that
the nature of language permits literature to avoid. When we read
a character's thoughts, or a narrator's remarks, we know that
it is being proposed that the character is thinking exactly what
his words mean that he is thinking. Context may well add implicit
meaning to the explicit, but implicit and explicit meaning are
both there in the discourse because words and sentences can make
propositions that can be seen in each other's lights. But in
film we are given no one's words or sentences to take as sources
of propositions. In fact, nothing is being proposed, because
images and sounds, like rocks in the stream, propose nothing.
Rather, we are being "offered a subject" for observation, so that
the words and images in the film mean all that their context lets
them mean, but propose nothing on their own.

When a character speaks, we are observing his behavior.
We are not being told that he does what he does. We see him do
it. Is the meaning what he says? Who knows? It may be more
meaningful that a car passes as he says it. Still, no one
proposes that the car passes; it simply passes. We have to work
out the meaning. When the camera moves, is it to leave what it
leaves or find what it reveals? Who knows? We have to think
about what we left and what we find, and about all aspects of
the images of leaving and finding. But the sentence, It is
raining, is an exact vehicle for the proposition that it is
raining. If, somewhere else in the discourse, someone says or
implies that the sun is out, there is no doubt where the interest
arises--from the gap between the two propositions, both of which
are part of the discourse. In consequence of what the words mean,
we can confidently say that someone is saying something about
something.

It is important, then, to emphasize that it is not clear
that any aspect of a film signifies or communicates anything
whatever. We may say that film, like literature and music but
unlike painting, has sequence. Or that film, like literature
and representational painting but unlike music, often represents.
Or that film, like music and painting but unlike literature, does
not primarily signify, but does have qualities, including
qualities of representation emergent from every aspect of its
parts and the ordering of their relations. There just isn't any
reason to think that we should trace the cognitive purport or
meaning of a film, since there is no more reason to find a speaker
in film than there is to find one in a painting or a piece of
music. We have no duty to find the point-source of a film's
meaning. But we have every duty to see and hear it fully, to
take in and organize and relate every aspect of its design and
subject, including those aspects and connotations that are quite
comprehensible, though quite unnecessary, to describe in terms
of cultural codes.

But if describable, explicable meaning, which depends on
something being said by somebody about something, is an illegal
import to film, that by no means says that the word meaning

has no place in film criticism.  Beardsley is careful to preserve
the distinction we have drawn between the describable meaning
of literature and the describable qualities of painting and music
and, we add, film, and indeed to see the web of meanings as what
must be described ("explicated") in the verbal arts, whereas
qualities and relations are what are to be described in the other
arts.  But while we must not see painting, music, or film as
offering proposition-vehicles, still Beardsley points out that
painting and music and, again, film

> have an important characteristic that is so close to being
> propositional that the distinction is hard to preserve.
> A visual or auditory design presents itself with every sign
> of being a human artifact, something thought out
> intelligently and ordered by a being like ourselves:  it
> has an air of purposiveness and directedness about it. . . .
> It has a point of view in a larger sense, which we might
> call its attitude; it represents the subject as regarded
> by one who has certain thoughts and feelings.

The way of seeing in Hals's Governors and Lady Regents may
not be their only drama, but it is very clearly in the paintings
as an air of directedness, an attitude.[20]
     Also in literature, as Beardsley treats its interpretation,
meaning turns out to be a matter of the kind of reading that is
not primarily linguistic analysis of the discourse.  Rather
(exactly as with painting and music), a literary work's meaning
is put in terms of the same air of having an attitude, a
directedness, a quality of contemplatability in light of an
attitude against which it plays, and which it manifests.  This
attitude is often to be assigned to an implicit narrator.  But
literary meaning itself is not equivalent to the narrator's
attitude, but rather amounts to "the total attitude of the work,
the basic point of view, [which often] extends beyond, and even
contradicts, the set of beliefs in the mind of the narrator" (that
is, what we would ordinarily call the purport or meaning).
Therefore, Beardsley concludes, "the implicit Reflections of the
work are either predications purportedly believed by the speaker
or the ironically suggested contradictories of purported
beliefs."[21]  And these "implicit Reflections" of the second
sort are difficult to distinguish from the attitudes in painting,
or from meaning in its ordinary and desirable sense.  They, too,
lack a point-source, despite the origins of the discourse's
meaning in language and its implications of a narrator.  The
novel's attitude, a product of all the aspects of its relations,
implications, connotations, and design, is exactly like the
painting's.  Its discourse may create the fictional world and
a narrator who proposes it, but such a world and such a narrator
are in their turn offered us as subjects.  Our observation of
them can turn back on the propositions from which we infer their
existence.  Their meaningfulness, like the meaningfulness of the
representational painting that, however, has no discourse, is

a regional quality of the whole, and not, like the meaning of
the discourse itself, a coded and decipherable message. The
painting may have the quality, yet lack the narrator and the
message. So may the film.

Something very like this argument is implicit, I think, in
Metz's analysis of filmic discourse in Film Language, though
his commitment to a communication model makes him both try to
defend the case with what Brian Henderson has shown to be an
inapplicable dependence on commutation tests, and to urge that
finally filmic discourse does amount to a kind of code. But the
point to which Metz's logic leads him is avowed in at least one
important claim in his subsequent book, Language and Cinema.
In that book the crucial insight is that, whereas system is to
code as text is to message, and whereas every code is a system
and every message a text, the inverse of this second pair of
propositions is not true. There are, says Metz, systems and texts
(e.g., films as wholes) that are not codes or messages, but that
are singular. "Code" suggests that more than one message could
be sent; "message" suggests that more than one code could be found
for it. The singular textual systems qualify as systems and texts
by virtue of something different from codes and messages, namely,
though Metz, clinging to a communication model, cannot draw the
conclusion, the emergence of qualities from their totalities.
This is a meaning not decipherable nor decodable nor dependent,
like the meaning of language, on the rules of combinations of
parts, but simply an attribute of this system, this text as such,
a property of its relations.[22]

Even if we should decide (as recent linguistics argues we
should not) that language leads us along an endless chain of
signifiers while one sign gives birth to another as its
interpretant, and that the process is what meaning is, we would
have no excuse not to allow that this process would govern the
interpretation, though not the description, of painting and film
as well as of literature. It is the air of directedness that
gives rise to the quality artworks can have, the quality of
suggesting-the-appropriateness-of-interpretation, of suggesting-
assignment-of-meaning. It is the possession of that quality that
leads us to ask what they might properly be said to mean, yet
not to equate meaning with a narrated cognitive purport. And
when we ask about such meaning, we begin to think, as Metz does
when he considers filmic discourse, of difference, of what else
might appear in this place, of combinations within and under
higher levels--of all the operations, in short, of teasing out
meaning with which we are familiar as the semiotic legacy of
structural linguistics. But now it is plain that these meanings
are not the result of describing the discourse, but are simply
interpretations of the web of connotations from which emerges
the air of directedness.

Clearly, then, if we take a film as having the air of being
a human production with an attitude, then we find at once that
(while we must not take it as a literal discourse) we need not

consider only its "limited range of rhetorical and dramatic
effects," its "illusion," the way it "plays directly on our
feelings." It can be taken as <u>an occasion for reflection on</u>
<u>the attitude that it embodies</u>, in all that attitude's relativity
to what it is directed toward, what discourselike interplay with
its alternatives in all their connotative richness it implies.
To see an attitude in a painting or film is thus to be in that
world where "something is being said . . . about something,"
though not literally, and not by somebody. This is a world of
quasi discourse and hence of contemplatability. Taking a painting
or a film that way is coming to comprehend its "implicit
Reflections" by exercise of will and intellect through which,
as with literature, we can "actively fill" the virtual world it
presents.
        Our argument that the film, the painting, and even the world
of the literary work are meaningful in a sense only metaphorically
connected with the kind of literal meaning emergent from a
discourse should enable us to emphasize emergent qualities of
images, structure, and stories, without having to think of such
qualities as having been selected from any storehouse of
linguistic possibilities where ways of sending messages are laid
up, and yet also without having to think of them as simply
provided by direct resemblance to the world.

## The Point-Source in the World

        But the relation between the storehouse of <u>la langue</u> and
the actualities of <u>les paroles</u> raises more issues than the
question of whether artworks are discourses that send messages.
In the first semiology it was generally assumed that the messages
sent and the meaning assignable to an implicit speaker should
be thought of as choices by an individual. The language of
criticism based on such semiology, like Saussure's speaking about
<u>parole</u>, is usually unself-consciously intentionalistic. Lotman
is, again, simply more explicit than most in his emphasis on
semiotics as the study of how "an artist has an infinite (rather,
a very great) number of possibilities in choosing <u>how</u> to render
an object," and of how the artist has a "choice from a certain
number of alternative possibilities which, in their totality,
comprise the inventory of elements of a given level."[23]
        Thus, semiology, in one strand of its development, treated
objects like films and verbal discourses as a human being's
choices from a storehouse. But in another part of the
semiological forest, it came to be argued that the storehouse
of language is not only what a language user chooses <u>from</u>, but
what he or she chooses <u>with</u>. It is the language itself that
permits what can be said in it. And this conception calls into
serious question any simple notion like Lotman's of assignment
of meaning to the chooser. The foundations of a second semiology
developed along lines not explicitly followed by Saussure, though
implicit in his presentation, and made use of by Lévi-Strauss
and extended by Lacan and Althusser. This second semiology

emphasized the sense in which the storehouse, and not the language
user, should be thought of as doing the choosing and hence
creating the meaning of speech acts.  In this view it is the
social world, the sole possessor of the totality of any language,
that is to be emphasized as the point-source of messages, rather
than the language user, who chooses the language in which to send
his or her message.  The consequence of this emphasis is to lead
us again to analyze the communicator, the one who signifies.
But now this one is not a human addresser of a message, but rather
the world itself.  It is both that other, whose discourse is the
unconscious, and that language that speaks through man.[24]

Discourse sends a speaker's, a chooser's, message.  But who
is this speaker and what sort of thing is his or her choice?
From the start, many understood Saussure to imply that the speaker
is _constituted_ by the language in which his or her messages
are sent, so that language itself speaks.  The idea of a finally
personal point-source of behavior in a "subject," or "self," in
a freely choosing sender of messages that translate freely chosen
thought into the terms society provides for its transmission,
is denied.  With it, of course, is denied the appropriateness
of terms like "will and intellect," or "reader's imagination,"
as terms for faculties and operations of critic or creator.  Lacan
is at the center of this line of argument.  And Lacan, says Sherry
Turkle, "denigrates 'humanistic' philosophy and psychology that
treat man as an actor who wills his action and instead sees man
as a submitting object of processes that transcend him."  What
she goes on to call "Lacan's affirmation of the centrality of
language to thought" implies again that _all_ human behavior is
discourse, but that the sender of its message is not the
"subject," who thinks he or she sends it, but "the other" who
sends it through him or her, the "society [that] enters the
individual as the individual enters the world of symbolic speech"
and provides a point-source for the actions of "the ego [that]
is not autonomous, but subordinated and alienated to the objects
(people and images) with which it has identified during its
development.[25]

Thus discourse derives from an imaginary ego and a symbolic
language--clearly the somebody who says something about something
is no simple chooser, of Lotman's sort, but is the world, the
other.  The concrete individual is site and object of the dynamics
involved, and the individual's "practice is seen as the
interaction of new objective contradictions with a subject formed
in the place of old contradictions and old representations of
contradictions."[26]

Film is, then, a product of, and would appeal to, what the
world makes people.  And by two routes this argument challenges
our claim for meaning as emergence of the contemplatable.  First,
the attack on the subject undercuts the validity of what we might
wish to say concerning what we see, and implies our duty to break
free from what ideology makes us.  Somehow we must observe our
bondage and, later, infer from it _theory_ that will enable us
to intervene in the course of our own response.

Second, even if we do not feel that, in Louis Althusser's terms, we must construct "scientific" theory in order to achieve an "epistemological break" with "ideology,"[27] there is a second route of attack on meaning as contemplatability, along with its implications that art objects are properly understood through attention to their capacity for inducing aesthetic experience rather than to the medium of their presentation. This attack says that human beings are formed by what the world is to respond to the world's different classes of objects (among which would be film, literature, language) in the terms under which society has carved them off from each other. It follows that we ought to fight the fight proper to each class of objects, drawing the correct criticial distinctions among members of those classes. Thus we should, on the one hand, distinguish the policy (the politique) of our involvement with language proper from the policy of our involvement with art objects, and, on the other, distinguish the politique (within consideration of art objects) of our approval of film or literature that implies the propriety of the epistemological break from any possible counterpolicy that would permit submission to the wiles of art objects whose implications cozy up to ideology.

Even before Lacan's claim that the unconscious is structured as a language, and hence itself speaks through us as language does, it was clear that the Saussurian concept of language had consequences for criticism. In that conception, language and other semiological processes found people memorizing sentences and other linguistic forms and then, in acts of parole that may themselves become parts of the storehouse of langue, either copying them with minimal substitutions, or forming new constructions by operations of analogy--if I can say "apple-corer," I can create "pimple-corer."[28]

Understanding utterances thus means recognizing them as belonging to the storehouse of memorized constructions with their minimal extensions and substitutions. Understanding a unit means seeing where it fits the possibilities of what such units can be. We know what things mean because we've seen them or their close kindred enough to know how they work in society. Linguistics and semiotics, as sciences, simply chart the regularities in the social systems people recognize. The only alternative to this passive re-creation of the shape of the systems that social custom imposes upon our organizing habits is a critical activity, an intervention into the social understanding that such systems amount to what we do (and should) take reality to be.

Thus Ben Brewster could quote Peter Caws as early as 1966 presenting as "the position of the structuralists" the "metaphysical question of the subject which has been considered to be a product of language, posterior to language." As important as shifters, to Brewster's argument that structuralism is not applicable to film criticism is thus the special relation among language, literature, and criticism that he observes in Barthes's

literary criticism. This relation must be seen as grounding a
politique concerning literature absolutely different from any
politique concerning film.[29]
    Brewster argues that it is the point of structuralism that
because the subject is constituted by language yet participates
in the social process of creation of la langue by acts of
parole, everything we say becomes part of la langue, including
what we say about literature. Hence the critic is part of what
he or she criticizes (namely, language), and hence it follows
that criticism itself is a politique that embodies and extols
its own writing. Literary criticism is a part of language,
of what it criticizes, in a way film criticism can never be,
simply because the film critic is not making films when he or
she writes. Structuralism, as a politique, is unavailable to
film criticism: even if film critics make a difference to future
film production, their writing is not part of that production.
Literary criticism, however, becomes part of the literature it
comments on simply because literature is writing. It is
language, modified and re-created by speech.
    Likewise, the argument goes, the film viewer is debarred
from that sharing of the film that would be analogous to the
sharing of the language possible to the reader of literature
because of shifters. Reading and understanding amount to activity
in the symbolic mode, which is itself what makes la langue both
continue synchronically to be what it has come to be through
people's acts of parole that teach it to each other, and also
to change diachronically into what it evolves toward by those
subtle modifications enacted through analogy and other variants
of parole on la langue. The film viewer does not act in the
symbolic mode. The reader, however, is at play in the fields
of the signifier. He or she is involved in words, a creator of
la langue through his or her reading insofar as the reading
modifies his or her portion of the social possession, language.
Because a participator in la langue, he or she speaks for that
society, that other, which is language and which speaks itself
through him or her. The politique of structuralist criticism
is, therefore, to extol by its practice of active reading--by
S/Z, for instance--the awareness of this process of symbolic
activity, to praise works whose parole is such that it must
be taken in terms of the langue of which it reduces the
redundancy, so that we must read it as writing and not as a window
on the world. Or it may, by revealing how readerly writing
pretends not to be simply about its own language, extol the
writerly by reconstituting the reality of that evasive
readerliness in light of the writerliness it ought to be. So,
Barthes turns "Sarrasine" into a play of signifiers in spite of
itself, recaptures it for the writerly while revealing the
shortcomings, the pretense, involved in taking it any other way.
    The nature of film, in Brewster's view, prevents that play
of signifiers. Film must be what realistic, i.e., readerly,
literature tried to pretend it was, a source of impressions that

we have access to the world, to something other than its own
language.  No criticism of it (criticism being a form of writing)
is possible.  Only submission to it or critique of that submission
is possible.  We can extol the writerly in literature even by
such indirections as recuperative praise of a readerliness altered
in the very process of intervention in its language, as Barthes
does with "Sarrasine."  But we can only expose the inevitable
readerliness of film:  "Sarrasine" becomes something new and
wonderfully writerly with S/Z, because the language of S/Z
becomes part of "Sarrasine."  But Young Mr. Lincoln is merely
revealed in its inconsistencies by Cahiers's critique.  Balzac's
language will never be the same after Barthes, but Ford's film
remains.

The film viewer, under this argument, is thus doomed to be
merely the consumer of the film, and, if he or she plays
productively with signifiers, it is only with imaginary
signifiers.  The viewer is unable in theory or in practice to
become part of what he or she views, to enter into its imaginative
play as shifters allow, or to constitute the film language that
he or she is constituted by as is the literary reader.

Still, as we have seen, the first semiology distinguished
between image discourse (inevitably imaginary) and filmic
discourse (cultural, symbolic).  This distinction suggests access
to the same kind of politique on the part of critics and
filmmakers as is praise/creation of the writerly in literature.
If the distinction does not overcome the problem of shifters or
of a viewer's access and contribution to the language of film,
still it permits us to find in certain films a quality of
reflexivity, of self-consciousness of themselves as films, and
hence to distinguish them as works that admit that they are about
their own "language" from those that pretend they are not.

Metz's Film Language itself culminated in such a
politique in the article "The Modern Cinema and Narrativity."
There is a tendency in recent semiotics of film ever more overtly
to view its goal as intervention in film practice, through
distinguishing films (often called "classic") that are said to
be properly read only in terms of their presumed appeal to
audiences' (false) subjectivity, to their (ideologically
determined) sense of reality, from films--usually Godard's, but
called "writerly" or "post-modernist" whatever their provenance--
that must be read, if they are to be understood, in terms of their
critique of what F. E. Sparshott called the "bias of exposition"
that film has always had toward the naturalistic.[30]  These
films, it is argued, have a kind of meaningfulness that is not
an embodiment of anything.  Their meaning is like that
"rhetorical" aspect of literature that Paul de Man extols as the
proper object and method of literary criticism, unsubsumable to
logic or the world, inexplicable under grammar.  These films are
textual sites for operations of deconstruction and interpretation
in terms of socially determined systems and practices of
signification--of involvement with which practices the criticism

that critiques it, as Cahiers made so plain in its insistence on its sharing of S/Z's practice in treating Young Mr. Lincoln, must be self-aware.[31]

This distinction is not, Stephen Heath has argued, in principle one between art films and popular films. Rather, on the one hand, are any films that allow one to respond to them in any way at all that accepts them as "the expression of reality with reality." And, on the other hand, are films that emphasize by their practice, by their refusal of illusions of naturalization, that proper response should be a matter of understanding meaning rather than responding to effects. Here the proper motive of film criticism, like that of any activity whatever, is taken to be the imperative to escape ideology by the epistemological break that permits exposing the illusions of the subject and hence answers to the "concern," as Northrop Frye would put it, for socialist revolution, theory and practice in this view not being detachable from each other.[32]

The modernist critics have sought to blast through film as film, round and smooth as an egg (as Bazin says of certain virtually unauthored Westerns, which he wishes to preserve against auteurism's neglect), and to deconstruct it into text, as Walter Benjamin sought to blast through history, round and smooth as an egg under its ruling class castration, and to deconstruct it into the "tradition," which is always remade in every encounter with it.[33] These critics would base criticism on a fundamental operation of exposure of those films which are readerly, in all their falseness of appearance, their insidiousness of appeal, their status as parts of the ideological apparatus for the interpellation of the subject that Althusser defines. And they would extol only those films that insist by their "practice of cinema" on the recuperation of the signifier as such.[34]

This argument is based on sand. It is an indefensible assumption that because it is possible for many viewers to think that there is a difference in contemplatability between films that embody the world and films that don't, critics must accept that distinction too. Further, it is indefensible that critics should contemplate the writerly, but merely report on the insidious blandishments of readerly films.

If there is one thing we are sure of, and on which all schools of criticism agree, it is that no film simply embodies the world. Even Bazin's notion of the "filter" that film places before reality guarantees that the film the filter lets through will be what Beardsley calls an "object manqué," and will in some metaphoric sense belong to the world of signs as well as revealing signs of the world.[35] And no film is better than any other, more or less exposable or extollable, on grounds of the degree to which its surface calls attention to its membership in that world of signs. What does distinguish them, no matter what their style, is the degree to which the qualities that emerge from the fusions and implications of their connotations and suggestions are such as to induce aesthetic experience, the degree to which they simply have that richness (in some combination of dimensions) which makes them worth thinking about, engaging with, contemplating.

The degree to which films have this capacity is, we argue, only assessable through observation of the films themselves--no a priori rules whatever can determine it, whether rules like "be as distant from the norms of representation as possible" (Arnheim), or "be ambiguous" (Bazin), or "be revolutionary" (Eisenstein, Eagleton) or "reflexively concern the practice of cinema" (Heath). A film is good if it's good, and you can only tell by looking. But you don't look solely with some imaginary system that you mistakenly think puts the world in your head, as it is argued that people think they do; rather, you look with your whole mind, keeping in mind that what you're looking at is a movie--as much an occasion for contemplation as any novel.

## On the Subject

There is one other aspect of what Brewster calls the structuralist case that its proponents would claim as decisive in a refutation of our claim that meaning is the consequence of aesthetic experience of the contemplatable. We must refute it. This is the basic case against the subject, the case that "we" don't properly look at all. It is argued that the idea of meaning that we have been advancing is indefensible, as is any idea of meaning that attaches it to the qualities or implications of the objects that bear it, whether the meaning is conceived as a standing for, i.e., a semiosis, or, as we urge, as an emergent quality of whole designs that have relatability to human concerns but that do not signify the relations that can be observed. Structuralists reject our case because, they say, the response to something as meaningful is a response of an alienated subject, of an illusory center of consciousness that is simply a socially induced and shaped formation, a site of intersection for the codes that traverse it and give it its false sense of self.[36]

In this view, neither discourses nor what we have called quasi discourses can have meaning or other qualities--rather, they simply mobilize those processes of substitution and repression that society has imposed upon individuals, turning them into subjects. A film or a sentence or an argument will have its meaning revealed only when what is explained about it is how it promises to satisfy audience impulses that are never avowed, but in terms of which every occasion for response must, though indirectly, be seen. We might say that meaning is a process of reaching for what we repress as we reach for it, what is always present as something deferred, what is only to be explained as an occasion for illusion.

The argument is that as socialized human beings what we do-- including what we think, and therefore what we think of films-- displays under a proper analysis our wish for a primeval plenitude or power. Our every organization of response, however, reveals how that wish has been given up, negated, in consequence of the

"non" of our Father, and replaced, in consequence of the "nom"
of our Father, by a series of substitutions. These substitutions
stand for each other in a chain, but are always reducible to the
substitution of our father's--society's--prohibition/valuation
and authority for our vision of being the phallus that our mother
wishes she had.

The set of values that we accept and internalize as our
definition of ourselves is society's law, or "ideology." We have
the illusion of access to the power of decision, of recognition
and awareness, when we join the sociality and become its
creature. Whatever we think we say on our own, we say as the
world's representatives--the meaning of every act is simply that.
No sign, no thought, no meaningful gesture, or formal pattern,
bears any true relation to the wishes it purports to express,
but only to that endless pattern of substitutions that we entered
into when we accepted in place of the phallus, the Name of the
Father.

The dependence of this view on the Saussurian picture of
the nature and structure of language is plain. Language, in the
Saussurian picture upon which Lacanian psychoanalysis depends,
is an inventory of organizations of differences among formal
possibilities on various levels (e.g., a phonemic level, a level
of syntagmas or words, a level of syntactical formations), and
it is characterized by the double possibility, at every point
and on every level, of combination and of substitution of the
organizations possible at that point. Words may replace each
other or may be added to each other under various constraints.
To know an utterance as a permissible item in a given language
is to know what other words might have been used at each point
in its string and to know what difference it would have made to
use others. Learning a language is thus largely a matter of
memory and a kind of primitive data processing of difference,
a matter therefore of submitting ourselves to the discipline under
which, if we are to communicate with others who have also
submitted themselves to this discipline, we must link sounds and
meanings in terms others also agree to abide by.

Clearly, the "axis of selection" (to use Roman Jakobson's
term) along which replacements can be made for words in the speech
string is the axis of substitution, the location of metaphor--and
here we return to Lacan, for whom entry into the world of symbolic
processes is accomplished by submission to the discipline of
substituting one thing for another.[37] The unconscious itself,
in fact, is a social product, a language in the sense that it
is a storehouse of items substitutable for each other, from which
what is chosen amounts (like the first substitution) to a
renunciation of something much more personal and rewarding to
the individual, something oceanic and fulfilling rather than
truncated, carved-off ("castrated"), conventional, utilitarian,
social.

A language use, like any other human act, is thus, it is
said, a gesture of submission to the ideology that decrees that
any more directly expressive sort of conduct (whatever it could

be--our fantasies alone know, and they aren't telling.  How could
they?  In what language could they speak?) would be not only
ineffective but wrong, a violation of the Law.  The less alienated
impulse for which they substitute, like the original wish for
which the Name of the Father substitutes, is and must be
repressed (otherwise we might seek to express it and fall out
of language entirely), leaving only its traces in the
unconscious.  There it continues to seek its natural release along
the only paths available to it, creating metonymic chains of
metaphoric substitution that entirely compose the structure of
that unconscious (as in a Saussurian storehouse they compose a
language) and that keep it always involved in the very processes
of its own subjugation to the social world whose acceptance
brought it into being.
     The Lacanian addition to Saussurian linguistics, then, is
the notion that what substitutes for what else might be said
represses other speech, whereas for Saussure saying one word
rather than another mobilizes the difference the one makes, rather
than the other, for the addressee of the speech act involved.
Understanding language, for Saussure, is analyzing the statistics
of possible combinations of the items in the storehouse of
language.  But understanding that "language" which is the
unconscious is, for Lacan, revealing the repressed, the
unspeakable, the unreachable meaning that every utterance covers,
the meaning that is the oceanic fantasy of being the phallus,
the desire of the Mother.  To reveal the ways of the unconscious
is not to reveal our deepest being, but rather to reveal the
alienated, socialized construction of substitutions, carvings
off, repressions, castrations, with which we have replaced that
deepest being--which being is, however, only finally a fantasy,
a baby's dream.
     Truly understanding utterances, or discourses, then, in the
Lacanian view amounts to deciphering in them the traces of what
they cover up.  By attention to echoes, possible wordplays, gaps
in sense, meaninglessnesses, we discover what it is that in their
condition as discourse they can never express.
     The qualities of speech acts or any other symbolic acts,
such as the making or viewing of films--acts that can be taken
as standing for something, as linking the concrete reality of
some expressive substance to the equally concrete (though mental)
reality of some expressed substance--are preeminently the
qualities of evasion.  Things say what a social world lets them
say.  We know that world takes as its membership fee the
channeling and reduction of meaning into absolutely artificial
courses that reduce what we might be and feel to what the
dynamics of that world's systems of power permit us to be and
feel.  Things do not say what the motives that lead to their
saying wished they might say, yet it is the motives that lead
to their saying that give the energy that made it possible that
they could be said.  Those motives are subverted, their imagined
meaning castrated.
     And that means that the proper understanding of the thing

that says always has two aspects--one in which what it says is
read in context of the social organization of which it is an
example, and the other in which what it does not say, but wishes
it could, is read off from the fact that it hasn't said it. Take
a discourse or a film as a whole (one of the levels on which it
can be read in terms of the language of the unconscious or of
its various suborganizations such as narrativity), and one can
and should see it as a metaphor, that is, as a substitution of
one signifying form for another. In this metaphor we can detect
two qualities commensurate with these two aspects: a quality
of conventionality, and a quality of incoherence. It clearly
is, as metaphor, a member of a whole set of conventional types:
we have been there before, we know that this means exactly what
we have learned such things mean. But equally clearly, it doesn't
mean that: it isn't that, it pushes away from that meaning and
means . . . who knows what? A chain of other substitutions, none
of which can be sustained but behind which we feel the pressure
of the unspeakable, of what this metaphor yearns toward at the
same time as its existence as metaphor covers it up.

In the view we are reporting here, the goal of linguistic
analysis, or of literary or film criticism, must be the
recognition of this double aspect. This prevents the
misrecognition that it is the function of the objects themselves,
as objects in their various languages of culture, to misrepresent
as plenitude, presence of meaning. On the one hand, it is an
enormously appealing goal. Very little in this life is obvious,
and much that we take for granted is on reflection simply evidence
of our having brought into play assumption systems that won't
stand the light of day--assumptions of value, for instance, that
amount to ethnocentricity or class or sexual bias. But, on the
other, the goal is naive and misleading, and amounts not to the
expansion and enrichment of the human potential of film criticism
that it is clearly the motive of those who seek it to realize,
but rather a reduction.

We can see the problem with the position we have summarized
in two lights. First, language does not work as Saussure said
it did, as a storehouse of combinables and substitutables the
use of which is governed by memory and a primitive data processing
device for detection of difference. Hence there is no reason
to think of the operations of the unconscious as the operations
of language. While they may be the operations that Lacan
specifies, they are not the operations of language. The
possession of language is far less simply social than Saussure
saw, far more a matter of a native human endowment. It is simply
not explainable in terms of memory or data processing or the
carving-off of sounds and meanings in accordance with social
convention.

There is thus no reason to think of the metaphoric ability
as being at the center of the linguistic faculty. Nor of its
being entered into as an extension of the acceptance of the Name
of the Father, and hence of its carrying with it an Oedipal
burden, a stench of castration. Language use is not a matter

of repetition of learned forms with a little extension by analogy, but a matter of "creativity." Perfectly comprehensible <u>new sentences</u>, "uncontrolled by stimulus conditions though appropriate to situations," never before expressed, and capable of meanings that cannot be explained on the basis of extrapolations of the sort Saussurian linguistics or semiology proposes, are generated by every language user all the time. They are not recognized by auditors but rather are understood through processes of analysis by synthesis, the application of a logic ranging over representations (many of them indeed unconscious and never appearing on the surface of behavior). It is inconceivable that the rules for these processes could have been learned by young children through the application of a data-processing device operating upon memory. And they are so similar, in their forms, from culture to culture, that they cannot plausibly be thought of as constructions of ideology, or, indeed, as social constructs at all. Thus it is plausible that the meaning of discourse is, at least in linguistic contexts and most probably in those other contexts for which we have coined the notion of quasi discourse to admit a profound difference from the linguistic, at least in part a function of kinds of implication--of demonstration, suggestion, proper inference, etc.--that have nothing at all to do with a motive towards expressing the inexpressible desire for and of the Mother, but that may be thought of as aspects of human nature itself.[38]

## Plain Sense and Film

Language has a plain sense level that it is among the analyst's duties to take account of and to read off against the many other levels and aspects of the linguistic act. That plain sense level is the analogue of the level of implication in films on which they raise issues and develop formal and substantive variations and resolutions of those issues that establish attitudes towards them. We're not saying that we know in detail what the "linguistics" of this plain sense level is for film, but we are saying that we have a strong suspicion about what it isn't. It isn't an analogue to Saussurian linguistics, such as that which is suggested by Lacan and by those who seek conscientiously to apply the implications of the Saussurian/ Lacanian view to such systems as film and literature. If Saussure is wrong about language, then what is argued under Saussurian warrant for the unconscious and its involvement in human acts--for instance, that the reading of film must be a matter of deferment of meaning, since every other reading must--is at least not proved.

But we are certainly not saying that film, or literature, or language, are <u>less</u> complex than the semiological tradition would have them, or that there is <u>only</u> a plain sense meaning to a film or a discourse. While "ambiguities and mysteries" cannot be traced to the fixed virtualities of the Saussurian <u>langue</u>, that fact by no means entails that film can offer us rhetorical and dramatic effects but not meaning. The semiologists

are right that there is more to it than that, though they are
not right about the reason.  Our reliance on Beardsley is as much
a reliance on metaphor as is Barthes's on Lacan, and we are
arguing specifically that metaphor has a creative aspect like
the creative aspect of language use.  Unpacking a metaphor is
not a matter of tracing a message of castration and desire, not
a matter of finding the quality of incoherence behind which we
must feel (and seek to expose) the dependence on and ultimate
restatement of the desire for and of the Mother.  We are saying
that the web of organizations that film or literary images of
all sorts (formal ones and substantive ones, generic and
argumentative) enter into will indeed be incoherent, in the
entirely Beardsleyan sense that in many ways the parts of the
web will militate against each other's use as substitutions for
other ways of putting the same thing.  But that incoherence will
not simply express repression, but will rather carry qualities
of applicability and meaningfulness that enrich rather than
impoverish the surface sense of what it is they seem to stand
for.  There is no more reason to think of all these qualities
speaking to a Freudian unconscious than to think that none do.
Our position is that the human psyche is not simple, that no
simple principles are likely to explain it as a whole, and that
in the absence of such a general psychological theory as would
do so, there is far more reason to eschew dependences on
theorizings that are problematic at their roots than there is
to embrace them.[39]

We claim, then, that connotations interplay in a film in
many and complex ways, and that it is at least possible that they
might do so in such a way that, from and despite the complexity,
unusual qualities of relevance to various aspects of human
experience might well emerge from the proper subsets of exactly
the connotations that are at play in the particular film under
consideration.  Our argument is that there is not a well-grounded
general psychology, that there are films that have various
implicational aspects, that among these might well be an aspect
that we can equally well call (Beardsleyanly) attitude, or
(auteurianly) vision, or (semiologically) meaning, and that the
proof is in the pudding.  What follows, then, is an attempt to
trace, for a related set of films, the set of connotations
mobilized by story, style, imagery, and structure, and to present
the case that, in fact, this web does amount to something, that
it is, as a whole, a metaphor or substitution for an attitude
embedded in the films, an integrated set of qualities carried
by them and emergent from them, a set that deserves to be called
the films' meaning.


THE MEANING OF ANTONIONI'S TRILOGY

L'Avventura
        Central to Antonioni's films is a sense of the way a certain
willingness not to interact with others is encouraged by social

reality.  It appears that life will be easier if people do not
relate to others warmly and with concern, but rather adjust to
life by not asking too much of it, by convincing themselves that
emotional and other situations are in good order, even if, in
fact, they are not, and by deadening themselves to emotional
appeals even though they thereby deaden themselves to joy as
well.  The social environment encourages this deadening.  We
cannot blame people for succumbing to it, and we cannot be
surprised when most people succumb.  Yet from the perspective
of the good that presses against this hindrance, the perspective
of the kind of vitality that is everywhere suggested but nowhere
prevails in the films and that is perhaps most memorably rendered
by Monica Vitti in moments of the trilogy, people can be hurt
if not astonished.  It is that perspective which most often
Antonioni's films encourage us to share.  The films are filled
with _pain_ for innocents, and even for those not quite so
innocent, who feel wounded by the consequences of others' having
become absorbed into an orderly but cold social life.  The films
are also filled with characters' anxious, perhaps angry,
understanding of the way that modern society encourages the
adjustment that will hurt those who want more than merely that.

        We cannot call this sense of gap between slightly naive
wishes for fulfillment and the world that makes people give those
wishes up any simple name.  "Alienation" will suggest some of
it, as will "lack of communication," "dehumanization," even
"Antoniennui."[40]  Perhaps someone who intended to give a name
to the Antonioni quality would choose one of these words, but
one could never properly characterize it by means of one.  The
quality is precise, situational, very much a matter of clear
images of the world's attraction as deadening surface and of the
slightly naive individual's expectation that is doomed to be
dashed in a surface like that.  And this kind of precise
specification of feeling, through works that develop different
aspects of it, is exactly what an artist's vision can provide--it
is what an artist's vision is, and thus, the meaning of the films.

        A characteristic Antonioni scene, rendering the vision rather
directly, is of a usually female character expecting human
relationship in human contact, not getting it, and being amazed
and hurt.  Early in L'Avventura, Claudia approaches Anna's
father to commiserate with him on his daughter's disappearance.
Claudia is embarrassed at wearing the blouse that Anna has given
her--she thinks quite correctly that the father will think her
the kind of person who might well rifle Anna's things as soon
as possible--but she yearns to share with him her concern for
her friend.  But he, standing with Anna's Bible in his hands,
and more as if to convince himself than Claudia, starts at once
to urge that since Anna had a Bible she cannot have committed
suicide.  That case is so flabbergastingly off the mark, it shows
so little understanding of the dynamics of the situation that
has caused Anna to disappear, that Claudia is thunderstruck and
flinches back from him before she flees.  She realizes that his
explanation is prompted by obscure needs and understandings of

his own, and not so much to respond to his daughter's loss as
to explain it in terms that will enable him to think well of her
and of himself. Claudia is aware of the reality of the
situation. She sees the sadness of Anna's having been compelled
to disappear and the misery of the father's having lost her.
But those to whom she reaches out with her natural response are
not as aware as she is. They are ruled by other concerns. They
are in a different world from Claudia, and it horrifies her to
discover this.

Similarly, when Claudia first arrives at the hotel at
Taormina, she must face, as Sandro's mistress, the group who were
on the boat when Anna was in that role. In an understandable
reflex, she tries not to let Patrizia glimpse her in the lobby
of the hotel and to stave off the inevitable questions--"Did you
find Anna?" would only begin them. And when spotted, she takes
Patrizia away from the crowd, to a privacy that will make the
necessary self-exposure intimate and bearable. But Patrizia sits
with her like a casual acquaintance, makes only polite remarks,
and asks none of the predictable questions, but is plainly
relieved when Sandro comes up and she can play the role of
introducer to the routine of the hotel.

Patrizia is simply not interested in integrating past and
present. She does not refrain through delicacy from asking about
Anna, but rather because for her, Anna being gone, it is as if
Sandro's time with Anna never existed. When Claudia goes to
Patrizia's room to look for Sandro later that night, Patrizia
counsels only that acceptance of whatever happens that we would
expect from her, given her own casual switch in the same company
from the gigolo Raimondo to her husband Ettore. Patrizia's
failure even to consider evaluation of conduct under a criterion
of personal commitment amounts to moral numbness. Claudia's
progress lies in coming to be more like her, to accept
uninvolving, uncommitting, and impermanent relations with people.

But Anna's father's almost willful obtuseness and Patrizia's
anaesthesia are not the only forms of substitutive strategem in
the characters of Claudia's world for the kind of authenticity
in personal relations that it is to be wished that a person could
take for granted. Throughout the early part of the film Corrado's
cruel squelching of his wife Giulia is painful. In the search
for Anna, we see him turn decisively away from Giulia's glancing
appeal in a way similar to (though far more intentional than)
Sandro's later rejection of Claudia in the hotel room at Noto.
Corrado's cruelty is so gratuitous that it bespeaks a depth of
loathing that must simply override any responsiveness to a
moment's demands. At least, the cruelty makes comprehensible
Giulia's funny and painful acceptance of seduction by the young
painter later.

We do not, of course, see why Corrado is so hard on Giulia.
It seems so little motivated that we must guess that through it,
he, too, compensates for other disappointments in his life by
simply taking them out on her. But we see clearly that, in

accepting the painter, Giulia is herself responding far more to
her having been scorned and hurt by her husband than by any
positive feeling for the young man. And this pattern of defensive
response, of actions caused not by desire for their objects but
by some intention to compensate for life's general or particular
disappointments, is what Claudia, like the other Antonioni
heroines, finds in the world around her. Against these
compensatory actions Antonioni sets the authentic wishes of his
principal characters, till they too are ground down.

The trilogy begins this way, with a compelling lesson to
Claudia that if she is to survive she must become as little
expectant of personal fulfillment as the others in her world.
Could anyone--perhaps someone more sophisticated, less naive--
find warrant for expectation of anything else in life than this
pained reduction of hopes? La Notte, second of these three
films, asks that, and answers with an ambiguous perhaps. Can
we see the semiproffer of La Notte as a generalization, as what
we can expect for ordinary human relationships that are carefully
and hopefully tended? Eclipse says not.

Of course, the principal teacher of the reductive lesson
to Claudia is Sandro. He has little idea how sexual relations
might be linked to emotion. Anna remarks to him on the island
just before she disappears, "I don't feel you anymore." Amazed,
he asks, "Not even yesterday at my house? You didn't feel me
then?" Anna replies, entirely accurately, "You always have to
drag things down." He drags things down not from malice, but
from incomprehension of an alternative. With both of his
mistresses it happens that first Anna, then Claudia evinces some
reluctance to make love on demand. Sandro each time asks blankly,
"Perché?" ("Why?"). Each time the woman realizes that he simply
doesn't understand her feelings and she is miserable. Anna beats
at him and repeats, "Why? Why?" and Claudia understands how,
for him, all human relationships are like the "adventure" he tells
her they are having. L'Avventura is, of course, the Italian
word for temporary affairs.

Sandro's incomprehension and his misuse of emotional
relations come not from thinness of spirit, but from his being
flooded with and dominated by a sense of failure in his own life.
Everything he does is compensatory for his sense of personal
failure. What counts in his life is his sense of having sold
out when he switched from architectural design to estimating costs
of school construction. It is clear that Claudia is at best a
substitute for him, that she is only a momentary appeal that he
finds no reason to resist. On a deeper level, the substitution
itself brings on resentment of her as a woman, connected by that
very fact, in the value structure of these films that have at
their centers a sensibility that is, conventionally imaged as
feminine, with the kind of sensibility that Sandro has given up
with his creative career.

Thus Sandro, walking out in Noto, muses on the difference
between his own professional life and the kind of creative

experience that must have underlain the building of the city, which is an amazing baroque fantasy in stone. He sees a drawing, unattended for a moment, that perfectly captures a single architectural detail on one of the buildings--a detail of a feminine, shell-like arch, reminding us, if not of such an orgy of shells as Sternberg's Anatahan, perhaps of Fellini's treatment of Venus's shell in connection with Maddalena in La Dolce Vita and with Susy in Juliet of the Spirits. Sandro spitefully mars the drawing by spilling ink on it, and confronts the student artist in an envious, compensatory display of machismo that pretends to assert superiority when it is actually the most agonized inferiority that Sandro feels. Passing a line of most un-Fellinian seminarians, who must also reproach him with a sense of innocence bartered away, Sandro returns to the hotel and Claudia. He closes the shutters on the painful Noto scene and tries simply to force Claudia into sex, in obvious substitution for any direct resolution of the complex of unhappy feelings roused by his experience of architecture, youth, creativity, sensibility, and the loss of them.

Sandro is as resentful of women, of all that arches and shells stand for, as is Steiner in La Dolce Vita. But whereas Steiner turns his resentment on himself in suicide, Sandro turns it on shell symbols and on Claudia. Claudia is, for him, compensation for loss; she is an opportunity for an adventure who comes to him from that very world which, by providing opportunities, has seduced him away from what he regretfully feels he might more assertively have made of his talents. His awareness, then, is reflected not only in a predatory attitude to Claudia as representative of that world--his hostility is clear in the sadistic aspect of his sexuality and also in his readiness to betray her--but also in a programmatic generalization of what she stands for. Sandro elevates his moral flabbiness to a philosophy of overreceptivity to life's chances, of being moved by every breeze. "I'm not resisting," he says to Claudia on the train, as she resists the developing attraction because of her sense of obligation to Anna. "Then it's out of our hands," he says in the paint shop, that being for him sufficient reason to go on with the developing adventure.

The hindrance of the film is thus plainly symbolized in Sandro's history. He elected a career that is socially and financially profitable, but that is premised (as is the career that opens up for Giovanni in La Notte) on the renunciation of the kind of immediate vitality represented by Noto. What the film presents for us to contemplate as its negatively valued conception of reality--what it is for things to be askew--is exemplified in the fact that in this world a person like Sandro can seem to succeed exactly by doing not only what makes him miserable, but also what betrays the talent and sensitivity of his best self. This is the kind of world where insensitivity to the best qualities brings rewards in precise moral register with what has earned them.

Claudia, as symbol for Sandro of the interchangeable blandishments by which he is seduced and reproached and as symbol for us of a vibrant reality gone to waste in Sandro's world, is thus defined by her victimization by Sandro. We cannot take Claudia as the good we see her in terms of (though undoubtedly an aspect of her character exemplifies it) because she is the victim of its defeat. But the film does in fact suggest a human image of that good, even though the character must seem a little unreal in a world where it is inevitable that the good will be squelched in active people. A character who is not squelched must be a bit removed from action, distant from the human norm in the same way that Noto is distant from the contemporary architectural norm. Noto is set as an alternative in its contrast with the modern town Claudia and Sandro find so oppressive before they arrive at Noto. In a world this bad, the good must have the quality of wish-fulfillment rather than mimesis.

The human representative of the good is the old man who lives in the cottage where Sandro and Claudia and a few others spend the night waiting for Anna. He enters self-assuredly and, without even being asked, defines himself in his social relations, shows pictures of his family on the walls, and tells about them in relationship to himself. He contrasts in every respect with the rich people who, mobile but rootless, meet and relate only for business purposes—it characterizes their values that one of them can tell his host that his home would make a good mental clinic. During the search of Lipari, we come back several times to views of this old man watching these ephemeral, alien creatures with amazed interest. And we remember another scene in which rich people invade a poor man's shack. In Red Desert Max has sold the fishing shack to the worker from his plant, and it is Iole (the name both of Max's boat and the worker's womanfriend) who puts the industrialists in their place. The rich people snicker about sexual aids, and Iole remarks that some people like to talk about certain things, but others like to do them. In fact, the rich wind up destroying the shack, since they cannot work out a way to have the orgy they fantasized. As destruction substitutes for sex in that scene, so sex substitutes for architecture in L'Avventura—but for the old man on his island, there are no substitutes for the directness of a life in tune.

Claudia is like that old fisherman, in her directness of feeling and her sense that it is right to cling to and honor the claims of the past. She wishes to let them go only under the great stress of significant new feeling, of allegiance. Thus when Sandro returns to her from the encounter with the student and Claudia says to him, disengaging herself from his attack, "I want just what you want, Sandro, but . . . ," both the claim and the reservation are accurate. She accepts her human nature and its needs, which impel her to seize the ongoing moment for the joy it can bring, but which also entice her to believe in Sandro's fidelity to her when he was able to forget so promptly her predecessor, Anna.

Claudia is pathetically blinded by her wishes and by the act that Sandro puts on. With great delicacy of feeling, she refuses to go with Sandro into the Trinacria Hotel at Noto where they have heard that Anna may have gone. She feels that it should not seem to Anna, if she is there, that Claudia has caught Sandro and is now insisting that he catch up with Anna only to break it off with her. Claudia is sure that it is she, herself, whom Sandro really loves, that true feeling has come upon them both in these odd circumstances, and that the morality of its cultivation must be tended with care. But we suspect that Sandro might equally likely stay with Anna if she were there or go again with Claudia if she pulled hard enough. Claudia indeed wants what Sandro wants, a meaningful life that she images in terms of affection and sex and fun. But her wish comes from the depths of a completely different character, one that can be troubled by conflicting commitments and scruples and delicacies of feeling for another.

Thus it is, in one sense, weakness in Claudia to be attracted to Sandro--she puts her hand on his when he kisses her even in the boat, though she is horrified at her involvement in the seemingly inexorable relation that is coming upon her. But in another sense, she is completely forgiveable. Sandro is saying to her, "This is the real thing at last!" How can we blame her for believing him? If it is the real thing, then she responds rightly to it, going out of herself into a joy that is quite genuine. Antonioni does not blame a woman's desire or pleasure, but makes it clearly natural and right. We would not have Claudia be other than she is in her ready sexuality, her willingness to fall for Sandro.

And it would be childish moralism that would blame Claudia for any supposed infidelity to her friend Anna. She could observe, and had been specifically told, how unsatisfactory the relation between Anna and Sandro had been. She had no reason to doubt the honesty of Sandro's sudden attraction to her. And she might reasonably think that it must be a strong attraction indeed, one that might develop into a lasting relationship, or else surely Sandro would not approach her so quickly after Anna's disappearance--except that she is wrong, and Sandro is simply unfaithful both to Anna and to his own life.

Far from being blameworthy for her belief in the strong attachment that she develops for Sandro, Claudia's responsiveness, openness, joy, and flirtatiousness in the hotel room at Noto show what human relations and feelings should be like. Her happiness stands out from the coldness of the others in the film, from the attitudes of Patrizia and Sandro and Ettore and Giulia and the rest, as waking life stands out from a nightmare. It is in this sense that we can say that Claudia embodies the good. The film's world, the representation that emerges from its audio-visual surface, is suffused with a human quality of vibrant joy during Claudia's playful dance for Sandro, which takes its place in the network of the film's qualities--its shadings of attitudes and

expectations, its dynamics of feeling--as simply the point of
maximum value from which every other quality is a falling away.
And Claudia's rendered experience is so important a condition
of the emergence of that quality that, by a kind of shorthand,
we can say that she embodies it, almost that her vibrancy is the
film's good.

And when the nightmare returns, when Sandro suddenly shows
his preoccupation and does not respond to Claudia's joyous
clowning, but simply sits looking at his own inner demons, the
moment is truly horrible.  As Claudia puts on her display of what
it is like to be happy, he plays along for a while, especially
while she is looking at him.  But as she continues, full of
certainty that he is thinking of her as she is of him, he drops
his head and loses himself in his general sense of failure.  She
finishes her routine, saying with a flourish, "And tell me that
you love me," looks down at the audience she was so sure was
enthralled, and sees that he is somewhere else in his mind.  He
looks up blankly, her face falls, and we realize that she suddenly
understands that she is not there for him at all, that she is
only an object by which he can try to forget his failures, just
as Anna was.  The bottom falls out of the world, for her and for
us.  And the worst of it is that he means her no real harm, that
for him there is nothing happening but an adventure and so no
reason to relate to her at all.  We have seen Claudia make herself
vulnerable to a man who is as far from her in quality of mind
and feeling as Anna's father had been as he thought about her
Bible.  Claudia has joined the beckoning situation with the most
proper reluctance and moral reticence, and it suddenly turns and
rends her.  One does not need to make up sharks--as, indeed, Anna
had said.

The betrayal with Gloria Perkins at the end, when Claudia
is sleepy and Sandro's glands suggest dalliance, is well prepared
for, and Claudia's shock is only the last in the series we have
observed.  We must not think that when Claudia accepts Sandro's
unspoken apology she recognizes that she is as much to blame for
her betrayal of Anna as he for his betrayal of her:  Claudia
believed that she had been overwhelmed by a reciprocal emotion
for Sandro, and surely Sandro owes her more than he owes Gloria
Perkins, for whom no one believes he feels anything whatever.
Claudia should not see herself even parodied in Gloria Perkins.
Similarly, we should not think that Sandro, too, has some
understanding at the end, a momentary commitment through the
appreciation of Claudia, after all.  Sandro's tears are as facile
and changeable as his love, and as he treats Gloria Perkins when
he sees Claudia looking at him, so he would have treated Claudia
had Anna appeared over her shoulder.  He is capable of being
caught up in a momentary realization of how incapable he is of
making a commitment that can govern his behavior.  But Claudia's
shock of recognition is that she is more capable of fidelity than
he.

There has been a gathering web of pressures on Claudia to

commit herself to the developing feeling of her relation to Sandro, followed by the sudden realization that the commitment is to someone who is unworthy of it. The gathering web is expressed also as a figure of style: the principal visual sequence on the island is the accretion of people around the mystery of Anna, the empty sea and the islands gradually becoming filled with a gaggle of helicopters, boats, and functionaries. It is in clearest opposition, by the modernity of such things as hydrofoils, to the ancient security of the island and its old man. The gaggle collects as if out of nowhere for the kill. Similarly a horde of men collects in Palermo around Gloria Perkins, men like those who collect around, strut before, and intimidate Claudia as she waits for Sandro before the Trinacria Hotel. Gloria Perkins had intended to collect the men around her, with the ridiculous display of her split seam, whereas Claudia, who could here as elsewhere wrongly be seen as like her, is not calculating, but is delicately waiting for Sandro to work things out with Anna. But the collection of men around her, like the gaggle on the island that leads to the shock of Anna's father with Anna's Bible, leads to another shock, again of the sort we began by arguing as representative of the film. This time, it is the shock of Claudia's seeing what a trick of perspective makes her (and us) think is Anna, accompanying Sandro out of the hotel. At that Claudia turns and flees to the paint store around the corner, as she fled Anna's father and as she will flee Sandro himself when confronted with the unimpeachable truth of his identity with those strutting men who also lusted for Gloria Perkins. As always, Claudia's delicacy, openness, and appropriateness of feeling, the manifest good of the film, come against and are dashed by the exemplars of the hindrance, as in moments when she is left gasping at the difference between her quality of involvement with life and that of those in whom she had thought to put her trust.

These moments are so devastating and so strong that there is a simplified, almost allegorical quality to this first film of the trilogy, as if at first glance outlines were sharper, oppositions more marked, qualifications less obvious, than the later films, having had more time to make allowances and distinctions, will allow them to be. A progression in the trilogy will thus be toward a proper reduction of the oversimplification, a view less uncritical of the woman, more sympathetic to the man. L'Avventura is a first approximation, like a musical statement of theme, that, though by no means disavowed by what follows, is more important for the variations to be worked on it than for itself. Though we have seen that Claudia is so embedded in the film's world that she must be said to suggest if not to embody its good--its set of connotations that add up to a positively valued conception of reality--still the story is virtually that of personality or selfhood itself, surrounded by beings of another order entirely, like the Vices which press upon the Soul in a Mystery Play. This selfhood is made to become sickeningly, heart-rendingly aware of the tremendous gulf between what seems the

most normally human directness of feeling and the tangle of lies,
self-indulgences, repressions, proprieties, substitutions, and
defenses by which the beings of the other order seem most of the
time to live.
      There is anguish for the central character, and even a
certain pity for the lost ones like Sandro around her.  The
anguish and pity play against each other, defining the gulf,
establishing the terms in which personality must operate and
suffer, and keeping our attention focused, by the very static
quality of the opposition, on the importance but great difficulty
of achieving a satisfactory sense of relation with an unresponsive
world.

La Notte
      In La Notte, as in L'Avventura, there is a strong sense
of longing for a fulfillment that seems to be unavailable.  The
characters tend to withdraw protectively into numbness, or to
seek what even they at least partly understand to be inadequate
substitutes for what eludes them.  But there is a difference.
In L'Avventura, Claudia's availability for feeling, virtually
an image for the good in the film, comes to grief against Sandro's
quite different attributes of character, virtually an image for
the film's hindrance.  Clearly Lidia, in La Notte, has had the
same capacity for feeling as Claudia--indeed younger Valentina
has it still--and Lidia's capacity presses against her husband
Giovanni's inadequacies in the same way as Claudia's against her
lover Sandro's.  Still, there are no surprises for Lidia, who
is nonetheless in the same central position in the film's
perspectival structure as Claudia in L'Avventura.  Lidia is
herself divided and cold as Claudia never is.  She rejects
Giovanni's needs as ruthlessly as he does hers and far more
consciously, more embitteredly, than even Sandro, Claudia's.
The strand of L'Avventura that Lidia plays out is not so much
Claudia's squelching by Sandro as what was the less stressed
element of the earlier film, Giulia's mutually self-destructive
symbiosis with Corrado.
      Valentina, too, exudes, along with the Monica Vitti vitality
("Monica, c'est la joie de vivre," as Antonioni once said),
a dark despair.  Once she lost everything, she says, but will
not tell us when.  She feels ironies alien to Claudia, pretending
to be only a playgirl when she is not.  She is already defensive
and wounded, whereas Claudia becomes that way.  And Giovanni,
too, as divided as the other two, is not a failed artist suffused
with the sense of his betrayal of his art, but a successful and
highly intellectual writer overcome with the way in which his
art has failed him.  With it he feels out of touch.  He has no
life but his work, and that seems empty of value.  He looks for
a way to convince himself that he can stand to sell out--and
cannot find one.
      Thus, though like L'Avventura it sets thwarted humane
impulses against a depersonalizing modernism, La Notte does
not so much attach those opposed values to different characters,

one value for each, as it presents all of its characters as at
the same time victims and antagonists of the world they
constitute.  In all of the characters, each in his or her own
way, we see the issue of the pressure towards expression of
feeling as it opposes the tendency towards being closed down by
bitter experience and the exigencies of social life.  The problem
is made equally clear for each character, and is set up for us
at the very beginning.  Tommaso, the dying friend of Lidia and
Giovanni, shows both in his character and his plight why one
cannot, as L'Avventura might be taken to imply one could, trust
for salvation to being committed, idealistic, responsive, and
good.

Various glances between Lidia and Giovanni as Tommaso talks
to them show that the Pontanos feel reproached by the depth of
Tommaso's feeling for them, but also that they recognize the ways
his affection has blinded him to the reality of their
relationship.  Thinking that his disease gives him a lucid
detachment, he reflects on how his presence spoiled many evenings
in their contented home--that every signal tells us can never
have been more contented than is the relationship we now see.
He tells his mother proudly how the Pontanos are his only
friends:  yet Giovanni admits to Lidia that he never cared much
for Tommaso, and Lidia was annoyed, we later learn, by Tommaso's
emotional pressures on her.  Here at the hospital she refuses
to sit down, to smoke (it would confirm that she was relaxed and
informal), or to respond to Tommaso's quiet appeals.  Yet her
careful refraintment from catering to the dying man seems somehow
more respectful than Giovanni's observing him even as he
apparently warmly chats and shares literary talk.

Giovanni's slightly troubled concern seems almost like the
placations of the hospital, against which the agonies of Tommaso's
helpless pain stand out like something improper.  Tommaso remarks
that the hospital is too much like a nightclub, upon which a nurse
brings in a bottle of champagne (Fig. 9.1).  The drinking
together, the leaving of this wasted life by a good person whose
very goodness has made him pathetic and a bit ridiculous, is too
painful for Lidia to stand.  She refuses to take a glass.  But
Giovanni and Tommaso's mother do, and, as Antonioni cuts to a
high shot of the frozen tableau, Lidia is overcome by the ironies
of this social scene so out of touch with the emotional realities,
and leaves abruptly.  And Giovanni observes the helpless hunger
of Tommaso's farewell to her as he had observed the pathetic
attempt Tommaso made to make contact with the nurse who had
brought the champagne.  Tommaso's love for Lidia is so obvious
we hardly need to be told about it at the end of the film.  We
need hardly be told at the end, either, that Giovanni found
Tommaso's vulnerability so great that he took no pleasure in the
compliment of Lidia's preferring him to Tommaso.  On every score
he is full of pity for the dying man, whose plight is a metaphor
of the consequences of a lack of the toughness the world seems
to demand.

One can understand, then, how Giovanni, shaking his head

sadly as he leaves the futility of Tommaso's room, should respond
to the lust of the apparently nymphomaniac young woman who reaches
out for him in longing and gratitude and delight.  Her hunger
for fulfillment is at least that rebelliousness, that assertion
of self, that Tommaso has always failed to exhibit.  The brutality
of the attendants who come in and slap the woman into submission
again is the other aspect of the nightclublike hospital that
brings you champagne when you behave (Fig. 9.2).  We may feel
that Giovanni, in responding to the young woman, takes advantage
of a driven creature's illness.  But Lidia, nonetheless, too
coldly rejects him as disgusting her when he, much upset by the
incident, tells her about it.  It simply does not adequately
characterize Giovanni, as Lidia seems to think, to say that he
responds to a sexual or literary opportunity.  He has been
troubled by the pathos of Tommaso's absurdly yearning
selflessness, and troubled also by the impersonality of the young
woman's desire for him, its quality as itself a symptom of
disease, yet also as a justifiable attempt to overcome the
conditions of repressive life.  The pair of cases symbolize his
own dilemma:  be like Tommaso, a patsy of the world, or like the
young woman, perhaps more assertive but thereby depersonalized
and even more vulnerable.

Giovanni's sophisticated awareness of the bind between
absurdities of selflessness and selfishness has led him, as we
can infer from what others say of his writing, to expression of
that awareness, and also, as we can observe ourselves, to
emotional detachment from any other aspect of his life.  His work
consumes his life, yet despite the success promised his latest
book at the publisher's party, the fulsome vacuity of his admirers
there and at the Gerardinis' party seems insufficient reward for
that form of involvement.  When he returns to his apartment,
Giovanni can find no interest in work, in reading, in his mail.
He falls asleep on the couch.  And when he startles awake sometime
later, he can only look for Lidia--who obviously matters to him
in a way which does neither of them any good--and stand on his
balcony in the depersonalizing cityscape to await her call.  A
neighbor voices trivia about a spoiled weekend, and we see her
turn back to feed birds in a cage that, in the same position in
the left foreground, is echoed later at the Gerardinis'.  There
Giovanni is offered a job by the industrialist, and we cut at
once to a shot of a birdcage on the lawn.  The forms of dependence
are obviously the same.  Giovanni looks for an escape, but
Gerardini's offer is no real alternative.  It amounts, even as
a substitutive alternative that denies responsiveness, to exactly
the kind of numbness and capture that a writer's life of awareness
and its expression also yields.  We may be tempted to think
Giovanni another Sandro, selling his artistic birthright for a
mess of pottage.  But the way both commitment to art and the
temptation to cynical self-aggrandizement lead to futility forces
us to see a difference.  Sandro is the world's problem, but
Giovanni its victim.

Lidia's leaving the publishers' party in disgust at its
artificiality and at seeing Giovanni's picture on the book jackets
all around her, and walking through Milan, is her form of search
for the vitality that life with Giovanni so obviously lacks.
And just as he is torn between his artist's awareness with its
consequent misery and the desire to join what that awareness tells
him is the horrible wave of the future, so Lidia is divided
between a desire for the kind of life with Giovanni as an artist,
of which the letter she reads at the end shows the lost richness,
and a desire to join more apparently vital forms of social life
from which, however, she both shrinks and is debarred, much like
her husband.

There is intensity of feeling all around Lidia on her walk,
but also a strong sense of there being no place for her—if she
can share in that intensity at all, it is only as victim. She
is pleased by the autonomy of a man eating a sandwich and of men
who walk laughing by her, but they give her only perfunctory and
sexually appraising glances. A man reading in a window and the
cabby who waits for her are as neutral, but somehow as ominous,
as the man who sells grey fruit in Red Desert (Fig. 9.6). The
working class adolescents by whose fight she is attracted and
then appalled perceive her as an object with the same aggressive
masculinity as seems to have inspired the fight. There is, in
fact, a pervasive sexuality to the imagery throughout her
adventure. The amateur rocketeers are concerned with thrust,
and their rockets are prefigured in the concrete phallic posts
through which Lidia weaves her way. In an image that prefigures
the enveloping of Ugo and Corrado by steam as they stand
tranquilly in the factory yard in Red Desert, the rocketeers
are enveloped in the smoke of the rocket. We see the image of
envelopment of this sort again in Eclipse in the cloud that
chills Vittoria, and preeminently in Red Desert, in the fog
that terrifies Giuliana as she sees her friends concealed by it,
and in the yellow smoke through which birds, she tells Valerio,
learn not to fly. The image connotes a condition of being at
one with an essentially hostile force in the modern world that
is frighteningly different from what the principal character can
achieve. The overwhelming force that attracts but alienates has
a kind of fascination that is evidenced in the treatment of the
rockets in a series of progressive close-ups. We see this
treatment again, forceful but frightening, in the ending sequence
of Eclipse.

Women, too, are involved in the sexual imagery: a foodseller
offers Lidia a hotel room for the assignation she postulates Lidia
is making; as Lidia pays the cabby, a woman in the background,
talking to a friend, molds her figure with her hands as she
apparently describes a provocative costume. With all this
evidence of the attractions of sexuality and of its ominous
quality when unconnected with real emotional life, Lidia calls
Giovanni to come and see the rockets where they visited as lovers
in better days. But the rocketeers are finished by the time

Giovanni arrives. Lidia's situation may be intolerable, but there is no world of vitality outside the situation waiting for her to come and join it. As for Giovanni in the hospital, for Lidia, too, there is a bind: be the passive victim of your husband's images, or like the young woman be the more active victim of the world's insistence on its own established patterns. You get champagne if you are obedient, but you get slapped into submission if you rebel.

Though we observe in the film a crisis in which Lidia decides she no longer loves Giovanni, it is clear that she wishes she could. It is not as a last resort that she returns to Giovanni, but because their relationship should fulfill her, and it is largely his doing that it does not. After the walk through Milan, Lidia offers herself to Giovanni and is hurt that he, having taken refuge in an utterly private, polite unavailability, ignores her naked in her bath. She models her new dress proudly for him and responds with revealing quickness to what she hopes will be more than a perfunctory peck on her shoulder as he hooks her dress. At the nightclub they visit (their first outing in years, and she has had to beg for it), Giovanni would rather absorb himself in the fantasies of the adept but pointless strip-teasing dance than attend to Lidia. She makes a genuine effort to reach him, and it is as painful as Sandro's failure of Claudia at Noto (which, in the film's organization, it closely parallels) that Giovanni should refuse to be reached.

The dance involves the dancer's drinking a glass of wine from a contorted posture. Lidia notices the glass in her own hand as she watches, and puts down the glass in distaste as she apparently reflects on her own place in Giovanni's fantasies. She is impelled to try to make a better form of contact with him. She "dances" her fingers over to the jewel in her purse (one thinks of the jewel lost from Valentina's compact later) and then appeals to Giovanni with a reminiscence of the jeweled cufflinks he is wearing. He rejects the appeal nastily (he wants to watch the act, he says), but she persists, giving a dazzling display of the attractions of her character as she mimes a thought rising to the top of her head. Giovanni utterly rejects her—he shakes his head: "These silly women"—and returns to the act. Lidia then won't tell him what her thought is. (Later we learn it is that she no longer loves him.) She suggests they go to the Gerardini party that she had hoped to avoid by going to the nightclub. She simply gives up hope for Giovanni, at least for the moment. She has good reason, for his rejection of her appeals is evidence of a far more deadened sensibility than her rejection of his appeals when he tried to share with her his trouble over the young woman in the hospital. And his turning away from contact to attend to the dance is for the purpose of avoiding emotional relations with his wife, whereas her turning away from the publishers' party is for the purpose of enriching emotional relations with her husband.

Though Lidia has been rebuffed in her attempt to relate to

Giovanni in anything like the ways suggested to her by the
vitality she has observed, she twice tries to reach Giovanni at
the Gerardinis' party. It is clear that everything conspires
to drive the couple apart. An option of fashionable infidelity
is presented to Lidia in Roberto, who (probably incited by Lidia's
childhood "friend" Berenice) keeps crossing her path and looking
meaningly at her. Lidia flees Berenice's first introduction to
Roberto. A few minutes later, beside the swimming pool with
Giovanni, Lidia turns to flee the approaching Gerardinis and goes
over towards the silly asses splashing in the pool. But the
option of that sort of childish pleasure is not possible to her.
Roberto moves between her and the more innocent players, exactly
as he will later prevent her jumping into the pool with them and
lead her off in the hope of seducing her (Fig. 9.8). But Lidia,
not ready to equate playfulness with infidelity, goes quickly
and sits with her husband and her hosts.

But that artistic sensibility for which Lidia married
Giovanni, and that she still treasures over the mores of the
fashionable life to which she was born, Giovanni is intent on
casting off. Gerardini talks nonsense about the artist's
compulsive vocation, and when Lidia urges the accuracy of the
description of Giovanni as truly dedicated, Giovanni stops her
with that barely suppressed savagery with which husbands tell
their wives they are saying the wrong thing. He is intent now
on denigrating art and flattering Gerardini. I'm not so
important, he says, you industrialists are the genuine artists--
and he says it with a vitality we see in him nowhere else in the
film, a veritable eagerness for damnation. It hurts Lidia's
feelings, of course, and she soon leaves with the similarly
repulsed Mrs. Gerardini to wander the party some more. In fact,
she passes Roberto giving her more meaning looks as she politely
leaves Mrs. Gerardini greeting a new guest.

Lidia goes upstairs, and during the crowd game with
Valentina's compact (Giovanni has left Gerardini, gone to the
house, and found Valentina), she sees Roberto again, looking up
at her, and then (in obvious response, a turning away from this
beckoning alternative), she calls the hospital and learns that
Tommaso has died a few minutes earlier. Looking down into the
atrium again, she sees Giovanni and Valentina kiss (Fig. 9.11).
The similarity of angle to her earlier view of Roberto implies
that this infidelity might make a reason for her own. She wanders
miserably onto the balcony.

Lidia is ready to share the grief over Tommaso with her
husband, to whom Tommaso is supposed to have meant as much as
he did to her. But Giovanni is up to something else, and Lidia's
appeal, as when sitting with the Gerardinis, falls on deaf ears.
The dynamics by which Lidia is led to Roberto's car are
brilliantly sketched. Giovanni comes upstairs from that kiss
with Valentina, and learns as Gerardini takes him away for the
job offer that she is the industrialist's daughter. Valentina
walks off with her mother and, looking up at Lidia on the balcony,

learns by her mother's addressing Lidia as "Mrs. Pontano" that
Giovanni is married.  The camera stays with Lidia, however, after
Valentina's disturbed reaction.  Lidia sits miserably at a table
on the balcony, her jeweled purse prominent in the shot, while
Giovanni, having left Gerardini, walks out to her.  He says
something about the beauty of the estate (he is trying out the
thought, half for her and half for himself, of accepting
Gerardini's offer to "live as we live"), and she responds
politely.  But she thinks of Tommaso and her face falls while
she turns her head.  Giovanni--probably thinking that this
neurotic woman is about to recall him to some emotional obligation
he is not interested in meeting right now--moves to the balcony
wall.  He sees Valentina, who sees him and runs out of sight.
Lidia brings herself together to appeal to him, and rises to tell
him about Tommaso, to turn these developments from their disaster
course, to reassert the continuity in their lives among these
crossed purposes and failing intents.  But he is moving towards
the door to follow Valentina (we see only his shadow, symbolically
enough), and simply excuses himself from attending to Lidia in
another painful rebuff.  From that point Lidia's return to the
dance floor below and her being finally taken away by Roberto
are as if inevitable.

Lidia is divided, then, between the intellectual's life that
is failing her and the hedonistic alternative that finally
disgusts her.  The world beckons, and she cannot respond.  It
is exactly like Giovanni's division:  he is miserable as the
intellectual he is, seeing the future in hands like the
Gerardinis'.  But he is as repulsed by the prospect of living
among the industrialists as Lidia is by the prospect of affairs
with men like Roberto.

The woman named Resy is the best of the Gerardinis' lot,
as it appears to Giovanni, yet her ridiculous notions of
intellectuals simply annoy Giovanni.  Resy wants sentiment, and
cannot imagine any truth to the story he tells her of a hermit
who becomes an alcoholic.  Gerardini, who thinks his industries
are works of art, has a huge mural of a machine in his study to
prove he is right.  Guido, the lecherous guest Mrs. Gerardini
greeted as Lidia left her and passed Roberto, tells without self-
irony about how Hemingway had said he would shoot him on sight
if Guido ever tried to pay him a visit.  It proves Hemingway's
forcefulness, Guido thinks, and the writer is admirable because
he has made money, no matter what he may say.  Giovanni mutters,
in response to Guido's remark that money is easy to put up with,
that it is not easy to say what an intellectual can put up with,
and he seems thoroughly and finally to reject this social world
when Roberto (no doubt smarting from having been rejected by
Lidia) tells him that democracy means taking things as they are.
It reminds us of Sandro's "then it's out of our hands," and
Giovanni is clearly refusing to become like Sandro.  He rejects
what he recognizes as the quotation (he told Lidia earlier that
at this point in his life he has a good memory but no

originality), saying that it was written in despair but that
Roberto quotes it in satisfaction. How indeed can Giovanni enter
this world? He would have to do it in despair. It is so
satisfied with itself that membership in it could only be a source
of constant anguish. It is as impossible for Giovanni to "live
as we live" as it is for Lidia to accept Roberto.

La Notte would be more like L'Avventura than it is,
however, if the world the Pontanos' emotional quality will not
let them enter were not itself divided. Just as both Giovanni
and Lidia are divided between a comprehension of the world that
detaches them from it and a longing to give up the misery of that
detachment and sink into the offered flow of affluent, self-
aggrandizing, soul-destroying modern life, so is Valentina. It
is the irony of Giovanni's turning to her that she is like Lidia.
Lidia came from this social class to Giovanni, the two women dress
alike, each shows flashes of the same sort of vital delight, and
we observe Valentina reading as, Lidia tells us, she herself used
to read. When Giovanni reproaches Valentina with having too
thoroughly aligned herself with the Gerardinis' world when she
twitted him during the compact game for being a bleeding-heart
intellectual, she responds in a charming contriteness (which he
by no means merits, using his intellectual's status, as he does,
to one-up her) by asking him to read with her. And, of course,
she does display a sensitivity in the tape recording she plays
for Giovanni that she cannot deny to herself by saying that it
is merely a talent for observation.

But Antonioni is rendering a bind in this film, between
observation of the modern world's development and the
powerlessness to affect it that tempts people, forgiveably, to
submit to what they cannot defeat. Giovanni tells Valentina that
his "crisis" is that he knows what to write but not how to write
it, i.e., from what perspective or with what intention to make
a statement to an envisionable audience about how to cope with
his perceptions. It is not at all clear, then, that there can,
in fact, plausibly be more than a talent for observation--unless
the writer's "compulsion" can amount to Tommaso's ability to blind
himself to the facts. And, indeed, the content of Valentina's
tape expounds the film's divisions as clearly as anything in it.

On the tape she reports on the sounds in nature, on hearing
the rustle of a tree and wishing to believe that it comes from
within the tree and is not imposed by the listener, and on how
other sounds intrude on the stillness such observation brings--to
which other sounds one must submit oneself like a floater to the
waves. The relationship between peace and intrusions has
characterized the sequence. Valentina was happy playing her game,
she says; now she is melancholy again. Obviously, the social
reality intruded on her like sounds on stillness. Giovanni is
married; any relation between them is contaminated by his games
and by her identity as her father's daughter. There can be no
"stillness" in this developing relation when so much of its
context makes one suspect ulteriority.

We know Valentina is right:  she stands to Giovanni for an
escape from the reality of his commitments, not for a new
fidelity.  And she has shrunk from his signals of personal
interest as if they were attacks, even before she learned how
similar to the fighting punks' interest in Lidia his approach
to her must be taken to be.  Twice when he played the compact
game she flinched from meaning remarks of his.  And she tells
him twice, too--when he comes to her room she tells him love is
a fraud, creating emptiness around us.  And when he, having heard
the tape, tells her they will see more of each other because he
has been offered the job, she replies, only seemingly not to the
point, that when she tries to communicate with someone, love
disappears.  Clearly "love" itself is like those "useless sounds"
on the tape, an anodyne, a way to sink into substitution for
understanding the real case.  Communication drives out love
because it makes us understand the substitute; the love itself
drives out communication and creates emptiness.

But of course the sounds, the love, do intrude.  Valentina's
defense is, like Giovanni's and Lidia's, to try to deaden herself,
accept the world (like a floater, the waves) the rejection of
which is so hard to sustain.  She pretends the playgirl:  when
Giovanni tells her his crisis she toughens up, rises and dabs
perfume and strikes a flapper's pose and asks why he should tell
little her these things when all she cares about are horses and
cars and parties.  Interested in nothing else? he asks.  And she
deflates:  "Everything," she answers, aware of how she must
truncate that interest to live at all.  And it is then that,
Angelo the servant bringing more candles and illumination
following, she plays Giovanni the tape showing the nature and
quality of that interest.

When the tape is over, Valentina rises again, plays with
a wire toy on her arm in intended protective coldness as she tells
Giovanni how love drives out communication.  When he rather
fulsomely replies, "I need you," to her ironic remark that he
needs a young girl to get him going again (clearly he resists
understanding, he actually wants "love" and not communication),
she mockingly retreats from him--she likes him, but what has he
offered her except what she knows is false?--yet takes his dare,
stupid as it is ("What are you afraid of?"), and stands her ground
for him to kiss her.  Half knowing better, Antonioni's heroines
(Claudia and Vittoria are like this, too) accept what the world
pressures them into with an innocence for which we cannot but
forgive them.  It is the world we blame, and it is for the doomed,
but vital, readiness to submit to it that we love the heroines.
One submits to the alien and intrusive sounds.  What else is there
to do?  But the lights come on again and Valentina takes it as
a proof:  "See how ridiculous this is?"  And as foolishly (though
less painfully) as when interrupted with the young woman in the
hospital, Giovanni can only follow Valentina as she goes back
to the party.

In a sense, then, Valentina saves Giovanni from truncating

himself by false attachment to her, just as Lidia saves herself from Roberto. And when Lidia returns and Valentina dries her and speaks with her, it is as if her refusal of Giovanni has earned her the friendship of both Pontanos. It pleases both Lidia and Valentina that they do not have to soul-search in any conventional way with each other. Lidia is pleased to hear Valentina announce that her vices are new (it amounts to her saying she is not a homewrecker) and her life miserable, though Lidia tells her she is too young to know the weight of useless years. A bond is made between them. It seems almost perverse to Valentina that this couple should feel for her exactly because she has resisted and refused them, and that they should suggest they be friends, that she visit them. But, after all, it is the identification of her quality that she has not fallen in with the wrong suggestions—there are few enough who can tell that "this is ridiculous," that communication is better achieved in silence than through intrusive and self-interested mutual revelation.

Giovanni steps forward and caresses her cheek. The complicity, the sense of having earned membership in a fellowship of despair, is by no means wholly appealing: Valentina steps aside from him. But Lidia comes forward in her turn and kisses her. No wonder Valentina says they have exhausted her between them, and that, after they leave, with a wonderfully resigned yet tensely active gesture of her foot sideways to a floor-level switch, she should turn the light out on herself, leaving herself a silhouette in the dark, latent, self-contained, dynamic, and resigned to her unfulfillment in the very awkwardness of her pose, submitting like a floater to the waves (Fig. 9.27).

There are mysteries to Valentina, and it may be that with that doused light she suggests a suicide that we can also infer from her portentous statement that she will return from vacation much later this year. Valentina cannot but recognize that her choices are those of the other two: to be a playgirl and repress that awareness that there is a life of trees and silence that represents the only value there is, or accept that knowledge and be as divided by it as are Lidia and Giovanni. It is a sad prospect, but in a strange but distinct way we are pleased at the communion that develops among these three. "Communication" has indeed driven out "love," and all three of these characters both sympathize with each other's natural attempts to achieve such satisfactions as it seems only natural to require of the world, and also respect each other's awarenesses of the uselessness of such attempts.

It seems finally, then, the nature of the modern world itself that brings these people down. The lucidity of awareness of the three characters is extraordinary, and there have been no delusions, no deep truncations of understanding among them as there are in the other films of the trilogy. If these three people are miserable, then sensitive intelligence and precise awareness of the value life's options present doesn't save us from misery. The Antonioni quality is strong here: we see the

pressure, the desire for joyous fulfillment by characters who
seem only to be able to try to reach it by reducing their goals,
accepting trivialized and reduced relationships because of the
robotlike inhumanity of the world around them.  And there is
strong evidence in the film's style itself for arguing both that
Antonioni renders a depersonalizing force in the world under which
all of the characters suffer, and that Valentina, left behind
in darkness, has less of a chance to prevail against the
tendencies in things than Lidia.  In L'Avventura characters
made their destinies by moral choice; here objects seem to
dominate, and both nature and the personality itself seem under
attack.

   As Lidia and Giovanni drive up to the hospital a large crane-
operated shovel falls in the street, making them swerve (Fig.
9.5).  In the hospital room a helicopter flies by low in the sky.
Lidia watches it entranced, and later watches jet planes that
we hear zoom low over her.  She objects of the jazz band at the
end that it is absurd that they should play as if the day would
dawn brighter for it.  There is, in that fashion, a pervasive
sense of the human replacing the natural with slick surfaces and
fantasy gratifications. Games replace feelings:  in the Gerardini
house we constantly see checkerboard floors, even a checkered
blanket next to the band at the end (Figs. 9.7, 9.8, 9.9).  Slick
architectural forms replace more comfortable ones.  The film's
first (and brief) shot is of an old building utterly unlike
anything we see later, replaced at once with a long track down
the Pirelli building that gives equal weight to reality and to
its reflection in a constantly changing, but ever the same,
architectural surface (Figs. 9.3, 9.4).

   The Bietti house of the Gerardinis is opulent, but its most
marked feature is its atrium downstairs in which, surrounded by
glass, grow some trees.  This is Valentina's favorite spot, as
if she tries for those trees but is withheld from them by the
conditions of her life as she is withheld from positive
relationships by those conditions too.  In the windows that
surround the trees we constantly, in the scenes between them,
see Valentina and Giovanni reflected--there is even a tendency
for the shots to emphasize the reflections' disappearing (Figs.
9.9, 9.10).  One gets the sense that the characters are already
parcelled out, like Milan in the Pirelli building, between their
reality and their reflections, and that they may be lost at any
minute, may disappear entirely.

   In Eclipse, as we shall see, an important imagistic
progression is indeed toward the disappearance of the characters.
But Eclipse is prefigured even more strongly in the way that
architecture is divided from trees by the glass walls of the
Gerardini house.  Valentina is no Gloria Perkins, but the fact
that Lidia is the right partner for Giovanni, the person to whom
his commitment belongs, is indicated in the fact that Lidia is
treated consistently in terms of trees and the availability of
exterior nature, as Valentina is treated in terms of reflections
and the interior of her house.  Despite a few reflections of Lidia

(Fig. 9.6), and despite Valentina's attaching life's most positive values to trees' self-generating rustle--and after all, the basic opposition of this film is between the oppressive world and the divided characters, not among the characters themselves--Lidia is directly and insistently associated with the trees from which, contrariwise, the walls of Valentina's house insistently separate her.

It is in this sense Lidia who moves toward the good that in this film is never imaged directly, that is squelched by the hindrances of modernism, and that, squelched, is present only in our strong sense of its absence. We can see both that the film reflects the structure of L'Avventura, with Lidia heroine like Claudia, and that it implies, by lowering of the structured terms, a darkened theme:  Lidia merely reaches toward the good that, at certain moments at least, Claudia bears in herself. Sandro is Claudia's hindrance, but the truncated modernism for which he stands squelches both Lidia and Giovanni--and for that matter, unlike Gloria Perkins, Valentina, too.

At the close of her walk through Milan, Lidia walks into the yard of a church.  Giovanni finds her there standing next to a vine-covered tree (Fig. 9.15).  Lidia is greatly interested in his response to the place.  He is surprised at his own nostalgia for it.  They used to come here, they say, and it touches Giovanni that the context of their earlier relationship has remained unchanged when the relationship has changed so much. He holds Lidia's shoulder in friendly intimacy as he calls her forward from the tree and reflects on the scene--it is the only time he touches her other than perfunctorily until the end of the film.  Although Lidia remarks that the area will change, and although Giovanni himself notices that the railroad tracks that were in use when they were there are overgrown, still the clear effect is of the appearance of a kind of value in the surface of the film that is the object of its longing throughout.  And this effect is intimately associated with trees, and moreover with Lidia's dealing with someone from beside a tree.  These associations will add great force to the end of the film.

That things have changed and that qualities are lost of youthful bravado; the sense that nothing ends; the feeling of overriding love in which past, present, and future are reflected: these are all concepts from Lidia's last exposition to Giovanni when she reads him his early letter to her.  Taken together, they are the components, the surface manifestations, of the complex attitude that is the film's principal hindrance, and they are constantly emphasized, varied, combined and recombined.  Lidia tells Valentina that she doesn't know how heavy the burden of useless years is; on the walk in Milan, in a ruin where a baby cries and Lidia, who prizes any human feeling, getting so little sense of it from her world, comforts it smilingly, she stops by the door and we see a close-up of a broken clock and then of Lidia's hand peeling some rotted paint from a ruined wall.  Those railroad tracks seem much to the point, then, when Lidia and

Roberto, enclosed in his car in the rain and driving slowly along through dark and light--it is a wonderful image of interest and security, and relates richly to the lights and candles of the Gerardinis' house and even to the nymphomaniac young woman's blowing out of Giovanni's match at the beginning--come to the flashing light of the railroad signal and stop the car and get out. A train comes by and Roberto, making his move toward seduction, starts to kiss Lidia. She is again at that point standing by a tree, and the rain, the enclosed car, the train, the tree, the flashing light, add up to the setting for exactly that romance of the lack of which Giovanni's remark about the disused track takes notice. But the time has gone, and Roberto, a substitutive sexual opportunity, is not Giovanni. For Lidia, as she says succinctly, it is "not possible," and she has Roberto return her to the party.

As the party ends, Valentina has in a sense been brought into the world of Lidia and Giovanni, as we saw. But in another sense, they retreat from her world as Lidia retreated from Roberto. They leave her in her darkened room to walk across the park and golf course to the place where trees assume their final significance. As they walk along, Lidia hurts Giovanni's feelings by suggesting that he take the position with Gerardini that he has been offered. His duties would be to join the firm, write a history of it that will, the industrialist believes, unite labor and management by teaching the workers its history and that of Gerardini, its founder, and in return "live as we live." Lidia feels rightly that it would simplify Giovanni's life to take such a job, and Giovanni stops, hurt by her acceptance that he might do it, while she walks on ahead. But he has not earned the right to be hurt at a low opinion of himself that he has done everything to encourage. He walks on after a second's pause, and we see the couple move forward as a pair to a position beside a pair of trees (Fig. 9.16).

There is then a cut to an extraordinary shot, a moderate high angle on the pair of trees and the couple, in which the shapes of the trees match the outlines of the people as they stand, awkwardly and stiffly but as if giving more attention to their words than to the stylishness of their demeanor, and speak of Tommaso, who Giovanni only now learns has died while he was "playing" (as Lidia puts it) with Valentina (Fig. 9.17). At first it is hard to tell exactly how the trees and the people are associated, although that the outlines of trees and people resemble each other is clear (there is some shifting of position that keeps the similarity-pairings fluid). But as Lidia explains her mixed feelings for Tommaso's efforts at her self-improvement she steps forward, isolating herself in a frame apart from Giovanni, to whom we cut for his reactions. Now it is clearer: in the frame with Lidia is the straight tree trunk (Fig. 9.18); in the frame with Giovanni is the crooked one (Fig. 9.19). As the emotional underpinnings of the action become explicit here at the end, the characters are distinguished even as their unity as a couple is emphasized: they are associated with trees, but differently.

As Lidia finishes speaking of Tommaso (of how he loved her and of how she would have accepted him while he tried only to improve the mind merely numbed by the reading that was supposed to amend the mindless life to which she had been born), she steps forward to another tree, a birch with leaves and branches hanging down beside its trunk. She drapes the leaves around herself to face Giovanni and to tell him, with all the force of the image that should have fitted her and that he should have understood and treasured, that she no longer loves him and therefore wishes she were dead (Fig. 9.20). It is a powerful moment, to which the whole film has led--one sees what Lidia should have been, once was, and what Giovanni and she herself have lost.

The awkward stances of the couple by bare trunks, the graceful stance of Lidia by the leafy one--these do not end this ending sequence. Both people sit down by a sand trap, looking over the golf course at the dawn. Giovanni articulates his correct understanding that he has taken from Lidia and given nothing, although she, of course, has asked too little. As he suggests they cling to what they have and says he loves her still, she takes from her purse a folded paper and reads him a passage from, it seems, a love letter. It shows him how little relation his "loving her still," as he says he does, bears to love as it is possible to feel it. The lover sees his mistress asleep, and thinks of her meaning to him. As she reads, Antonioni cuts between the couple, and we see Lidia's face, expressive in its yearning emotion (Fig. 9.21), and Giovanni's, as he is reproached by the strength of feeling in the letter but at the same time repulsed by it too, finding it a bit fulsome, a bit jejune (Fig. 9.22). But as Lidia reads, those instructive medium close-ups are interspersed with other shots. She reads how the lover thinks of the life in her throat, and we are shown a closer shot of her torso, her throat and shoulders, and we feel the vibrancy the letter praises (Fig. 9.23). She reads on, of the intensity of his feeling, and we are shown a close-up of her hands and knees as she reads the letter (Fig. 9.24). The increasing closeness of the special shots between the normal ones brings us into her experience and renders that personal intimacy that the film has so horrifyingly lacked.

We have been held away from loved bodies, from awareness of the person. We come to know Lidia here at the end, to feel with her the kind of involvement in life that the film's presentational norms have squelched as they have tended toward awkwardness, to the posed middle distance, even to reflection and to disappearance of the image. Lidia finishes her reading and the camera dips further yet and tilts up to her face under the sky and leaves and branches of the birch tree (Fig. 9.25). And we realize, as we see this human face in its natural context, the depth of rage this film bears against the concerns for financial advancement, for the easy life, for decorum, in a

society that encourages even in its best minds misery as the
dominant quality of their reflections on it.  It was towards those
trees the film worked all along, and against them that its whole
world presses.
   The walking, standing, now sitting couple has yet further
to go.  As Giovanni to his amazement hears that he wrote the
passage himself--and hence realizes how far from its quality of
feeling his life as a writer has brought him--he reaches for Lidia
with much of the anguish (and none of the grateful incredulous
surmise) of the young woman in the hospital.  He pulls Lidia down
with him to the sand pit; she protests she does not love him,
but she means that she is defending against the knowledge that
he does not love her.  Yet he has learned from the letter the
value of the assertion of love that seemed so easy before Lidia
read it.  He will not now say he loves her, but only tells her
to be silent when she asks him to say it.  Yet not saying it is
far more expressive than saying it had been.  Lidia resists for
a while, then kisses him and seems to tolerate the embraces,
perhaps to accept them.  We are seeing a dropping back in order
to advance, a return to attempting contact instead of taking it
for granted; we are seeing the creation of love from the materials
of anguish, the act that is always in Antonioni necessary, and
seldom achieved in his films.
   As the couple shifts into this new phase of their encounter,
Antonioni cuts the camera back decorously once and then (as
Giovanni seems to grope for Lidia in preparation for an act of
love) further still--and this second cut sets the couple under
a pair of trees that from this angle almost overlap and that are
leafy and full (Fig. 9.26).  The camera tracks left, first
covering the couple with the trees and then finally leaving both
couple and trees in order to pan to the long shot of a low hedge
with the golf course beyond that closes the film.  But the
implication is clear.  Giovanni may be crooked and Lidia
straight.  Neither may love the other in any richly rewarding
way at this exact instant in their relationship.  But to be in
nature, working at what they can only hope they can forge into
love, is better than to be in the modern house that encloses trees
within itself, and in the context of which human reflections tend
to disappear.
   The unifying of the couple under the trees, first awkwardly
and then more intimately, counters the sequence that poor
Valentina has suffered.  When Giovanni first saw her, we saw both
of them reflected in different planes of the glass walls of the
atrium (Fig. 9.9).  And when the camera moved to bring Giovanni
into the room in direct unreflected image, it picked up Valentina
separated from him by the V formed by the bases of two of the
trees (Fig. 9.12).  Then when, after the party game, Giovanni
reproaches Valentina with flightiness and, indicating to her that
he understands how she might hunger for affection, kisses her,
Lidia from the balcony above sees the kiss next to the two trees
(Fig. 9.11) under their forms, as at the end she and Giovanni

are (Fig. 9.26). But as Lidia watches, and Valentina kisses
Giovanni as he kissed her, they move left towards the stairs—and
instead of being together, they stop and stand separated by beams
of the house, visually decapitated by one beam and separated by
others (Fig. 9.13). And we can see that these acts and attempts
at communion are doomed.

Similarly, when Giovanni finds Valentina in the atrium during
the storm—they meet here for the first time since learning each
other's family relations—she passes behind pillars to tell him
to pay his "debt," incurred under the rules of the compact game,
by going back to his wife. He fatuously says Lidia sent him to
her, and that it is too dark to find Lidia. As Valentina responds
to this portentous imagery with the sad understanding it deserves,
she walks with Giovanni back to the glass walls of the atrium,
there to tell him that she was happy playing the game with him
but that now, with the usual philandering, social, financial
complex of motives having intruded, she is sad again (Fig. 9.10).
As they walk, they are divided by a post of the house in the same
way (Fig. 9.14). The trees can hardly remain trees here. They
become contaminated by their contact with the human, and they
divide people. Indeed, we see in the image that what Gerardini
makes of his world imprisons his daughter and separates her from
meaningful contact with others.

The images we have been discussing are, I think, the dominant
ones in the dense thematic web Antonioni weaves. As we suggested,
the characters are set against, but also related to, the images
of their world in a way different from that shown in
L'Avventura. We have here a stiff, awkward, and oppressive
visual norm, with images of the worst it can come to (the film's
hindrance) and the best (its good). The characters are all hemmed
in by that norm, yet each is related to different aspects of it,
so that even within their common victimization we can see that
some have better chances than others. But all are mixed—we have
here no simple fable of victim and villain, but rather an evenly
distributed network of temptations and understandings and
defenses. The underlying Antonioni story—of the pressure of
feeling seeking for fulfilling outlet in the world, its painful
squelching, and a retrenchment—is thus rendered by all the
characters' sequences rather more than, as in L'Avventura, by
the single sequence made up by their interplay. But we can see
that it is, though suffered by each of the characters rather than
inflicted on one of them by others, the same story.

The fact that our sympathies are more evenly divided has
thematic consequences. On the one hand, the story is more
optimistic than L'Avventura. It is based on an interplay among
the motives of people who are equals, rather than on tormenting
discoveries of spiritual inequality, and it develops through the
active working out of individual destinies rather than through
more passive sequences of people being seduced or cajoled into
a particular fate. Since we see the characters resist temptation,
apply ironic perceptions to situations, struggle to assert

nonverbal communication, La Notte at least implies that there
are options for conduct among which one can choose.
    But, on the other hand, La Notte is harsher in its
implications than L'Avventura.  It presents us fewer hedges
to the universality of the story than Claudia's innocence and
Sandro's especially wounded case suggest.  The flow of feeling
is more muted, constrained, mixed.  One does not sink into it,
as one does into L'Avventura, for the painful pleasure of
the fairy tale.  One could go either way from La Notte
(appropriately, for the second part of a trilogy):  towards self-
determination and a way of coping with modern depersonalization
through treasured personal relations; or towards defeat by the
seductiveness of a world where the artworks are machines and the
hospitals are nightclubs.

Eclipse
    In La Notte our sympathies are divided among characters
who try to achieve some mastery over their lives in a society
to whose blandishments they are drawn, but that they realize can
only betray them.  After it, Eclipse focuses our sympathy, and
returns us to as simple a structure as L'Avventura's.  As
simple, and similar:  Vittoria is drawn despite resistance into
an affair with Piero, but rather than being released by the
relationship she is constricted by the new one exactly as she
had been by the one she fled.  Piero seems different, but turns
out to be like Riccardo, the lover from whom we see her part at
the film's beginning.  Piero offers no greater vitality in human
relations despite his bustling activity and simple enthusiasm.
The distrust Vittoria feels for his involvement in the unreality
of the stock exchange, and his sharing of its materialist values
so that he cares more for his smashed car than for the drunk who
died in it, turns out to be justified.  There is much to love
especially in the natural world, but the approach to society for
which Piero stands (and that we have seen in less extreme form
in Sandro and in the Gerardinis) prevents our finding or savoring
it.  All must be manipulated, reduced to human scale, brought
under control.  But the world's vitality, what we can share with
others if we allow feeling to develop according to natural
rhythms, is thus withdrawn from the characters and replaced by
anxious egotism.  The next step from the final misery of Piero
and Vittoria is the complete rejection of feeling by adjusted
people, and their classification of human warmth as neurosis,
which we observe in Red Desert.
    Looked at as a whole, the trilogy suggests in its complex
middle part La Notte that the assertiveness to which the
characters are driven by the manifest failures of their attempts
to find contentment in submission to a world they can only despise
might prevail.  Our knowledge of human communion might set us
free even in the midst of the world's pressures against it.  But
the trilogy's end reasserts what its beginning had implied:
feeling itself becomes contaminated by the attitudes that our

position in the modern world makes natural. It is hard to see
ourselves standing together against the easy reductions of
ourselves, at the kind of cost La Notte made apparent. Thus
the rich three-part perspective on almost equal characters of
La Notte is, in Eclipse, reduced again to the simpler form
of L'Avventura. Eclipse settles the question of which of
La Notte's eventualities is most likely, by rendering a form
of feeling in which a high quality of longing is brought to
nothing by the pressures of the world against it. It is
Vittoria's perspective we share, then, as we shared Claudia's.
The sequences of the story and of the developing symbolism of
objects and stylistic devices are the sequences of her options,
choices, and submissions.

From the start, Vittoria tries to achieve a feeling of
relatedness to natural objects, to simple experiences, and to
other people, through slow growth of selfless feeling and
enjoyment. And from the start this yearning for authenticity
is opposed by selfish and exploitative egotism and by reduction
of nature to a scale that falsifies it. Vittoria tries to
treasure authentic responsiveness, but is forced to accept too
rapid development of the relationships to which she would like
to attach her responsiveness, and hence becomes vulnerable to
betrayal from those in whom proper feeling has not achieved its
grounding. In the process she is absorbed into the kind of
sequence her oppressors have demanded. It is as if she is lost
from connection with the natural objects, the places of the heart,
around which she has tried to build the kind of web of
associations of value that could form the bases of true
relations. There is a tendency through the film for her to
shrink: we are told she is losing weight; she puts a coin in
a scales as she watches the losing investor who draws flowers; she
tells Piero she is smaller now than she was at fifteen. Finally
she disappears from view. She resists, but she is made to
change.

Vittoria becomes, in the end, the inexpressive wounded
creature she had been with Riccardo in the beginning. Soon she
will be a cast-off like Piero's former mistress, whom she calls
"the beast." The beast began as a blonde, too, Piero tells us,
and he rejects her because she dyes her hair (Fig. 9.41). At
the end, where we expect to see Vittoria meet Piero by appointment
at their treasured place, we see only a succession of dark-haired
young women of increasing slovenliness. And before that end we
see Vittoria, in the penultimate shot we have of her, through
the grate outside Piero's office where we had seen him cast off
"the beast" (Fig. 9.42). Surely Vittoria becomes one of these
young women. Having submitted to Piero's demands, she is surely
the prisoner of his rhythms at the end.

But the film begins with Vittoria's rejection of the impasse
human relations can come to, as she leaves Riccardo. It is as
if Lidia finally left Giovanni; for Riccardo, like Giovanni, is
an intellectual, and the way he inhabits his apartment gives us

a strong sense of the desiccation of that tradition of intellectual modernism for which he stands. At the start, Vittoria holds an empty picture frame on a table, takes a full ashtray out of it, and frames a small metal sculpture in it. A pan up to her sad face reveals the aimlessness and futility of the framing gesture, but a glance at an old map on the wall seems to give her no more orientation. As if oppressed by the claustrophobic quality of the cluttered room and the dead silence, Vittoria goes over to the curtain, pulls it aside, and looks sadly out at a corner of vegetation so that she is reflected in the window as if she were Valentina (Fig. 9.28). Overcome (it seems by the contrast between the outdoors and the pressures on her in this room), she sinks foetally into the sofa; but then, with a sympathetic but determined look she rises, goes past Riccardo, and tells him she is leaving.

Riccardo begs her to stay, and though she clearly sees no purpose to it, she seems to agree. In a sad tidying gesture, she takes some empty coffee cups out of the room. But Riccardo is offering nothing. When Vittoria returns, Riccardo is sitting as if frozen in his chair. She backs away almost in panic—what is he asking of her, if he wants her to stay but is dead to her?— and turns with a gasp of fear as she sees herself in a mirror, as depersonalized as he. Quickly she goes to the other wall and opens the curtain there. But she sees herself reflected in that window too, and the window is dominated by a mushroom-shaped water tower which gives no relief (Fig. 9.32). It is strongly suggestive of the truncation of natural forms that, it is the film's metaphoric point to show, distorts the human relations that must take place in its context. As we shall see, the African savannahs in the pictures which delight Vittoria are reduced in her world to clusters of fossilized or painted grasses. The African spears (Fig. 9.36), with one of which Vittoria plays, are changed from being extensions of a person's feelings to being oppressors of them in the flagpoles that dominate Vittoria's feelings like the water tower (Fig. 9.38)—and even the flagpoles are swallowed up in architectural forms as they are changed to stumpy reinforcing rods that only barely manage to obtrude from the side of a building (Fig. 9.39). The wind in the trees is reduced to the fan with which we first see Riccardo, and then to the tiny portable fan Piero carries into the stock exchange. The point is general: emotional relations themselves are truncated, made hard and domineering like that water tower rather than human-scaled and receptive like the open water barrel into which Vittoria drops a deeply valued piece of wood.

As Vittoria stands by the window looking out at the tower, Riccardo suddenly comes into the frame and, oppressing her psychically as the tower oppresses the visual scene, grapples for her and asks for sex "this one last time." It is the only alternative to sitting dead in his chair of which he—and it turns out Piero, too—is capable. Vittoria shrinks away, of course. There is no offer to her here, no intention of any sharing, but

only a pressure towards sexuality that is somehow supposed to
carry a symbolic weight it can't sustain. One doubts Riccardo
fully understands it, but at least he knows he has not related
correctly to Vittoria when she reminds him that she was happy
when she met him. His face falls, just as Piero's face will later
fall when he partly understands Vittoria's deadly serious remark,
"I wish I didn't love you, unless I could love you more." Both
men have only sexuality, and a chain of conventionalities
involving "love" and marriage, to imagine as a good, and both
can be reproached by the sense that there should be a deeper
communion for which their inadequacies unfit them.

     Both men react defensively but aggressively to their inklings
of being reproachable, and they do so in such similar
conversations with Vittoria as to make clear how little change
she effects in attaching her affections to one rather than the
other. The opening scene with Riccardo, at the close of the
relationship, continues with Riccardo acting angry with Vittoria
after she rebuffs him. He returns from shaving (brushing past
Vittoria as if she weren't there) and then demands to know whether
her point is that she doesn't love him or that she won't marry
him, and asking, too, when it was that she stopped loving him.
It is clear that in this context of emotional estrangement such
questions are simply unanswerable, and Vittoria can reply only,
"I don't know," to all of them.

     It is much later, and at the beginning of their relationship,
that the similar scene between Vittoria and Piero takes place.
It seems very different: it is the first scene following
Vittoria's seduction rather than a scene following a refusal of
sex. But the point is plainly that the seduction, far from
engendering communion, results in a truncation of the relations
between Piero and Vittoria. The truncation is visual as well
as emotional. The scene opens with a shot of Piero's body,
decapitated by the left edge of the frame, while in the background
is an angular, harsh, and ugly modern church, itself truncated
of the dome it ought to have. But when Piero and Vittoria had
been courting before the seduction, in the background as they
walked about, had been a church with a softly rounded dome. When
Piero, then, rises into the frame--getting his head back, though
what he then says is that he feels as if he were in a foreign
country--he at once starts asking just such questions as Riccardo
had asked. Would they get along? Does she want to marry him?
Why does she go out with him if she's not sure? He misunderstands
a turn of phrase (taking "I don't miss marriage" to mean she
doesn't look back on it longingly, rather than that she doesn't
look forward to it longingly) in a way possible only between
people who don't know each other well. And when Vittoria flinches
under the inappropriate questions, he rounds on her with the
domineering instruction not to reply "I don't know." But, as
it had been with Riccardo, it is the only answer possible. Since
Piero has pressed her as he has, the terms of the relationship
have been set in a pattern as wrong as the one that had come to

characterize the relation with Riccardo.  No wonder she says at
that point, "I wish I didn't love you, unless I could love you
more."
    Vittoria, in her instinctive way, knows that there is in
Africa a simplicity that civilized complications overwhelm.  She
tries to lead the men in her life to the good she understands,
to a sharing of moments of joy of which a more lasting bond might
be the natural outcome.  But they demand sexual submission, a
definition of love that is linked to it--one thinks of Sandro's
incomprehension that Anna should not love him after their sex
together--and an orientation to marriage.  And the hindrance
embodied in this reduction of emotional richness to such
conventional expectations is what prevails in the story of
Vittoria and in the story of the tendencies in modern life for
which it stands.
    Vittoria is full of pity for Riccardo's awkward attempts
to reestablish intimacy between them even as she leaves him--to
drive her home and then to walk with her, to talk about the beauty
of the morning, to romp as if happy through weeds in the pathside,
to ask her to breakfast, to shake hands with her at parting.
Vittoria sees his pain, and sees, too, the sad absurdity of his
presenting his profile as he leaves, not looking back, preserving
a shred of dignity.  But there is (as there was with Sandro's
love for Claudia--and Sandro had explicitly presented his profile
to Anna) an aggressive component to his treating Vittoria as badly
as he does.  We saw him vary between dead hostility and sexual
grappling.  And late that night Vittoria is waked by Riccardo
at her window.  He rattles the apartment door viciously, and
Vittoria calls a friend on the phone.  She wants him to help
Riccardo, to be close to him.  The friend immediately starts his
own offensive--"I'd rather be close to you"--and we see Vittoria's
frustration and annoyance that what motivates men seems simply
to be these egotistical mixtures of aggressiveness and demeaning
humility that prevent any direct communication of emotional needs.
    There is no way for Vittoria to reach out to what she
understands is Riccardo's misery, or to bring anyone else to
help.  Every motive around her is self-interested.  We learn that
her mother, for instance, has sanctioned her affair with Riccardo
because he can loan money to cover her margins at her broker's.
It seems as if the only fulfillments are to be moments in nature,
either alone or in selfless play; yet there is always pressure,
as Vittoria is sought by men who insist on dominance, away from
the natural.  To call the friend, for example, Vittoria goes into
an inner room of her apartment and turns on a lamp.  On the other
hand, after Riccardo went into the bathroom to shave, rebuffed
by Vittoria, she had opened the other curtain in the apartment,
revealing the shrubbery of which we had had a glimpse, and had
turned out most of the lights in the apartment.  In Piero's
parents' apartment, too, Vittoria remarks that they seem to live
in the dark, and goes to the windows for some natural light.
From those windows, however, much like Giuliana in Red Desert

looking from Corrado's window, Vittoria sees only images alienated
from herself, so that she accepts Piero's advances as at least
counter to them, just as Giuliana accepts Corrado's.

What is outside seems in Eclipse unpromising in certain
respects, but it is all that can oppose what is indoors. As
Vittoria tells Riccardo finally that he has not made her happy,
she stands by a table lamp, her face taking half the screen and
the lamp the other half, while the fan in the apartment blows
her hair. We can understand why, after she has sent Riccardo
away and gone into her own apartment, Vittoria should go upstairs
and stand by her window (we see it in long shot from outside)
while she looks at a wall of blowing trees and foliage outside.
Vittoria is striving for natural, and not artificial light; for
the outdoors that rebuffs her, and not the indoors that makes
false appeals. This is one aspect of the film's profoundest
thrust of feeling, which on the level of the emotions of the story
amounts to Vittoria's striving for tranquility and spontaneity
as against being sexually pressed and oppressed.

It is clear, when Vittoria opens the second curtain in
Riccardo's apartment, that shrubbery stands for an alternative
to what the mushroom tower represents. But it seems at first
as if the stock exchange may be the way to reach that alternative,
since its vitality and Piero's are at least different from
cultural lethargy and Riccardo. The first scene in the bourse
has great verve, and Piero's clever turnover of a large profit
from an overheard order to a slower-moving older broker is
exhilarating by contrast with the agonizingly slow scene with
Riccardo that has preceded it. But the causes of Vittoria's
instinctive resistance to Piero are made plain at once. We see
the couple divided, during the minute of silence for a dead
colleague, by a huge pillar of the building (the effect is like
Vittoria next to the lamp at Riccardo's—and indeed like Lidia
dwarfed by a huge building in Milan during her walk), and we see,
too, Vittoria's ironic notice that, although a friend has died,
Piero is most impressed by the cost of the minute. It prefigures
Vittoria's notice of his greater concern for his car than for
the drunk who has died in it.

But the most important function of the scene is to show how
Vittoria's mother is "obsessed" (as Vittoria later calls it) with
her investments. It is a function of Vittoria's desire for
"simplicity" that she should feel, as she explains to Piero, that
she is neither terrified of poverty like her mother nor, the
reciprocal of that fear, obsessed with desire for wealth. She
tells Piero in exactly that context that she is sure her mother
has forgotten her father, that the concern for winning on the
exchange has consumed her. It is as weighty a moment as any in
the film when later, in Piero's parents' apartment as he tries
to explain to Vittoria how the exchange catches you up, "gets
you," if you become involved in it, she looks at him—we hold
a long time on Vittoria's quizzical, doubtful, sympathetic face—
and asks, "What gets you?" Concern for inordinate winning,

unreality, replacement of natural rhythms with unnatural, people
with objects, serenity with perpetual motion:  these get you,
and they get Vittoria only a little differently, through the man
of the exchange, than her mother through the exchange itself.

Obsessed like that, her mother, Vittoria realizes, is utterly
useless as a source of advice or consolation about her breakup
with Riccardo that morning.  She lies about it when her mother
asks.  Vittoria, we see, is very much on her own, and the scenes
that follow complete the first half of the film's structure by
showing what Vittoria wants from and can offer life--that is,
what a person alone can ask and get on his or her own--and by
showing that independent pleasures are inadequate.  Having left
the hopelessly artificial Riccardo, Vittoria builds a set of
feelings for objects in the world, elements which can delight,
in which one can ground oneself.  And naturally, in the second
half she tries to bring the richer, more complex human
relationship with Piero into the slow maturing of her integration
with the possibilities of her world.  But he, contaminated,
incomprehending, fails her--Vittoria's integrity is destroyed,
the objects are left, and she is lost to them.

We saw the tendency toward foliage in the opening scenes.
Vittoria, before Riccardo drove up behind her, reached out and
swept some weeds with her carried sweater in a pleased gesture
of relation with them, an instant of integration of character
with its purposes.  After she leaves her mother at the bourse
Vittoria goes shopping, apparently, for we see her return in the
evening to her apartment with a plaque of a bundle of weeds.
It feels as if she is making the best of what she is reduced to
as she sadly but intently traces the fossil outline (Fig. 9.33):
it is too much like the outline of the mushroom tower for comfort,
and even, in the curve she first traces, suggests the line of
the street lamps outside, one of which provides the film's last
terrifying image (Fig. 9.35).  That specific line, a vertical
with a leftward curve at its upper end, becomes a dominant image
in Red Desert, as a line of paint or a pipe, abstracted even
further from its natural form.  We see bundles of flowers or
grasses again, too:  the losing investor (in fact he draws
flowers, but petals only, not bunches) comes into the apothecary
and we see him next to a large vase of flowers.  There are small
prints of bundles of flowers shaped the same way behind Vittoria
as she apologetically turns off the radio whose reports of the
exchange she had foolishly thought to please Piero by playing
as if he, the expert, could learn anything from them.  And as
Vittoria walks toward the bedroom where she will be seduced in
Piero's parents' apartment she stops, holding her torn dress,
before a set of doors dominated by etchings of sprays of flowers
like that (Fig. 9.31).  They are associated, then, with a longing
for nature, and a capture and reduction of it by artifice, that
link closely with the capture of the individual by the social
for which Vittoria herself stands.

As Vittoria pounds a hanger for her plaque she wakes her

friend Anita, who comes in to visit her.  Vittoria confides her
misery at breaking up with Riccardo and, standing at her window,
confides, too, that things and men seem sometimes all the same.
It seems a response to this sad sense of disjunction from one's
life that Marta, from her apartment across the courtyard, should
call the two women to come and visit her, and that they should
develop together through their actions imagery of the socially
and personally vital.  Modes of fulfillment that are alternative
to the beckoning attachment to a man are being tried out here,
and Vittoria's visit with Marta and her airplane ride have much
the sense of Lidia's walk through Milan.  Marta, who was brought
up in Kenya and loves it there, clearly stands to Vittoria for
involvement with a kind of naturalness that she finds missing
in her own life.  Vittoria likes the elephant foot and the skins
on the floor, the pictures of Kenya on the walls and the picture
in a book of a baobab tree like a natural version of the mushroom
tower.  As Marta speaks of the savannahs we see a picture on the
wall, rolling grasslands, a tree--the camera pans the picture
and comes to rest on a group of three lions totally at one with
their natural surroundings.

The scene is full, for Vittoria and for us, of a sense of
longing, of love of place, of uncomplicated natural beauty.  And
the feeling Vittoria has is immediately expressed in her wondrous
dance.  She picks up a spear and dances with it, full of joy and
excitement (Fig. 9.37).  We notice that Marta seems uncomfortable
as the spear is in the frame next to her, and finally, as Vittoria
and Anita continue to dance, Marta stops them.  She turns on the
light (again that association of artificial light and the
repression of the natural) and tells them not to act like natives.

Slowly their joy fades.  They take off their ornaments, and,
as they lie on the bed together and talk, they learn the
hindrances to responsiveness to the simplicity of the exotic.
Marta is a racist.  She is terrified of the natives, thinks them
apes--she cannot stand to see even fantasized what they stand
for to her.  She tells Vittoria when they walk outside that she
loves Kenya and wishes she were there, that in Italy she never
goes out of the house and misses the people at home.  Vittoria
gently twits her:  "You mean the apes?"  We have been given a
clear picture of what joy is, and yet its social context is as
oppressive as Vittoria's.  Marta, who lives in Kenya, is incapable
of incorporating its vitality into her life, and is stuck in a
sad nostalgia, more constrained even than is Vittoria.

A perfect imagistic rendition of what Vittoria has learned
from Marta's case immediately follows the squelched dance.
Marta's dog escapes and the women chase it.  Marta's husband will
be furious if the dog is gone, we are told, and when Vittoria
finds it and it walks around her on its hind legs, she is
delighted, involved in the comicality in that engrossed and vital
way of hers.

But the implications come home to her.  We see her rise into
the frame struck serious by a strange sound.  She goes to it and

comes into the frame of an extraordinary perspective shot (Fig.
9.38). The sound is of flagpoles shaking gently, their lines
slapping against them. Vittoria is dwarfed by them. She backs
up next to a grotesque Pan-like statue that towers over her
too--we see her move between its legs in a high shot before she
looks up at it. And then she stands under it and glances first
up at the flagpoles, then down at the poodle. Those poles, which
echo the shape of the spears in the African pictures, dwarf
Vittoria as the tower does Riccardo's apartment. Clearly she
is not in control of spears like the natives, but rather in her
world their equivalents, the flagpoles, dominate her. The dog
dancing on its hind legs is a better image for Vittoria than the
lions of the African savannahs. And the dog (and Marta who is
charged with its care) is under a man's domination as Vittoria
is under domination by flagpoles and the Pan statue. Rather than
a free creature, she is a domestic animal, a figure of fun.

As the spears reappear as reinforcing rods, so the Pan statue
reappears. A statue quite like it is revealed as Vittoria walks
into Piero's parents' apartment and Piero locks the door behind
her. The statue supervises her seduction mockingly--we note that
Vittoria gives a sad recognition to a bust of a woman as she walks
through the apartment after Piero tears her dress, acknowledging
that in the very physical setting of the apartment the preordained
roles are played out in the statuary. The whole sad foreknowledge
is in Vittoria's eyes as, under the Pan statue's legs, she looks
up at the flagpoles and down at the poodle.

The airplane ride to Verona that follows Riccardo's rattling
at Vittoria's door is tinged by some of the sadness of the evening
before, but not by much. Vittoria's delight in the trip is
obvious, in the sheer magic of getting off the ground, the
slightly anxious but perfect landing, and particularly the flying
through the cloud, which the pilot does in response to Vittoria's
request. Vittoria turns her head with enthusiasm to hear that
the cloud is stratified of snowflakes and raindrops. Flying
through it is not so good: it gets dark in the plane, and chill.
Anita, who we have seen before, as now, touch herself in the
self-absorbed fashion of the people on the monorail in Fahrenheit
451, rubs her arm while in the cloud. Water condenses on the
wing in a slightly ominous line. But Vittoria is thrilled with
it. The anxiety in the cloud is relieved as the plane comes out.
Perhaps experience is stratified like that too; it is possible
that things go dark for a moment and become light again. It is
not until Red Desert that the birds learn not to fly through
the clouds of poisonous smoke at all.

At the Verona airport, Vittoria is as happy as she is ever
to be. That is a fact not untinged with a sadness of its own,
for the fact that relationships with people at the airport are
much reduced is what makes them manageable for Vittoria. At the
door of the little airport bar sit two black men, as different
in their submissiveness from the Kenyans of the previous scene
as could be. One of them looks up at Vittoria and then politely

drops his eyes.  In the bar a man sees her, says, "Hello,"
invitingly (he seems to be an American), and shakes his head only
a little sadly when Vittoria smiles but does not join him.  She
sees two men talking quietly in an arbor, and two others talking
over beers on the terrace.  The peace of the scene is obvious,
and it is sad that Vittoria is so reduced by the pressures of
her life that she can like best those casual encounters in which
she has no part, and that have no women in them.

What pleases Vittoria most is the simple, open, sun-drenched
ambience.  She stands by the wing of the plane after the others
walk in and watches entranced as a plane practices an approach
and soars up again.  She looks at jet trails in the sky.  She
settles into a lawn chair before some shrubbery on the terrace,
in another appearance of that major image, and tells Anita with
a sigh of contentment that she likes the place.  We had seen that
she did, and why; the reductions here make her in tune with her
surroundings, not alien from them.  And we are shown her
in-tuneness (her "atonement" Joyce would say) in this scene in
an expressive pair of shots with a strong effect:  Vittoria walks
directly away from the camera towards the airport building, and
Antonioni cuts directly to a plane moving away from the camera
at just the same angle, its propeller blowing the long grasses
beside it as it goes.  Vittoria is equated with the plane, and
the wind in the blowing grass is rich with evocation for us, too.

The openness and contentment of the airport scene is sharply
altered with an abrupt cut that, it turns out, begins the
sequences that make up the film's second half, the sequences of
the relationship between Vittoria and Piero.  The cut is from
the serenity of Vittoria's face before shrubbery to bars at the
gate of the bourse.  And promptly Piero and his boss walk along
beyond those bars, Piero showing him a little battery-powered
electric fan that seems a trivializing reduction of the airplane
propellers we have just seen.  And this second, amazing sequence
at the bourse completely reverses the implications of pleasing
vitality that were there in the first.  As the long sequence
develops and the market falls, Antonioni give us ever more sharply
etched shots of the panic that replaces the usual benign
pandemonium on the floor.  Piero is, of course, involved in it
like everyone else, and he is disgusted, throwing up his hands,
inspecting his nails, realizing that nothing can be done.  But
he is not overwhelmed.  He fools a man by tapping him on the
shoulder so he will turn the wrong way for a joke.  He talks to
a man about a callgirl the man apparently provided him--the
customer is concerned with his losses and reproves Piero, who
accepts the reproof knowing that it is in the nature of investors
to be intense about fluctuations that he takes as normal.  And
it is the customers who are destroyed.  Vittoria's mother is
superstitious, spiteful, emotionally drained, angry:  she blames
the fall on politics, she throws order books angrily at tellers,
she storms out with a group of fellow-sufferers, apparently to
complain to someone, even as Vittoria tells her she hates to see
her like this and urges her to come home.

So when Piero offers the submissiveness of the man who draws
flowers as a model, Vittoria has doubts of him.  She notices that
Piero never stops moving--why should he, he asks, just as when
he visits Vittoria's apartment that night he asks why they should
waste time.  She notices that he overfamiliarly pats a woman on
the buttocks, and that he seems too uncaring about the man who
draws flowers.  She notices especially that Piero has no answers
to her questions about the stock exchange's unreality, about where
the lost money goes.

A relationship is developing between the two, and Vittoria
is surely attracted to Piero's secure involvement in his life,
so different from Riccardo's insecurity.  But his life and values
are very questionable, and it is hard for Vittoria to find a way
to relate to Piero other than simply to submit to him.  As they
go to his car she tries to buy him a chamois for it, but he has
one already.  At her mother's she shares with him her pleasure
in thinking about herself as a young girl.  It is painful ("God,
how I've changed") but fun to lie on her small bed.  Piero,
however, sits beside her and tries to kiss her.  That is not what
Vittoria has in mind.  She has no reason to kiss him, and she
shrinks from his embrace, to his annoyance.  We notice, too, that
her room is full of books--she is highly though unpretentiously
cultured, speaking, for instance, four languages that we know
about--and that Piero's childhood room has no books at all, but
only a ship model (spars now askew through neglect), a set of
tasteless framed posters of face cards, and a trick pen which
disrobes a picture of a woman as one inverts it.  The naiveté
of the trick pen at the same time reminds Vittoria of the casual
insistence of his orientation to sex, and of his essential
innocence about personal relations.  With his experience of his
lower-class mistress and of callgirls, he does not know how to
behave with Vittoria, and her response is a distinct tolerance
so that he can learn, as well as a distinct doubt that he will--as
indeed he does not.

Vittoria's mother comes home just as Vittoria squirms out
from under Piero's attempted embrace, and the mother talks sadly
to Piero about her losses.  Vittoria tries again to offer him
something, this time the radio news, and is again rebuffed.
Finally, they having nothing to say to each other, Piero sinks
into an overstuffed chair and falls dead asleep.  It is the first
indication of his surprising similarity to Riccardo; he has
pressed Vittoria sexually, it has come to nothing, and his
response is to become dead to her.

The two are, nonetheless, attracted to each other, but there
are these internal signs of difficulties to come, and some
external signs as well.  After Piero rejects his girl, "the
beast," a priest walks in front of him as he goes over to his
car to go visit Vittoria, slowing him a little.  Similarly, he
sits lost in thought a moment before he starts the car:  is there
a relationship to fidelity that he is not sustaining?  Is it
entirely right to move from one woman to another quite so
smoothly, so entirely forgetting the immediate past?  The priest

suggests a context that makes an insistence in the background
of the film from this point: a priest walks in front of Vittoria
and Piero on the way to Piero's parents' apartment; Vittoria sees
nuns from that apartment's window. They seem to reprove the
couple for a certain inability to integrate their relationship
into life's natural sequences. And similarly, all the shots of
children seem to reprove in the same way: a little boy passes
in front of Riccardo and Vittoria walking; a nurse and baby pass
Piero and Vittoria several times; a group of children come to
play in the sprinkler about to be turned off at the end. The
sexual relationship into which Vittoria and Piero enter fails
to achieve emotional grounding and to function as an integral
part of a commitment ranging over all aspects of the personal
life, of which commitment to sexual union can be sign and
sacrament. Therefore images that connote the elements of the
emotional life with which sexuality can be connected by means
of that grounding--the moral, social, and spiritual values
symbolized by religion, the values of family solidarity, and the
succession of the generations symbolized by children--visually
contradict the couple, seem virtually to reproach Vittoria and
Piero for not being in tune with them. These images throughout
the rest of the film render possibilities of integration the
couple fails to reach.

There is, then, in the external world beyond Vittoria and
Piero--in the frame with them, but separate from them--at least
a conception of the good (not that it is asserted, by that fact,
that individuals can be expected to achieve it), from which
Vittoria and Piero seem to be cut off even as they develop the
relationship toward what should be manifestation of that
conception. And that sense of being cut off from the conception
of the good is explained in the internal dynamics of the
developing relationship. Almost as if it were itself an organism
with a life of its own, the relationship reaches toward communion,
adjusts the reservations, interests, and personal styles of its
participants, opens up the hope of fruition, yet displays the
signs of what may and does prevent it. Callow freshness, the
style of this relationship, can after all go either way, to become
openhearted spontaneity and attuned responsiveness, or
incomprehending and thin-spirited failure of empathy. And it
is between these two qualities that Vittoria and Piero are, during
the agonizing/exhilarating development of their relationship,
poised.

Vittoria is more pleased to see Piero outside her window
than she had been to see Riccardo, though that he appears there,
as Riccardo had, chills us a little and is an internal sign of
coming trouble--perhaps, we realize, Riccardo and Piero aren't
as different as it had seemed we should suppose. Though the drunk
who elegantly and foolishly salutes her pleases Vittoria too,
she likes to tease Piero and to flirt: again, perhaps Piero and
the drunk, both of them likeable in their silliness and both a
bit vulnerable and out of control, are not entirely different.

But it is we, watching a movie, who are attuned to possibilities of meaning that there is no reason for Vittoria, living a life, to entertain.  And it is we who will be troubled, on her behalf, by the similar echoes when Piero calls her the next day to come and see his car raised.  She finds that, whereas he is appealingly attracted to her, his car is more important to him than the fact that the drunk died in it.  There is a possibility of something turning out right here, but also much that is wrong.  Bystanders rush over to see the car and its dead occupant and press the couple in a way that makes Vittoria feel claustrophobic.  A boy even falls into the lake with much the heedless gesture of one of the Gerardinis' roisterers falling into the pool in La Notte.  And it was the quality of that recklessness that had made it appropriate that Roberto virtually rescue Lidia from participation in it.

Though the press of people is no less a problem for Vittoria than the Gerardinis' hedonists were for Lidia, Piero is not so obviously a false alternative for Vittoria as Roberto was for Lidia.  He is more unused to being thoughtful than incapable of it--it is what makes Vittoria and us think she can make something of him--and he is not utterly insensitive to the fate of the drunk.  He immediately realizes the insensitivity of his response and promises to sell the car that now has such bad associations.  Vittoria is more amused than offended with his gaucherie, especially when he awkwardly says that talking to her is not wasting his time because he had to be here to see about the car anyway.  She is tolerant, and willing to teach him how to act.  Their walk through the district (the rounded church in the background) is basically to her rhythmn, as she starts to build the relationship seriously, to learn to enjoy him and give him a chance to enjoy her in the building of shared experiences.

The images of this scene are so important, so much the basis for what Piero and Vittoria could feel for each other later, that, after his insistence and her loss of choice destroy their chance, the mere reference to the elements of the web exacts a wrenching tribute of pain.  We look down on them through pine branches as they walk underneath, in as complete a moment of people united in the context of foliage as the film presents (Fig. 9.29).  Piero smirks like a little boy when he looks into Vittoria's accidentally unbuttoned blouse and sees her underwear (it is another sign of his social inexperience), but a few minutes later notices how unbothered Vittoria is as she notices and does the button up.  With one of those typically Vittorian laughing gasps of delight, she goes over to a sprinkler and splashes Piero by putting her hand in its flow.  She darts away, and we are shown her coming around a palm tree with her face surprisingly fallen after that instant.  The film's tensions are articulated here: by the joy of life Vittoria is pressed to these flirting playful games.  But she fears that their feeling betrays, that they may lead to repetition of what she has suffered before.  Virtually upon biological demand Vittoria becomes that poodle dancing on its hind legs whose act had first delighted and then saddened her.

The reservations in the scene, the images for sudden awareness of how life's best moments are contaminated by their true places in a larger context and by their likely outcome, at this point are an undercurrent only. Piero and Vittoria continue their walk: to a terrace where, reminding us of the Verona airport, in the context of Coca-Cola signs people listen to pleasant jazz on a jukebox. Piero and Vittoria like the music, and as she walks past the jukebox Vittoria swerves a little to touch it, to make the kind of contact with it she did with the weeds by the pathside as she walked alone from Riccardo's.

At her apartment building, Vittoria whistles and hides, laughing delightedly as Piero shrugs to the cyclist, who has stopped for the whistle, to indicate that they want nothing of him. The whistle is like Piero's tapping the man on the shoulder in the bourse, and the shrug is like Vittoria's to the following traffic as she paid her cab and held up traffic for a moment, earlier in the film. Vittoria calls poor Marta who, always at home, is available to come and pop the balloon with her African rifle to the couple's admiration and her own pleasure. Piero asks Vittoria not to go in quite yet, and they walk on, to a street crossing. Piero tells Vittoria that he will kiss her on the other side and, the camera over their shoulders as they walk on the crosshatches that mark the walkway, they come up to the center line (Fig. 9.43). Vittoria says they are halfway across and continues, thoughtful, aware of the consequences, of the division point in the relationship, over to the other sidewalk.

It is a construction site and it will become imagistically the most important spot in the film (Fig. 9.34). Piero, passing the water barrel that will be the film's very locus and symbol of value, walks quietly over and turns, leaning on the fence that surrounds the site. He does not press Vittoria, and the moment is auspicious. She joins him, a step away: she looks up, and we see what she sees as the screen fills with blowing tree limbs, a vegetative richness warranting the moment, joining the emotional development of the couple with the suggestions of value the film has built all along (Fig. 9.30). Vittoria turns and smiles gently, welcoming just that kiss that the dynamics have justified. Piero kisses her, as gently as is deserved, and she shrinks away only when he starts to press, to overdo it.

Piero looks a little wry, as when she had shrunk from him before, but she is in no sense rejecting him. She says she will go now, not to reject him, but because there has been enough. There have been promises made and justifications for the promises established, in the conditions which led up to the kiss, and promises and justifications need maturing, development, reflection. To memorialize the moment, Vittoria drops a small chunk of wood from the fence (it bears all the weight of the film's instant of maximum promise) into the water barrel and walks

past it down the street toward her apartment.  For the only time
in the film, its good is directly rendered:  an object in the
world bears and gives warrant for the human feeling that through
its symbol both floods over the natural world and is given
integration into the universal order by it.

But at this very instant of maximum value, it starts to go
sour.  As Vittoria says she will leave, we hear (the film's first
nondiegetic music) a piano note that is the start of the ominous
score that followed the "Twist" sung raucously behind the titles
and that ends the film with an abrupt, harsh crescendo.  We follow
Vittoria with the camera, and we see her turn quickly to wave
goodbye, to reassert those promises, and to reassure Piero that
there is no rejection here but only development.  She is sure
he is emotionally with her, just as, at exactly this point in
L'Avventura, Claudia is sure Sandro is with her.  But the
outcome is the same as in the earlier film.  When Vittoria turns,
the corner is empty.  Piero could not wait, could not be still
for a moment, could not learn.  Vittoria will not be allowed to
let the rhythms of the relationship develop for her and Piero.
"Put out or lose" is the message Piero sends.

That night Vittoria calls Piero on the phone.  We see him
reading the paper and talking with someone else.  The busy line
also tells Vittoria something of what the situation is.  Piero
gets out of bed, filling the screen with parts of his body in
the way that will culminate in his headless torso lying across
the frame, to pour a sleeping draught for himself.  The phone
rings, and he answers, "Pronto," and as apparently no one
speaks, he shouts it again into the receiver, banging it down
abruptly when he gets no answer.  There is simply going to be
no doing of things at rhythms different from those he feels
right.  He will not learn from Vittoria how to relate to the more
subtle but solid rhythms we have seen the world offer, but will,
to borrow Anna's language about Sandro, "drag things down."  And
as we cut from his banging the phone, we see Vittoria's
realization of it:  first, from behind, a high shot of her sadly
sitting on her bed, and then, in close-up, her melancholy face,
show she knows the terms.  She fights back tears, she seems in
a despair of which we can understand the cause.

It must be that she accepts the terms of her undoing, for
it is a different Vittoria who appears at the corner to meet
Piero, presumably the next afternoon.  To the accompaniment of
that ominous piano note, the camera pans as she walks behind a
pile of geometrical plaster pipes and open-ended boxes (much like
the piles of retorts and bottles whose close-up symmetry,
replacing the human with abstract shape and color, opens the last
scene of Red Desert) (Fig. 9.51).  In a low shot she passes
one of the streetlights that will take on such ominous
implications later.  The shots we get are portentous, but we will
wish that we could have them again as we have them here, when
at the end they are repeated without the people for whom we care.

There are still hopes here, but the whole is more ominous, the possibilities are beginning to be squelched. In long shot we see Vittoria walk over toward the water barrel, in front of the matting-covered building being constructed. She checks for her stick of wood--yes, it is still there, the continuities are available, all is not yet lost--but as she looks around, instead of blowing trees, she sees the reinforcing rods emerging from the side of the building (Fig. 9.39). The camera follows and pans as Vittoria walks around and stands by several posts that cut the screen vertically in a visual effect deeply associated with Riccardo earlier in the film but of which we have seen little since (Fig. 9.53). A sulky comes into the frame and the camera pans with it and picks up Piero, who comes over to Vittoria and greets her (Fig. 9.55).

Vittoria is reserved with him, and he is a little apologetic. He tosses a matchbook in the water barrel, and she quickly separates it from her chunk of wood (Fig. 9.57). He tells her he has ordered a new car, and she moves away from him in a little spasm of pain for what she observes of his sensibility. But she is resolute, she knows what is required: she agrees as if making a contract to go to his place, "casa tua," though she procrastinates a bit, stopping to look at a handsome young working-class man who walks past. Piero likewise looks at the nurse with the baby carriage, as the nurse adjusts her stockings as they pass. One feels the emotional integration of the day before has been lost to a degree, that the couple is controlled by this sequence rather than controlling it, is led by events. And a priest passes as they turn to go, reminding us of the rejection of "the beast." It is clear that a new phase is beginning, and it is strongly suggested that it is not a good one.

At Piero's parents' apartment Vittoria is out of place, submissive, and unhappy. The Pan statue supervises the entrance. The apartment is full of pictures, different from Riccardo's, since, though some are sentimental and cheap, others are attractive, but still dominating this life as Riccardo's culture dominated his (and Vittoria with it). Vittoria sits in a hall, as if a servant or a guest of lower social class than the owners. She moves docilely but stiffly when Piero asks her to. Piero seems to have meant more formality, an assertion of greater concern and respect than the totally exploitative taking of a mistress to which we presume he is used, in bringing Vittoria here to his parents' rather than to his own apartment, but the tone of the place is oppressive. Everything seems to make Vittoria cheap, which she is not, and to deprive Piero of the self-assurance that is among his main appeals, leaving only that awkward assertiveness which is what hurts Vittoria most. As Vittoria walks in, a woman appears in the window of a house across the street and moves away at once as if disapprovingly, leaving the window in stark blackness. There is tremendous pressure

towards placement of this relationship between Vittoria and Piero
in contexts that reduce it from the self-generated richness we
had seen begin to underpin it the day before.

Thus Vittoria is pleased when Piero's chocolate box is
empty--it allows a lightening of the mood, a return to something
closer to spontaneity--and she is displeased as it seems to
develop that they almost formally, as if they owed it to each
other, question each other about what they have done when they
were apart. There is no need to know each other to love, Vittoria
says (meaning that such "knowledge" as where one ate dinner is
not germane, intrudes on the emotional reality), perhaps no need
to love at all (meaning that the reality is tenuous and may well
be destroyed by such placement in language). It feels as if
Vittoria is being trapped. And again, to preserve the lightness,
the spontaneity of the developing feeling between them, she pulls
a window between them and kisses the glass dividing them, as he
does, too (Fig. 9.45). It is _referential of_ sexual passion,
it says that she hopes for and promises a personal involvement
with him but is not ready now to have heavy breathing and passion
overwhelm the reservations she feels about the stock exchange,
about the similarity within difference of this dark bourgeois
ambience to Riccardo's more modern but equally dark and oppressive
one, about the quality of inexorability with which it seems that
she is required to be seduced.

But again Piero presses. He comes round the window, kisses
her hard, follows her as she pulls away again, and as he grapples
with her the light dress tears at the shoulder (Fig. 9.47). He
is, of course, mortified--he doesn't _want_ not to know how to
act--and she reassures him as she moves away, through the
apartment, past the etched grasses on the door (Fig. 9.31),
observing his room and its evidence of his obtuse adolescence,
into his parents' room (no doubt having in mind to look for his
mother's sewing basket to tack the dress). She observes the heavy
inevitability of the isolated oval pictures of his parents on
the wall (quite different from the happy picture of her own
peasant parents early in their marriage, before the war and her
father's death, which she looked at in her own mother's
apartment). She looks out the window, seeing the ordinary
reality, the terrible isolation of people in that world she is
asked to join:  nuns walking across the square, a family coming
out of church, a soldier leaning on a wall at a corner. It seems
too inevitable. This oppressive relationship takes her too far
from trees and open fields, from wind and flight, to solidity
and psychic closure. She refuses Piero admission as he asks for
it at the door.

But he comes around by another way, and Vittoria is pleased
at his game of surprising her. He even has better sense this
time, and lets her rhythms keep her at least a little in play.
The pathos and balance of the film is perfect here:  the social
and personal inevitability, everything represented by this

apartment and Vittoria's having come here because Piero has made
it so plain that she must if she is to see him at all, will
destroy this couple. Yet they are brought together by the
affectionate feeling that leads to games and to delight, and
thence to that sexuality that will be captured by this world,
that will reduce the quality of feeling that led to union into
the social expectations and demands Piero will impose as Riccardo
did before. Vittoria's instinctive search for immediacy, for
subtle union with the natural world and the authentic in people,
cannot hold out against what must become of her natural mode of
expressing it. And the point generalizes: we have botched our
world by our anxious dominance of it, so that what should free
us binds, what should join us severs, what should give us identity
makes us disappear.

It is not the fault of the lovemaking itself that this couple
is doomed, but rather the fault of having come to this lovemaking
by the blackmail of Piero's having become unable (at the
suggestion of his whole society) to stop pressing Vittoria as
we have seen him do. The pressure of feeling should lead us to
oneness with a vital world of delight if we could learn to handle
it as Vittoria instinctively does, with a kind of reserve within
which "everything" could come to sing and be alive like the rocks
and sand and sea of Giuliana's fable to Valerio in Red Desert.
Within that vital reserve in turn human relations could spring
out like the ships that brave the seas of this and other worlds
in that same fable. But those ships become plagued freighters,
the rocks become sludge, and biology betrays us into their
keeping. Through the rest of Eclipse, we see Piero and Vittoria
love each other as best they can: but the false grounding gives
them no chance. Having been failed as she was at that
construction site, Vittoria becomes Gloria Perkins herself,
becomes "the beast." Her love with Piero is its own substitute,
and for neither of them is there the better partner to return
to that there was in each of the films that preceded. Hence they
disappear, become other than they were to start, and we recognize
them no longer.

We learn how bad it will get immediately after the seduction,
as Piero badgers Vittoria about not being firm of statement about
her feelings, saying, "I don't know," to his questions in the
scene we have described. She feels caught, wishing for good
reason she didn't love him unless she could love him more. He,
feeling the truth of the remark, how some step in the development
between them has been falsely taken, understands why she says
it, and looks as guiltily hurt as Riccardo. But for the moment
these intuitions of their fate are countered by the vitality that
they bring and that they have achieved, certain though it is that
its context will ultimately destroy it. At Piero's office we
see them playing, having fun getting each other's arms out of
the way as they roll around on the couch, and imitating for each
other the affectations of pairs of lovers they have seen. It

leads Vittoria to a parody of her own seduction, as she acts out
Piero's moves when he seduced her.

She is laughing, as parodists should, at the conventionality,
almost stereotypy, of the actual moves that were dictated by
feeling, and the principal response is delight at the fun.  From
a position of security in the open sexuality they have come to,
Vittoria is laughing at the trauma of getting there.  And there
is no malice in the laughter.  She mimics every move:  she kisses
Piero through a window she pulls between them, and then comes
darting out from behind, grinning diabolically, to grab him and
kiss him (Fig. 9.46).  As he kissed her neck and shoulders while
she anguishedly half resisted and half accepted, so she now gets
him in an armlock and kisses his neck while he squirms and laughs
(Fig. 9.48).  As he pulled her down on the bed and kissed her
slowly, finally clutching the fabric of her torn shoulder over
her breast in his hand as the intensity increased (Fig. 9.49),
so now Vittoria laughing savagely pulls him to the floor and
poises herself over him, pouncing with her hand like a claw (one
remembers the lions on the savannah and notices the animal-print
dress she is wearing) arched over his shirt and grabbing it and
smothering him with kisses (Fig. 9.50).

The doubling of the experience is exactly what ought to prove
the relationship secure.  After natural resistances, the force
that through the green fuse drives the flower, drives the couple
together.  And it would be only healthy to be able to look back
and laugh at the symbols of that reticence so happily overcome
and of the assertiveness necessary to overcome it.  That is, the
doubling would prove it secure if the context were right, if the
flower had a natural air in which to flourish.  But the context
is not right, the grounding of the relationship is not secure,
and the ending of the film is another and far darker doubling,
this time of the elements and sequences where it all went wrong.

The transition to this end is signalled by intrusion of the
world usual to Piero's office.  As in the minute of silence at
the bourse a telephone rang insistently, making Piero twitch
towards it, so as Vittoria grabs Piero's lapel a bell (the
doorbell, it seems) rings and interrupts them.  It is late,
Vittoria says, and they settle their clothing and go toward the
door, with one last spasm of imitative fooling as Piero twines
his fingers with hers as he had done immediately after surprising
her in his parents' room.  Vittoria likes the reference, and bats
his hand away laughingly.  At the door to the back stairs, out
of which Piero had earlier pushed a ruined investor of whom he
required coverage for margins (the reference is insisted on by
similar cuts to long shot later as earlier), Piero and Vittoria
part.  She hugs him, first uncertain and then eagerly smiling
as she decides it is all right between them despite her doubts,
and they agree to see each other, not only every day, but also
this very night, at eight o'clock.  They kiss, but suddenly turn
toward us together, huddling with sad frightened faces, as if

knowing that the promise is illusory, that they haven't enough
in common, not a secure enough relation to the objects, the
society, the business of their lives, to guarantee the
preservation of the kind of happiness they have achieved.
     It is as if the world returns on both of them, then, as we
see the island of security they have built again in the context
that formed their way of building it.  In several intercut
sequences, we see each return to consciousness of the lives and
roles that they genuinely inhabit, and that Piero's insistence
on acting in terms of has guaranteed that they will not
transcend.  He walks back through the office, replacing first
four telephones on their hooks in the outer office and then, as
he walks dreamily past the billowing curtains where he has played
with Vittoria, sitting down at his desk and, more slowly,
replacing one and then another telephone there.  He bends over
his papers for a moment and then, hovering between two worlds,
leans back in his chair, uncertain in the transition between the
kind of life Vittoria has introduced him to, too late, and the
full-scale commitment (so much more unaware of alternatives than
Giovanni or even Sandro) to the kind of life that has ensured
that hers will not avail.
     Her return is to the bleakness his normalcy creates, and
she is less unknowing.  She comes down the stairs in a cold light,
and with a scaffolding visually pressing on her.  Leaning against
a diagonal beam of the scaffolding, she halts a moment, as visibly
shaken as when hanging up the phone on Piero's loud "Pronto."
What can she be thinking save how, despite such momentary riches
as she has just garnered, there is not sufficient wealth in their
relation's ore to make it any more worth mining than the relation
with Riccardo?  As she goes out into the street (down past one
last intrusive beam that presses her visually as the spear had
pressed Marta) it is like a return from fantasy to reality.  As
her mother had been jostled by people in the bourse when her
financial bubble burst, so Vittoria is jostled by people passing
in the street.  She goes to the grating over an entrance like
the one by which Piero had rejected "the beast," and we quickly
see the connection as the camera shoots to her through that
grating with trees beyond her across the street (the first time
we have seen them there).
     It is clear that what we have seen amounts to the denial
of the earlier sequence.  We had hoped that what trees and wind
and nature meant could be absorbed to the characters and become
the grounding for their lives.  But clearly it has worked the
other way.  The absorption has been of Vittoria to the social
sequence demanded by Piero, simply another version of the one
that she fled at the start.  The trees are left behind, as
Vittoria withdraws from them to whatever sad fate is hers, with
Piero or without him.
     The camera tilts up to lose her and to see only the trees
through the grate.  As if to recapitulate the film, there is a
cut to the other side of the grate so that we see the trees
without it, and pan right to pick up Vittoria's face.  As she

had looked up at the flagpoles and down at the poodle, she looks
up sadly at Piero's office and then down at the street, and turns
and walks out of the frame and the film, leaving the trees there
for a moment without her.

That we have lost her and the values she came to stand for
is made abundantly clear in the last sequence, doubling what we
have seen before and advancing the action towards our assurance
that, in fact, Piero and Vittoria are lost to us, and certainly
in some sense to each other as well. The sequence takes place
around the construction site where it all went wrong, and gives
us image after image of that place while time passes, eight
o'clock comes and goes as night falls, and Piero and Vittoria
do not meet each other there as they had promised. Instead, the
familiar images about which we had cared are replaced by others,
different from but reminding us of those we have seen. We see
the shots we cared about with the people we loved withdrawn from
them, and then we see their replacement with other people about
whom we care less. Finally it is a depersonalization of the world
caused by the socially induced failure of that feeling that
strived to come forth but that was finally withdrawn from it,
leaving strangers, the artificial, and suggestions of social and
political collapse.

We see first the nurse the couple passed when leaving that
corner, and then, after a shot of the pipes and boxes Vittoria
had moved behind (Fig. 9.52) we see the corner, Vittoria absent,
and then the water barrel with the matchbook still in it, but
Vittoria's stick no longer visible (Fig. 9.58). The camera tilts
up as it had done before, but Vittoria is no longer next to the
posts as before (Fig. 9.54). The reinforcing rods from the wall
are there, though, and a new shot of a construction of bars
follows a shot of them, as if emphasizing them and showing how
what they stand for overcomes (Fig. 9.40). The sulky comes by
again, but the camera picks up, not Piero, but rather the nurse
walking tranquilly across the sadly empty street (Fig. 9.56).
We see the crosshatches and the center line, but instead of our
couple, a stranger walks briskly across (Fig. 9.44). We see the
important shot of the blowing trees again (though this time a
little darker, more like the trees Vittoria just left), and then
a high shot of the street a little further up from where Vittoria
met Piero by the lake, at which point we had had a very similar
high shot. The camera tilts down to show us the crosshatches
and corner of the construction site: the magic is going from
the scene, we are starting to have a clearer sense of it in its
topography, and as a place like any other.

The good is going out of the scene, in fact. We see the
building in long shot, as we had in the earlier sequence, but
this time Vittoria is missing. Suddenly we see the water barrel
with the water starting to drain from it. We follow the water
down to a gutter and a drain; soon much of the value will not
be there. A woman looks for someone and waits, and an
unfashionably dressed young woman on the corner looks anxiously
for someone. A man gets off a bus reading about how peace is

bad in a newspaper the headline of which concerns atomic war.
Children in the street approach the sprinkler that has been so
important to the couple, but a workman comes over and with
heartbreaking finality turns the sprinkler off.  Its stream
sputters to a halt, and what stood to us for Vittoria's best hope
is gone, though water drips pearly from the trees.

New people, harsher scenes, start to be evident.  In a
succession of three progressively closer shots we see a distant
building, its jagged balconies taking half the screen as did
Vittoria's building when she stood at the window before trees.
The shot is like the earlier one, but colder.  On the roof two
strangers watch jet trails in the sky as Vittoria had watched
them in the windy airfield of Verona with a completely different
feeling for us.  The sequence of scalings then switches the other
direction, and instead of being brought in we are backed off.
We see first in close-up the water barrel continuing to empty,
and in extreme close-up the texture of the concrete over which
the water flows.  It yields to a similar extreme close-up of a
human cheek, as if the textures were the same, as if people were
becoming alien like objects rather than integrating objective
with human value as we had hoped.  From that cheek several shots
take us back:  an eye, a whole face, a full figure shot as the
man turns and leaves the corner, a stern man we have not seen
before.

Our perspective is becoming more fluid as we lose our sense
of recognition of this world, but at the same time feel more and
more that it is an ordinary world, the one we live in, a world
from which the moral charge has been drained like the water from
its barrel.  We see the lamps on the street, a dark-haired, plain,
and harried young woman behind bars; and the artificial lights
come on in that way we have learned to associate with the
undesirable, the loss of the natural.  People get out of busses,
walk in groups down the street.  We look closely:  we think we
recognize a turn of the head here, a swing of leg there.  But
none of them is Vittoria or Piero.  They pass the water barrel
without a glance (it is empty now), and then the traffic is over.
We see the building in darkness with a lonely light over the water
barrel, and we pan right to the street lamps (Fig. 9.35)--and
end with a close-up of one light, radiance in radiance.  We hear
a roar of the music that began the film, as if it now ends the
world.

It is, of course, metaphoric that in the very evening of
the delight in Piero's office, the couple should be lost to each
other.  It would likely take a bit longer (it took years with
Riccardo), but it is so inevitable that it is as if it happens
at once.  What we have called the Antonioni sequence has
occurred.  The feeling of longing for natural vitality has pressed
out into the world, sought its fulfillment elsewhere than in
sexual relations, tried for communion on terms that the man of
the couple could not meet, and finally, after various substitutive

and imposed alternatives, has been reduced to far less than it had hoped to be--so far, in fact, this time that the very energy that was invested in the trilogy with Claudia's young enthusiasm for her boat trip on the magic sea is finally literally lost, as water itself is turned off and drained away. The world finally forms characters like Piero, who cannot adjust to the natural values in things with a sure enough submission to their rhythms to avoid destroying them, and like Vittoria, whose instinctive longings are not proof against the contaminations of what she is offered, what is pressed upon her. There is simply no more holding out. From here we have only, in Red Desert and Blow-Up and Zabriski Point, the sad acceptances of Ugo and Thomas, the impotent attempts at making a difference of Corrado and Mark and David, the helplessness and fantasy of Giuliana and Daria.

Vittoria is lost to us. We see at the end the eclipse of our hopes for preservation of a sense of vitality in life through effort at personal relations. Eclipse is a metaphor of sexual submission as personal and social defeat, a fable of the individual, hence of ourselves and of the social world we make, forced by the very terms of the life we have constructed towards acceptance of just those relationships that will keep us from the fulfillment for which we entered into them. Instead of characters in nature struggling in the dawn, Eclipse (and the trilogy) ends with only a struggling light on the film's location of greatest value, and with the atomiclike radiance of the artificial light that eclipses the natural.

The failure of the relationship between Piero and Vittoria thus amounts to a disappearance of the possibilities of character of which at the end of their film Claudia and Sandro had still a conception, and for which Giovanni and Lidia struggled again. With Piero's and Vittoria's absorption into the kind of dynamics that had destroyed the relation between Vittoria and Riccardo in the beginning, it is as if the last chance to hold out is lost. There is nothing more to be said about trying to blend personal relations and the kind of vitality that Vittoria could feel before, and independent of, her seduction. Vittoria's defeat is the eclipse of character by modern society.

In one sense, of course, the Antonioni vision of this eclipse is sad and disturbing in all its versions, a vision of feeling denied and communion lost. Yet in another sense, the quality, especially of the trilogy, but also of that astonishing body of Antonioni's work from Il Grido through Red Desert, is not exclusively gloomy. Of course, the films are about the loss of value in the world, and its causes in social, political, and technological errors about human nature and people's place in reality. That is what Antonioni saw in the early 1960s as the current plight, and he must, like any artist, tell what he sees. But the attitudes emergent from aesthetic wholes are not, after all, statements about how things are out there in the world in

the same way as are the assertions of expository writing. As
we have argued, the meaning of Antonioni's films, as of any
aesthetic objects, lies in the pattern of the qualities that
emerge from the aesthetic surface (the design and its world),
that embodies and concerns that issue about the nature of things
that the work raises as its ostensible subject or theme—most
precisely, meaning lies in the iconicity of qualities and the
pattern they make up with qualities and patterns of human
experience. Thus a chorus may say, "The moral of our story has
been that we should count no man happy until he is dead"—but
no one should believe the chorus, or carry that point away from
Oedipus the King. There has been more to it than that, having
to do with the way feelings have been invested in the immediate
dynamics of the struggle by those characters the tenuousness of
whose happiness the chorus tries to tell us is the only point.

The extraordinary sense of the value that is squelched,
though it is squelched in the story, is what we carry away from
Antonioni, a kind of exhilaration both at the richness of the
picture offered of emotional/aesthetic value in the context of
what opposes it, and at the delicacy and sureness of the sequence
in which the issue is developed. It is his specific quality of
feeling we will learn if we watch an Antonioni movie correctly—if
we must name it, we have used the Joycean "atonement," and it
will do. We learn what it means to detect, feel, and enter
imaginatively into what lies latent, waiting for us, in people,
situations, and even objects. We learn how things bear an
instruction and a reward for us when we manage to take them
correctly, when we are up to them.

On the strictly positive side of the Antonioni quality, we
learn from every gesture of every character, and indeed from every
succession of images, to entertain the attitude that the most
plausible explanation of virtually all motivations is a generous
wish for union, a breaking down of barriers, an overcoming of
alienations. Antonioni's is a world straining passionately to
the good, and the vividness with which what merely is quivers
with the inner force of its energy towards what ought to be surely
is its dominant quality.

Moreover, that quality is as memorable as it is, exactly
because in the films' fables the good is articulated in the fact
that it is brought to nothing by contamination from social
expectations, impositions of selfishness, overconcern for blinding
assumptions. These contaminations we are also ready to
contemplate, both as plausible aspects of social reality as we
know it, and as metaphoric and iconic of certain hindrances,
resistances, intransigencies that have exactly the place in the
pattern of general human experience that they have in the pattern
of issues developed in these films. What the good is, in the
films, is defined by the fable of its not being achieved, by its
remaining strained after, latent, known in its absence. It is
the attitude that the heroines in the films ought to be able to

feel as characterizing their own dealings with their world, the quality of feeling of which they are capable yet which they cannot sustain.  And because they cannot, what we are left with is the vivid apprehension of the good in tension with the no less vivid apprehension of the plausibility with which a fable can render its not being manifested.  To experience the tension is to have interpreted the films' meaning, and by that very interpretation to have come to appreciate their value.

W.C.

NOTES

1. Roger Shattuck, "How to Rescue Literature," New York Review of Books, April 17, 1980, p. 34.
2. Four Screenplays of Ingmar Bergman (New York:  Simon and Schuster, 1960), p. xvii.
3. Christian Metz, Film Language (New York:  Oxford Univ. Press, 1974), pp. 78-79, 111.
4. Stephen Heath, "Film/Cinetext/Text," Screen, 14, no. 1/2 (1973):  112.
5. For "storehouse," see Ferdinand de Saussure, Course in General Linguistics (New York:  McGraw-Hill, 1959), pp. 13-14; for Peirce's "interpretants," see Paul de Man, "Semiology and Rhetoric," in Textual Strategies, ed. Josué V. Harari (Ithaca:  Cornell Univ. Press, 1979), pp. 127-28; Umberto Eco, A Theory of Semiotics (Bloomington:  Indiana Univ. Press, 1976), pp. 68-72.
6. Metz, Film Language, pp. 78, 63; Metz, Language and Cinema (The Hague:  Mouton, 1974).
7. Monroe C. Beardsley, Aesthetics:  Problems in the Philosophy of Criticism (New York:  Harcourt Brace & World, 1958), pp. 237-38, 117-18, 409-22; the final phrase is cited by Paul de Man, "Semiology and Rhetoric," p. 130.
8. Beardsley, Aesthetics, p. 127.
9. Beardsley, Aesthetics, p. 375.
10. John Berger, Ways of Seeing (London:  BBC and Penguin, 1972), pp. 10-16.
11. André Bazin, What Is Cinema?, vol. 2 (Berkeley:  Univ. of California Press, 1971), pp. 35, 99.
12. Frank B. Ebersole, "Seeing Red in Red Things:  The Question of Common Properties," Things We Know:  Fourteen Essays on Problems of Knowledge (Eugene:  Univ. of Oregon Press, 1967), pp. 3-17.
13. Leonard Bernstein, The Unanswered Question (Cambridge:  Harvard Univ. Press, 1976), pp. 125-54, 179; Beardsley, Aesthetics, p. 337.
14. Roland Barthes, Elements of Semiology (New York:  Hill and Wang, 1967), pp. 41-42; for Marxist analysis, see Eco, Theory of Semiotics, pp. 24-26; for Lacanian analysis,

see Anthony Wilden, System and Structure: Essays in Communication and Exchange (London: Tavistock, 1972), esp. p. 29.

15. Barthes, Elements of Semiology, p. 54.
16. Manuel Alvarado, "Photographs and Narrativity," Screen Education, no. 32/33 (1980): 7-8.
17. Jurij Lotman, Semiotics of Cinema, Michigan Slavic Contributions, no. 5 (Ann Arbor: Department of Slavic Languages and Literature, Univ. of Michigan, 1976), pp. 1, 3.
18. Noam Chomsky, Rules and Representations (New York: Columbia Univ. Press), pp. 229-30.
19. Ben Brewster, "Structuralism in Film Criticism," Screen, 12, no. 1 (1971): 49-58.
20. Beardsley, Aesthetics, p. 378. Perhaps it needs no pointing out--but then again perhaps it does--that if an object has an air of directedness, that fact no more entails our obligation to seek its author, or his intention, than our obligation to find its narrator.
21. Beardsley, Aesthetics, pp. 415-16.
22. Brian Henderson, A Critique of Film Theory (New York: E. P. Dutton, 1980), pp. 160-200; Metz, Language and Cinema, pp. 74-79.
23. Lotman, Semiotics of Cinema, pp. 13, 34.
24. For these developments, see Rosalind Coward and John Ellis, Language and Materialism (London: Routledge and Kegan Paul, 1977).
25. Sherry Turkle, Psychoanalytic Politics (New York: Basic Books, 1978), pp. 49-50, 54.
26. Coward and Ellis, Language and Materialism, p. 9.
27. Louis Althusser, For Marx (London: NLB, 1977), pp. 249, 252.
28. For such analogies, see Barthes, Elements of Semiology, pp. 50-51; for Saussure's as a linguistics of memory, see Noam Chomsky, Language and Responsibility (New York: Pantheon, 1977), pp. 50, 51, 97, 156.
29. Brewster, "Structuralism in Film Criticism," p. 50.
30. Heath, "Film/Cinetext/Text," pp. 122-24; Henderson, Critique of Film Theory, pp. 62-81; Laura Mulvey, "Visual Pleasure and Narrative Cinema," Screen, 16, no. 3 (1975): 6-18.
31. De Man, "Semiology and Rhetoric"; Henderson, Critique of Film Theory, pp. 218-25; "Editorial," Screen, 20, no. 4 (1980): 7.
32. Heath, "Film/Cinetext/Text," pp. 102, 122; Northrop Frye, The Critical Path: An Essay on the Social Context of Literary Criticism (Bloomington: Indiana Univ. Press, 1971), p. 36.
33. Unpublished lecture by Terry Eagleton, "Exploding History," The University of Oregon, spring, 1980; For Bazin, see "La Politique des Auteurs," in The New Wave, ed. Peter Graham (Garden City: Doubleday, 1968), p. 154.

34. Heath, "Film/Cinetext/Text," p. 104; for interpellation of the subject, see Louis Althusser, "Ideology and Ideological State Apparatuses," Lenin and Philosophy (London: NLB, 1971), pp. 121-73.

35. Bazin, What Is Cinema?, vol. 2, p. 98; Beardsley, Aesthetics, p. 529.

36. Among others, Althusser, Lenin and Philosophy, pp. 127-86, 195-219; Turkle, Psychoanalytic Politics, pp. 47-68; Wilden, System and Structure, pp. 483-84; Wilden, "Lacan and the Discourse of the Other," in Jacques Lacan, The Language of the Self (Baltimore:  Johns Hopkins Univ. Press, 1968), pp. 159-311; Mulvey, "Visual Pleasure and Narrative Cinema"; Coward and Ellis, Language and Materialism, pp. 93-121.

37. Roman Jakobson, "Closing Statement:  Linguistics and Poetics," in Style in Language, ed. Thomas A. Sebeok (New York:  The Technology Press of Massachusetts Institute of Technology and John Wiley and Sons, 1960), p. 358.

38. Chomsky, Rules and Representations, pp. 221-39.

39. For the creative aspect of metaphor, see Paul Ricoeur, "Metaphor and the Main Problem of Hermeneutics," in The Philosophy of Paul Ricoeur, ed. Charles E. Reagan and David Stewart (Boston:  Beacon Press, 1978), pp. 134-48.

40. Andrew Sarris, The American Cinema:  Directors and Directions 1929-1968 (New York:  E. P. Dutton, 1968), p. 146.

# C H A P T E R
# 10

## Toward a
## Cartesian Aesthetics

The lights come up at the end of The Most Dangerous Game,
Thierry Kuntzel says, and I wonder, "What did I come to see?
The Most Dangerous Game replies that I came to see." That
is what is left. It is "the fate of 'popular' films: they, too,"
like the story on which Freud based his reflections on the
uncanny, "leave an impression, a few narrative fragments,
sometimes a few images. They are 'silly'; the strange impression
they create--the void contained within the 'loop' described"--is
what can only be filled by "what I go to see (again) with each
new film; my own desire--endlessly repeated--for re-presentation."
It is, we agree, what does happen, for instance, when the lights
come up at the end of Raiders of the Lost Ark, which even
implies an argument that that is how it should be: after raising
and ignoring the doubling of hero and villain, and the need for
comeuppance for a hero who takes the substance of his quest as
mumbo jumbo, the film leaves us seeing "history itself" set aside
in Citizen Kane's cellar. That is what always happens. Destiny
works its magic; its husk, its ark, is rightly set aside; we are
left having seen, as in The Most Dangerous Game, "in the course
of the film itself . . . nothing other than what I had already
seen when I was informed that it was about to begin"--figures
filled the screen and bore us away with them into its space, there
was a rush of jeopardy and assured triumph, a comeuppance for
a traitor, a flood of seeings and hearings which, if anything
so implicational, are quoted in order to mock old notions of
meaningfulness. We saw the world turn into signs and lived among
them.[1]

Daniel Dayan argues that as language to literature, so "the
system of the suture" to film. While the patterns of narrative
exist (patterns of filmic discourse, Metz calls them), they are
known through their enunciation, through image discourse, which
bears us away from reflection on their significance. And, the
Dayan case goes, since language is ideologically determined and
determining, so that whatever is narrated must have all the
implications of the medium that narrates it, therefore the

shot/reverse shots of suture, its sentence-equivalents, mean all
and only what sentences finally mean, i.e., the placement within
ideology of the "subject," the present absence borne away into
the film space. That subject is thus fixated in the "gaze,"
defined by and living out from its Imaginary world.[2]

Mainstream narrative cinema, in short, means only what the
social being of those who think they watch it (but who are as
much watched by as watching, who are, as Lacan says, "in the
picture") determines that it shall mean. All the rest is cover
story and illusion, manifest rebus for the latent significations
of the desire of the Other; criticism of a cinema like this is,
of course, necessarily demystification, exhortation to a writerly
and scientific alternative through theory.

It is the multiform errors in this view that we have tried
to dispel in our "counter-theory." For that the lights go up
and we find only that we came to see is not what happens when
the lights go up on Eclipse or The Searchers, or (to be clear
that value belongs not merely to a valorized cinematic past) on
The Last Metro, or It's Alive, or The Godfather, or The
Long Riders. We may have come to look, but we can also think.
Memory of what is worth remembering is no useless husk to be put
away and forgotten; rather, it can and should inform our lives.
Modern film theory denies a difference between The Most Dangerous
Game and Young Mr. Lincoln. It says audiences come to see,
see they do, and that's all there is to it. "The pretexts of
'artistic' and 'documentary' films (the author's work, great
aesthetic works, important messages) are just so many attempts
made by cinephiles to deny the instinctual roots of their desire
to look," according to Kuntzel. All the more in popular films.
What we should do, then, Metz says, is to think not about the
films that let us look--what can we say but that they let us do
it?--but about what is interesting in the fact that we do it,
the very fact that as adults we use our grown-up skills for such
guilty pleasures. The film for us, Metz says, is like "the
uninterpreted dream, the fantasy, the symptom [, which] are all
symbolic operations. . . . Thus as a beginning it is absolutely
essential to tear the symbolic from its own imaginary and to
return to it as a look." That is, we can and must think about
film viewing and construct its science.[3]

But isn't it plain? Modern film theory is yet another way
of being able to dismiss the movies, to fail to see the trees
for the forest, to say that since Raiders of the Lost Ark fails
the probe of thought, so then must Young Mr. Lincoln, and all
we can or should do is psychoanalyze ourselves for the dynamics
of our pleasure. If we deal with films at all, we should not
hesitate to "force their texts," construct their systems without
regard to weightings, emphases, or implications of qualities
emerging from the manifest designs of their compositions, for
these are illusions of manifest content anyway; even if they were
not they would not be the film's, but rather our own (hence to

do with as we choose, to deconstruct along what lines we will),
since "'Manifest' does not mean that this structure is a given--
the textual system is constructed by the analyst" and "text
and system thus differ from one another as an actual unfolding
from an imputed intelligibility."[4]

But we urge that films have that intelligible system and
that we may observe it, though, of course, we may instead permit
ourselves to be sutured in the gaze and to respond with culturally
determined looking. So we argue against the notion that something
in the nature of social language determines how we shall take
and what we should say about films. We think there is more to
human cognitive processes and what they permit of aesthetic
experience than can be explained with such automatism. And as
to what should be said about aesthetic experience, we think it
is wrong to search for the meaningfulness of the parts of
aesthetic objects in terms of the categories we see those parts
under, what we recognize them as, the "codes" to which they
belong as expressions. Instead we think the terms for the
attribution of significance should be of the compositions, in
all their complexity, that the parts articulated by those
compositions make up--which is not to deny that each part making,
and each part made, may be recognizable as a member of a category
and hence itself connote. After all, the Citizen Kane allusion
at the end of Raiders of the Lost Ark, like the Straight
Shooting allusion at the end of The Searchers, simply gives
us one more thought about the attitude of the whole film's quasi
discourse. The discourse of these images implies much, including
much about movies. But that does not mean that what we get is
a "re-presentation" of what we've had before, though what we
get may use such recognizable representations in giving us what
we have now. A film's giving us what it does and meaning what
it means and being worth thinking about or not depends on all
its qualities of design and implication. Our "primary cinematic
identification" with our looking could not replace the specific
film we saw--it was to see it that we came, and our argument
here is that such seeing properly involves much thinking. Why
should we admit that the worst possible viewing experience
determines what we should say about a film?[5]

Semiology, as we have said, has a strong case (Jurij Lotman
to our mind makes it best, and his "structural semiotics" of
"secondary modelling systems" is a heuristic for Beardsleyan
analysis) for a sophisticated view of the connotative force of
cinema's own reality as cinema--the relation of images to each
other and to other images, the relations of stories and story
parts to each other and to what other stories they might be,
including those we expect of them themselves. Yet the virtues
of this view are entirely congruent with that version of classical
aesthetics we have urged, namely an objectivist, realist,
instrumentalist, nonsemiological, antiintentionalist, part/whole
aesthetic based on arguments for the validity of concepts of

aesthetic experience, emergent human regional qualities, and the inexhaustibility of metaphor conceived as concept rather than as fact of language alone.

But on the other hand there are consequences that are not so benign of the "theoretical" side of semiology that derives conclusions of theory and practice from presumptions like Dayan's and stemming from the same arguments. We have tried to suggest as a grounding common to our own New Critical practice and the analysis of singular textual systems of Lotman and of Metz (though not to the theory with which Metz supplements and modifies his analysis), a "Cartesian aesthetics," which is neither impressionistic nor semiological, but rather symbolic in a sense following Dan Sperber, theoretical but not scientistic, grounded in a psychology to which psychologists themselves might assent. A central proposition of a Cartesian aesthetics might be that aesthetic value is to the philosophy of art as grammaticality is to the philosophy of language. Both aesthetic value and grammaticality are terms for capacities in things and both are investigated in the same way. Linguistics investigates the intuition of grammaticality and postulates structures to model it, and aesthetics investigates aesthetic experience and postulates the structures that model it.

What is the theoretical side of this aesthetics, and how is it grounded in what psychology? Something must be said about these questions, because we have insisted on the importance of arguments about language (a subject which does have a theory, or at least some well-developed parts of one) in our dealing with film (a subject which manifestly does not). Our claim has been that film meaning is a function of aesthetic experience, since meaning is a regional quality of the whole film and since aesthetic experience is the "isolated" experiencing of exactly such qualities in objects like films considered as whole objects that contain their own connotations. What is the relation between "theory" and a claim like that? Lacking a specific deductive theory like transformational-generative grammar, what psychological "theory" can support our case?

We must first think about theories. We can say that we have a theory about something and mean that we have some notions concerning the reasons it is the way it is. Or we can have a theory of something and mean that we can offer a set of primitive terms, axioms, and postulates that permit us to construct statements about the phenomena we would like to account for, which statements are in fact the accountings possible under the theory. Such accountings are explanations of what is modelled by the theory in its primitive terms under the "explanatory principles" provided by the entire theory, the relations among terms and axioms and postulates.[6]

Of course when one sets the sort of standard for "theory" implied by the second sort of usage here it is obvious that no film theory is a serious candidate for meeting it. In this, film theory is no different from sociological theory or literary theory. Chomsky points out that, like sociology, "literary criticism also has things to say, but it does not have explanatory principles. Of course ever since the ancient Greeks people have been trying to find general principles on which to base literary criticism, but . . . I'm under the impression that no one has yet succeeded in establishing such principles."[7]

But it is not such principles that film theory has sought. If we had them they would generate descriptions of a set of films with the sort of precision with which generative grammar describes a set of sentences in a language, and would be themselves describable formally in such a way that all and only the set of such objects as those that are defined by its terms would be described using them. Structuralist theories merely report on and elaborate regularities among patternings of surface data. But patterns and regularities are only interesting if the rules derived from them predict the distinction between well-formed and ill-formed formulas within a system. Even the most significant structuralist theories fail to do this. As Philip W. Davis concludes: "Like Saussure's theory, Hjelmslev's ends by characterizing objects we would want to call languages but also some we would not." Accounting for the objects in which patterns can be discerned by explicit sets of rules for generating what are in relevant aspects their models, is and always has been completely beyond structuralism and all its derivatives.[8]

But film theory, when not confusing itself with methodologies pretending to be theories, has consisted of theories in the other looser sense, theories about something rather than a theory of something. Film theorists have thought they were theorizing when they were providing (to quote Chomsky's recognition of what sociology does offer though it does not offer theory) "observations, intuitions, impressions, some valid generalizations perhaps."[9] They have provided these especially when drawing inferences about film from claims about matters (mostly genetic) bearing on films in some more or less direct way: ideology, psychoanalysis, some notion of reality under which film can seem to make more sense, be carved off from other things according to the premises derived from the observations, intuitions, impressions, and valid or invalid generalizations belonging to the speculations of the prior field. In "The Imaginary Signifier," Metz, for instance, seeks to find cinematic specificity exactly where the film viewing experience can be described in terms of psychoanalytic process. The experience of the viewer of at least the mainstream narrative Hollywood film is to be forced along the suturing lead of the identifications the film provides, so that it is by imaginative (and Imaginary) sharing of the objects of the fable good and bad that a Hollywood film is understood in the only proper way. What is specific to mainstream cinema is exactly this capture of the viewer's gaze in regressive object relations.

There is what amounts to critical consensus on this view.
We have seen it in the important theoretical readings of films
such as the Cahiers Editors' "Young Mr. Lincoln," Laura
Mulvey's work on filmic pleasure, and Thierry Kuntzel's on The
Most Dangerous Game. Pure theorists--Stephen Heath, Brian
Henderson--add their arguments to the reader/theorists' for a
distinction between mainstream and avant-garde cinema on the basis
of the picture. And it is presumed by less theory-minded workers
in the field as well. For instance, the avant-garde filmmaker
Scott Bartlett presumes it in discussing the difference between
mainstream and avant-garde films:

> Hollywood is always going to make a film with characters
> with whom the audience is meant to identify, make that leap
> and then move around within the fairy tale, while an enormous
> percentage of avant-garde films are direct experiences.
> Abstract or otherwise, they present a set of images on the
> screen which are transmitted directly to you, the viewer.
> The communication is not between two characters within the
> film but between the filmmaker and the film viewer.[10]

It amounts to an orthodoxy, then--Hollywood films differ
from other what Kuntzel calls "orders" in that audiences respond
to them differently, taking them for object relations and
Imaginary identifications and not for thought. And we know this
because psychoanalytic theory tells us how we are set in place
as observers of things like films by ideology and the logic of
the gaze.

To argue that a generalization from psychoanalysis has some
bearing on aesthetic experience in general and the film experience
in particular is not really to propose a theory. But it is
certainly to suggest a picture of how we should imagine films
to work. And that is fair enough. The rules for pictures are
different. Their duty is not to generate models of their objects
that will describe all of and only those objects, but to be
congruent with what else is known or understood as the most
plausible guess about those aspects of reality that have bearing
on them. If there isn't yet a general psychology in which a true
theory of aesthetic experience can be required to ground itself,
in the way that linguistics can be required to ground itself in
fundamentals of mathematics, still there is no excuse not to
require that claims made about film be in line with psychology,
which obviously has a bearing on it.[11] Our duty is to make
sure of "general consistency," in Louis Breger's phrase, within
our own picture of our own field, with what is most plausibly
suggested by the best available picture of the fields that impinge
on our own--especially those whose arguments we use to support
our own.[12]

We come then to the substance of our objection to "film
theory" as a current orthodoxy. Its picture of film, whether
process or system, enunciation or enouncement, at every point

appeals to the composition or implication of the Saussurian
picture of language. And that picture is not generally consistent
with what is now known about language--for instance, about the
kind of knowledge that native speakers have and for which
linguistic theory may be called to account--so arguments built
on Saussure are not consistent with it either.

Chomsky describes the limitations of the Saussurian picture
as deriving from inadequate "models of competence." Chomsky's
most deeply weighted examples are always of evidence for the
knowledge of language people have that cannot be accounted for
by what he sometimes calls "shallow" explanations. He argues
that much explanation requires postulating "knowledge without
grounds," and suggests that "a central part of what we call
'learning' is actually better understood as the growth of
cognitive structures along an internally directed course." It
is absolutely clear that no Saussurian system could possibly
account for the kinds of knowledge people have of language. All
arguments about mental function must begin from that fact.[13]

Moreover, Saussure's picture of language acquisition is
consistent with Freud's picture of memory acquisition (and
probably, though less surely, with Freud's picture of language
acquisition), so that Lacan is justified in arguing that Freud's
unconscious is structured as a Saussurian language. But what
we know of how language is actually structured, along with what
that implies about the endowment of creatures that can learn
language as human beings do, casts the gravest possible doubt
on those arguments of Freud's and Lacan's that make use of the
picture of Saussurian language. The arguments that are most
crucial, and that are especially undercut, are for a picture of
a primitive state of the human infant in which, before a data-
processing procedure has associated words and images of experience
and stored them along associative routes in memory in consequence
of repression, there is only an experience of lack, of a gap to
be filled with re-creation of a wished-for oceanic identity
between self and object, a primitive plenitude to which
structureless state it is the goal of all human symbolizations
(including those of the Imaginary) and desires to return.[14]

Suppose that is wrong. Suppose there is not, lurking beyond
each and every one of our memories, a need to create an image
of recollection of what Norman N. Holland calls the primal "bath
of bliss," an image appropriate to the lacks articulated by that
memory.[15] We think it is wrong, though our objection is in
no sense to the notion of regression, or to the idea that much
old business clings to and modifies our thoughts in the
unconscious. Our objection is to the notion that every memory
and thought is to be conceived as mobilizing and explained by
stand-ins for the primitive lack. The notion seems entirely
antithetical to Freud's view of ego processes (including
unconscious ones) like language, and is patently antithetical
to what Chomsky has shown of language, i.e., that it is not so
conceivable, but rather in large measure innate.

If the Lacanian picture of development is wrong, then clearly
as profound a set of changes would need to be made in our picture
of the relation between our cognizing present and our influencing
past as the set that derives (to take another example with
profound implications for modern film theory) from the recent
implication of empirical psychoanalytic research that the cause
of passing through the Oedipus complex is not castration anxiety,
but rather the recognition of the father's desire to be nurturing
and cooperative.[16] If the former set, where then the Symbolic
as alienation from a dream of primitive plenitude and the
Imaginary ego's action in it as a struggling along a chain of
signifiers in search of a "lost object"? (To be explicit, out
of court is where.  The human processing of symbols, in at least
one major aspect of its functioning, language, is not such a
struggle but is rather the largely unconscious operation of an
innately specified device based not on difference but on
biological structure ensuring its growth as surely as biological
structure ensures we'll all grow kidneys to use.  If there is
even one such "Symbolic" system, then the whole structure deriving
from a psychology based on the tabula rasa and the processing
of difference collapses.  And it seems evident that there are
many more than one.)  And if the latter set, where then the
warrant for notions of the patriarchal unconscious and that
fundamental distinction between male and female thinking, so dear
to Freud with his notions of woman as the less moral man?  Also
out of court, surely.

If these and other changes are required in the Saussurian/
Lacanian/Althusserian picture because of intuitions and valid
generalizations (if not theories) with which our picture of human
nature ought to be generally consistent, then it is easy to see
how a different status for the notion of aesthetic experience
not characterized by emphasis on difference, absence, repression,
castration, alienation, and lack might be implied.  The
intellectual's proper effort, in that case, would not be the
deconstruction of proposals that are themselves paperings-over
of the lacks, in order to reveal their derivation along the chain
of signifiers from alienations of Symbolic and then in turn
Imaginary from primal Need.  We have tried to suggest something
of what that effort ought to be with regard to film.

In general, it is clear that the picture of human nature
that modern discoveries suggest must include emphasis on the
biologically innate structure of people's approach to the world
and hence on the copresence, in an adult's cognizing mind, of
the results of his or her developmental history and the inherited
autonomous structures making that history possible.  But as
Richard Wollheim points out, the Lacanian tradition insists on
the entire separation of the mental from the biological, so not
only is there no place even for those instincts that Freud
conceived of as being at the root of experience, but also there
is no place for any notion of innate structuring of the human
animal's cognitive processes.  For Lacan, unconscious knowledge

is entirely the result of experience, since (as Wollheim interprets him) "everything that is in the unconscious has to find its way there; it must first get symbolized, and only then is it ripe for repression."[17]

This view is virtually an article of faith with Lacan and all structuralists. Lacan's "drives" are, as mental, in effect drives towards meaning for the individual; they drive towards satisfaction of Need for a particular mental representation, either that of the filled gap or its derivatives, e.g., the organ defined, the plenitude of the other, the integrity of the subject. See, for instance, this from Stephen Heath, the most concise summary of Lacan I know:

> Language is the condition of the unconscious, which latter is a concept formed on the trace of what operates to constitute the subject. Caused in language, which is division and representation, the subject is taken up as such in an interminable movement of the signifier, the process of the symbolic, and in a structure of desire, the implication of the subject's experience of division, of lack, in language. Hence the importance of language for psychoanalysis as the site of its object, unconscious desire; to grasp language as the condition of the unconscious is to insist on desire in language and to make the subject the term of a constant construction and representation, outside of the expression of any unity, biological included.[18]

If words have meaning, these imply that the Lacanian position they summarize is (yet another) desexualization of Freud--Freud is not, in this view, about libido, he is about society and the ideology of its language. That is not how Freud sees it.

But this view is exactly that dependence on Chomsky's "shallow explanation" of a simple data-processing device (the one that can tell difference), upon which Chomsky has always urged that it was the fundamental inadequacy of structuralism to depend. Such a device is not a "schema," even in Ulric Neisser's sense of the term, and it cannot provide in principle an accounting for the kind of knowledge human beings have of, for instance, the rich details of language or of many other objects of representation by mental organs (e.g., binocular vision).[19]

Indeed, despite Neisser's qualms about accepting a fully Chomskian view of innateness, he acknowledges some "specificity of the initial schemata (i.e., the degree to which human beings are innately endowed . . . )" and that activities like speech perception and, indeed, all human activities of gaining knowledge of the world "require some initial schema to get them under way; the perceptual cycle must occur before it can develop."[20] In fact, his argument at every stage requires presumption of an often very richly detailed initial structuring of the schemata with

which, he surely rightly argues (like F. C. Bartlett, and like
Miller, Galanter, and Pribram), the perceptual cycle samples the
world for information used to modify the schemata and hence act
as guide for continuing action--action attended, in certain of
its aspects and phases, by that quality it has of being
conscious. This cycle involves the direction, by complexly
structured schemata, of explorations of the information offered
to perception:

> My perception will always be guided by some general cognitive
> map as well as by a specific perceptual schema. . . .
> Ordinary perception relies heavily on the mutual support
> of these different levels of interaction with the
> environment. So does behavior, for that matter. Actions
> are hierarchically embedded in more extensive actions and
> are motivated by anticipated consequences at various levels
> of schematic organization.[21]

We have no idea how richly detailed our cognitive and
emotional schemata innately are, though we can expect that it
will turn out that they are more detailed than we are used to
thinking. But even lacking the theories we may perhaps someday
achieve, by reserving a place in our picture for variable innate
structures for our schemata we can make plausible a picture of
human mental functioning (including watching films) that, beyond
the question of the initial state of the cycles of action,
perception, and cognition, is very close to Neisser's. This
picture will be entirely compatible with those we infer from
Beardsley, Chomsky, and Dan Sperber, but fundamentally
inconsistent with the pictures of Saussure, Lacan, and Screen.
Generally speaking, our picture is of schemata governing
and constituting our approach to the world, and governed in turn
by a system of interconnections among their separate parts and
plans. This integrating system we can call (following Neisser's
earlier use) an "executive," and it is a place therefore as much
for our subjectivity as for autonomous functions like circulation
of the blood. Our picture is of ourselves as evolved and
developed, engaging a world with which we have a multitude of
plans for coping. Governed by those plans, we explore the world,
and we modify plans at every level and at every instant with the
results of the explorations. Some aspects of the plans involve
following rules, and some involve changing them in light of the
changing situation with which it is the purpose of the plans (a
purpose established, as Jacques Monod has so decisively shown,
not by dialectic, but rather by chance and necessity) to
cope.[22]
Clearly, as Dan Sperber has shown, not everything in our
cognitive plans is "semiotic," a matter of mobilizing meanings
that are the matchings of images of expression and content in
the mind of the ideology-established subject. A semiotic system,
"independently of all external input, . . . generates the
sentences of the language it describes" by a grammar. "All

sentences, the whole language, are contained in its grammar,"
which is "an apparatus that enumerates (in the mathematical sense
of the term) the sentences of a language.  In this respect, a
grammar differs from other mental apparatuses in which the set
of parts that constitutes them cannot be enumerated."  "No grammar
. . . generates by itself the set of myths, any more than the
mechanism of visual perception generates by itself the set of
possible perceptions," because "no one could conceive of making
a grammar out of possible visual stimuli; these stimuli are
generally limited by input conditions (such as wavelength and
intensity) and cannot be enumerated."  But "under certain
conditions, every object of thought can elicit a symbolic
evocation; thus the set of symbolic phenomena is not enumerable
and can be defined only by input conditions.  Consequently, the
mental apparatus that underlies symbolic activity is of a
completely different type from that which underlies linguistic
activity."[23]

Thus, much mental action is not a matter of achieving
recognition, but of creation (in the sense that language use is
creative) of representations of reality dependent on its nature
and what we make of it, and not on a finite set of established
meanings.  Rather than one of a culturally defined relation
between signs and meanings manifesting itself on the site of the
subject, then (as in the general picture of semiology), our
picture of the film interaction is a relation between observer
and observed in which the whole person--grown, evolved, developed,
full of old business in the unconscious yet also of capacity to
use and integrate autonomous ego functions like language,
perception, judgment--creates, from what the film implies in all
its relations and emergences, a representation of the information
it carries and a plan to act on it (for fantasy gratification,
contemplation, gathering of evidence, whatever).

Aesthetic experience should thus be conceived as an
experience that a person can choose to have or not, by choosing
what schemata to use in extracting from the objects of their
exploration the information the objects contain.  By rejecting
the idea that our responses to film are those of what Metz in
"The Imaginary Signifier" calls a "deluded ego," and hence that
they must be seen as involuntary, conditioned, necessary,
"determined" responses, we enable ourselves to urge that informed
experience appropriate to its objects, but not determined by them,
is possible.[24]  And this picture enables us to insist, with
Beardsley, on the study of aesthetics as a study of what people
ought to say about art objects if they choose to attend to them
as having the capacity to induce aesthetic experience, rather
than a study of what they must say about that experience on
the grounds that it is determined to be experience of a particular
sort by their fixation in the gaze.  We are insisting that film
study should not be of how people respond to films, but rather
of what ought to be said about films.

But we need to make aesthetic experience, if it is not a
delusion of an alienated subject, congruent with ordinary

experience and a choosable version of it. The first thing is
to establish that there is anything like information in objects
like films, which are clearly in some sense metaphorical, having
as much the status of discourses (or quasi discourses) about the
world as of objects within it. But there is nothing surprising
about the embedding of perception of "irrational" objects in the
general cognitive psychology. Sperber, as an anthropologist,
takes "as symbolic all activity where the means put into play
seem to me to be clearly disproportionate to the explicit or
implicit end, whether this end be knowledge, communication, or
production. . . . In short, the criterion I use in the field is
in fact one of irrationality." In effect, symbolism is a
mechanism for "rethinking" "defective conceptual representations
that are submitted to it" like the self-controverting inputs of
metaphor. In fact, "those conceptual representations that have
failed to be regularly constructed and evaluated constitute the
input to the symbolic mechanism. In other words, the symbolic
mechanism has as its input the defective output of the conceptual
mechanism."[25]

    We "pick up" (as James J. Gibson says) information that the
world provides about what is true of things. That is, before
they are evaluated by the conceptual and symbolic mechanisms,
perceptual schemata are mobilized. Neisser reports with approval
Gibson's view that "the observer perceives simply by 'picking
up'" "the complex structural properties of the optic array,"
for instance. "This structure specifies those objects; the
information about them is in the light." "The organism is not
thought of as buffeted about by stimuli, but rather as attuned
to properties of its environment that are objectively present,
accurately specified, and veridically perceived." Neisser's work
adds to rather than contradicts Gibson's by insisting on
postulation of "cognitive structures . . . that prepare the
perceiver to accept certain kinds of information rather than
others and thus control the activity of looking," just as
Sperber's adds to it by enriching our understanding of one of
the schemata, the symbolic mechanism as a set of plans, that comes
into play when the contents of cognition are of a certain
sort.[26]

    What we do with the information that the world provides is
to try to square it with the formulations of our "encyclopaedia"
of "knowledge about the world." The contents of this
encyclopedia, says Sperber, "may be expressed in the form of a
set of synthetic propositions" that are "true or false according
to the state of the world" and concerning which "no semantic rule
determines their truth-value."[27] But of course much of what
is true about things, in terms of the statements we might make
to express it, is not "articulated to" statements about
encyclopedic knowledge "as are the latter among themselves."
Sperber goes on:

    Any synthetic statement implies and contradicts others.
    Our knowledge about the world is formed by organizing

statements according to these relationships, by accepting
a statement only with its implications--at least the most
evident ones--and similarly, by avoiding contradictions.
Experience shows that encyclopaedic knowledge is not immune
to incoherences and contradictions, but all practical life
is based on a continuous effort to avoid or correct them.
[But] Symbolic statements are not articulated in the same
way, and similar efforts are not made with them. Not that
they are incoherent among themselves, but their coherence
is of another variety, and they co-exist without difficulty
with encyclopaedic statements that contradict them, either
directly or by implication.[28]

Much of what we take to be true of things, then, seems not
quite to fit the network of all else that is true: a smell
reminds us of . . . what?; my friend seems to mean something,
but not what he says; leopards are Christians and observe the
fast days of the Ethiopian Orthodox Church, but they are likely
to eat your sheep on Wednesdays and Fridays, which are fast
days.[29] Information like this, Sperber says, we have to put
"in quotes," and we use the plan to "focalize" our exploratory
plans on the ways it doesn't fit in order to "evoke" accounts
of what doesn't fit that will have a certain truth to them. The
"evocational fields" that have this certain truth to them are
parts of other plans than those that dictate the compilation and
squaring of the statements in the encyclopedia. These are plans
for coping with a world not all of which, in fact, makes the sort
of sense it makes to see, to call again on Bazin's wonderful
image, that a rock in the stream may be a stepping stone to the
other side.[30]
The rock in the stream is more like a landmark than a sign
of a crossing--and that is to say that it is a symbol. As Sperber
says, "A landmark is not a sign but a clue which serves
cognitively to organize our experience of space." In general,
"Symbols are not signs. They are not paired with their
interpretations in a code structure. Their interpretations are
not meanings." "Symbolism conceived in this way is not a means
of encoding information, but a means of organizing it. A symbolic
opposition must not be replaced by an interpretation, but placed
in an organization of which it constitutes a crucial element,"
and "each symbolic element suggests some interpretations not of
itself, but of the set in which it finds its place"--it suggests
it by means of the innate symbolic mechanism.[31]
When we pick up information under a plan, and the information
doesn't fit our day to day cognitive map, and yet also doesn't
seem to be veridical like the leopard's obedience to the rule
of Wednesday fasting, then we may apply to that information our
aesthetic schema; we can evoke what, if we fed it back into our
encyclopedia as veridical, would be the sort of symbolic
knowledge that we don't articulate to the other propositions of
the encyclopedia, but rather carry as separate (though veridical,

not metaphorical) understandings of the world. Much of the time
we do not feed aesthetic knowledge back into the encyclopedia
as symbolic knowledge, though of course we may. When we keep
it "in quotes," for contemplation, isolated and at Bullough's
"aesthetic distance" from our ordinary concerns and our plan to
cope with them, it is the substance of what we describe as
"aesthetic experience," which is thus simply a name for the
consciousness we have of attending to our exploratory behavior
when we don't mean to use its results to guide action other than
the action of continuing to explore it.

        A representation of the aesthetic object thus comes to be
in our encyclopedia in quotes, and we work out how it is valid
and suggestive in the same way we do a figure like "a rolling
stone gathers no moss." We use both the commentary that is
entered with it from the culture (its connotations, including
the ways we learned to do criticism of objects like that) and
that which comes from our experience, and we let ourselves be
open to the object's own implications, its own capacity for
application to the world it helps to order.[32] Aesthetic
experience is thus virtually perception of the object—in a usage
extended only a little from Susanne Langer we might call it
"virtual perception"—though on such a deep level as to include
many aspects of motivation as well. It is perception of which
we have urged that it is appropriate to interpret the meaning,
in a sense Sperber would accept. Sperber's case provides the
mechanism for understanding individual differences in the
recognition of qualities, without obscuring either the cultural
grounding of the qualities or the sense that they nonetheless
are rooted in something deeper than culture, something permitting
the intelligibility of such patterns as those we have proposed
in our specific theory of the shape of sequences (and
implications) of issues and attitudes centering on good and
hindrance, drawback and hedge.

        Of course this virtual perception is "deeper" than the
perception that we use for guiding locomotive exploration, for
all the reasons that Norman Holland urges for saying that we
"regress" to the state where the boundaries of self and object
are blurred.[33] It is consistent with our picture to assent
to that, and to think of the connotations of the object at which
we are looking as including all of its applicabilities to
primitive and internal concerns as well as to those social and
external ones that are the semiotics of social convention.
Aesthetic experience, we agree, is depth experience, whether it
is experience of structure and design or of the representational
worlds of works. The human qualities of perceived objects,
whether we are using them for aesthetic experience or observing
them while following other plans, are simply the applicabilities,
concerning the information picked up from the object, to the
schemata for aesthetic experience that are governing our
introjection of the object, our regression to a position of object
relations with it, our isolation (from the Symbolic, in Lacan's

terms), our aesthetic distance from contingency when in touch
with it. The deeper these schemata are, of course, the more
generally derived they are from human experience, and thus the
less culturally specific, the more "universal," as it is sometimes
forgotten that Freud pointed out. Hence aesthetic experience
can be, as Holland (no objectivist) and Beardsley (objectivist,
indeed) would agree, consoling and enriching exactly as it enables
us to feel more in touch with the world of oneness we have at
any ordinary moment lost simply because, in any ordinary moment,
we concentrate on making something of that world by carving its
parts off for our use.[34]

But again, this assent to a picture of aesthetic experience
as putting us in touch with a world that is prior to "difference"
must not be assent to a picture that is out of phase with what
is actually known of such a world. It is not, Freud implies and
Holland states, a world of unity of self and object, or a world
prior to acquisition of cognitive structures. We are born with
such structures, with the capacity for object recognition and
probably even with "some degree of what used to be called empathy,
the automatic reaction to another person's physical state, [which]
is built into our perceptions" so that "we see the tenseness of
the throwing arm rather than infer it," as Gombrich argues.[35]
We have a rich cognitive endowment, though how rich we do not
know in any detail except for language. And as we watch a film,
we do so not with our childish selves, but rather with our adult
selves evoking many of the connotations we established in
childhood as well as many others—so the introjected film is one
we rightly consider from mature viewpoints too, viewpoints from
which issues of morality and verisimilitude, of elaboration and
subtlety of temporal and spatial design, for instance, become
more richly articulated by their unusual linkage with more archaic
patterns of concern.

Hence our best picture of the psychic state in which the
work of art is introjected as a subsystem of our egos is not the
portrait of a place where all is fantasied to be one, but of a
place where, in the condition of basic trust that Erik Erikson
describes as the proper skill of the infant in the oral stage,
things may seem (and may seem, since we have cognitive
structures under which they can seem) to be delightfully
themselves—vivid, intricately related to what else our schemata
for detailing the cognitive map tell us we will find by looking
and by our interlockings of encyclopedic and symbolic
knowledge.[36] What we observe from here, from this "place,"
must be those concepts that are metaphors in the broadest sense,
described (through their applicability to other plans) in the
other terms they evoke with which, as we contemplate them, we
can handle them for maximum pleasure of the particular isolated,
distanced, kind that is aesthetic experience.

It will not have escaped the semiologically minded reader
that our picture of the relations within the aesthetic object
of its perceptual design and the connotations that link its

qualities is like Umberto Eco's picture of the relations among signs and interpretants in A Theory of Semiotics, which in turn is like Metz's treatment of textual systems in Language and Cinema.  But with one difference:  locked into a conception of signification, by which there must be a signifier expressing in some sense a signified, the relations between signs and interpretants are those of what is sometimes called a "chain of signification."  As Eco says, "I shall assume that all the denotations of a sign-vehicle are undoubtedly its interpretants, that a connotation is the interpretant of an underlying denotation, and that a further connotation is the interpretant of the one underlying it."  But if it is not a matter of signification at all, but rather of evocation of what Sperber calls a "new conceptual representation" that finds the certain truth to it of a defective conceptual representation, then nothing underlies or precedes anything else and we have not semiosis, not communication nor messages, but rather objects with qualities, the objects of Beardsley's aesthetics.  Semiology errs in its oversimple picture of mental functioning, its premature assumption of automatism, and its unjustifiable reliance on Saussurian notions of the social storehouse of meanings as exhausting the explananda of complex cultural artifacts.  Otherwise, the first semiology applied to film is a useful organization of the factors bearing on cinematic structure.[37]

The things we observe from the place of aesthetic experience, then, may seem to be 1) complete in themselves, thus crisp with the Beardsleyan unity, 2) linking to and commonly patterned with other attendable schemata and thus intricate with Beardsleyan complexity, 3) analogous with a multitude of objects useful for various plans of perception and action, thus suffused with the applicabilities to those plans that are their human qualities. Aesthetic experience is the deep experience Holland says, but at all levels it amounts to that exploration of relations and attendabilities that we have called contemplatability when considering the capacities of its objects.  Some of that contemplatability may derive from specific, perhaps innate, plans for seeing objects exactly that way--namely, in depth, isolated, for the sake of metaphoric resonance (like all symbolism) that is nonetheless especially handled always in quotes, i.e., held out, simply entertained through the capacity of the organism to "turn round upon its own schemata and to construct them afresh."[38]

Exercising this particular aspect of the human skill is attaining aesthetic experience, which is real, yet different from other experience, but generally consistent with general cognitive psychology, and characterized by exactly those attributes to which we come with Beardsley from the direction of philosophy, attributes of primary responsiveness to unity, complexity, and intensity of human qualities.

From the point of view of psychological theory (in the looser sense), we have returned to the main points we have made all

along, most importantly to the ideas of the reality of the
aesthetic object and of the aesthetic experience that it is its
special capacity to induce. Fantasies and defenses belonging
to that object as introjected are, we have seen, only in part
socially determined, and though they are among the connotations
that we ought to count as belonging to the work, they are not
what we ought primarily to concentrate on in analyzing it. It
is, after all, as Holland says, "within a rind of our ordinary
selves" that the inner connotative core of the artwork functions
like a dream of our own, a laying down of the gaze
(dompte-regard) of the Other. And those ordinary selves can
tell, about artworks, not only the resonance of their
connotations, but also the qualities of their designs, their
implications, values, dramatic and narrative structures, world
views and in general fusions of all parts into compositions from
which emerge qualities of all sorts.[39]

There is no reason, given the general psychology we have
suggested, to think of these qualities as having that relation
to the inner connotative core that Freud shows stands between
a manifest dream content and its latent dream thoughts, namely
the relation of the product of distortion vis-à-vis the true
meaning it distorts. There is no reason to think we observe the
film as if in an Imaginary dream from which we wake and wonder
where we were and are. Rather, we see it in an especially
cognizant kind of waking--that is, when we are seeing it as it
can be seen, for we have the option, after all, to see it
incorrectly. To see it correctly is to be in a condition more
like the scientist's imaginative identification with his object
than the baby's.[40] It is the qualities that emerge from whole
compositions, and not the relevancy of Imaginary objects to
connotation systems (or to the ideologies that determine them),
which ought to be the objects of our multilayered contemplation.
We have urged that social being does not determine such
consciousness in any very simple way.

Perhaps our argument comes down to these two points, which
seem to us the most important to reassert in the current climate
of film criticism. The first point is that, in fact, what ought
to be most emphasized about films is the polysemy of their
coding systems, the inexhaustibility of their metaphoric
emergences, exactly as Barthes, Metz, Cahiers, and Henderson
urge, but not because "the textual system" that reveals such
polysemy "is constructed by the analyst." Rather, it is in
the film, and contemplated by the viewer whose presentation of
the art object is in fact a properly observant one--to alter
Beardsley's words only a little, "to understand a film is simply
to see it and hear it in the fullest sense, to organize its sights
and sounds into wholes, to grasp its filmic and image discourses
as textural and structural patterns, to perceive its kinetic
qualities and, finally, the subtle and pervasive human qualities
that depend on all the rest."[41]

And the second point follows from this. It is that since

there is no imprisonment in or determination by an Imaginary signifier for any film viewer, there is the chance to do the best he or she can do with the whole psyche in observing and contemplating what is there in the film. It follows that there are no films that especially permit this more than others by a cinematic specificity of one sort or another. It is simply not the case that in avant-garde as opposed to mainstream films, "The communication is not between two characters within the film but between the filmmaker and the film viewer," because there is no sense in which any such identification with communicating characters or with the "gaze" created in human socialization is demanded of any film viewer at all. Film viewers may see films badly, and no doubt many do. But what will distinguish films from each other is not their insistence through a generic style on a scientific way of reading them, as opposed to an ideological submission, but rather simply how well they repay in their individual ways and to their individual degrees the attention that it is a modern presumption to permit only to films by Godard. Godard's films and Antonioni's are fine, and Straub's and Huillet's, and Rocha's too, to name some other favorites whose conventions are not those of mainstream cinema. But also Ford's and Hitchcock's, Ray's and Borzage's. It is an empirical question, then, and a good one: What repays your attention? The range of the answer is what we've tried to suggest and defend in this book.

W.C.


NOTES
1. Thierry Kuntzel, "The Film-Work, 2," Camera Obscura, no. 5 (1980): 63.
2. For the concepts of "gaze" (or "look," "regard," or [French] "regard") and "suture," see Daniel Dayan, "The Tutor-Code of Classical Cinema," in Movies and Methods, ed. Bill Nichols (Berkeley: Univ. of California Press, 1976), pp. 438-51; for basic exposition of the gaze, see Jacques Lacan, The Four Fundamental Concepts of Psycho-Analysis (New York: W. W. Norton, 1978), esp. pp. 65-119.
3. Kuntzel, "The Film-Work," p. 68; Christian Metz, "The Imaginary Signifier," Screen, 16, no. 2 (1975): 16.
4. Kuntzel, "The Film-Work," p. 55; Christian Metz, Language and Cinema (The Hague: Mouton, 1974), p. 76.
5. Metz, "Imaginary Signifier," p. 58.
6. See Philip W. Davis, Modern Theories of Language (Englewood Cliffs: Prentice-Hall, 1973), pp. 1-12; Ernest Nagel, The Structure of Science (New York: Harcourt Brace & World, 1961), pp. 1-153; for the rationalist position on the role of theory in observation and the necessity for "abduction" in achieving explanation, see N. R. Hanson, Patterns of Discovery (Cambridge: Cambridge Univ. Press, 1961); Noam

Chomsky, "A Review of B. F. Skinner's Verbal Behavior,"
Language, 35 (1959): 25-58; Noam Chomsky, "Explanatory
Models in Linguistics," in Logic, Methodology and Philosophy
of Science, ed. Ernest Nagel, P. Suppes, A. Tarski
(Stanford: Stanford Univ. Press, 1962), pp. 528-50, esp.
pp. 528-31 and 534-37.

7.  Noam Chomsky, Language and Responsibility (New York:
Pantheon, 1979), p. 56.

8.  Davis, Modern Theories of Language, p. 68. For underlying
problems in structuralism, see Jonathan Culler,
Structuralist Poetics: Structuralism, Linguistics, and
the Study of Literature (Ithaca: Cornell Univ. Press,
1975), pp. 20-31.

9.  Chomsky, Language and Responsibility, p. 56.

10. Mitch Tuchman, "Scott Bartlett in Hollywood," Film Comment,
17, no. 3 (1981): 48.

11. Note that J. A. Miller's argument on suture, "Suture
(elements of the logic of the signifier)," Screen, 18,
no. 4 (1978): 24-34, is not that grounding, though it
purports to be--it merely analogizes the 0 in a series of
numbers to the cognizing subject in its representations.

12. Louis Breger, "Dream Function: An Information Processing
Model," in Clinical-Cognitive Psychology, ed. Louis Breger
(Englewood Cliffs: Prentice-Hall, 1969), p. 195.

13. Noam Chomsky, Language and Responsibility, pp. 50-51; Noam
Chomsky, Language and Mind, Enlarged ed. (New York:
Harcourt Brace Jovanovich, 1972), p. 25; Noam Chomsky, Rules
and Representations (New York: Columbia Univ. Press, 1980),
pp. 30-42; for the decisive examples, see Rules and
Representations, pp. 42-43, 83-84, 191-95, and Noam Chomsky,
"On Cognitive Structures and Their Development," in Language
and Learning: The Debate between Jean Piaget and Noam
Chomsky, ed. Massimo Piattelli-Palmarini (Cambridge:
Harvard Univ. Press, 1980), pp. 35-52.

14. For clear exegesis of Lacan's picture of developmental
psychology, see C. McC. [Colin MacCabe?], "Introduction,"
in Metz's "Imaginary Signifier," pp. 7-13; for treatment
of the period prior to self-object discrimination and its
relation to later mental stages, see Norman N. Holland, The
Dynamics of Literary Response (New York: Oxford Univ.
Press, 1968), pp. 34, 77-79.

15. Holland, Dynamics of Literary Response, p. 16.

16. Seymour Fisher and Roger P. Greenberg, The Scientific
Credibility of Freud's Theories and Therapy (New York:
Basic Books, 1977), p. 221.

17. Richard Wollheim, "The Cabinet of Dr. Lacan," New York
Review of Books, January 25, 1979, pp. 38, 40.

18. Stephen Heath, "Difference," Screen, 19, no. 3 (1978):
63.

19. Ulric Neisser, Cognition and Reality (San Francisco: W.
H. Freeman, 1976), pp. 55-56.

20. Neisser, Cognition and Reality, p. 163.
21. Neisser, Cognition and Reality, p. 113; for schema and correction in representation and perception in art, see E. H. Gombrich, Art and Illusion, 2nd ed. (Princeton: Princeton Univ. Press, 1961), pp. 73-90, 270-75.
22. Ulric Neisser, Cognitive Psychology (New York: Appleton-Century-Crofts, 1967), pp. 295-96, 279-305; Jacques Monod, Chance and Necessity (New York: Knopf, 1971), pp. 33-40, 146-80.
23. Dan Sperber, Rethinking Symbolism (Cambridge: Cambridge Univ. Press, 1975), pp. 23, 82; Dan Sperber, "Remarks on the Lack of Positive Contributions from Anthropologists to the Problem of Innateness," in Language and Learning, ed. Piattelli-Palmarini, p. 248.
24. Metz, "Imaginary Signifier," p. 55.
25. Sperber, Rethinking Symbolism, pp. 4, 41, 140.
26. Neisser, Cognition and Reality, pp. 18-19, 20.
27. Sperber, Rethinking Symbolism, pp. 91-92.
28. Sperber, Rethinking Symbolism, p. 94.
29. Sperber, Rethinking Symbolism, pp. 115-40.
30. Sperber, Rethinking Symbolism, pp. 123, 141-46.
31. Sperber, Rethinking Symbolism, pp. 33, 85, 70-71.
32. Sperber, Rethinking Symbolism, p. 104.
33. Holland, Dynamics of Literary Response, pp. 75-96.
34. Sigmund Freud, The Interpretation of Dreams, in The Basic Writings of Sigmund Freud (New York: Modern Library, 1938), pp. 296, 307-11, 497.
35. E. H. Gombrich, "Standards of Truth: The Arrested Image and the Moving Eye," Critical Inquiry, 7 (1980): 268-69.
36. Erik Erikson, Childhood and Society (New York: W. W. Norton, 1963), pp. 247-51.
37. Umberto Eco, A Theory of Semiotics (Bloomington: Indiana Univ. Press, 1976), p. 70; Christian Metz, Language and Cinema (The Hague: Mouton, 1974); Sperber, Rethinking Symbolism, p. 142.
38. F. C. Bartlett, Remembering (1932; reprint, Cambridge: At the Univ. Press, 1967), p. 206.
39. Holland, Dynamics of Literary Response, p. 87.
40. Monod, Chance and Necessity, pp. 156-58; Arthur Koestler, The Sleepwalkers (New York: Universal Library, 1959), p. 519.
41. Monroe C. Beardsley, Aesthetics: Problems in the Philosophy of Criticism (New York: Harcourt Brace & World, 1958), p. 337.

# BIBLIOGRAPHY

The bibliographic entries that follow are intended primarily as a selective guide to reading and research. References cited in the notes are only repeated here if they are essential to a fuller understanding of the theoretical context wherein we write. Likewise, we refer only to particular chapters or essays in cases where the essay by itself is of particular importance. With few exceptions we cite only the most readily available source or edition. More complete references, where necessary, are already in the notes.

Althusser, Louis. *Lenin and Philosophy and Other Essays*. Trans. Ben Brewster. London: NLB, 1971.
———. *For Marx*. Trans. Ben Brewster. London: NLB, 1977.
Andrew, J. Dudley. *The Major Film Theories: An Introduction*. New York: Oxford Univ. Press, 1976.
———. *André Bazin*. New York: Oxford Univ. Press, 1978.
Arnheim, Rudolf. *Film as Art*. Berkeley: Univ. of California Press, 1957.
———. *Art and Visual Perception: A Psychology of the Creative Eye: The New Version*. Berkeley: Univ. of California Press, 1974.
Barthes, Roland. *Elements of Semiology*. Trans. Annette Lavers and Colin Smith. New York: Hill and Wang, 1967.
———. *Writing Degree Zero*. Trans. Annette Lavers and Colin Smith. New York: Hill and Wang, 1968.
———. *S/Z*. Trans. Richard Miller. New York: Hill and Wang, 1974.
———. *The Pleasure of the Text*. Trans. Richard Miller. New York: Hill and Wang, 1975.
———. *Image/Music/Text*. Trans. Stephen Heath. New York: Hill and Wang, 1977.
Bartlett, Frederic C. *Remembering: A Study in Experimental and Social Psychology*. 1932. Reprint. Cambridge: At the Univ. Press, 1967.

Bazin, André. "La Politique des Auteurs." In The New Wave.
    Ed. Peter Graham, pp. 137–55. Garden City: Doubleday, 1968.
————. What Is Cinema? Trans. Hugh Gray. 2 vols. Berkeley:
    Univ. of California Press, 1967 and 1971.
————. Le Cinéma de La Cruauté. Paris: Flammarion, 1975.
Beardsley, Monroe C. Aesthetics: Problems in the Philosophy
    of Criticism. New York: Harcourt Brace & World, 1958.
————. The Possibility of Criticism. Detroit: Wayne State
    Univ. Press, 1970.
Belsey, Catherine. Critical Practice. New York: Methuen,
    1980.
Bennett, Tony. Formalism and Marxism. New York: Methuen,
    1979.
Berger, John. Ways of Seeing. London: BBC and Penguin, 1972.
Bernstein, Leonard. The Unanswered Question: Six Talks at
    Harvard. Cambridge: Harvard Univ. Press, 1976.
Bettetini, Gianfranco. The Language and Technique of the Film.
    The Hague: Mouton, 1973.
Bordwell, David, and Kristin Thompson. Film Art: An
    Introduction. Reading, Mass.: Addison-Wesley, 1979.
Branigan, Edward. "Formal Permutations of the Point-of-View
    Shot." Screen, 16, no. 3 (1975): 54–64.
Breger, Louis, ed. Clinical-Cognitive Psychology: Models
    and Integrations. Englewood Cliffs: Prentice-Hall, 1969.
Britton, Andrew. "The Ideology of Screen." Movie, no. 26
    (1978–79), pp. 2–28.
Brower, Reuben Arthur. The Fields of Light: An Experiment in
    Critical Reading. 1951. Reprint. New York: Oxford Univ.
    Press, 1962.
Burch, Noel. Theory of Film Practice. 1973. Reprint.
    Princeton: Princeton Univ. Press, 1981.
————. To the Distant Observer: Form and Meaning in the
    Japanese Cinema. Berkeley: Univ. of California Press,
    1979.
Burke, Kenneth. Counter-Statement. Chicago: Univ. of Chicago
    Press, 1957.
Cameron, Ian, ed. Movie Reader. New York: Praeger, 1972.
Campbell, Joseph. The Mythic Image. Princeton: Princeton
    Univ. Press, 1974.
Caughie, John, ed. Theories of Authorship: A Reader. London:
    Routledge and Kegan Paul, 1981.
Cavell, Stanley. "Leopards in Connecticut." The Georgia
    Review, 30 (1976): 233–62.
————. The World Viewed: Reflections on the Ontology of
    Film. Enlarged ed. Cambridge: Harvard Univ. Press, 1979.
Chomsky, Noam. Syntactic Structures. The Hague: Mouton, 1957.
————. "A Review of B. F. Skinner's Verbal Behavior."
    Language, 35 (1959): 25–58.
————. Aspects of the Theory of Syntax. Cambridge: M.I.T.
    Press, 1965.

————. Cartesian Linguistics. A Chapter in the History of
     Rationalist Thought. New York: Harper and Row, 1966.
————. American Power and the New Mandarins: Historical
     and Political Essays. New York: Random House, 1969.
————. Problems of Knowledge and Freedom: The Russell
     Lectures. New York: Vintage, 1971.
————. Language and Mind. Enlarged ed. New York: Harcourt
     Brace Jovanovich, 1972.
————. Language and Responsibility. New York: Pantheon,
     1979.
————. Rules and Representations. New York: Columbia Univ.
     Press, 1980.
Coward, Rosalind, and John Ellis. Language and Materialism:
     Developments in Semiology and the Theory of the Subject.
     London: Routledge and Kegan Paul, 1977.
Culler, Jonathan. Structuralist Poetics: Structuralism,
     Linguistics, and the Study of Literature. Ithaca: Cornell
     Univ. Press, 1975.
     . Ferdinand de Saussure. New York: Penguin, 1977.
Davis, Philip W. Modern Theories of Language. Englewood
     Cliffs: Prentice-Hall, 1973.
Dayan, Daniel. "The Tutor-Code of Classical Cinema." In Movies
     and Methods. Ed. Bill Nichols, pp. 438-51. Berkeley:
     Univ. of California Press, 1976.
De George, Richard T., and Fernande M. De George, eds. The
     Structuralists: From Marx to Lévi-Strauss. Garden City:
     Anchor-Doubleday, 1972.
Dickie, George. Aesthetics: An Introduction. Indianapolis:
     Bobbs-Merrill, 1971.
Durgnat, Raymond. Films and Feeling. Cambridge: M.I.T.
     Press, 1971.
Eagleton, Terry. Marxism and Literary Criticism. Berkeley:
     Univ. of California Press, 1976.
Eco, Umberto. A Theory of Semiotics. Bloomington: Indiana
     Univ. Press, 1976.
Edelson, Marshall. "Language and Dreams: The Interpretation
     of Dreams Revisited." In The Psychoanalytic Study of the
     Child, 27, pp. 203-82. New York: Quadrangle, 1973.
————. Language and Interpretation in Psychoanalysis. New
     Haven: Yale Univ. Press, 1975.
Ehrmann, Jacques, ed. Structuralism. Garden City: Anchor-
     Doubleday, 1970.
Eisenstein, Sergei. The Film Sense. Ed. and Trans. Jay Leyda.
     New York: Harcourt Brace, 1947.
————. Film Form: Essays in Film Theory. Ed. and Trans.
     Jay Leyda. New York: Harcourt Brace, 1949.
Ellis, John M. The Theory of Literary Criticism: A Logical
     Analysis. Berkeley: Univ. of California Press, 1974.
Erikson, Erik. Childhood and Society. New York: W. W. Norton,
     1963.

Fisher, Seymour, and Roger P. Greenberg. The Scientific
    Credibility of Freud's Theories and Therapy. New York:
    Basic Books, 1977.
Fodor, Jerry A. Psychological Explanation: An Introduction
    to the Philosophy of Psychology. New York: Random House,
    1968.
Fodor, Jerry A., and Jerrold J. Katz, eds. The Structure of
    Language. Englewood Cliffs: Prentice-Hall, 1964.
Freud, Sigmund. The Basic Writings of Sigmund Freud. New
    York: Modern Library, 1938.
Fredericksen, Don. "Jung/Sign/Symbol/Film. Part I." Quarterly
    Review of Film Studies, 4 (1979): 167-92.
————. "Jung/Sign/Symbol/Film (Part II)." Quarterly Review
    of Film Studies, 5 (1980): 459-79.
Frye, Northrop. Anatomy of Criticism: Four Essays.
    Princeton: Princeton Univ. Press, 1957.
————. The Critical Path: An Essay in the Social Context of
    Literary Criticism. Bloomington: Indiana Univ. Press,
    1971.
Gibson, James J. "The Information Available in Pictures."
    Leonardo, 4 (1971): 27-35.
————. The Ecological Approach to Visual Perception. Boston:
    Houghton Mifflin, 1979.
Gombrich, E. H. Art and Illusion. 2nd ed. Princeton:
    Princeton Univ. Press, 1961.
————. "Standards of Truth: The Arrested Image and the Moving
    Eye." Critical Inquiry, 7 (1980): 237-73.
Gombrich, E. H., Julian Hochberg, and Max Black. Art,
    Perception, and Reality. Baltimore: Johns Hopkins Univ.
    Press, 1972.
Goodman, Paul. The Structure of Literature. Chicago: Univ. of
    Chicago Press, 1954.
Grant, Barry K., ed. Film Genre: Theory and Criticism.
    Metuchen, N.J.: Scarecrow Press, 1977.
Greenberg, Harvey R. The Movies on Your Mind. New York:
    Saturday Review Press-E. P. Dutton, 1975.
Hall, Calvin S. A Primer of Freudian Psychology. New York:
    New American Library, 1954.
Hanson, N. R. Patterns of Discovery: An Inquiry into the
    Conceptual Foundations of Science. Cambridge: Cambridge
    Univ. Press, 1961.
Harari, Josue V., ed. Textual Strategies: Perspectives in Post-
    Structuralist Criticism. Ithaca: Cornell Univ. Press,
    1979.
Harrington, Michael. Socialism. New York: Saturday Review
    Press, 1970.
Hartman, Geoffrey H. Saving the Text: Literature/Derrida/
    Philosophy. Baltimore: Johns Hopkins Univ. Press, 1981.
Hawkes, Terence. Structuralism and Semiotics. Berkeley:
    Univ. of California Press, 1977.

Heath, Stephen. "Film and System: Terms of Analysis." Screen,
    16, no. 1 (1975): 7-77, and no. 2 (1975): 91-113.
————. "Narrative Space." Screen, 17, no. 3 (1976): 68-112.
————. "Difference." Screen, 19, no. 3 (1978): 51-112.
Henderson, Brian. A Critique of Film Theory. New York: E. P.
    Dutton, 1980.
Hess, John. "Auteurism and After." Film Quarterly, 27, no. 2
    (1973-74): 28-37.
Hirsch, E. D., Jr. Validity in Interpretation. New Haven:
    Yale Univ. Press, 1967.
————. The Aims of Interpretation. Chicago: Univ. of Chicago
    Press, 1976.
Holland, Norman N. The Dynamics of Literary Response. New
    York: Oxford Univ. Press, 1968.
Hollander, Ann. Seeing through Clothes. New York: Viking,
    1978.
Jakobson, Roman. "Closing Statement: Linguistics and Poetics."
    In Style in Language. Ed. Thomas A. Sebeok, pp. 350-77.
    New York: The Technology Press of Massachusetts Institute
    of Technology and John Wiley and Sons, 1960.
Jameson, Fredric. The Prison-House of Language: A Critical
    Account of Structuralism and Russian Formalism. Princeton:
    Princeton Univ. Press, 1972.
"John Ford's Young Mr. Lincoln." By the Editors of Cahiers
    du Cinéma. In Movies and Methods. Ed. Bill Nichols,
    pp. 493-529. Berkeley: Univ. of California Press, 1976.
Kitses, Jim. Horizons West: Anthony Mann, Budd Boetticher,
    Sam Peckinpah: Studies of Authorship within the Western.
    Bloomington: Indiana Univ. Press, 1970.
Koestler, Arthur. The Act of Creation. New York: Macmillan,
    1964.
————. The Ghost in the Machine. New York: Macmillan,
    1967.
Kracauer, Siegfried. Theory of Film: The Redemption of Physical
    Reality. New York: Oxford Univ. Press, 1960.
Kuntzel, Thierry. "The Film-Work." Enclitic, 2, no. 1 (1978):
    38-61.
————. "The Film Work, 2." Camera Obscura, no. 5 (1980),
    pp. 7-69.
Lacan, Jacques. The Language of the Self. Trans. Anthony
    Wilden. Baltimore: Johns Hopkins Univ. Press, 1968.
————. Ecrits: A Selection. Trans. Alan Sheridan. New
    York: W. W. Norton, 1977.
————. The Four Fundamental Concepts of Psycho-Analysis.
    Ed. Jacques-Alain Miller. Trans. Alan Sheridan. New York:
    W. W. Norton, 1978.
Lane, Michael. Introduction to Structuralism. New York: Basic
    Books, 1970.
Lane, Robert E. The Liberties of Wit: Humanism, Criticism,
    and the Civic Mind. New Haven: Yale Univ. Press, 1961.

Langer, Susanne K. Feeling and Form: A Theory of Art Developed from Philosophy in a New Key. London: Routledge and Kegan Paul, 1953.

―――. Philosophical Sketches. 1962. Reprint. New York: Mentor-New American Library, 1964.

―――. Mind: An Essay in Human Feeling, I. Baltimore: Johns Hopkins Univ. Press, 1967.

de Lauretis, Teresa, and Stephen Heath, eds. The Cinematic Apparatus. New York: St. Martin's, 1980.

Leach, Edmund. Claude Levi-Strauss. New York: Viking, 1970.

Lemaire, Anika. Jacques Lacan. Trans. David Macey. London: Routledge and Kegan Paul, 1977.

Levi-Strauss, Claude. The Raw and the Cooked: Introduction to a Science of Mythology, I. Trans. John and Doreen Weightman. New York: Torch Books-Harper, 1970.

―――. "The Structural Study of Myth." In The Structuralists: From Marx to Levi-Strauss. Ed. Richard T. De George and Fernande M. De George, pp. 169-94. Garden City: Anchor-Doubleday, 1972.

Lewis, C. S. An Experiment in Criticism. Cambridge: Cambridge Univ. Press, 1961.

Lotman, Jurij. Semiotics of Cinema. Trans. Mark E. Suino. Michigan Slavic Contributions, No. 5. Ann Arbor: Department of Slavic Languages and Literature, Univ. of Michigan, 1976.

Lovell, Alan. "Robin Wood: A Dissenting View." Screen, 10, no. 2 (1969): 42-55.

―――. "The Common Pursuit of True Judgment." Screen, 11, no. 4-5 (1970): 76-88.

Lovell, Terry. Pictures of Reality: Aesthetics, Politics, and Pleasure. London: British Film Institute, 1980.

Lyons, John. Noam Chomsky. New York: Viking, 1970.

MacBean, James Roy. Film and Revolution. Bloomington: Indiana Univ. Press, 1975.

Machery, Pierre. A Theory of Literary Production. Trans. Geoffrey Wall. London: Routledge and Kegan Paul, 1978.

Mast, Gerald, and Marshall Cohen, eds. Film Theory and Criticism: Introductory Readings. 2nd ed. New York: Oxford Univ. Press, 1979.

Metz, Christian. Film Language: A Semiotics of the Cinema. Trans. Michael Taylor. New York: Oxford Univ. Press, 1974.

―――. Language and Cinema. Trans. Donna Jean Umiker-Sebeok. The Hague: Mouton, 1974.

―――. "The Imaginary Signifier." Screen, 16, no. 2 (1975): 14-76.

―――. "The Fiction Film and Its Spectator: A Metapsychological Study." New Literary History, 8 (1976): 74-105.

Miller, George A., Eugene Galanter, and Karl H. Pribram, eds. Plans and the Structure of Behavior. New York: Holt, Rinehart & Winston, 1960.

Miller, Jacques-Alain. "Suture (elements of the logic of the signifier)." Screen, 18, no. 4 (1978): 24-34.

Monod, Jacques. Chance and Necessity: An Essay on the Natural Philosophy of Modern Biology. Trans. Austryn Wainhouse. New York: Knopf, 1971.

Mulvey, Laura. "Visual Pleasure and Narrative Cinema." Screen, 16, no. 3 (1975): 6-18.

Münsterberg, Hugo. The Film: A Psychological Study. 1916. Reprint. New York: Dover, 1970.

Murray, John C. "Robin Wood and the Structural Critics." Screen, 12, no. 3 (1971): 101-10.

Nagel, Ernest. The Structure of Science: Problems in the Logic of Modern Biology. New York: Harcourt Brace & World, 1961.

Neale, Stephen. Genre. London: British Film Institute, 1980.

Neisser, Ulric. Cognitive Psychology. New York: Appleton-Century-Crofts, 1967.

———. Cognition and Reality: Principles and Implications of Cognitive Psychology. San Francisco: W. H. Freeman, 1976.

Nichols, Bill. Ideology and the Image. Bloomington: Indiana Univ. Press, 1981.

Nichols, Bill, ed. Movies and Methods: An Anthology. Berkeley: Univ. of California Press, 1976.

Oudart, Jean-Pierre. "Cinema and Suture." Screen, 18, no. 4 (1978): 35-47.

Perkins, V. F. Film as Film: Understanding and Judging Movies. Baltimore: Penguin, 1972.

Pettit, Philip. The Concept of Structuralism: A Critical Analysis. Berkeley: Univ. of California Press, 1975.

Piattelli-Palmarini, Massimo, ed. Language and Learning: The Debate between Jean Piaget and Noam Chomsky. Cambridge: Harvard Univ. Press, 1980.

Pratt, Mary Louise. Toward a Speech Act Theory of Literary Discourse. Bloomington: Indiana Univ. Press, 1977.

Pye, Douglas. "Genre and Movies." Movie, no. 20 (1975), pp. 29-43.

Ricoeur, Paul. Freud and Philosophy: An Essay on Interpretation. Trans. Denis Savage. New Haven: Yale Univ. Press, 1970.

———. The Rule of Metaphor: Multi-Disciplinary Studies of the Creation of Meaning in Language. Trans. Robert Czerny, with Kathleen McLaughlin and John Costello, S. J. Toronto: Univ. of Toronto Press, 1977.

Rosenblatt, Louise M. The Reader/the Text/the Poem: A Transactional Theory of the Literary Work. Carbondale: Southern Illinois Univ. Press, 1978.

Rothman, William. "Against 'The System of the Suture.'" In Movies and Methods. Ed. Bill Nichols, pp. 451-59. Berkeley: Univ. of California Press, 1976.

Ruesch, Jurgen, and Gregory Bateson. Communication: The Social
    Matrix of Psychiatry. New York: W. W. Norton, 1951.
Sarris, Andrew. The American Cinema: Directors and Directions
    1929-1968. New York: E. P. Dutton, 1968.
de Saussure, Ferdinand. Course in General Linguistics. Trans.
    Wade Baskin. New York: McGraw-Hill, 1966.
Scholes, Robert. Structuralism in Literature: An
    Introduction. New Haven: Yale Univ. Press, 1974.
————. "Narration and Narrativity in Film." In Film Theory
    and Criticism. 2nd ed. Ed. Gerald Mast and Marshall Cohen,
    pp. 417-33. New York: Oxford Univ. Press, 1979.
————. "Language, Narrative, and Anti-Narrative." Critical
    Inquiry, 7 (1980): 204-12.
Smith, Barbara Herrnstein. On the Margins of Discourse: The
    Relation of Literature to Language. Chicago: Univ. of
    Chicago Press, 1978.
Sperber, Dan. Rethinking Symbolism. Trans. Alice L. Morton.
    Cambridge: Cambridge Univ. Press, 1975.
Thompson, Kristin, and David Bordwell. "Space and Narrative in
    the Films of Ozu." Screen, 17, no. 2 (1976): 41-73.
Tudor, Andrew. Theories of Film. New York: Viking, 1974.
Turkle, Sherry. Psychoanalytic Politics: Freud's French
    Revolution. New York: Basic Books, 1978.
Weismann, Donald L. The Visual Arts as Human Experience.
    Englewood Cliffs: Prentice-Hall, n.d. [1974].
Wilden, Anthony. System and Structure: Essays in Communication
    and Exchange. London: Tavistock, 1972.
Wimsatt, W. K., Jr. The Verbal Icon. Lexington: Univ. of
    Kentucky Press, 1954.
Wittgenstein, Ludwig. Philosophical Investigations. 3rd ed.
    Trans. G. E. M. Anscombe. New York: Macmillan, 1973.
Wollen, Peter. Signs and Meaning in the Cinema. Enlarged ed.
    Bloomington: Indiana Univ. Press, 1972.
Wollheim, Richard. "The Cabinet of Dr. Lacan." New York Review
    of Books, January 25, 1979, pp. 36-45.
Wood, Robin. "Ghostly Paradigm and H.C.F.: An Answer to Alan
    Lovell." Screen, 10, no. 3 (1969): 35-48.
————. Personal Views: Explorations in Film. London: Gordon
    Fraser, 1976.

# INDEX

The following index entries are far from exhaustive. They are designed as guides to the primary substantive topics and discussions of the book. Relatively incidental references to films or books are generally not indexed, nor are note references except where a note presents additional points of argument. Certain index categories have been interpreted somewhat loosely to accord with variant usages in related contexts. Under "Qualities," for instance, are indexed references to "Regional qualities" and "Human qualities." Similarly, film titles are generally listed by directors, as are book titles by authors. In every case the principle of inclusion and categorization involves the overall logic of the views we are urging.

<u>William Cadbury</u> holds degrees from Harvard and the University
of Wisconsin.  He taught and published in the areas of Victorian
and modern literature from 1961 to 1969 in the Department of
English at the University of Oregon, and in film history,
criticism, and theory from 1969 to 1975 in that department.  From
1975 to the present he has taught in the film studies area of
the Department of Speech at the University of Oregon.

<u>Leland Poague</u> holds degrees from San Jose State College and
the University of Oregon.  He has taught literature and film
criticism at the State University of New York at Geneseo and at
the University of Rochester, and is presently a member of the
Department of English of Iowa State University.  He is the author
of four books of film criticism, the most recent a study of Howard
Hawks.  Much of his research for the present book was undertaken
while participating in a National Endowment for the Humanities
seminar directed by David Bordwell of the University of
Wisconsin-Madison.